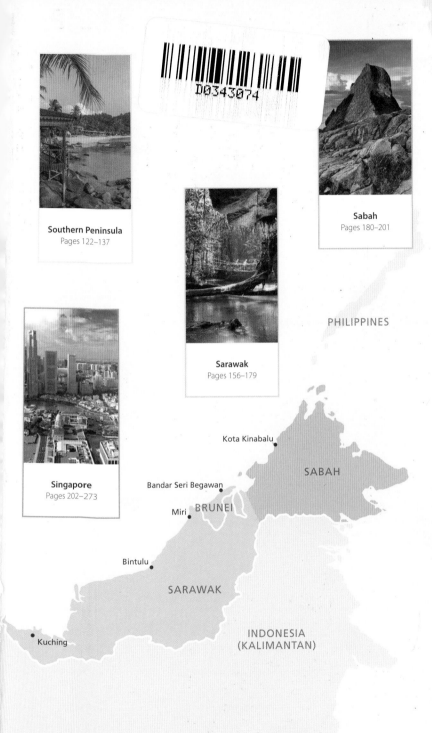

PHILIPPINES

Kota Kinabalu

SABAH

Bandar Seri Begawan

Miri BRUNEI

Bintulu

SARAWAK

INDONESIA
(KALIMANTAN)

Kuching

EYEWITNESS TRAVEL

MALAYSIA & SINGAPORE

EYEWITNESS TRAVEL

MALAYSIA & SINGAPORE

LONDON, NEW YORK,
MELBOURNE, MUNICH AND DELHI
www.dk.com

Managing Editor Aruna Ghose
Editorial Manager Ankita Awasthi
Design Manager Priyanka Thakur
Project Editors Sandhya Iyer, Shonali Yadav
Project Designers Neha Beniwal, Shipra Gupta
Editors Jayashree Menon, Ipshita Nandi
Designers Pramod Bharti, Anchal Kaushal
Senior Cartographic Manager Uma Bhattacharya
Cartographer Alok Pathak
Senior DTP Designer Vinod Harish
Senior Picture Researcher Taiyaba Khatoon
Picture Researcher Sumita Khatwani

Contributors
David Bowden, Ron Emmons,
Andrew Forbes, Naiya Sivaraj, Richard Watkins

Consultants
David Bowden, Nick White

Photographers
Demetrio Carrasco, Nigel Hicks, Linda Whitwam

Illustrators
Chapel Design and Marketing Ltd, Arun Pottirayil,
T. Gautam Trivedi

Printed and bound in China

First American Edition, 2008

15 16 17 18 10 9 8 7 6 5 4 3 2 1

Published in the United States by
DK Publishing, 345 Hudson Street,
New York, New York 10014

Reprinted with revisions 2010, 2013, 2016

Copyright © 2008, 2016 Dorling Kindersley Limited, London
A Penguin Random House Company

A catalog record for this book is available from the Library of Congress.

ISSN: 1542-1554
ISBN: 978-1-4654-4005-1

Floors are referred to throughout in accordance
with American usage; ie the "first floor" is at ground level.

MIX
Paper from
responsible sources
FSC
www.fsc.org   FSC™ C018179

**The information in this
DK Eyewitness Travel Guide is checked regularly.**
Every effort has been made to ensure that this book is as up-to-date as possible at
the time of going to press. Some details, however, such as telephone numbers,
opening hours, prices, gallery hanging arrangements and travel information,
are liable to change. The publishers cannot accept responsibility for any
consequences arising from the use of this book, nor for any material on third party
websites, and cannot guarantee that any website address in this book will be a
suitable source of travel information. We value the views and suggestions of our
readers very highly. Please write to: Publisher, DK Eyewitness Travel Guides,
Dorling Kindersley, 80 Strand, London, UK, WC2R 0RL, or email: travelguides@dk.com

Front cover main image: Thean Hou Chinese Temple, Kuala Lumpur

◀ The entrance to Batu Caves, the largest cave temple in Malaysia

Contents

Figure of temple guardian, Tua Pek Kong
Temple, Sibu, Sarawak

Introducing
Malaysia and
Singapore

Interior of the Inverted Dome Pavilion,
Islamic Arts Museum, Kuala Lumpur

Malaysia Region By Region

Boats and jet-skis off the beaches of Batu Ferringhi

Travelers' Needs

Survival Guide

Chinese ceramic vase at the National Museum, Kuala Lumpur

Singapore Area By Area

The grand Raffles Hotel in Singapore

HOW TO USE THIS GUIDE

This guide helps you get the most from your visit to Malaysia and Singapore. It provides detailed practical information and expert recommendations. *Introducing Malaysia and Singapore* maps the countries, sets them in their historical and cultural context, and describes events throughout the year. Each region has its own chapter, with its history and important sights described using visuals and maps. Information about hotels, restaurants, shops and markets, entertainment and outdoor activities is found in *Travelers' Needs*. The *Survival Guide* has tips on everything from making a telephone call to using local transportation.

Putting Malaysia and Singapore on the Map

The orientation maps show Peninsular Malaysia, Borneo, and Singpore, in relation to their neighboring countries. In this book, Malaysia is divided into six main regions that are each covered in a full chapter. Singapore has its own chapter, which is further split into the key sightseeing areas.

A locator map shows the country in relation to other countries.

Malaysia Region by Region

Each region has a map at the start of the section. The key to the symbols is on the back flap.

Sights at a Glance lists the chapter's sights by category, such as Towns and Cities, Areas of Natural Beauty, Islands and Beaches, and Parks and Preserves.

1 Introduction

The landscape, history, and character of each region are described here, including an account of how they have changed over the centuries and what they have to offer to the visitor today.

2 Regional Map

This map shows the road network and gives an overview of the topography of the entire region. All the sights are numbered and there are also useful tips on getting around by plane, train, boat, and car.

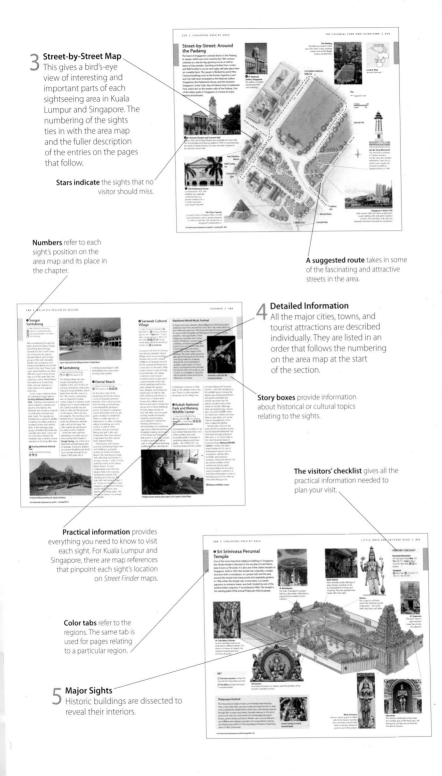

3 Street-by-Street Map
This gives a bird's-eye view of interesting and important parts of each sightseeing area in Kuala Lumpur and Singapore. The numbering of the sights ties in with the area map and the fuller description of the entries on the pages that follow.

Stars indicate the sights that no visitor should miss.

Numbers refer to each sight's position on the area map and its place in the chapter.

A suggested route takes in some of the fascinating and attractive streets in the area.

4 Detailed Information
All the major cities, towns, and tourist attractions are described individually. They are listed in an order that follows the numbering on the area map at the start of the section.

Story boxes provide information about historical or cultural topics relating to the sights.

The visitors' checklist gives all the practical information needed to plan your visit.

Practical information provides everything you need to know to visit each sight. For Kuala Lumpur and Singapore, there are map references that pinpoint each sight's location on *Street Finder* maps.

Color tabs refer to the regions. The same tab is used for pages relating to a particular region.

5 Major Sights
Historic buildings are dissected to reveal their interiors.

INTRODUCING MALAYSIA & SINGAPORE

DISCOVERING MALAYSIA AND SINGAPORE

The tours on the following pages each offer a mixture of historical sights and modern attractions as well as, in most cases, places of natural beauty such as national parks and islands. Though the tours are designed with geographical proximity in mind, Malaysia's wildlife areas are necessarily rural or remote, so may require a half-day road journey (or a short flight) to reach. For Borneo, package trips that include pre-arranged stays in longhouses or visits to jungle reserves are a very worthwhile option. Four itineraries focus on Peninsular Malaysia and Singapore, and three on Borneo; the longest tours last roughly a week. Domestic flights make it feasible to combine many itineraries, and Brunei is a possible overland extension to the Northern Sarawak tour.

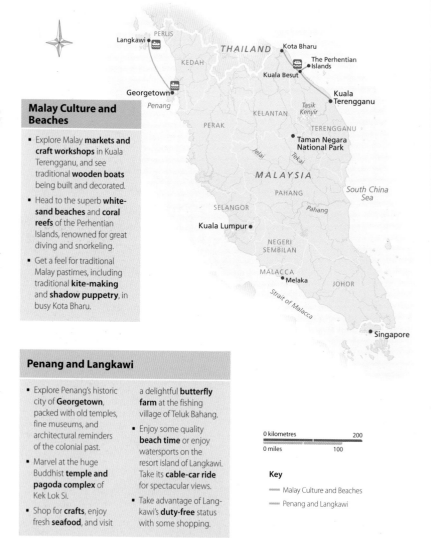

Malay Culture and Beaches

- Explore Malay **markets and craft workshops** in Kuala Terengganu, and see traditional **wooden boats** being built and decorated.

- Head to the superb **white-sand beaches** and **coral reefs** of the Perhentian Islands, renowned for great diving and snorkeling.

- Get a feel for traditional Malay pastimes, including traditional **kite-making** and **shadow puppetry**, in busy Kota Bharu.

Penang and Langkawi

- Explore Penang's historic city of **Georgetown**, packed with old temples, fine museums, and architectural reminders of the colonial past.

- Marvel at the huge Buddhist **temple and pagoda complex** of Kek Lok Si.

- Shop for **crafts**, enjoy fresh **seafood**, and visit a delightful **butterfly farm** at the fishing village of Teluk Bahang.

- Enjoy some quality **beach time** or enjoy watersports on the resort island of Langkawi. Take its **cable-car ride** for spectacular views.

- Take advantage of Langkawi's **duty-free** status with some shopping.

0 kilometres 200
0 miles 100

Key

━━ Malay Culture and Beaches
━━ Penang and Langkawi

◀ Detail from Nikhrodharam Thai Temple at Alor Star, Northwest Peninsula, Malaysia

A Week in Sabah

- Immerse yourself in the friendly bustle of **Kota Kinabalu**, with its lively seafront markets.

- Book a river trip in the Klias Wetlands to spot shy **proboscis monkeys** and twinkling fireflies.

- Try **white-water rafting** on the Padas River, or visit the **Mari Mari Cultural Village** to learn about life among Sabah's tribes.

- Walk forest trails in the shadow of **Malaysia's highest peak** in Kinabalu National Park, looking out for pitcher plants and slipper orchids, then soak those tired muscles at **Poring Hot Springs**.

- Check out Sandakan's **Chinese temples** and busy waterfront.

- Support animal rescue work at the sanctuaries for **orangutans** and **sun bears** at Sepilok, and spend a night in a **jungle lodge**.

- See nimble locals climb poles to harvest the raw ingredient for **birds'-nest soup**.

Gunung Kinabalu, the mighty mountain that lies at the heart of the Kinabalu National Park

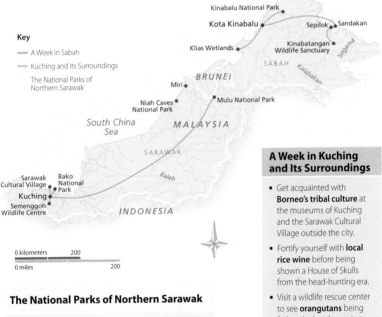

Key

— A Week in Sabah

== Kuching and its Surroundings

The National Parks of Northern Sarawak

Kinabalu National Park
Kota Kinabalu
Sepilok • Sandakan
Klias Wetlands
Kinabatangan Wildlife Sanctuary
Segama
SABAH
Kalabakan
BRUNEI
Miri
Mulu National Park
Niah Caves National Park
South China Sea
MALAYSIA
SARAWAK
Baleh
Sarawak Cultural Village
Bako National Park
Kuching
Semenggoh Wildlife Centre
INDONESIA

0 kilometers 200
0 miles 200

The National Parks of Northern Sarawak

- See one of nature's most awesome spectacles, as **millions of bats** emerge at dusk from the caves of Mulu National Park.

- See **ancient rock art**, boat-shaped "death ship" coffins, and spectacular natural rock formations as you go underground to explore the caves.

- Refresh yourself with a spot of **river-bathing** after a jungle trek.

- Admire the handicrafts and exotic jungle produce brought to Miri's **markets** by indigenous people.

- Extend your stay with a two-day side trip to fascinating **Brunei**.

A Week in Kuching and Its Surroundings

- Get acquainted with **Borneo's tribal culture** at the museums of Kuching and the Sarawak Cultural Village outside the city.

- Fortify yourself with **local rice wine** before being shown a House of Skulls from the head-hunting era.

- Visit a wildlife rescue center to see **orangutans** being fed, and take a boat trip to spot rare **river dolphins**.

- Spend a couple of days at the superb **Bako National Park**, with its cute family of **proboscis monkeys** and lovely beaches.

- Be a guest at an **Iban longhouse**, with an overnight stay to allow you to learn more about your hosts' traditional way of life.

Kuala Lumpur, Taman Negara, and Melaka

- **Duration** Five days, with two nights spent at Taman Negara National Park.
- **Airports** Fly into and out of Kuala Lumpur (KL).
- **Getting around** Taman Negara can be accessed by car, or by public bus via Jerantut, but the trip offered by many KL tour operators by coach to Kuala Tembeling, then river boat to Kuala Tahan, is highly recommended. In monsoon season (Nov–Mar), it is worth checking conditions at Taman Negara before travel.

Day 1: Kuala Lumpur
Explore around **Merdeka Square** (see pp66–7), the old heart of Kuala Lumpur, with its colonial and Moorish-style architecture and the **Masjid Jamek** (Jamek Mosque) (see p68). For lunch, head for bustling **Chinatown** (see p70), walking via the **Central Market** (see p69), now devoted to craft shops. In the afternoon, head over to the **National Museum** (see p72) and the adjacent **Perdana Botanical Gardens** (see p72) and explore the delightful **Butterfly Park**. Try to get to the **Menara KL** tower (see p80) by late afternoon for fine sunset views over the city from the top, then pick a restaurant for dinner in the surrounding **Golden Triangle** (see p80).

Massive statue of the Hindu god Lord Muragan at the entrance to the Batu Caves

Day 2: Kuala Lumpur and Batu Caves
Book ahead to enjoy the view from the skybridge between Kuala Lumpur's iconic **Petronas Towers** (see p78) then see the nearby **Aquaria KLCC** (see p79). Make an afternoon excursion to the **Batu Caves** (see p96) on the city's outskirts. Return for an evening stroll around **Little India** (see p76).

Day 3: Taman Negara
Make the journey to Malaysia's largest national park, **Taman Negara** (see pp144–5). Arriving at Kuala Tahan in the afternoon, the energetic can make for the **canopy walkway** for an overview of the stunning surroundings. Or, relax and sign up for a guided night trek to see the nocturnal creatures of the rain forest.

Day 4: Taman Negara
Park staff can offer advice to help you choose from many outdoor activities: a jungle trek on one of the shorter trails, climbing, caving, a boat trip, or a guided wildlife-spotting tour, perhaps to see elephants or some spectacular birdlife.

Day 5: Back to Kuala Lumpur
On your return, immerse yourself in city life again with an evening taking in the sights, sounds, and smells of famous food street **Jalan Alor** (see p76), or at the glitzy **Suria KLCC** mall (see p79) at the Petronas Towers.

> **To extend your trip...**
> Wildlife-lovers will find a longer stay at Taman Negara rewarding. Or, if not intending to see Penang, spend two days in **Melaka** (see pp128–33), with a similar mix of old temples, colonial buildings, and shophouses.

Three Days in Singapore

- **Arriving** The MRT metro system will whisk you from Changi Airport to downtown in 30 minutes.
- **Moving on** Changi Airport has excellent connections with many Malaysian cities, and is also served by express buses (to Kuala Lumpur by bus takes at least 5 hours). Malaysian trains out of Singapore are slow and not recommended, except for the sleeper services.
- **Book ahead** for the Universal Studios theme park.

Day 1
Morning Explore Singapore's historic old quarters, beginning with the **Colonial Core** along the Singapore River, around the **Padang** (see pp214–15) and **Fort Canning Park** (see p223). Take your pick of the museums, such as the **Peranakan Museum** (see p222), **Asian Civilisations Museum** (see p216), and grand **National Gallery** (see p217).

Traditional gateway to Chinatown in Kuala Lumpur

For practical information on getting around, see pp330–39

Relaxing on Pantai Cenang, one of Langkawi's white-sand beaches

Afternoon Head to the most atmospheric of the old districts, **Little India**, to look around the exuberant **Sri Veerama-kaliamman Temple** *(see p235)*. Nearby is **Kampong Glam** *(see pp232–3)*, the heart of Muslim life in the city and home to the **Masjid Sultan** mosque *(see p234)*. Spend the evening at the **Gardens by the Bay** *(see p217)*.

Day 2
Morning Visit the **Singapore Botanic Gardens** *(see pp246–7)*, including the spectacular National Orchid Garden.

Afternoon Explore **Chinatown**, being sure to see the **Buddha Tooth Relic Temple** *(see p225)* and **Thian Hock Keng Temple** *(see pp228–9)*. In the evening, head to **Singapore Zoo** for its Night Safari *(see p244)*.

Day 3
Thrill-seekers can easily spend the whole day on **Sentosa** *(see pp250–51)*, Singapore's theme park/resort island, where **Universal Studios** holds pride of place. Or, spend the morning at the gentler **Jurong Bird Park** *(see p245)*. From the Bird Park, it's a short train journey to the Chinese folklore theme park of **Haw Par Villa** *(see p248)*. Then take a trip to Sentosa in the late afternoon to visit **Underwater World** and **Fort Siloso** *(see p250)*. Have a sundowner at the beach, then head back downtown to spend the evening browsing the high-end shops of **Orchard Road** *(see pp238–41)*.

Penang and Langkawi

- **Duration** Six days, extendable by spending more time on Langkawi.
- **Airports** Fly into Penang and out from Langkawi.
- **Getting around** Ferries sail between Georgetown and Langkawi; flights are faster.
- **Book ahead** Ferry tickets are best bought a day in advance.

Day 1: Georgetown
Explore the colonial center of **Georgetown** *(see pp106–11)*, including **St George's Church** and **Fort Cornwallis**. Visit **100 Cintra Street** in Chinatown *(see p110)* with its Peranakan museum and curio stalls, then explore the mini-water village of the **Weld Quay Clan Piers** *(see p106)*. Dine in **Little India** *(see p108)*.

Day 2: Georgetown and Around
Explore the best of Penang's clan temples, the **Khoo Kongsi**

(see p107) and take in other places of worship such as **Kapitan Keling Mosque** *(see p108)*. Take the tour of the **Cheong Fatt Tze Mansion** *(see p111)* then perhaps have a look around the grand old **E & O Hotel** *(see p111)*. Visit the giant **Kek Lok Si Temple** complex *(see p113)* in the afternoon, and spend the evening atop nearby **Penang Hill** *(see p113)* to see Georgetown light up at night.

Day 3: Georgetown and Around
Head to the **Penang National Park** *(see p115)* for a few hours of jungle trekking, or spend the morning at the temples of **Wat Chayamangkalaram** *(see p118)* in Pulau Tikus. Then head to **Teluk Bahang** *(see p114)* for the **Penang Butterfly Farm** and **Forest Recreation Park**. Relax on the beach at **Batu Ferringhi** *(see p114)* in the late afternoon.

Day 4: Langkawi
Catch a morning ferry or flight to **Pulau Langkawi** *(see pp118–9)*. Spend the rest of the day on Cenang beach, perhaps indulging in water sports like paragliding. Stay on Langkawi.

Day 5: Langkawi
Head up the **Langkawi Cable Car** *(see p121)* to Gunung Machinchang for amazing views over a forested valley. Drop by Pantai Cenang's **Underwater World** aquarium *(see p121)*. In the afternoon, take an island-hopping trip to **Pulau Dayang Bunting** *(see p121)*.

Day 6: Depart Langkawi
Grab another morning on the beach before flying out.

The graceful Kapitan Keling mosque in Georgetown

Malay Culture and Beaches

- **Duration** Five days. Keen wildlife spotters should spend an extra night at Taman Negara. Alternatively, extend the itinerary to a week by adding on Melaka. Note that the east coast is a seasonal destination: avoid the stormy northeast monsoon (Nov–Mar).

- **Airports** Fly into Kuala Terengganu and out from Kota Bharu.

- **Getting around** Hotels and tour operators in Kota Bharu and Kuala Terengganu can arrange transfers to and from Kuala Besut, where Perhentian Islands boats depart. Water taxis run around and between the islands. A taxi is useful for visiting Kota Bharu's scattered craft workshops.

- **Book ahead** Book accommodation on the Perhentian Islands at least ten days in advance if intending to stay during a local holiday or school break.

Beautiful 19th-century architecture of the Istana Jahar in Kota Bharu

Day 1: Kuala Terengganu

In the center of sleepy **Kuala Terengganu** *(see p147)*, see the **Pasar Payang** produce market and the small temples and boutiques of Chinatown. Head just outside town to one of Malaysia's most architecturally striking museums, the **Terengganu State Museum Complex**, designed to look like a series of monumental Malay houses. In the afternoon, visit the few surviving traditional boatyards at **Pulau Duyung** *(see p149)*, also just outside the town, where Malay craftsmen still produce wooden fishing boats and sailboats.

Days 2 & 3: The Perhentian Islands

Leave in the morning for the tiny seaside town of Kuala Besut to catch a boat to the **Perhentian Islands** *(see p148)*, the most down-to-earth and likeable of Malaysia's resort islands. They have a wide range of accommodation, although Perhentian Besar is the better of the two islands for more mature travelers or those with families. Take your pick of dive packages or hire a snorkel and fins for a couple of hours. It's worth hopping between islands to eat at different restaurants.

Day 4: Kota Bharu

Return to the mainland in the morning and head north to **Kota Bharu** *(see pp152–3)*, a conservative but likeable city with a strong Malay flavor. In the center, drop by the enjoyable **Pasar Besar**, a market packed with colorful fruits and vegetable stalls, and the beautiful **Istana Jahar** *(see p152)*, built as a palace in traditional wooden style but now a museum of royal traditions and customs. Also visit the **Gelanggang Seni** (Cultural Center) *(see p153)* to learn about old-fashioned Malay pastimes; ask about shadow puppetry shows in the evening.

Day 5: Kota Bharu

See the city's craft cottage industries – tourist offices can provide details of which ones are currently best to visit – including silversmiths producing filigree jewelry, and traditional kite-makers. Either depart in the afternoon or visit more museums, such as the **Istana Batu** *(see p152)*, a former palace now used as a museum of royal paraphernalia, and the small **World War II Memorial Museum** *(see p153)*.

Landing jetty at Coral Bay beach on the Perhentian Islands

For practical information on getting around, see pp330–39

A Week in Kuching and Its Surroundings

- **Duration** Seven days.
- **Airports** Fly in and out of Kuching.
- **Getting around** Many of the highlights are rural and it is best to book a package trip; spare time in Kuching can be spent consulting tour operators. Some sights are straightforward by public transport, including Bako National Park, reached by bus and then boat. Shuttle buses leave from central Kuching for the Sarawak Cultural Village.
- **Book ahead** Recommended for Iban longhouse stays and accommodation at Bako National Park (through Sarawak Forestry in Kuching).

Traditional Orang Ulu longhouses, some of which offer accommodations

Day 1: Kuching and Sarawak Cultural Village

Wander through the delightful riverfront area of central **Kuching** (see pp160–63), lined with colonial-era monuments, before getting acquainted with Borneo tribal culture at the **Sarawak Museum** (see p160) and **Textile Museum** (see p160). Make an afternoon excursion to explore beautiful examples of authentically styled tribal longhouses and observe the skilful craftsmanship of indigenous communities at the **Sarawak Cultural Village** (see p165), a folk museum outside the city.

Day 2: Semenggoh, Anna Rais, and the Santubong River

Watch orangutans being fed at the **Semenggoh Wildlife Centre** (see p167) south of Kuching in the morning. From here buses run to the **Anna Rais** longhouse community of Bidayuh people (see p167), where you are likely to be invited to sample rice wine and see a house of skulls dating from the head-hunting era. Returning to Kuching, take a **Santubong river cruise** (see p315) in the late afternoon to look for rare dolphins.

Day 3: Bako National Park

Head to the superb **Bako National Park** (see pp168–9), with its endearing **proboscis monkeys**. There are trails that can take up the rest of the day, some leading to fine beaches, while others go up and across a plateau covered in unusual scrub forest. At night you can sign up for a guided trek through the jungle, looking for snakes and other creatures.

Day 4: Bako and Kuching

Spend the morning at Bako. Returning to Kuching, go down to the lively **Waterfront** (see p162) to browse shops and stalls and perhaps visit the **Chinese History Museum**. Linger outdoors and you may catch one of the city's scenic sunsets.

Days 5 & 6: Iban Longhouses

Book a package trip to an **Iban**

Iban women weaving in the Nanga Sumpa longhouse in Sarawak

longhouse (see p173) east of Kuching. With a stay of two nights you will get to know the inhabitants, who may have traditional crafts for sale. The package will usually include **jungle treks** and **river boat trips**, perhaps to waterfalls or other swimming spots.

Day 7: Kuching

Return to the city; if there's time before your departure, visit the **Tua Pek Kong** temple (see p162) or the kitsch **Cat Museum** on the northern outskirts (see p163).

> **To extend your trip…**
> Fly from Kuching to spend extra days in the Mulu National Park, following the suggestions at the start of the Northern Sarawak itinerary (see p16).

Boardwalk through the swampy mangrove forest in Bako National Park

Longboats moored in a creek near Clearwater Cave, Mulu National Park

The National Parks of Northern Sarawak

- **Duration** Four days, with the option to extend to a week by visiting Brunei.

- **Airports** Fly into Mulu National Park and out from Miri. If including the Brunei extension, fly out from Bandar Seri Begawan.

- **Getting around** This itinerary can largely be followed independently using flights and taxis. For Niah Caves National Park, arrange a taxi through your hotel to take you there in the morning and collect you at an arranged time.

- **Book ahead** Flights to and from Mulu National Park. For Brunei, book a two-day package at the Ulu Tembu-rong National Park on arrival in Bandar Seri Begawan.

Day 1: Mulu National Park
Fly into Mulu National Park (see pp176–7) in the morning. Once you've checked into your accommodations, register at the park headquarters to book guided trips around the extraordinary show caves. Don't miss the spectacular **Deer Cave** (see p176), with stunning rock formations and – at dusk – vast flocks of bats emerging from the cave mouth.

For practical information on getting around, see pp330–339

Day 2: Mulu National Park
In the morning, take a boat ride to view more of the caves: the **Wind Cave** is packed with stalactites and stalagmites, while **Clearwater Cave** (see p176), thought to be the longest in Southeast Asia, impresses with its vastness and subterranean river. Bring bathing gear for a river swim outside the caves once the tour is over. There are trails, the lofty **Canopy Skywalk** (see p177), and one or two other caves to occupy the rest of the day.

Day 3: Miri
Fly to **Miri** (see p174) in the morning. Spend the afternoon wandering around its compact center, visiting Tamu Muhibbah, one of the markets where exotic jungle produce is on sale, then catch a taxi up to the hill behind the town to visit the **Petroleum Museum** (see p177), telling the story of Miri's oil boom.

Day 4: Niah Caves National Park
Make an early start, ideally leaving Miri by 8:30am for a day trip to the **Niah Caves National Park** (see p174), nearly two hours' drive away, with jungle trails and caves of archaeological significance. These are also the source of edible swiftlet nests and bat guano for fertilizer, both of which you may see workers harvesting. Bring torches for the caves, notably the dark passages of the aptly named Great Cave. The farthest cave is the Painted Cave, named for its wall paintings.

To extend your trip...
Spend three days in **Brunei** (see pp178–9), a 4-hour bus ride from Miri. The highlights of the capital, Bandar Seri Begawan, are the opulent **Omar Ali Saifuddien Mosque** and the sprawling **Kampung Ayer**, a village built on stilts over the Brunei River. After a night in the capital, book an overnight excursion to the **Ulu Temburong National Park**, with several trails and an impressive canopy walkway at treetop height for wildlife spotting.

Mist-shrouded forest seen from the entrance to the Great Cave, Niah National Park

A Week in Sabah

- **Airports** Arrive at Kota Kinabalu; depart from Sandakan.
- **Getting around** Sabah has a good bus network, but many highlights are remote and it is best to book guided or organized tours locally. For Kinabalu National Park, it is worth chartering a taxi for the day or asking the driver who takes you there to return to collect you. Fly from Kota Kinabalu to Sandakan.
- **Book ahead** Book Sepilok and Kinabatangan tours before arrival in Sandakan.
- **Note on safety** Check your government's current travel advisories for this area before planning trips to some parts of Sabah *(see p183)*.

The Sabah Museum, Kota Kinabalu, designed in the style of a Rungus longhouse

Stark high-altitude landscape on Gunung Kinabula, high above the tree line

Day 1: Kota Kinabalu and Klias Wetlands

Kota Kinabalu *(see pp184–5)* is a compact town, easily seen on foot. The main attractions are the **Sabah Museum** *(see p184)* with its ethnographic exhibits such as a village showing the traditional dwellings of Sabah's tribes; and the town's waterfront markets, selling produce and crafts. In the afternoon, head out to the **Klias Wetlands** *(see p186)* for an escorted boat trip through the mangrove forests. There's an excellent chance of seeing bulbous-nosed proboscis monkeys, and most tours linger in the evening to try to spot fireflies, which flash in unison.

Day 2: Kota Kinabalu and Excursions

Either book an exciting but not too challenging rafting trip down the **Padas River** *(see p187)* or acquaint yourself further with Sabah's tribal cultures at the **Mari Mari Cultural Village** *(see p188)*, where you can try rice wine and be given a tour of the various longhouses. Back in Kota Kinabalu, ascend **Signal Hill** *(see p184)* in the late afternoon for a scenic vista over the town from its observation platform.

Day 3: Kinabalu National Park

Head out to the **Kinabalu National Park** *(see pp190–91)* and spend the day walking the trails at the foot of the mountain. The Bukit Tupai trail affords a great view of Mount Kinabalu. Late afternoon, visit the nearby **Poring Hot Springs** *(see p191)* for a relaxing soak.

Day 4: Sandakan and Sepilok

Fly to **Sandakan** *(see p196)* in the morning and check out the waterfront with its boats, markets, and Chinese temples. Join a package trip out to **Sepilok Orangutan Rehabilitation Center** *(see p196)*, where you can see the animals being fed. If possible, join a tour that includes the neighboring **Sun Bear Conservation Center** *(see p196)*, which helps rehabilitate orphaned bears, and the Rainforest Discovery Center, with jungle trails and a suspension bridge.

Day 5: Sandakan and Kinabatangan

Visit Sandakan's **Agnes Keith's House** *(see p196)*, a beautifully preserved shrine to the American writer who helped publicize Borneo in the 1930s, and the **Sandakan Memorial Park** *(see p196)*, commemorating Allied war dead who perished on a forced march in 1944. In the afternoon, join a two-night trip to the **Kinabatangan Wildlife Sanctuary** *(see p197)*, where there are excellent jungle lodge accommodations.

Day 6: Kinabatangan River

Spend the day on **river trips** to spot proboscis monkeys and wonderful birdlife. Many packages include a visit to the **Gomantong Caves** *(see p197)*, populated by swiftlets and bats, where you may see the edible swiftlet nests being harvested.

Day 7: Sandakan

Return to Sandakan to fly out.

Kingfisher spotted on a boat trip down the Kinabatangan River

Putting Peninsular Malaysia on the Map

Bordered by Thailand to the north and connected to Singapore in the south by a causeway and a bridge, Peninsular Malaysia occupies the extreme south of mainland Southeast Asia, lying between 2 and 7 degrees north of the Equator. Off the west coast is the Strait of Malacca, while the east coast looks out onto the South China Sea. The majority of Malaysia's 29 million inhabitants live on the peninsula, heavily concentrated on the west coast, which includes the capital, Kuala Lumpur. A mountainous ridge runs down the center of the peninsula, separating the densely forested and sparsely populated east coast from the west.

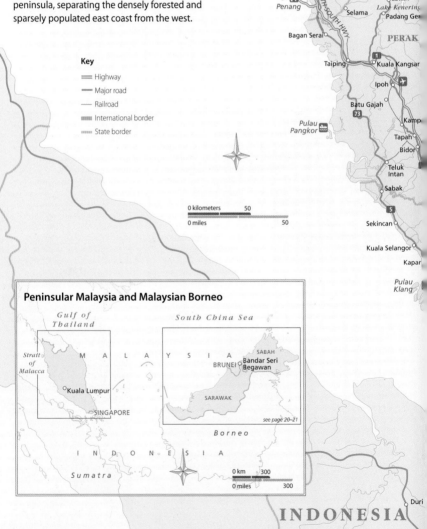

Key

— Highway
— Major road
--- Railroad
▪▪▪ International border
▪▪▪ State border

0 kilometers 50
0 miles 50

Peninsular Malaysia and Malaysian Borneo

Gulf of Thailand

South China Sea

Strait of Malacca

M A L A Y S I A

SABAH

BRUNEI Bandar Seri Begawan

Kuala Lumpur

SARAWAK

SINGAPORE

see page 20–21

I N D O N E S I A

Borneo

Sumatra

0 km 300
0 miles 300

INDONESIA

Duri

Putting Malaysian Borneo on the Map

Generally referred to as East Malaysia or Malaysian Borneo, this half of Malaysia comprises the states of Sarawak, the largest in Malaysia, and Sabah, which together occupy more than half of the country's 127,445 sq miles (330,000 sq km). The states are located in the northern part of Borneo, the world's third-largest island, which they share with tiny Brunei and Kalimantan, Indonesia. Borneo lies about 373 miles (600 km) east of Peninsular Malaysia, from which it is separated by the South China Sea. The region is rich in natural resources, particularly oil and gas, and much of it is covered by rain forest and is sparsely populated. Of a population of 6 million people, most live in the provincial capitals, Kuching in Sarawak and Kota Kinabalu in Sabah, while many indigenous communities occupy remote outposts in the interior of the states.

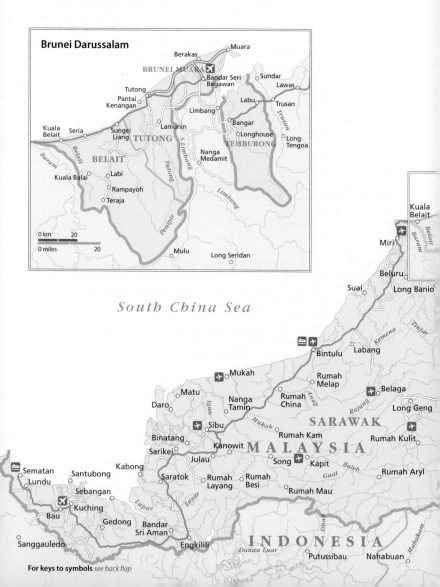

For keys to symbols *see back flap*

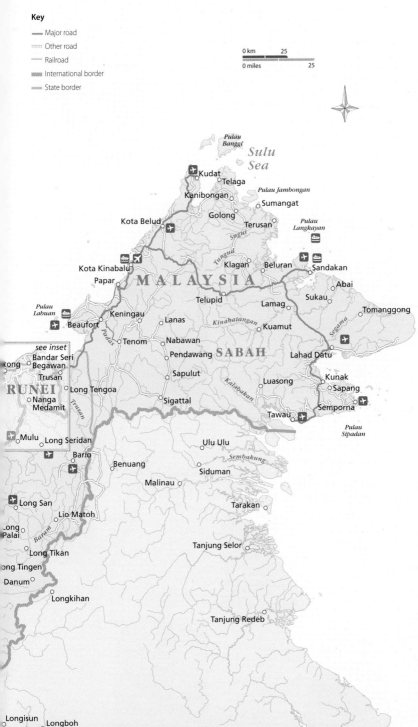

Landscape and Wildlife

Although separated by the South China Sea, Peninsular Malaysia and Malaysian Borneo form a part of the Sunda Shelf, a tectonic plate that once joined them in a single land mass. As a result, they share many geological features such as mountains, river networks, pristine offshore islands, and some of the world's oldest rain forests. These rain forests provide a habitat for a wealth of flora and fauna, including more than 15,000 types of flowering plants and nearly 200,000 species of animals. Among these are well-known endemic species, such as the orangutan, proboscis monkey, and rafflesia. Singapore retains pockets of primary rain forest in its northern region, while three-quarters of Brunei is still covered by native forest.

The *tualang* tree, one of the tallest plants in Malaysia

Rain Forests

The rain forests of Malaysia are about 130 million years old and nurture a phenomenal range of plant life, from the 262-ft- (80-m-) tall *tualang* tree to an array of ferns, mosses, fungi, and orchids. They also provide a home for orangutans, proboscis monkeys, tapirs, binturongs or Malay civet cats, and honey bears, as well as hundreds of species of birds and butterflies.

Malaysian tapirs are distinguished by their black and white coloring and pig-like snout. These vegetarian mammals are most active at night.

The orangutan is the only great ape found outside Africa. These red-haired primates now face extinction and are rarely seen in the wild.

Limestone Outcrops

Many of Malaysia's mountains are formed of limestone, often rising dramatically out of the surrounding plain and containing massive cave networks caused by erosion. The most spectacular limestone outcrops are found in Sarawak's Niah Caves *(see p174)* and in Mulu National Park *(see pp176–7)*.

Bats, such as the wrinkle-lipped bat, are common residents of limestone caves. Each evening, millions of bats take flight, filling the sky with a fantastic display.

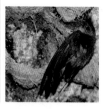

Cave swiftlets are unusual birds that use echolocation to navigate the pitch-dark interiors of the caves. White nest swiftlets are prized in Malaysia for their edible nests.

Malaysia's Endangered Species

Malaysia's population has doubled since the 1970s, and the growing demand for living space is gradually destroying the habitat of several wildlife species. In greatest danger is the Sumatran rhinoceros, whose numbers are now thought to be fewer than 100. Several other species, including the clouded leopard, Asian elephant, and the country's national animal, the tiger, have also seen a dramatic decline. Among marine life, leatherback turtles and dugongs face a similar threat.

The Sumatran rhinoceros is critically endangered. Its last remaining habitats include Sabah and Endau-Rompin National Park *(see p143)*.

Clouded leopards, tawny or silver-colored cats, are hunted for their pelt, teeth, and bones, the latter being used in traditional Asian medicines.

Coastal Plains

The west coast of Peninsular Malaysia constitutes a long plain that provides an ideal environment for human inhabitation. These plains were the site of the earliest British settlements. Most of the country's important towns and cities, such as Kuala Lumpur, were established here.

Offshore Islands

The seas around both Peninsular Malaysia and Malaysian Borneo are studded with stunning islands, many of them surrounded by coral reefs that sustain an incredible wealth of marine life. Divers are drawn to islands such as Tioman and Sipadan to observe the thriving underwater world.

Mangroves are trees and shrubs that form swampy forests in saline coastal waters and provide a vital habitat for a number of wildlife species such as the proboscis monkey.

Dugongs take their name from the Malay word *duyung*, which means mermaid. Persistent hunting has resulted in the near extinction of these large sea mammals.

Fiddler crabs are critical to the wetland environment as they help aerate the soil by their feeding action. Males have asymmetrical and often brightly colored claws.

Coral reefs, formed by tiny marine animals called polyps and other organisms, are beautiful living structures. They are essential to the preservation of marine life.

Marine Life

The waters around both Peninsular Malaysia and Malaysian Borneo contain a huge diversity of marine life that attracts divers and snorkelers from around the world to gaze at brilliantly colored parrotfish, lionfish, and clownfish flitting around the vibrant coral reefs. For much of the year, the superb clarity of the water makes it easy to spot even the tiniest fish. The Malaysian government has designated 38 of its coral islands as protected areas to preserve their unique and biologically sensitive ecosystems.

Snorkeler examining underwater life on a coastal reef

Sea anemones, named for a species of garden flower, are brightly colored, predatory animals that eat fish, mussels, and zooplankton.

Coral Life

Over 350 species of coral have been identified in Malaysian waters, making the country's reefs some of the most diverse in the world. Sadly, they are under threat from sediment build-up caused by ongoing logging, blast and cyanide fishing, and anchoring.

Gorgonian fan corals reach up to 16.5 ft (5 m) in height in the warm waters of the tropics, filtering out the plankton and zooxanthellae on which they live.

Brain corals are usually found in colonies and bear an uncanny resemblance to the human brain.

The star coral has a stone-like calcium skeleton and star-shaped polyp.

Yellow soft corals, so called because of their lack of a hard external skeleton, have polyps with eight tentacles, and come in a stunning kaleidoscope of colors.

Sunflower corals have long polyps tipped with stinging tentacles to catch plankton.

Mandarin fish live camouflaged in broken coral bottoms eating small crustaceans called copepods. The male is larger than the female and has a spiked dorsal fin which it uses to threaten other males.

Coleman shrimp, always found in pairs, live on the toxic fire urchin. They clear a resting area of poisonous spines and sit protected from predators.

Clownfish live in a symbiotic relationship with sea anemones, which defend them from predatory fish.

Sea ferns are a type of gorgonian coral with varied shapes and colors.

The lionfish, a reef dweller of spectacular appearance, is a deadly killer, armed with venomous spines that it uses to stun small fish.

Sea horses are unusual in that it is the males that give birth. Many species are almost transparent and hard to spot. Their use in Chinese medicine has put them under threat of extinction.

Lettuce coral is named for its green color and spiraling plates that resemble a growing lettuce.

Turtle Conservation

Until recently, turtles were among the most conspicuous forms of marine life in Malaysia. Of the four species of turtle known to breed in these waters – the green, the hawksbill, the olive ridley, and the leatherback – only the green is now commonly seen and the leatherback is an endangered species. There is ample evidence that human intervention is destroying the habitat and damaging the life cycle of these turtles. Throughout their lives, adult turtles are prone to getting caught in fishing lines and nets, while the increasing development of beaches has adverse effects on the numbers of nesting females, eggs, and hatchlings.

Green turtle swimming in the warm waters near Malaysia

Shoals of big-eye trevallies in the South China Sea

Peoples of Malaysia and Singapore

The indigenous people of Malaysia settled in the region some 40,000 years ago. Owing to its key position on maritime trade routes from around 2,500 years ago, the region acquired a large immigrant population. Today, Malays form 51 percent of the country's 29 million inhabitants, with the Chinese making up about a quarter, and the Indians about 7 percent. Indigenous groups comprise the remainder of the population. By contrast, the Chinese form a strong majority in Singapore, where there are fewer Malays and Indians.

A group of Orang Asli, the indigenous people of Malaysia

The Malay

The largest ethnic group of Malaysia is, by definition, a Muslim group. Believed to have arrived on the peninsula from Sumatra, the Malays began converting to Islam in the 15th century, owing to the rise of the Malay sultanates. Today, they predominate on the east coast of Peninsular Malaysia, while in Singapore, they constitute about 14 percent of the population.

Malays celebrate Hari Raya Puasa, also known as Hari Raya Aidilfitri *(see p58)*, the Muslim New Year. Here, Prime Minister Najib Razak joins other dignitaries in traditional Malaysian finery.

Traditional Malay culture revolves around village compounds called *kampung*, where inhabitants farm, fish, and practice crafts. Today, many Malays have migrated to urban centers.

The Chinese

Originally from southern China, most Chinese immigrants arrived in Malaysia during the 19th century to work as laborers in the burgeoning tin-mining industry. Since then, they have dominated all aspects of commerce and today, Malaysia has several Chinatowns, where Chinese businesses thrive. In Singapore, more than three-quarters of the population is Chinese.

The Peranakans, also known as Straits Chinese or Baba-Nyonya, are a community born out of marriages between Chinese and Malays from the 16th century onwards.

Chinese traders can be seen selling artifacts in Kuala Lumpur. The Chinese have historically played a major role in the Malaysian economy.

South Asians

Indians have been trading with Malaysia for over 2,000 years. However, most Malaysians of Indian origin settled here, like the Chinese, during the 19th century. Although the immigrants came largely from southern India, there are also people of northern Indian descent, notably the Sikhs.

Asian women of Indian descent sell handmade silk at market stalls in Kuala Lumpur. The ethnic enclaves of Little India *(see p76)* and Brickfields are packed with such stalls.

A rubber tapper of south Indian origin collects latex from a rubber tree. Indians have also traditionally been employed on tea estates.

Indigenous Peoples of Malaysia

The indigenous peoples of Peninsular Malaysia, the Orang Asli, are among the minority of the peninsula's population, and generally live in its more inaccessible areas. In contrast, indigenous tribes make up half the population of Sarawak and 66 percent of Sabah. Many of these groups, including the Iban and Bidayuh of Sarawak, live in longhouses and hold animist beliefs. Some, like the Kelabit and Bajau, have converted to Christianity or Islam. The tribes of Sabah, such as the Kadazan Dusun, are traditionally agriculturalists, but most other groups were semi-nomadic hunter-gatherer communities. They are now being encouraged by the government to live in towns and villages.

The Bajau are predominantly Muslim and are the second-largest ethnic group in Sabah. Noted horsemen, the Bajau dress in elaborate costumes at the annual Tamu Besar in Kota Belud (see p59).

The Penan, the only true nomadic indigenous group in Malaysia, are skilled hunter-gatherers. Of the 10,000 individuals living in the upper Rajang and Limbang areas of Sarawak, only about 200 are truly nomadic.

The Rungus are an indigenous people of northern Sabah. They are skilled in beadwork, weaving, and gong-making. Rungus people live communally in longhouses around Kudat (see p189).

The Kadazan Dusun are the largest ethnic group in Sabah, made up of a number of subgroups, constituting about 25 percent of Sabah's population. They traditionally wear black silk outfits on festive occasions such as the Dusun Harvest Dance.

The Bidayuh, or Land Dayaks, build their longhouses on hillsides, rather than near water as the other groups in Sarawak do. The third-largest of Sarawak's indigenous peoples, they predominantly inhabit the region around Kuching (see p165).

The Orang Ulu, or upriver people, is an unofficial generic name for about 27 small and ethnically diverse groups, such as the Kayan and Kenyah, living in the interior of Sarawak.

Bumiputras

The Malaysian authorities make an important distinction between migrant peoples and the *bumiputras*, or sons of the soil. The latter group includes all Malays and indigenous peoples of the country. This recognition was brought in as part of the New Economic Policy, following race riots in 1969, to boost the *bumiputras'* economic standing in society. It is much criticized by the Chinese and Indian migrants as racially discriminatory, though some argue the policy has ultimately led to more stability as it gave rise to a rich Malay group, whose financial interests lie in maintaining political and economic harmony.

The Iban, also known as Sea Dayaks, are the largest ethnic group of Sarawak. They have an enduring reputation as fierce warriors and good hunters. The men are often heavily tattooed.

Islam

While Malaysia is home to people of many different faiths, Islam is the official religion. So closely bound is Malay cultural identity with Islam that the Bahasa Malaysia phrase for adopting Islam, *masok melayu*, means "to become a Malay." Arab and Indian-Muslim merchants, who doubled as missionaries, began converting the local population from the 11th century onwards. Most Malay Muslims are orthodox Sunnis of the Shafi'i school but there are also smaller numbers of Shia Muslims and Sufi mystics. Just over 60 percent of Malaysia's population is Muslim; in Singapore, they form around 14 percent of the population.

Domes are a characteristic feature of all mosques. They are generally onion-shaped structures and are often crowned by a crescent moon, the universal symbol of Islam.

The courtyard of a mosque is designed to accommodate a large number of worshipers. This courtyard at Johor Bahru's Sultan Abu Bakar Mosque holds 2,000 people.

A minaret is a lofty tower usually located in one of the corners of a mosque. From here the *muezzin*, or caller to prayer, summons the faithful five times a day.

Islamic Architecture

Despite the flamboyant exteriors of some Islamic architecture, its real beauty lies in the inner spaces of the courtyard and rooms. This has often led to it being called the architecture of the veil. With its gleaming golden dome and striking minarets, Ubudiah Mosque (right) in Kuala Kangsar is among Malaysia's finest mosques.

This crenellated arch at Kapitan Keling Mosque *(see p108)* in Georgetown, Penang, is Moorish in style, borrowing from the architectural tradition of Islamic Spain and the North African Maghreb.

Colorful Islamic tilework is characterized by intricate geometric patterns and graceful floral motifs. Traditional Malay Muslim houses and mosques are adorned with these tiles.

Islamic Faith

Islam, which means "submission to the will of God" in Arabic, was founded by the Prophet Muhammad at Mecca in Arabia, in AD 622. The principle of Islam rests on an unshakeable faith in a single deity, Allah, and on his word delivered by Muhammad in the Koran. The five pillars of Islamic faith are shahadah, *witnessing that there is only one God;* salat, *performing the five daily prayers;* sawm, *fasting during the month of Ramadan;* zakat, *the giving of alms; and* hajj, *performing the pilgrimage to Mecca at least once in a lifetime.*

The Koran is the central religious text of Islam, believed to be the inspired and immutable Word of God. Divided into 114 units and written in the Arabic script, it is often memorized verbatim by the faithful.

Salat is the name given to the obligatory prayers that are performed five times a day. The faithful always pray in the direction of Mecca. Salat is believed to establish a direct link between the worshiper and the worshiped.

Wuzu is the first step of the ablutions performed before commencing the *salat*. This is an essential act of spiritual and physical cleansing, as no prayer is acceptable without the complete *wuzu*.

Islamic Art

Architecture and calligraphy are the two most distinctive and elegant art forms in Islam. Both have developed to levels of great sophistication because of the general prohibition of representational art forms. The hadith, *or Traditions of the Prophet Muhammad, decree that "the house which contains pictures will not be entered by the angels." Geometry also plays a major role in both architecture and calligraphy.*

The Jawi script is a Malay variant of Arabic writing. It is one of the two official scripts in Brunei and is also used in Malaysia and Singapore, particularly in religious calligraphy.

Zapin is a traditional Malay folk dance, with dancers usually performing in pairs accompanied by Islamic devotional chanting. Believed to have been introduced by 14th-century Muslim missionaries from the Middle East, it is commonly performed in Johor Bahru (see p134).

Batik, the art of wax-resist dyeing on textiles, is commonly used to pattern garments such as sarongs with bright designs. The most popular of such designs are floral prints (see p36).

Hinduism and Buddhism

Hinduism and Buddhism are the major religions of Malaysia and Singapore's South Asian and Chinese communities respectively. Although Hinduism dates back at least 1,500 years in both countries, the religion only took root when contract laborers from India were recruited to work in rubber and coffee plantations in Malaysia in the late 19th and 20th centuries. Buddhism became a permanent feature in Malaysia and Singapore after Chinese immigrants spread the religion to every part of the country in the 19th century.

Monk praying at a shrine of Kuan Yin, goddess of mercy

Hinduism

Hinduism in Malaysia and Singapore, complete with its many rituals and deities, is directly taken from Indian Hindu traditions, especially those of southern India from where most Indian migrants originated.

Statues of deities are enshrined at the central altar.

Fresh flower garlands are used to venerate the gods.

Devotees come to temples for individual or communal *puja*, or worship, ritual occasions, and to make offerings to honor the gods.

Offerings may include flowers, incense, and fruits such as coconuts, which are sprinkled with holy water during prayers.

Components of a prayer ritual include frankincense, myrrh, and other aromatic combustibles.

Hindu priests are Brahmins who belong to the highest of the four main castes. They tend to the temple and officiate at ceremonies.

The gopuram, or entrance gateway to Hindu temples, is often multitiered and elegantly decorated with colorful sculptures from the vast pantheon of Hindu gods.

Shaivism

Shaivism is a form of Hinduism which worships Lord Shiva as the main manifestation of the supreme being. His consort, Parvati, and their two sons, Murugan and Ganapati, are also worshiped by Shaivites. Shaivism grew prominent in Malaysia and Singapore as the Indian immigrants who settled there in the 19th century were mainly from southern India where the worship of Shiva is popular. The Sri Shivan temples in Singapore and Malaysia are especially revered by Shaivites.

Vibrant portrait of Lord Shiva

Buddhism

In both Malaysia and Singapore the Chinese communities follow the Mahayana school of Buddhism practiced in China, Japan, Korea, and Vietnam. The Thais of Singapore and the Orang Syam, or indigenous Thais of Malaysia, follow Theravada Buddhism, practiced in Thailand, Laos, Cambodia, Myanmar, and Sri Lanka. Buddhism in both countries is a fusion of different beliefs. In Singapore it is combined with Confucianism, Taoism, and ancestor worship. Buddhism is also personalized and centers around Kuan Yin, the goddess of mercy. Belief in luck and filial piety are also central features of Buddhism.

Buddhist monks shave their heads, wear saffron robes, and generally go barefoot to indicate a life of austerity.

The Buddha's halo, or nimbus, commonly depicted in Buddhist art, signifies enlightenment and spiritual development.

An urna, or a small protuberance between the Buddha's eyes, represents the "third eye" of spiritual vision, a mark of a holy man.

The Buddha is often depicted with a serene expression and a faint smile.

The wheel-turning pose represents the Wheel of Law, or *dhammachakra*, set in motion by the Buddha's first sermon at Sarnath, India.

Bare feet with both soles turned upward and resting on opposite thighs signifies meditation.

The Buddha's hair is generally arranged in the form of snail-shell curls, and surmounted by an *ushnisa*, or topknot.

Elongated earlobes are thought to be the result of heavy earrings worn by the Buddha as a prince.

A simple monk's robe represents the Buddha's life of renunciation.

The cross-legged posture is the position in which Buddha is most commonly portrayed.

Devout Buddhists burn incense and make offerings at temples across Malaysia and Singapore to show respect to the Buddha, the *sangha*, or order of monks, and the *dhamma*, or teachings of the Buddhist canon. Offerings often include fruit and flowers. Worshipers usually ask for good health and prosperity.

Principles of Buddhism

Despite the existence of two main schools and different sects that have evolved over the centuries, the central principles of Buddhism are common to most forms of the religion. These include the Four Noble Truths; the Eight-Fold Path; *karma*, or the moral law of cause and effect, which is symbolized by the Wheel of Law, and *nirvana*, or enlightenment. The Mahayana, or Greater Vehicle, school stresses the role of the *bodhisattva* or religious adept who, having gained *nirvana*, voluntarily renounces it to enlighten others. The Theravada, or Lesser Vehicle, school emphasizes the role of the *arhat*, or worthy one, who has attained *nirvana*.

Buddhist Wheel of Law

Secular Architecture

The traditional vernacular architecture of Malaysia and Singapore is mainly Malay and Straits Chinese, but a strong colonial influence is also apparent in buildings constructed during periods of British, Portuguese, and Dutch rule. In contrast, both countries boast stunning modern architecture, most prominently seen in their soaring skyscrapers. This is particularly true of Kuala Lumpur and Singapore.

The Singapore skyline is dominated by spectacular high-rise buildings

Straits Chinese

Straits Chinese architecture centers on the ubiquitous shophouse, found throughout Malaysia and Singapore. Buildings of this style were introduced by immigrants from the Guangdong province of southern China.

Overhanging floors protect pedestrians from the sun *(see p111)*

Characteristic gabled roof

Flower motif on a Peranakan shophouse tile.

Classic shophouses comprise a ground floor, whose street-facing portion is used to conduct business, and upper floors that serve as living quarters.

Traditional Malay House

The traditional Malay house tends to be raised on stilts, with extensions added when necessary. The house is centered around the *rumah ibu*, or main living room.

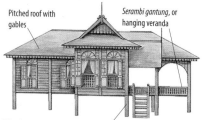

Pitched roof with gables

Serambi gantung, or hanging veranda

Stilts that protect the house from floods

The interiors are ventilated by many open spaces such as verandas and windows. Traditionally, the houses have wooden walls and thatched roofs.

Longhouses

Indigenous peoples of Sabah and Sarawak traditionally live in longhouse communities *(see p173)*, with each family occupying a separate apartment under a single contiguous roof. The entire structure is raised on stilts.

Longhouses commonly have a covered veranda, or *ruai*, which runs the length of the building, backed by a series of living quarters, or *bileks*. There is also a *tanju*, or open veranda.

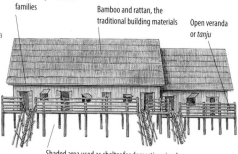

Living quarters occupied by individual families

Bamboo and rattan, the traditional building materials

Open veranda or *tanju*

Shaded area used as shelter for domestic animals

Minangkabau

The spectacular architecture of
the Minangkabau people,
concentrated in the state of
Negeri Sembilan, is chiefly
distinguished by upswept roofs
rising to pointed peaks that
represent the horns of a victorious
buffalo, or *minangkabau (see
p127)*. Traditionally, the roofs were
thatched with the fronds of the
nipa palm, but today they are
more usually shingled, or even
made from galvanized iron.

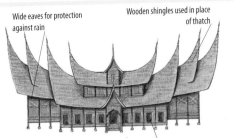

Wide eaves for protection against rain

Wooden shingles used in place of thatch

Windows permitting air circulation

Minangkabau houses, or *rumah minangkabau*, are recognizable by the distinctive style of their roofs.

Colonial Buildings

Colonial buildings in both Malaysia and Singapore
combine British Indian, Dutch East Indian, and
Portuguese styles, often combined with indigenous
Malay elements, Islamic motifs, and classical
European flourishes. Elaborate decorations and
wooden traceries lend individuality and style.

Classical façade

Grand entrance portico

Mock-Tudor bungalows are not
uncommon in the hill stations of
Peninsular Malaysia. These were built by
British plantation owners.

The Raffles Hotel in Singapore dates from
1887 and is named after Sir Stamford Raffles,
the founder of Singapore *(see pp220–21)*. It is
the epitome of colonial elegance.

Modern Architecture

Both Malaysia and Singapore are distinguished
by their steel and concrete skyscrapers, often
with façades of light- and heat-reflecting
mirrored glass. While contemporary buildings in
Malaysia incorporate elements of traditional
Islamic architecture, Singaporean designs
remain entirely modernistic.

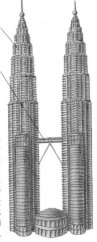

The 1,483-ft (452-m)-tall Petronas towers

Tower consisting of 88 floors, 10 escalators, and 76 elevators

Skybridge connecting the towers at 558 ft (170 m) off the ground

The Petronas Towers are Malaysia's most famous modern structures. With 88 stories, they are the tallest twin buildings in the world *(see p78)*.

The futuristic Esplanade – Theaters on the Bay, with twin
domes *(see p216)*, adds to Singapore's ultramodern cityscape,
in contrast with the city's traditional Indian, Chinese, and
colonial architecture.

Festivals of Malaysia and Singapore

Life in Malaysia and Singapore is punctuated with festivals, which are both frequent and spectacular. Although some festivals have a fixed date according to the international calendar, the Malay Muslim, Hindu, and Chinese traditions all set their festive days according to the lunar calendar *(see p321)*, making these celebrations movable events. Fortunately, the Malaysia and Singapore tourist boards regularly publish calendars of national and local festivals.

Giant banners in abundance, marking the beginning of the Chinese New Year

A traditional dinner with the entire family is perhaps the most important aspect of the celebrations at the New Year, which is also considered the time for new beginnings.

The dragon is a mythical beast symbolizing justice, wealth, and good fortune.

The colors used are predominantly red and gold, representing prosperity and long life.

Seven poles support the body, although more may be needed if the dragon is long.

Chinese New Year

The most significant festival for the Chinese is the Lunar New Year. In Singapore and in some parts of Malaysia, such as Kuala Lumpur, Ipoh, Taiping, and Johor Bahru, this 15-day festival is marked by chingay, a joyous street parade with lion dancers, stilt-walkers, giant banners, music, and colorful floats. Almost all the festival rituals are focused on bringing good luck and prosperity.

The leader of the team must be the most skilled and experienced of the dancers as the others follow him.

The display of fireworks in the night skies above the Petronas Towers is a spectacular highlight of the extravagant New Year's Eve celebrations in Kuala Lumpur.

The lion dance is a traditional dance form that dates back more than a thousand years. A pair of dancers trained in martial arts form the fore and hind legs of the lion, mimicking its motions.

Hari Raya Puasa

For Malay Muslims, the most important festival of the year is Hari Raya Puasa, also known as Aidilfitri in Malay, marking the end of the fasting month of Ramadan. Throughout the ninth month of the Muslim calendar, believers abstain from eating and drinking between sunrise and sunset. With the sighting of the new moon on the 30th day of the ninth month, Ramadan ends and the tenth month is ushered in with feasting on traditional fare such as ketupat, *or rice cakes, and* lemang, *or glutinous rice.*

Devout Muslim men start the day at the mosque for morning prayers, dressed in their finest clothes. Graves are cleaned and quarrels forgiven before the festivities begin.

The long, narrow body of the dragon is designed for sinuous movement.

Dragon dancers must be fit and need to practice regularly to put on a good show.

Muslim children light firecrackers on Hari Raya Puasa and are given *duit raya*, or gifts of money, in small green envelopes. For three days, family, friends, and neighbors visit each other.

Thaipusam

Celebrated by the southern Indian communities of Malaysia and Singapore, Thaipusam honors the Hindu god Murugan, youngest son of the gods Shiva and Parvati. It is held in the Tamil month of Thai (between January and February). The largest Thaipusam festival takes place at the Batu Caves, with over one million devotees and 10,000 tourists attending it. Worshipers shave their heads and undertake a pilgrimage along a set route, performing various acts of devotion along the way.

Kavadi carriers hold elaborately decorated metal frames called *kavadi*. Adorned with peacock feathers, these portable altars are attached to devotees with skewers pierced into the skin.

The Batu Caves *(see p96)*, dedicated to Lord Murugan, are one of the prime pilgrimage sites for Malaysia's Hindus. A spectacular scene unfolds at this site just outside Kuala Lumpur during Thaipusam, when pilgrims climb the 272 steps to the temple at the summit.

Arts and Crafts of Malaysia

Malaysia has a wealth of indigenous artistic traditions, many dating back centuries, but its arts and crafts have also been enriched by the cultural influences of Chinese, Indians, and other peoples. While Peninsular Malaysia excels at metalwork, Malaysian Borneo produces the most spectacular woodcarvings. Besides pottery, ceramic, brass, and silverware, a wide range of regional artistry, such as kite-making in Kota Bharu, is available. The country has a flourishing art scene, influenced by Hindu, Buddhist, Islamic, and Chinese cultures, and more recently by Western art.

Labu sayong water pots from Sayong, near Kuala Kangsar

Malayasian Textiles

Batik, which means writing in wax, is extremely popular in Malaysia, forming part of the Malay national dress. Among the best places to buy traditional batik is Kuching in Sarawak. The country's textile traditions also encompass fine silk and cotton cloth originally created for the royal courts. These include kain lemar, *or silk brocade interwoven with* ikat; kain sutera, *or woven silk;* kain songket, *or rich brocade; and* kain mastuli, *or heavy silk.*

Ikat cloth is made using a tie-and-dye technique on the threads before they are woven into elaborate patterns. Today, the best *ikat*, such as this decorative Iban blanket, comes from Sarawak.

Batik motifs are usually floral or geometric.

Melted wax is applied to the cloth to prevent dyes from penetrating.

Pua kumbu cloths are woven by the Iban for use in ceremonies and for decoration. Weaving is done primarily by women and the motif they use once showed their status. Today, motifs vary from plant and animal themes to more abstract patterns.

Songket Silk

The term songket *is derived from the Malay* menyongket, *which means to embroider with silver or gold thread. The metallic thread inserted between the silk strands stands out on the background cloth, creating a shimmering effect.*

Kain sutera is a type of *songket* used for sarongs traditionally worn on formal or ceremonial occasions.

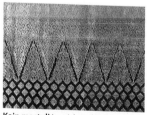

Kain mastuli is a rich and heavy variety of *songket* silk thread that is used when making traditional garments and decorative fabrics.

Woodcarving

Malaysian Borneo boasts the best and most varied forms of woodcarving in the country. Indigenous people of the region are known for their carving of spirit and totem figures, masks, and good luck charms.

Malay woodcarvers work deftly and with confident speed. Some of the best are found in Kuching and Kota Bharu.

Elaborate wooden masks are carved by the indigenous peoples of Malaysian Borneo to fend off evil and bad luck.

This gilt carving of a bat on the window frame of a Melakan house is a Peranakan symbol of good fortune.

A tribal grave post with a totemic figure is displayed at Kuching's Sarawak Museum.

Intricately carved shields were traditionally carried by Iban warriors into battle. The heavy wooden shields were often decorated with hideous faces to demoralize foes.

Metalwork

Traditional Malaysian silverware and jewelry has been influenced by the Peranakan. Metalware produced and sold in the markets of Penang, Melaka, and Kuching often shows considerable southern Indian influence. The products include gongs produced in Sumangkap (see p188), a range of brass items, and keris.

Brass is used for making household, decorative, and ceremonial objects. This brass screen in Kuala Lumpur's Sri Kanthaswamy Hindu Temple shows the intricate detailing that is typical of Malaysian craftsmanship.

Keris, or daggers, are weapons unique to Malay culture. They are said to possess magical powers that protect their owners and bring death to enemies.

Silverware of the finest quality is produced in Kelantan and Terengganu. Malaysian silverware is known for its intricate filigree work and designs.

THE HISTORY OF MALAYSIA AND SINGAPORE

The early history of the Malay peninsula is shrouded in mystery. But records of the subsequent centuries depict a great trading nation beleaguered by foreign invaders attracted by its abundant natural wealth and strategic position between the key maritime trade centers of India and China. Following their independence, Malaysia and Singapore have rapidly emerged as models of economic progress and modernization.

The discovery in 1958 of a human skull at Niah Caves in Sarawak and stone tools from Perak point towards human occupation of the region as far back as 40,000 BC. Findings of pottery and stone objects from both the peninsula and Malaysian Borneo, dating between 2800 and 500 BC, prove the existence of a Neolithic culture in this region.

Although few iron and bronze objects have been found in Malaysia, evidence in the form of huge Bronze Age Dongson drums links Peninsular Malaysia to northern Vietnam at around 500–300 BC. The drums, together with beads and pottery from India and China also found on the peninsula and dating back to the same time, indicate that international trade networks were already well established and foreign goods were being exchanged for the region's rich resources, including tin, gold, aromatic woods, and spices. So rich was this trade that the Indians seem to have referred to

the peninsula as *suvarnabhumi*, or the land of gold, from as early on as 200 BC. The growth of trade relations with India brought the coastal peoples of the Strait of Malacca into contact with Buddhism and Hinduism, as well as with Indian notions of kingship. For example, the Malay word for ruler, *rajah*, was borrowed from Sanskrit. Significant archaeological finds, such as Sanskrit inscriptions and Hindu and Buddhist statues (especially in Kedah in northwest Malaysia), suggest that Indian influence was well established in a number of settlements along the west coast of the peninsula by the 5th century AD.

Chinese trade was significant too, beginning from the 2nd century, via the Cambodian kingdom of Funan which extended its influence into the northern peninsula. The growing use of the sea to transport goods from western Asia to China gave further impetus to the emergence of port kingdoms in the Malaysian world.

Stone Age tools, Lenggong Museum

40,000–2800 BC Prehistoric Age

2800–500 BC Neolithic Age

500–300 BC Period of the Bronze Age Dongson culture in northern Vietnam

AD 1–99 Kingdom of Funan established in the lower Mekong Delta

200 BC Maritime trade links established between India and Southeast Asia; Hindu influences begin to spread across the region

AD 400–500 Increasing Southeast Asian trade with China

Dongson drum

2000 BC   1000 BC   0   AD 200   AD 400

◀ *Panoramic Sketch of Prince of Wales Island* by William Daniell, 1821

Srivijaya

The first of the port kingdoms to become a great pan-Malay confederation was the Hindu-Buddhist, maritime trade-based empire of Srivijaya. It emerged in the course of the 7th century and established its capital near Palembang in southeastern Sumatra.

Srivijaya evolved into a wealthy and powerful Malay kingdom, dominating maritime passages around the Strait of Malacca and the Sunda Strait (between Java and Sumatra), as well as the overland portage routes across Peninsular Malaysia as far north as Nakhon Si Thammarat in present-day Thailand. From its strategic position, Srivijaya was able to attract and monopolize overseas commerce between India and China, acting as a great entrepôt for Southeast Asian shipping as well as a source for rare and valuable goods, from scented woods to gold.

The rulers of Srivijaya developed methods of government which became popular with succeeding kingdoms such as Melaka. Paramount among these concepts was complete loyalty to the ruler, who was associated with divine powers – disloyalty was severely punished. While a mixture of Hinduism, Buddhism, and indigenous spirit belief was practiced in Srivijaya, it gained prominence as a center of Buddhist learning.

Srivijaya prospered until the 11th century, after which it began to decline, weakened by wars both with Java and the south Indian Chola kingdom. The power of the Hindu-Buddhist *rajahs* was also being undermined by Islam. At the same time,

Arrival of Arab merchants and missionaries in Southeast Asia

the increasing presence of Chinese ships encouraged Srivijaya's vassals to break away from Palembang's grip. By the late 13th century, the Thai kingdoms of Sukhothai and Ayutthaya had acquired considerable influence over the peninsula, as had the Hindu Majapahit empire of Java over southeast Sumatra.

The Spread of Islam

Islam came to Southeast Asia as a religion of trade, not one of conquest. Introduced by Arab merchants and missionaries around the 11th century, the religion spread rapidly across Peninsular Malaysia with Indian-Muslim traders. The Terengganu Stone, discovered in the peninsula's northeastern province in 1899, bears an inscription in the Malay Arabic script, suggesting that Islamic law was established here as early as 1303. However, Islam received its greatest boost when it was made state religion of the Sultanate of Melaka in the 15th century. Spreading to the farthest corners of the Melakan empire, Islam gradually came to be associated with the national identity of Malays.

700s Golden age of Srivijaya

Illustration depicting medieval Arab merchants

1000s With the arrival of Arab merchants, Islam spreads throughout the region

AD 700

AD 850

AD 1000

Thai Srivijaya-style Boddhisattva

992–1016 Wars between Srivijaya and Java

1025 Raids by Chola kings

The Rise of Melaka

Around 1400, Parameswara, the prince of Palembang, attempted to throw off Javanese domination over his realm by fleeing to Tumasik in present-day Singapore, before finally establishing a new kingdom at Melaka. Ideally located on the Strait of Malacca and within easy reach of the spice islands of Indonesia, the new state attracted trade from across Asia. In 1405, Zheng He, the great Chinese Ming admiral, launched his explorations of Southeast Asia and the Indian Ocean, and made Melaka the main outpost for his fleet. This helped secure a trade agreement with China as well as protection from its emperor against the constant threat of Siamese attacks. The city of Melaka became truly cosmopolitan: given the seasonal winds, ships from China, Japan, India, and Persia might spend at least a year in the port.

The spread of Islam in Melaka is believed to have taken place between 1425 and 1445, when Parameswara's successors made Islam the state religion and took the title of Sultan, thus giving rise to the Sultanate of Melaka. The adoption of Islam helped link Melaka to the vast Muslim trading world, and by the end of the 15th century it was the region's major entrepôt,

Plan of the city of Melaka by Pedro Baretti de Resende, c.1511.

dominating much of the Malay world. Though ties with the Imperial Court in China were fostered for added protection, the sultanate developed into an independent and centralized administration with the sultan as absolute ruler. He oversaw a fairly complex legal and administrative structure which ensured the stability of the kingdom. High-ranking officials of the state included the *bendahara*, or prime minister, the *laksamanas*, or admirals, who commanded the army and navy, the *temenggung*, or minister responsible for defense and justice, and the *syahbandar*, or harbor master. Government was formalized in the *Undang-Undang Melaka*, or codified laws of Melaka, which constantly evolved under successive sultans. The basis for Melakan law was threefold – Hindu-Buddhist tradition, Islamic tradition, and *adapt*, or indigenous tradition. Concurrently, Melaka became a center for Islamic dissemination throughout present-day Malaysia, Indonesia, and Brunei. The state's influence was reflected in the emergence of the Malay language as the language of trade throughout the region.

Relief of Zheng He, Chinese temple in Semarang, Java

			1425–45 Melaka ruler adopts Islam and takes the title of Sultan
	Sukhothai-style vessel with lid	1400 Parameswara founds the kingdom of Melaka	
1150		**1300**	**1450**
1238 Foundation of the Thai Kingdom of Sukhothai		1303 Terengganu Stone records the establishment of Islamic law	

Melaka tin coin, the earliest known indigenous coins of the Malay States

Portuguese Conquest

By the 15th century, the Portuguese were eager to challenge Venice's position as the sole suppliers of spices in Europe, as well as to break the monopoly of the Arab and Indian Muslim traders over the immensely valuable spice trade. In 1509, an initial Portuguese expedition under Admiral Lopez de Sequeira arrived in Melaka, but was driven off by the sultan's army. A much larger and better-equipped fleet, led by Admiral Alfonso de Albuquerque in 1511, succeeded in capturing Melaka after a 40-day siege, ushering in the era of European colonial powers in the region. Sultan Mahmud Shah escaped to the interior of the peninsula, where his elder son, Muzaffar Shah, eventually established the Sultanate of Perak in the north, and his younger son, Alauddin Riyat Shah, founded the Johor Sultanate in the south. This period also saw the rise of the Sumatran state of Aceh as a regional power. Although Melaka remained a Portuguese colony for over a century, the period saw a three-way struggle between Aceh, the sultanates of Johor and Perak, and the Portuguese for the control of Melaka, which lasted most of the 16th century.

Alfonso de Albuquerque

The Dutch Era

The new kingdom of Johor faced its own share of assaults, from both the Portuguese and Aceh, and it was not until the arrival of the Dutch, toward the end of the 16th century, that it succeeded in consolidating its position.

Looking to protect itself against its enemies, the sultan forged an alliance with the Dutch. In 1602, all the Dutch trading enterprises in Asia combined to form The United Netherlands Chartered East India Company (VOC), which recognized the need to seize control of Melaka to gain monopoly of the spice trade. In 1640, the Dutch, with the help of the Sultan of Johor, attacked Melaka and after a year-long siege succeeded in displacing the Portuguese. In return for its support, Johor was granted trading privileges and by the end of the 17th century it had grown into a powerful kingdom. At the height of its power it controlled southern Peninsular Malaysia and part of eastern Sumatra.

When the Dutch took over, much of Melaka lay in ruin owing to the 1640–41 siege. During their rule, the Dutch rebuilt the city and many of these structures survive to this day. Among the prominent buildings is the Stadthuys *(see p128)*, the oldest Dutch building in Southeast Asia.

Dutch ships attacking a Portuguese vessel on the Indian Ocean

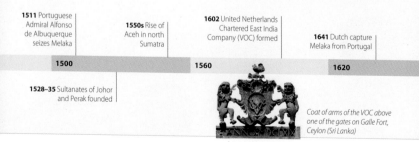

(see p128)

1511 Portuguese Admiral Alfonso de Albuquerque seizes Melaka

1550s Rise of Aceh in north Sumatra

1602 United Netherlands Chartered East India Company (VOC) formed

1641 Dutch capture Melaka from Portugal

1500

1560

1620

1528–35 Sultanates of Johor and Perak founded

Coat of arms of the VOC above one of the gates on Galle Fort, Ceylon (Sri Lanka)

Dutch merchant and VOC ships at Jakarta, 17th century

Yet, over the next 180 years under the Dutch, Melaka's prosperity declined as the new colonial rulers concentrated on developing their main base at Batavia, which is now Jakarta in Indonesia.

Borneo

Until the arrival of the British, the areas that now comprise Sarawak, Sabah, and the tiny, oil-rich state of Brunei had little to do with the Malay peninsula. Most of Borneo, as well as part of the neighboring Sulu Archipelago (present-day Philippines), was ruled by the powerful Brunei Sultanate. In 1704, during a period of internal unrest, Brunei appears to have ceded part of Sabah to the Sultan of Sulu in return for the latter's military assistance. The territory eventually passed to Malaysia via the British, but the Philippines tried to reclaim Sabah as their land after the formation of Malaysia in 1963.

Arrival of the British

Things changed dramatically in Malaysia with the arrival of the British in the 18th century. The British East India Company (EIC) needed a halfway base for their maritime trade with India and China. In 1786, Sir Francis Light *(see p109)* signed a treaty and acquired Penang from the Sultan of Kedah on behalf of the company and established it as a commercial and naval base. He also declared it as a free trading port and Penang soon thrived. After Europe's Napoleonic Wars (1800–15), Britain emerged as the leading power in Asia. In 1819, Sir Stamford Raffles *(see p44)* repeated Light's work at Penang with considerable success in Singapore, which also became a booming trade port. In 1824, Britain and the Netherlands signed the Anglo-Dutch Treaty dividing the Malay world, with the Malay peninsula passing to Britain and the bulk of the Indonesian Archipelago to the Dutch. Thus, Melaka passed to the British in exchange for Bengkulu on Sumatra, which went to Holland.

Initial British policy towards Malaysia was determinedly one of "trade, not territory," and also like the Dutch, but unlike the Portuguese, the British were not interested in spreading Christianity, but rather in free trade and profit. They limited their direct control to the Straits Settlements *(see pp44–5)*, formed in 1826. The Malay Peninsula became part of Britain's sphere of influence, but remained largely self-governing and independent.

British ships arriving to take control of Melaka in 1824

Sir Stamford Raffles

1704 Brunei cedes part of Borneo to Sulu

1819 Sir Stamford Raffles founds Singapore

1826 Formation of the Straits Settlements

1680	1740	1800

Detail of Borneo from Peter Plancius's chart of Borneo, 1595

1786 Sir Francis Light acquires Penang for the British East India Company

1824 Melaka passes to Britain under the Anglo-Dutch Treaty

The Straits Settlements

Between 1826 and 1946, the British Crown held a group of geographically separate territories consisting of Penang, Melaka, Singapore, Province Wellesley, and surrounding islands, under the collective name of the Straits Settlements. Colonial influence in the area, however, began as early as 1786, when the Sultan of Kedah ceded Penang to the British East India Company in exchange for protection from Siam and Burma. As other areas came under colonial power, they were built up to promote trade. The consequent close association of the region is still visible today in the racial and cultural ties of its mixed ethnic communities and the legacies of its architectural style and landmarks.

British East India vessel off Melaka, early 19th century

The British in Penang employed Chinese and Indian migrants, and sometimes indigenous Malays, as laborers on road construction projects throughout the island.

Colonization

The British did not arrive at the Straits Settlements in large numbers, instead establishing themselves as the ruling elite and employing migrants from India, China, and other parts of the British Empire to administer the new colonies and serve as soldiers, laborers, and tradesmen.

Chinese junks were used extensively for trade between the Settlements.

Stamford Raffles

Sir Stamford Raffles

One of the British Empire's most celebrated statesmen, Sir Thomas Stamford Raffles (1781–1826) began his career at the age of 14 as a clerk with the British East India Company in London. He worked his way up to become Lieutenant-Governor of Java in 1811 and was knighted in 1817. In 1819, Raffles signed a treaty with a local sultan, laying the foundation for modern Singapore. Also a founder and first president of the Zoological Society of London, he is remembered in the name of the largest flower in the world, the rafflesia.

Sultan Abdul Hamid Halim Shah of Kedah and his entourage in 1900. Like all sultans who reigned after the British took control of Penang in 1786, he had no real power in the island's government.

Trade

The Straits Settlements were acquired by the British to function as free trade ports, not to promote territorial ambitions. By establishing such ports, Britain sought to dominate trade routes between Europe and Asia.

Penang's first coin, bearing the British East India Company crest, was minted in 1787 in Calcutta. Sir Francis Light is said to have fired cannons loaded with coins into the jungle to coax laborers to clear it.

Spice plantations were set up in Penang to grow mace, nutmeg, cinnamon, and pepper, which were rare and valuable commodities in 18th-century Europe.

1/4 cent coins, bearing the sovereign's head, were first struck in 1826, the year the Straits Settlements passed into the hands of the British Government.

A new port at Singapore was envisaged by Raffles as a free port astride the sea lanes between Europe and the Far East. Today, it is one of the busiest ports in the world.

Culture

The Straits Settlements developed as a fascinating melting pot of cultures. Immigrants from Asia lived side by side with Portuguese, Dutch, and British settlers, as well as indigenous Malays.

Gas lighting was one of many innovations brought by the British to the Settlements.

Peranakan culture grew alongside the development of the Settlements. New customs were born out of the marriages between the Chinese and Malay, which blended the traditions of each culture. Peranakan weddings were 14-day affairs in which the couple wore Chinese dress.

Early Chinese settlers, as well as Peranakan men, wore their hair in distinctive long ponytails, or *queues*, well into the late 19th century. This was a sign of their allegiance to the Qing Empire.

Kling is an outdated name for early Tamil settlers originating from southern India. They formed the majority of South Asian migrants to the Straits Settlements.

A lithograph depicting the scene of a battle with pirates during James Brooke's rule

The Rise of the White Rajahs

Britain did not include Borneo in the Anglo-Dutch Treaty, preferring to concentrate their interests on the peninsula. By the late 18th century, Brunei was in decline and faced increasing unrest from the indigenous peoples as well as territorial claims from the Sulu Sultanate. In 1838, James Brooke, an explorer and former officer with the East India Company, set out to seek his fortune in the East Indies. En route he passed through Singapore and was asked by the British governor to deliver a message to Rajah Muda Hashim, Governor of Kuching in Sarawak. Brooke arrived in Sarawak in 1839 to find the territory in a state of revolt, with the indigenous Dayaks rising up against the Sultan of Brunei. He was enlisted to help the sultan and together they crushed the rebellion within a year.

James Brooke, the first White Rajah of Sarawak

As a reward, in 1841, the sultan made Brooke the Rajah of Sarawak, the first of three White Rajahs (*see p163*). Brooke, backed by British naval power, used his position to consolidate his rule over the indigenous people, as well as ward off unruly Malay pirates who wreaked havoc on the coast. Brooke's rule was remarkably progressive, and he sought to establish law and order as well as welfare for the local people. He gradually won the trust of the indigenous communities, although he faced and put down a rebellion by Chinese migrants in 1857. When he died in 1868, James Brooke was succeeded as rajah by his nephew, Charles Brooke (1829–1917), who was responsible for expanding the territory of Sarawak at the expense of the shrinking Brunei Sultanate. During his reign, Sarawak also became a British protectorate in 1888, with the Brooke family retaining control of the internal administration.

Expansion of British Control

In the mid-19th century, Sabah remained under the loose control of Brunei (with Sulu chiefs exercising authority at a local level). Enfeebled by internal disputes, Brunei sought to lease the territory, first to Claude

Signing the treaty for the cession of Labuan, Borneo, in 1846

1847 Signing of the treaty of Labuan

1865 Brunei leases Sabah to Claude Lee Moses, the American consul

1874 Treaty of Pangkor signed; first British Resident installed in Perak

1840 **1850** **1860** **1870**

1841 James Brooke becomes the first White Rajah

1857 Brooke puts down Chinese rebellion

Charles Brooke, second White Rajah of Sarawak

1868 Death of James Brooke, Charles Brooke succeeds

Lee Moses, the American consul in Brunei, in 1865, then to Baron von Overbeck, the Austrian consul in Hong Kong in 1875, and finally to Englishman Alfred Dent, who established the British North Borneo Company (BNBC) in 1881. In 1888, Sabah, along with Sarawak, came under British government protection. Like the White Rajahs, however, the company retained control of internal administration. A resistance movement started by Mat Salleh in 1895 against the company's rule was not defeated until 1905 (five years after Mat Salleh's death). Following that, Sabah remained a quiet colonial backwater.

British officials with the sultans of the Federated Malay States

At about the same time, the British began to refine their policies of non-intervention in the Malay peninsular states. The booming tin industry had attracted large numbers of Chinese immigrants to the states of Perak and Selangor. This led to ethnic clashes with the Malays, as well as to civil disorders caused by Chinese criminal gangs. Infighting also raged in various Malay sultanates. The British feared that another major European power, notably Germany, might exploit these weaknesses to gain a foothold on the Malaysian mainland. Hence, in 1874, through the Treaty of Pangkor, the first British Resident was appointed in Perak, whom the sultan agreed to consult on all issues except those involving Muslim religion and Malay custom. However, increased British control of judicial and financial affairs sparked unrest amongst the Perak Malays and led to the murder of the first Resident, J W W Birch, in 1875.

This revolt was quickly quashed, and the process of appointing British Residents continued. In 1896, the states of Pahang, Selangor, and Negeri Sembilan joined Perak as part of the British-controlled Federated Malay States, which were administered from the Sultan Abdul Samad Building in Kuala Lumpur. In 1909, under the terms of the Anglo-Siamese Treaty, the former Thai tributaries of Kelantan, Terengganu, Kedah, and Perlis, joined by Johor in 1914, came under the system of British Residents, becoming known as the Unfederated Malay States. Thus, together with the Straits Settlements and Sabah, Sarawak, and Brunei, British consolidation of power over Malaya was complete by World War I.

Sultan Abdul Samad Building, Kuala Lumpur

1877 Brunei renews lease on Sabah to Overbeck

STATE OF NORTH BORNEO · ONE CENT · *Stamp issued by the BNBC*

1888 British Resident appointed in Pahang

1895 Mat Salleh resistance movement begins in Sabah

1896 Creation of the Federated Malay States

1909 Unfederated Malay States formed

1880   **1890**   **1900**   **1910**

1881 Alfred Dent sets up the BNBC

1888 Sarawak and Sabah become British protectorates

1914 Johor joins the Unfederated Malay States

1877 Rubber tree introduced via Brazil, Kew Gardens, and Ceylon (Sri Lanka) to the Botanic Gardens in Singapore

Sir Frank Swettenham, first Resident-General of the Federated Malay States

A British rubber planter overseeing Indian workers, Malaysia

Colonial Life

Having taken charge of the entire peninsula, the British turned their energies towards developing a productive economy. Peninsular Malaysia emerged in the 20th century as the world's leading producer of both rubber and tin. In Borneo, Sarawak was a securely established and relatively prosperous territory by the time Charles Vyner Brooke took over as the third White Rajah in 1917, while Sabah was profiting from the timber, rubber, and tobacco industries. Large-scale immigration from India and China was encouraged to supply the workforce for the colonial economy. The Malays were recognized as indigenous people, but were largely encouraged to stay in their villages. By the late 1930s, ordinary Malays were less well off than the urban Chinese, and in danger of becoming a minority in their own homeland. The stage had been set for decades of racial tensions. Politicization and elite sentiment for independence along ethnic lines also began to grow. The advent of World War II ensured that colonial life would never be the same.

World War II

Troops of the Japanese Imperial Army landed on the east coast of the peninsula in December 1941. Within 2 months, they had conquered it, and Singapore and Borneo as well. For the next 3 years they would unleash a particularly ruthless regime. The *sook ching* (purification by elimination) massacres in the first months of Japanese rule involved the deaths of 40,000–70,000 ethnic Chinese in Singapore alone. About 75,000 Malaysians, mostly Indian Tamils, were recruited to work on the Burma–Thailand "Death" Railway. With malnourishment, appalling working conditions, and the brutality of the Japanese overseers, death rates escalated to 40 percent.

Japanese troops marching through downtown Singapore in December 1941

Some Malaysians resisted, notably the guerrilla units of the Malayan Communist Party (MCP), armed by British saboteurs in the underground Force 136. At the same time, to bolster their rule, the Japanese encouraged radical Malayan nationalists to organize paramilitary and political organizations. Hopelessly overstretched throughout Asia and the Pacific, Japanese rule had induced economic chaos in the Malay peninsula and Borneo by 1944. But it was the dropping of atomic bombs on Hiroshima and Nagasaki in August 1945 that finally forced Japan to surrender.

Charles Vyner Brooke

1930s Chinese begin to join the Malayan Communist Party

1941 Japanese invasion of Malaya and Singapore

| 1918 | 1923 | 1928 | 1933 | 1938 |

1917 Charles Vyner Brooke, third and last White Rajah of Sarawak (1917–46)

1926 Singapore Malay Union formed

HMS Prince of Wales, *sunk off the coast of Terengganu by Japanese bombers in 1941*

Declaration of independence from British rule by Tunku Abdul Rahman in August 1957

The Emergency

In the reoccupation, the first British step was to establish the Malayan Union in 1946. This united all the peninsular states into a central administration under British rule and granted equal citizenship rights to all ethnic groups. Singapore, Sabah, and Sarawak were to be governed separately as crown colonies.

The union was strongly opposed by the Malay population and led to the formation of the first Malay political party, the United Malays National Organization (UMNO). The Malayan Union was subsequently replaced by the Federation of Malaya, which excluded Singapore, and granted special rights to the Malays. However, the Chinese were dissatisfied with this development, and in June 1948, the Malayan Races Liberation Army (MRLA), the armed wing of the MCP, returned to the jungle under the leadership of Chin Peng to begin an insurgency against the British. So began the hard-fought Emergency.

Chin Peng's war was ultimately doomed. Few Malays or Indians supported the MCP, while the resettlement of 400,000 rural Chinese cut off the guerrillas from food and intelligence supplies. The MCP leaders finally fled to Thailand in the late 1950s, and by 1960 the government of independent Malaya declared the Emergency over.

Merdeka (Independence)

Parallel to their campaign against the MRLA, the British pursued talks with anti-communist Malay nationalists, promising independence. In 1955, elections were held to determine the government for the new country. This was won by the Alliance Party, formed by the UMNO, the Malayan Chinese Association, and the Malayan Indian Congress. On August 31, 1957, Malaya gained independence, with Tunku Abdul Rahman as its first prime minister. Sarawak, Sabah, and Singapore remained crown colonies, although Singapore became self-governing in 1959. In 1961, a new federation uniting the peninsular states, Singapore, Sarawak, Sabah, and Brunei, was proposed. Despite the opposition from Indonesia and the Philippines, the planned union went ahead, and Malaysia was proclaimed on September 16, 1963, but without Brunei, which opted out.

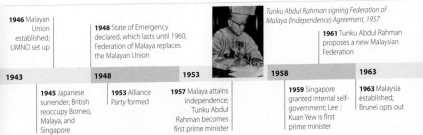

1946 Malayan Union established; UMNO set up

1948 State of Emergency declared, which lasts until 1960; Federation of Malaya replaces the Malayan Union

Tunku Abdul Rahman signing Federation of Malaya (Independence) Agreement, 1957

1961 Tunku Abdul Rahman proposes a new Malaysian Federation

1943

1948

1953

1958

1963

1945 Japanese surrender; British reoccupy Borneo, Malaya, and Singapore

1953 Alliance Party formed

1957 Malaya attains independence; Tunku Abdul Rahman becomes first prime minister

1959 Singapore granted internal self-government; Lee Kuan Yew is first prime minister

1963 Malaysia established; Brunei opts out

Malay Royal Regiment troops patrolling the streets of Kuala Lumpur following the May 13, 1969 riots

Konfrontasi

Both Indonesia and the Philippines immediately severed diplomatic relations with the new state of Malaysia. Indonesian president Sukarno began a policy of Konfrontasi, or confrontation, involving infiltration and sabotage. Indonesian armed troops crossed into Sabah and Sarawak, and even landed in Peninsular Malaysia and Singapore. Over the next 4 years the Malaysian army, backed by British, New Zealand, and Australian forces, defeated Indonesian attempts to subvert the new federation. Malaysia was thus established as a secure, internationally recognized state.

Inaugural meeting of ASEAN members in August 1967

However, in 1965, Singapore reluctantly left the Malaysian Federation due to continuing political disagreements and became an independent country. Still, the two neighbors remained closely associated. In 1967, Malaysia and Singapore joined the Association of Southeast Asian Nations (ASEAN) and were two of its five original members.

Ethnic and Economic Tensions

In the late 1960s, Malaysia and Singapore were still relatively impoverished by the effects of war and also riven with ethnic tensions. The departure of Singapore from the Federation of Malaysia ensured a Malay Muslim majority within Malaysia, but Malay politicians and the ethnic Malay population were still concerned by the economic power wielded by the Chinese. In 1967, the National Language Act was passed to ensure the primacy of the Malay language. The move was resented by the Chinese. Ethnic tensions first came to a head in Singapore, where there was rioting between the Malays and Chinese in 1964.

1963 Sukarno starts policy of Konfrontasi

1967 Malaysia and Singapore join ASEAN

1969 Race riots in Kuala Lumpur

1981 Mahathir Mohamad becomes Malaysia's fourth prime minister

1964

1974

1984

1965 Singapore leaves Malaysia and becomes an independent state

1970 Tun Abdul Razak takes over as Malaysia's prime minister; NEP introduced favoring the *bumiputra*

Offshore oil rig in Sarawak

In the 1969 general elections, the Alliance Party polled less than 50 percent of the popular vote, but retained its majority in the parliament. A celebration march by the opposition parties led to an outbreak of race riots in Kuala Lumpur on May 13, 1969, when hundreds of ethnic Chinese were massacred.

The Malaysian government, under Tun Abdul Razak, who had taken over from Tunku Abdul Rahman in 1970, was badly shaken. It responded by introducing the New Economic Policy (NEP) in 1970, which was designed to favor the *bumiputras (see pp26–7)* and improve their economic standing in society. At the same time, the authorities made it clear that no further racial attacks on ethnic Chinese would be tolerated. The Alliance Party also broadened its coalition to include members of the opposition and formed the Barisan Nasional (National Front), which continues to be in power today.

Kuala Lumpur's soaring skyline, dominated by the Petronas Towers, a symbol of economic prosperity

Malaysia and Singapore Today

Over the next 20 years, using a cautious mixture of financial inducements and firm paternalism, both Malaysia and Singapore remained peaceful. Malaysia prospered due to world demand for its rubber, palm oil, tea, and tin, and by the end of the 1970s, the development of light industries and the discovery of oil and natural gas reserves in the South China Sea provided an extra boost. A period of remarkable economic and social development in the 1980s and 1990s was overseen by Prime Minister Mahathir Mohamad, who came to power in 1981.

At its independence in 1965, Singapore seemed to face a bleak economic future.

However, under Lee Kuan Yew, Prime Minister from 1959 to 1990, it grew and prospered as a powerhouse of light industry and high technology. It also became one of the world's greatest sea ports.

In 2003, Abdullah Ahmad Badawi took over from Mahathir Mohamad as prime minister of Malaysia. He resigned in 2009 and was succeeded by Mohammad Najib Abdul Razak. In Singapore, Lee Kuan Yew's successor, Goh Chok Tong, was replaced by Yew's son, Lee Hsien Loong, in 2004. Both governments have now entered a less authoritarian era, although media and freedom of speech are still tightly monitored. In 2013 the Barisan Nasional coalition, led by Najib Razak, won their 13th victory in a row. The economies of both countries continue to surge ahead, as do standards of living and higher education, health, and social services.

Prime Minister Abdullah Ahmad Badawi

2006 Malaysia and Singapore fail to agree on new bridge project linking the two countries

2015 Death of Lee Kuan Yew; over a million Singaporeans queue to pay their respects in a week of national mourning

2007 Malaysia celebrates 50 years of independence

| 1994 | 2004 | 2014 | 2024 |

2003 Abdullah Badawi becomes Malaysia's fifth prime minister

2004 Lee Hsien Loong becomes Singapore's third prime minister

2011 Dr Tan Keng Yam Tony is sworn in as seventh president of Singapore

2009 Mohammad Najib Abdul Razak becomes Malaysia's sixth prime minister

MALAYSIA REGION BY REGION

INTRODUCING MALAYSIA

With its magnificent natural beauty and unique cultural heritage, Malaysia is a fascinating Southeast Asian destination. A relatively young country that celebrated 50 years of independence in 2007, it has progressed remarkably and has emerged as one of the most successful economies in Asia.

Situated at the crossroads of ancient maritime trade routes, Malaysia has long been a cultural melting pot. The bulk of the population lives on Peninsular Malaysia. While about half the country's 30 million people are of Malay origin, there are significant Chinese and Indian minorities, as well as many indigenous communities. The country's diversity is apparent in its social customs and festivals, and its many cuisines and languages.

Society and Politics

Malaysia is a constitutional monarchy, based on the political system of its former colonial ruler, Britain. In practice, however, there is more power vested in the executive branch of government than the judiciary. The country is headed nominally by a supreme ruler, a rotating position that is held for a five-year term by sultans of nine hereditary Malay sultanates, while the government is led by an elected prime minister, currently Datuk Seri Mohammed Najib Razak, who is assisted by a cabinet

of ministers. The government's two-tier parliament consists of a lower house with 219 elected representatives and an upper house with 70 senators. Elections are held every five years. Since independence, the country has been ruled by a multiracial coalition named Barisan Nasional (National Front), of which the United Malays National Organization (UMNO) is the largest political party.

Economy

From the early 1970s through the late 1990s, Malaysia transformed itself from an economy based on mining and agriculture to one dominated by manufacturing and exports, particularly of electronic components. Palm oil also continues to be one of the most important exports. Other prominent contributors to the economy are oil and gas production, timber, and tourism. The country has maintained steady economic growth over the past couple of decades, fueling rapid development in the major

The port and the stunning Masjid Negeri in Kuantan, Pahang

◀ Semporna Bay in Sabah

A pair of rhinoceros hornbills, the state bird of Sarawak, in the lush Malaysian rain forest

cities. Its main trading partners are the USA, China, and Japan, all significant sources of foreign investment. Malaysia's economy grew by 6 percent in 2014, one of the highest increases in Southeast Asia.

Environment

Malaysia, like many developing nations, faces its own set of environmental issues, including air and water pollution, deforestation, and the depletion of wildlife species. Although stretches of the country's ancient rain forests, and the wildlife they shelter, are protected in national parks, intensive logging is changing the face of the country, transforming jungles into barren hillsides. Fortunately, several international bodies, such as WWF, the global conservation organization, are very active in Malaysia and their persistent campaigning has at least slowed the rate of environmental degradation. Despite their efforts, the Sumatran rhinoceros and the leatherback turtle face extinction.

Culture and Arts

Malaysia's ethnic mosaic endows it with an infinitely varied and cosmopolitan culture, assimilating Malay, Chinese, and Indian customs, traditions, and beliefs, as well as those of its indigenous peoples. The ethnic diversity is also reflected in

the variety of religions followed here. Although Islam is the state religion, Buddhism, Hinduism, and Christianity, among others, are practiced freely. Traditional Malay performing arts, including the fascinating *wayang kulit*, or shadow-puppet plays, continue to thrive and can be seen during festivals or at cultural shows. Local pastimes such as kite-flying and top-spinning are still practiced, particularly on the east coast of the peninsula. The country has a vibrant handicrafts tradition, ranging from exquisitely woven textiles to basketware and woodcarving. Malaysia is also gaining a healthy contemporary art scene. Artists such as the collage specialist Yee I-Lann have exhibited in Hong Kong and New York.

Puppeteer maneuvering figures during a show

MALAYSIA THROUGH THE YEAR

With its blend of diverse ethnic groups and cultures, Malaysia hosts a range of festivals and events throughout the year. The country's religious festivals include the Islamic Hari Raya Puasa and Hindu Deepavali. Sporting events, such as Formula 1 racing, and traditional pastimes such as dancing and martial arts are also enjoyed. In addition to nationwide events, an array of state-specific festivals are celebrated. As many people visit family during major festivals, all forms of transport are congested. Many religious festivals are based on the lunar calendar, so dates can vary. Islamic festivals, for example, move forward by about ten days each year in relation to the Gregorian calendar. For exact dates, check with Tourism Malaysia.

January to March

Seasons vary little in Malaysia, with only the early months of the year distinguished by heavy rain on the east coast of Peninsular Malaysia. Still, spirits are far from dampened by the rain and festivals such as the Chinese New Year are celebrated with enthusiasm.

Chinese New Year (*Jan/Feb*), nationwide. The streets come alive to see out the old year and welcome the new, with dragon dances and Chinese opera performances. Debts are paid off, children are given presents of money, and mandarin oranges – a symbol of good luck – are eaten. Many shops and businesses close for a week.
Ponggal (*Jan/Feb*), nationwide. A Tamil (southern Indian) harvest festival celebrated by boiling rice, sugar, and milk until the pot overflows, symbolizing prosperity. This is offered to gods at Hindu temples.
Thaipusam (*Jan/Feb*), nationwide. A Hindu festival honoring Lord Murugan, in which thousands of devotees carry *kavadis*, or steel arches, attached to their skin by hooks, and walk in procession from the Sri Maha Mariamman Temple (*see p70*) to the Batu Caves (*see p96*), one of the largest temple caves in the country.
Federal Territory Day (*Feb 1*), Kuala Lumpur, Labuan, and Putrajaya. Malaysia's three federal territories put on parades, firework displays, and cultural shows.
World Kite Festival (*Feb*), Pasir Gudang, Johor. an annual event that attracts kite enthusiasts from around the world.
Hari Raya Haji (*variable*), nationwide. This Islamic festival celebrates the return of pilgrims from the Hajj to Mecca with prayers and animal sacrifices. This is a public holiday in the states of Kedah, Kelantan, Perlis, and Terengganu.
Chap Goh Mei (*usually Feb*), nationwide. The fifteenth day after the start of the Chinese New Year is marked by feasts and prayers.

Worshipers lighting candles at a church during Easter

Malaysian Open Golf Championship (*Feb*), nationwide. An international golfing event that takes place at the top golf courses in the country, including the Royal Selangor Golf and Country Club and the Kuala Lumpur Golf and Country Club.
Le Tour de Langkawi (*Mar*), Langkawi to Merdeka Square in Kuala Lumpur. Top cyclists from around the world compete over 10 day-long stages in Asia's version of the Tour de France.
Malaysian Grand Prix (*usually Mar*), Selangor. The world's fastest Formula 1 drivers compete at the Sepang International Circuit.
Easter (*Mar/Apr*), nationwide. The biggest ceremonies are held in Melaka with candlelit processions at churches on Good Friday, which is a public holiday in Sabah and Sarawak.

Formula 1 cars speed around the track at the Malaysian Grand Prix

April to June

This is the peak of the festival calendar especially for the Dayaks of Sarawak who celebrate the Gawai festival. Other highlights include the Buddhist Vesak.

Pesta Kaul *(Apr)*, Mukah. A festival of the Melanau fishing communities to mark the start of the fishing season. Dare-devil acts are performed on huge rattan swings.

Labuan International Sea Challenge *(Apr)*, Pulau Labuan. An international competition that includes fishing, swimming, and kayaking events.

Penang World Music Festival *(Apr)*, Georgetown. Over two nights this UNESCO World Heritage-listed city plays host to an annual music festival featuring a colorful assortment of local and international performances. In recent years, musicians from Spain, Germany, South Africa, and India have participated.

Prophet Muhammad's Birthday *(variable)*, nationwide. Processions and recitations of the Koran commemorate the birth of the Prophet Muhammad.

World Harvest Festival *(May)*, Sarawak Cultural Village, located near Kuching. A cultural extravaganza in anticipation of the Gawai festival, featuring dance and music.

Orang Ulu dancers in vibrant ethnic costumes at the World Harvest Festival

Sabah Fest *(May)*, Sabah. A cultural extravaganza incorporating dance, music, fashion, and food.

Colors of Malaysia *(May)*, nationwide. A month-long celebration of Malaysian culture, featuring parades, music, dance, and food.

Miri International Jazz Festival *(May)*, Miri. Musicians perform funk, fusion, Latin, and blues.

Tadau Kaamatan *(end of May)*, Penampang (Sabah). A festival for the Kadazan Dusun and Murut communities, who celebrate a successful rice crop by singing, dancing, and electing a harvest queen.

Vesak *(May/Jun)*, nationwide. The most important festival of the year for Buddhists, honoring the birth, enlightenment, and death of the Buddha.

King's Birthday *(1st Sat in Jun)*, nationwide. There are processions in Kuala Lumpur to celebrate the birthday of the king.

Gawai *(early Jun)*, across Sarawak. Marking the end of the rice harvest, this festival is the highlight of the year for the Dayaks of Sarawak and an occasion for feasting and dancing. There are many versions of Gawai, such as Gawai Padi, celebrated by the Bidayuh, one of the Dayak groups. It is an ideal time to visit a longhouse.

Fiesta San Pedro *(Jun)*, Melaka. The Eurasian community, who came here during the Portuguese occupation in the 16th century, decorate their boats to pay homage to St. Peter.

Penang International Dragon Boat Festival *(Jun/Jul)*, Penang. Long rowing boats race to honor the memory of Chinese poet Qu Yuan, who drowned himself in 278 BC in a protest against corrupt politics.

KL International Arts Festival *(Jun/Jul)*, Kuala Lumpur. A show-case for Malaysian art with some eye-catching street art.

Spectacular celebrations at the Colors of Malaysia festival

Average Monthly Rainfall (Kuala Lumpur)

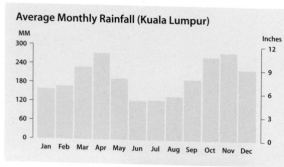

Rainfall Chart
Rainfall across the country is variable and it is difficult to show a national average. The wettest period for the east coast of Peninsular Malaysia and Malaysian Borneo is November to March. The west coast of the peninsula sees rain from April to October.

July to September

The focus of festivities during these months are Merdeka Eve and National Day at the end of August, and Malaysia Day in September. Other colorful and unique events include the Borneo Cultural Festival in Sibu, the Sarawak Regatta, and the Mount Kinabalu Climbathon.

Sabah International Folklore Festival *(Jul)*, Kota Kinabalu. Held at the Sabah Cultural Centre, this week-long celebration of folk dancing draws ethnic groups from around the world to give performances and hold workshops.

Borneo Cultural Festival *(Jul)*, Sibu. A week-long celebration of music and dance with participants that include local ethnic groups, and visiting performers from countries including China and Indonesia. The festival also attracts visitors from Thailand, Brunei, and nearby countries. Most events are held in Sibu's town square.

Fireworks display during National Day celebrations

Malaysia Mega Sale Carnival *(Jul to Sep)*, nationwide. Substantial discounts are offered on goods at shopping malls and stores.

Kuching Festival *(Aug)*, Kuching. This celebration of Sarawak's culture comprises concerts, exhibitions, theater performances, and food fairs, and lasts for a month.

Rainforest World Music Festival *(Aug)*, Sarawak Cultural Village, near Kuching. An annual global event featuring music workshops and performances by

musicians from around the world as well as rarely heard indigenous musicians *(see p165)*.

Merdeka Eve *(Aug 30)*, nationwide. Fireworks displays and cultural performances in major towns and cities herald National Day.

National Day *(Aug 31)*, nationwide. Parades, music shows, and competitions are among the celebrations that mark the anniversary of the country's independence.

Festival of the Hungry Ghosts *(Aug/Sep)*, nationwide. This Chinese festival is held to appease the spirits of the dead released from purgatory during the seventh lunar month. Joss sticks, candles, and paper money are burnt outside homes and Chinese street opera is performed.

Ramadan *(variable)*, nationwide. This is the Muslim holy month during which Muslims fast in daylight hours and eat only after sunset. Street stalls set up outside mosques in the evening offer many Muslim delicacies.

Hari Raya Puasa *(variable)*, nationwide. Also known as Aidilfitri, this Muslim festival marks the end of Ramadan, with feasts that feature special food preparations. Families get together and pay respect to their elders, and packets of money are given to children.

Sarawak Regatta *(Sep)*, Kuching. An annual regatta of paddleboat, powerboat, and canoe competitions on the Sungai Sarawak between the various indigenous people of Sarawak.

Malaysia Day *(Sep 16)*, nationwide. This national

Malaysia Mega Sale Carnival at Soga department store in Kuala Lumpur

Average Monthly Temperature (Kuala Lumpur)

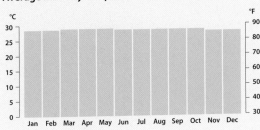

Temperature Chart
The temperature in Malaysia does not vary much. Hot and humid all year round, the temperature hovers around 30° C (86° F) during the day, with a slight drop in the evenings. The hill stations may get as cool as 15° C (59° F).

holiday celebrates Sarawak and Sabah joining the Malaysian Federation on this day in 1963. Expect government offices to be shut and shopping malls and restaurants to be packed.

October to December

Due to heavy rain and rough seas on the east coast, boat travel to small islands is tough. Some national parks are also closed. The two important religious festivals during this season are the Mooncake Festival and Deepavali. Although there are only a few Christians in Malaysia, Christmas is still a much celebrated event.

Mooncake Festival *(variable)*, nationwide. Also known as the Mid-Autumn Festival, this day is celebrated by the Chinese who exchange and consume mooncakes, made of lotus and sesame seeds, to mark the fall of the Mongol dynasty in China in the 12th century. In

Energetic dances at the KL International Buskers Festival

the evening, lanterns are lit and areas with large Chinese communities hold a colorful lantern parade.

Mount Kinabalu Climbathon *(Oct)*, Sabah. Most people take two full days to climb this massive mountain but the skilled climbers in this, the world's toughest mountain race, take less than three hours to complete the climb and descend.

Deepavali *(Oct/Nov)*, nationwide. The festival of lights commemorates Lord Krishna's victory over Narakasura, the triumph of good over evil and light over dark. Hindu homes and temples around the country are decorated with oil lamps to welcome the goddess of prosperity. Hindus pray for happiness and stability.

Tamu Besar *(Nov)*, Kota Belud. Held annually at one of Sabah's biggest markets and tourist attractions, Tamu Besar features cultural performances and handicraft demonstrations. The highlight, however, is to see Bajau horsemen, dressed in colorful traditional costumes. They ride their bedecked horses around town *(see p188)*.

KL International Buskers Festival *(Dec)*, Kuala Lumpur. For over a week, street performers from around the world, including musicians, dancers, comedians, jugglers, and acrobats, put on shows to demonstrate their talents.

Penang Chingay *(Dec)*, Penang. The Chingay parade is an attention-grabbing display which features skilled performers balancing giant flags measuring up to 12 m (40 ft).

Towering Christmas tree at a shopping center in Kuala Lumpur

Christmas *(Dec 25)*, nationwide. Largely unmarked in predominantly Muslim regions, Christmas is a major commercial event in the big cities. Midnight Mass is celebrated in churches.

Public Holidays

New Year's Day (Jan 1)
Chinese New Year (Jan/Feb)
Thaipusam (Jan/Feb)
Good Friday (Mar/Apr)
Birthday of the Prophet Muhammad (variable)
Labor Day (May 1)
Vesak (May/Jun)
King's Birthday (Jun)
Hari Raya Puasa (variable)
National Day (Aug 31)
Malaysia Day (Sep 16)
Deepavali (Oct/Nov)
Christmas (Dec 25)

Malaysia at a Glance

Malaysia consists of two geographical regions, Peninsular Malaysia and Malaysian Borneo, which are divided by the South China Sea. A range of mountains runs down the center of the peninsula, dividing the developed plains of the west from the more rural east coast. Malaysian Borneo, comprising the states of Sarawak and Sabah, is a land of rain forests and great rivers. Sandwiched between these two states is the oil-rich independent Sultanate of Brunei.

The Perhentian Islands *(see p148)* off the coast of Terengganu have pristine beaches and offer excellent swimming and diving in the clear waters of the South China Sea.

Cameron Highlands *(see pp98–9)* is the country's largest and most popular hill station, with a consistently pleasant climate, rolling hills, lush tea plantations, and a distinctively colonial character.

Taman Negara *(see pp144–5)*, Malaysia's largest national park, contains the peninsula's highest peak and an incredible variety of birds and wildlife.

Kota Bharu

Georgetown

Kuala Terengganu

NORTHWEST PENINSULA
(See pp92–121)

EASTERN AND CENTRAL PENINSULA
(See pp138–55)

Kuantan

KUALA LUMPUR
(See pp62–91)

Seremban

SOUTHERN PENINSULA
(See pp122–37)

South China Se

SINGAPORE
(See pp202–73)

The Sultan Abdul Samad Building *(see p68)* is one of busy Kuala Lumpur's most magnificent colonial structures. The city's other attractions include interesting museums, pleasant gardens, and lively local markets.

Seremban *(see p126)*, the state capital of Negeri Sembilan, is the center of Minangkabau culture in Malaysia. Striking buildings with roofs shaped like buffalo horns, such as the State Museum, can be seen throughout town.

Pulau Sipadan *(see pp200–201)*, off the east coast of Sabah, is surrounded by a coral reef and is rated among the world's top diving destinations.

Brunei's Sultan Omar Ali Saifuddien Mosque, an icon for the tiny Sultanate of Brunei *(see pp178–9)*, stands on an island in an artificial lagoon in the heart of the capital city of Bandar Seri Begawan.

Turtle Island National Park *(see p196)* is a prime spot for viewing the green and hawksbill turtles that come ashore to nest.

Kota Kinabalu

Tomanggong

Bandar Seri Begawan

SABAH
(See pp180–201)

Kunak

Miri

BRUNEI

0 km 150

0 miles 150

Bintulu

SARAWAK
(See pp156–79)

Saratok

Kuching

Engkilili

Mulu National Park *(see pp176–7)* has picturesque walking trails in a forested landscape rich in wildlife.

Kuching *(see pp160–63)*, the historic capital of Sarawak, is set on the banks of the Sungai Sarawak.

Lambir Hills National Park *(see p175)* protects the forested areas around Lambir Hills. Visited most often for its scenic waterfalls, the park reflects the natural heritage of Sarawak, a state that owes its considerable global significance to its many spectacular and species-rich forests.

KUALA LUMPUR

The capital of Malaysia, Kuala Lumpur, is the nation's biggest city with a population of 1.6 million people. A relatively young city, it has evolved from a humble town in the 1850s to the financial and commercial capital and principal gateway of the country. A vision of modernity with its skyscrapers and the best restaurants and nightlife in the country, Kuala Lumpur also possesses a rich cultural heritage that is revealed in its colonial architecture, temples, and mosques.

Kuala Lumpur sits in the Klang Valley, and its name, which means muddy confluence in Malay, is derived from its location at the point where the Klang and Gombak rivers meet. Established here in 1857, the city began as a ramshackle trading post for the burgeoning tin industry, and was constantly plagued by floods, fires, and civil wars. Chinese miners and traders formed a large part of its early population, governed by a Kapitan China, or headman. The most famous of them was Yap Ah Loy *(see p71)*, who was responsible for the city's early growth.

A building boom began when the British took control in the 1880s, and in 1896 Kuala Lumpur was made the capital of the newly formed Federated Malay States. A multiracial population began to settle here, congregating in ethnic enclaves that remain even today. In 1999, Putrajaya became the new administrative capital, but Kuala Lumpur remains the country's financial and commercial center.

Some of the country's rich history can be seen in the 19th-century architecture of the old colonial district and in neighboring Chinatown, with its incense-filled temples and chatter-filled *kedai kopi*, or coffee shops. Little India, Kampung Baru, and Chow Kit are the best places to find Indian, Malay, and Chinese cuisines. A closer look reveals that the city blends the old with the new. Flanked by glitzy shops and trendy bars, the Golden Triangle is the hub of the city's nightlife, while the Petronas Towers dominate the business district of KLCC. The Perdana Botanical Gardens are a perfect escape from the urban clutter.

Entrance to Chan See Shu Yuen Temple in Kuala Lumpur

◀ The stunning Petronas Towers and, below them, the upscale KLCC mall

Exploring Kuala Lumpur

Kuala Lumpur's old colonial core is centered on Merdeka Square, which is ringed with elegant colonial buildings. To the southwest are the tranquil Perdana Botanical Gardens. Across the river, to the east, Chinatown, Little India, Chow Kit, and Kampung Baru boast some of the best street markets. To the west is the Putra World Trade Center (PWTC), one of the city's convention and exhibition centers. Farther northeast is the modern Kuala Lumpur City Center (KLCC) dominated by the Petronas Towers. The Golden Triangle is the business and entertainment hub of the capital. Close by is the soaring Menara KL at the foot of which is the Bukit Nanas Forest Reserve, a patch of rain forest in the center of the city.

Sights at a Glance

Historic Streets, Buildings, and Neighborhoods

❶ Sultan Abdul Samad Building
❸ Royal Selangor Club
❽ Chinatown
⓬ Kuala Lumpur Railway Station
⓱ Carcosa Seri Negara
㉑ Little India
㉒ Jalan Tuanku Abdul Rahman
㉗ Petronas Towers
㉚ Malaysian Tourism Information Complex
㉛ The Golden Triangle
㉜ Menara KL and Bukit Nanas Forest Reserve
㉝ Badan Warisan

Museums and Galleries

❹ National Music Museum
❺ Kuala Lumpur City Gallery
⓮ *Islamic Arts Museum see pp74–5*
⓯ National Museum
㉔ National Art Gallery

Places of Worship

❷ Masjid Jamek
❼ Sze Ya Temple
❿ Sri Maha Mariamman Temple
⓫ Chan See Shu Yuen Temple
⓭ Masjid Negara
⓲ Thean Hou Temple
⓴ Masjid India

Shopping and Markets

❻ Central Market
❾ Jalan Petaling Market
⓳ Jalan Alor
㉓ Chow Kit Market
㉖ Kampung Baru and Pasar Minggu Market
㉘ Suria KLCC and KLCC Park

Islands

㊳ Pulau Ketam

Gardens and Themed Attractions

⓰ Perdana Botanical Gardens
㉕ Titiwangsa Lake Gardens
㉙ Aquaria KLCC
㉞ Kompleks Budaya Kraf
㉟ FRIM

Towns and Cities

㊱ Shah Alam
㊲ Klang
㊴ Putrajaya

For keys to symbols *see back flap*

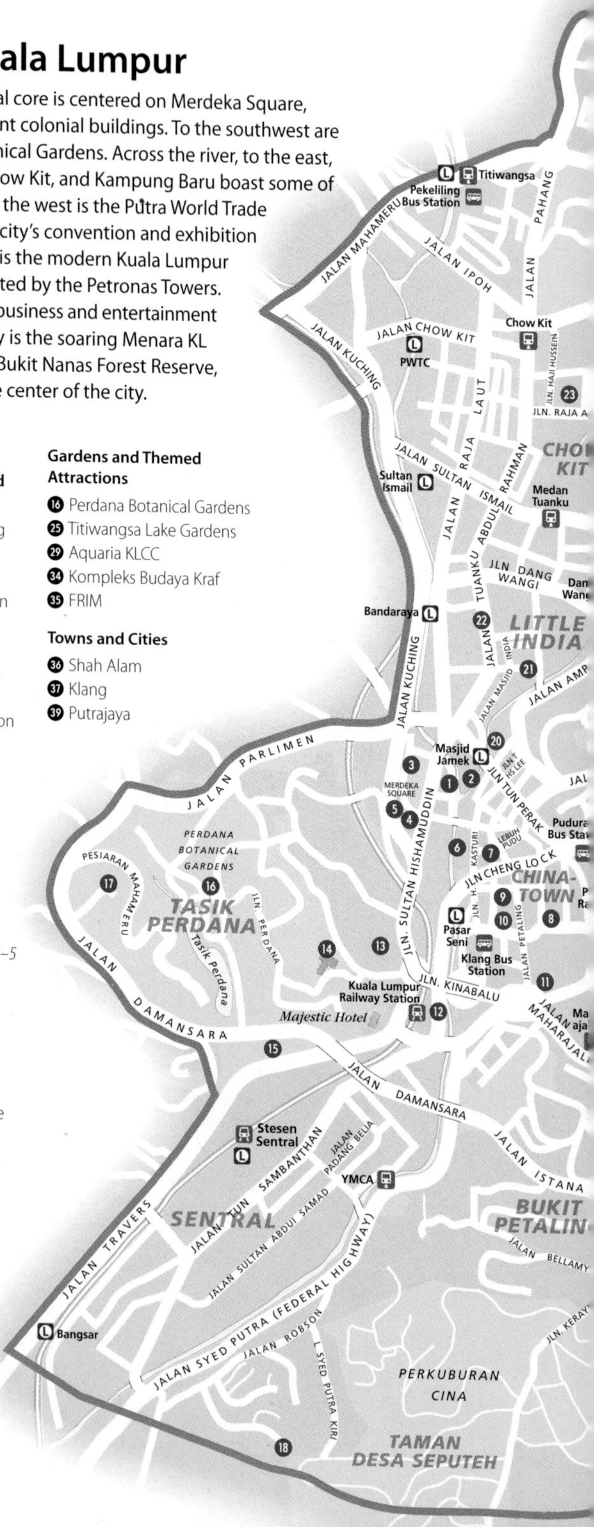

Beyond Kuala Lumpur

Getting Around

Exploring the city on foot is not advisable due to the heat, heavy traffic, air pollution, and a lack of sidewalks. The best option is to use the efficient public transport system. Stesen Sentral (KL Sentral Station) is the hub of the city's rail network, which consists of KTM, the national railroad system; Light Rail Transport (LRT); the monorail; and KLIA trains to and from the international airport. KTM Komuter trains are useful for out-of-town destinations such as Shah Alam, Klang, and Seremban to the south. KLIA Ekspres (KLIA Express) runs direct to KLIA airport and to the low-cost terminal at KLIA2. LRT and the monorail cover the city with many stops, as do Rapid KL buses, which offer an unlimited day travel ticket. Pudu Sentral and Terminal Bersepadu Selatan are the two main bus stations.

Key

- Major sight
- Highway
- Major road
- Minor road
- Railroad

The beautifully lit Thean Hou Temple at dusk

Street-by-Street: Merdeka Square

Located in the heart of Kuala Lumpur's colonial district, Dataran Merdeka, or Independence Square, is a vast rectangular grassy field that once hosted cricket matches and parades. Surrounded by the mock-Tudor Royal Selangor Club, the National Music Museum, St. Mary's Cathedral, and the Sultan Abdul Samad Building, the square offers a rare glimpse into the city's past. The venue for many national events, it was here that the Union Flag was finally lowered on August 31, 1957, when independent Malaysia was born. Today, the Malaysian flag flies at the southern end of the square.

Pitcher Plant Fountain
Standing in a small garden north of the square, this unique water feature is styled as a series of pitcher plants.

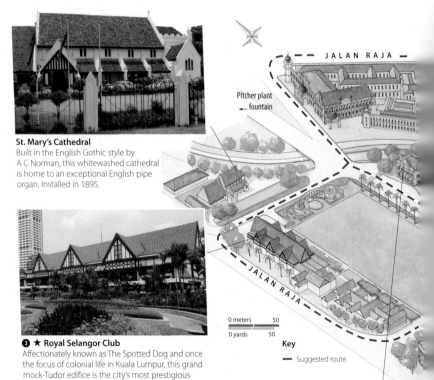

St. Mary's Cathedral
Built in the English Gothic style by A C Norman, this whitewashed cathedral is home to an exceptional English pipe organ, installed in 1895.

JALAN RAJA

Pitcher plant
fountain

JALAN RAJA

❸ ★ **Royal Selangor Club**
Affectionately known as The Spotted Dog and once the focus of colonial life in Kuala Lumpur, this grand mock-Tudor edifice is the city's most prestigious private club.

| 0 meters | 50 |
| 0 yards | 50 |

Key

— Suggested route

❶ ★ **Sultan Abdul Samad Building**
This flamboyant Moorish-style building dates from 1897. Dominating the eastern side of Merdeka Square, it now houses a division of the Malaysian High Court.

② Masjid Jamek
Built in 1909 in stately Mughal style, the Masjid Jamek, or Friday Mosque, is the oldest surviving mosque in the capital. It stands at the confluence of the Klang and Gombak rivers, where the city's first arrivals settled in the 1850s.

Locator Map
See Street Finder map 4

❻ Central Market
Once the city's main fresh produce market, the 1930s Art Deco building of the Central Market is now a shopping mall with Indian, Straits Chinese, and Malay ethnic arts and craft shops.

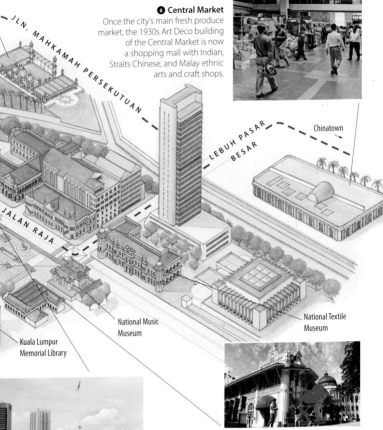

JLN. MAHKAMAH PERSEKUTUAN

LEBUH PASAR BESAR

Chinatown

JALAN RAJA

National Music Museum

National Textile Museum

Kuala Lumpur Memorial Library

The Flagpole
The 328-ft (100-m) high free-standing flagpole is believed to be the tallest in the world. The Malaysian flag is always flying here.

❺ ★ Kuala Lumpur City Gallery
Housed in a heritage building that dates to 1899, this gallery has displays on Kuala Lumpur's past, present, and future, including a huge model of the city complete with a sound and light show.

The Royal Selangor Club, once the focus of colonial life

❶ Sultan Abdul Samad Building

Jalan Raja. **Map** 4 E2. Ⓛ Masjid Jamek. B101, B109.

A magnificent Moorish edifice presiding over the eastern flank of Merdeka Square, the Sultan Abdul Samad Building was built in 1897 to serve as the headquarters of colonial administration and named in honor of the ruler of Selangor at the time. Designed by A C Norman, a British architect who also designed the nearby St. Mary's Cathedral, the building is made of red brick and white stone and draws upon Mughal, Egyptian, and traditional Islamic styles. Its architectural features include

Sultan Abdul Samad Building with its grand clock tower

elegantly arched windows, cupolas, an imposing porch, and a soaring 133-ft (41-m) clock tower, flanked by two smaller towers crowned with gleaming copper domes. Today, it houses the commercial division of Malaysia's High Court and although it is not open to the public (apart from a very small musuem that is of limited interest to the visitor), the striking façade of the building makes it one of the capital's most photographed landmarks.

❷ Masjid Jamek

Off Jalan Tun Perak. **Map** 4 E2. Ⓛ Masjid Jamek. B111. **Open** 8:30am–12:20pm & 2:30–4pm daily. **Closed** 11am–2:30pm Fri.

Standing at the confluence of the Klang and Gombak rivers, the site where Kuala Lumpur was founded, the beautiful Masjid Jamek is the city's oldest mosque. Masjid Jamek, which means Friday Mosque, was built in 1909 by architect A B Hubbock, who was responsible for many of the country's colonial cityscapes. The red brick and marble building, with three large onion-shaped domes, two minarets, and arched colonnades, was inspired by Mughal architecture. Surrounded by palm groves, and with unrivaled views downstream, the mosque forms a tranquil haven in the middle

of the city. The main prayer hall is open only to Muslims. Visitors to the mosque must be dressed appropriately with arms and legs covered, and women must cover their heads. Gowns are supplied free of charge and shoes must be removed before entering.

❸ Royal Selangor Club

Merdeka Square. **Map** 4 E2. **Tel** (03) 2692-7166. Ⓛ Masjid Jamek. B101, B109. Ⓦ rscweb.org.my

Established in 1884, the Royal Selangor Club was at the center of colonial social life in Kuala Lumpur. Expatriates and officials gathered here to relax, play billiards, and watch cricket on the padang, now a part of **Merdeka Square** (see pp66–7). The club also hosted traveling plays and musicals. In 1970, the original building was destroyed by a fire, which was soon followed by a flood. The present black and white mock-Tudor building, an authentic reproduction of the old club, was built in 1980. Still referred to as The Spotted Dog, the club remains the preserve of the city's elite and is open only to members. Theories about the origin of its nickname include one tracing it to a Dalmatian that belonged to a former member.

❹ National Music Museum

29 Jalan Raja. **Map** 4 E2. 🔲 Masjid Jamek. 🚌 B101, B109. **Open** 10am–4pm Tue–Sat.

Originally built in 1891 to house the city's first bank, this grand Mughal-style building at the southern end of Merdeka Square was for many years the home of the National History Museum, whose collection has now been merged with that of the National Museum (see p72). Since 2015 the building has housed the country's main music museum. Traditional instruments on display include giant *rebana* drums, *kompangs*, which are similar to tambourines, and the flute-like *sape* used by the Orang Ulu community.

❺ Kuala Lumpur City Gallery

27 Jalan Raja. **Map** 4 E2. **Tel** (03) 2698-3333. 🔲 Masjid Jamek. 🚌 B101, B109. **Open** 9am–6:30pm daily. 🅿️ 📷 📷 🌐 klcitygallery.com

Next door to the Music Museum is another fine old building. Formerly the Government Printing Office and then the National Library, now it houses an exhibition dedicated to the history of Kuala Lumpur. The highlight is a massive model of the city that includes new towers currently under construction that will come to dominate the skyline. Stopping outside the gallery is a tourist

The imposing façade of the National Music Museum

tram that will take you to local sights, and there are also horse and cart rides around the square.

❻ Central Market

Jalan Hang Kasturi. **Map** 4 E2. **Tel** 1300-22-8688. 🔲 Pasar Seni. 🚌 B101, B110, B112. **Open** 10am– 10pm daily. ♿ 📷 🌐 centralmarket.com.my

Housed in a powder-blue Art Deco building dating from the 1930s, the Central Market was formerly the city's main fresh-produce market. It was rescued from dereliction and reopened as a modern shopping complex in the 1980s.

Also known as the Cultural Bazaar, the building has arts and crafts shops that sell an array of products including woodcarvings, *batik*, pottery, paintings, and traditional kites. Prices tend to be high and haggling is necessary to get

reasonable deals. There are a number of other outlets that sell an eclectic assortment of goods ranging from guitars to ladies' wigs.

Upstairs, there is a good food court with separate counters offering dishes from various Malaysian states. A few restaurants are scattered on both floors. The Central Market is also a venue for free cultural performances.

❼ Sze Ya Temple

Lebuh Pudu. **Map** 4 F3. **Tel** (03) 2078-9052. 🔲 Pasar Seni. 🚌 B110, B111. **Open** 7am–5pm daily.

Located halfway down a narrow alley off Lebuh Pudu, the small Sze Ya Temple is built at an awkward angle to the road, a position said to have been decided by the principles of feng shui. The oldest Taoist temple in Kuala Lumpur, it was founded in 1864 by Yap Ah Loy, the third Kapitan China (see p71), who also funded its construction. Inside the temple, a statue of Loy is installed left of the main altar, while images of the patron deities Si Sze Ya and Sin Sze Ya occupy the back wall. The interior is filled with elaborate carvings and the smell of burning incense. The temple entrance is guarded by statues of fierce lions, a common feature in Chinese and Taoist temples, accompanied by statues of storks. For an extra charge visitors can have their fortunes told inside the temple.

Ornate interior of the Sze Ya Temple, one of the oldest in the capital

Gateway to Jalan Petaling in Chinatown

❽ Chinatown

Map 4 F3. ⓛ Pasar Seni. 🚌
Maharajalela. 🚌 B102, B110. 📷
Chinese New Year (Jan/Feb).

Kuala Lumpur's relatively small
but vibrant Chinatown is
roughly bordered by Jalan
Hang Kasturi to the west and
Jalan Sultan to the east, with
Masjid Jamek and the Chan See
Shu Yuen Temple marking its
northern and southern limits
respectively. The area is a maze
of narrow streets and alleyways,
dotted with small Chinese
temples and lined with old
shophouses, medicine stores,
and traditional family-run *kedai
kopi*, or coffee shops, where
locals gather to socialize.

At the heart of Chinatown
is **Jalan Petaling**, with its
bustling covered market and
crowded cafés. Numerous
modern shops and chain stores
add a contemporary touch to
this ethnic enclave. Chinatown
is also home to much of the
city's budget accommodation.
The area, however, is not
exclusively Chinese. Located

on Jalan Tun HS Lee, a major
thoroughfare, is the city's
principal Hindu temple,
Sri Maha Mariamman Temple.

❾ Jalan Petaling Market

Jalan Petaling. **Map** 4 F3. ⓛ Pasar
Seni. 🚌 B110. **Open** 10am–11pm.

The scene of the capital's
most famous and lively street
market, Jalan Petaling is a
covered string of stalls
specializing in fake designer
goods. Watches, clothes,
wallets, handbags, and a
profusion of pirated CDs
and DVDs are all sold openly.
There are few fixed prices,
and with initial offers often
set unreasonably high, buyers
are expected to haggle.
Interspersed with the stalls are
a few shops that sell an assortment of other goods such as
a variety of dried meats and
traditional medicines. At the
northern end is a traditional
wet market, full of interesting
sights and smells.

Jalan Petaling is just a normal
shop-lined street in Chinatown
until around 4 or 5pm every
day, when the area is closed off
to traffic and transformed into a
pasar malam, or night market.
Many of the daytime stalls pack
up and are replaced by food
stalls that sell a tempting array
of Indian, Malay, and Chinese
delicacies. Local souvenirs are
also available. Both the day and
night markets attract large
crowds and visitors should be
careful of their belongings.

Colorful *gopuram* of Sri Maha
Mariamman Temple

❿ Sri Maha Mariamman Temple

163 Jalan Tun HS Lee. **Map** 4 F3.
Tel (03) 2078-3467. ⓛ Pasar Seni.
🚌 B110. **Open** 6am–9pm daily.
📷 Thaipusam (Jan/Feb).

Established in 1873 as the
private shrine of a Tamil family
from southern India, Sri Maha
Mariamman Temple was rebuilt
on its present site in 1885.
Today, it is Kuala Lumpur's main
Hindu temple. The building is
said to be laid out in the form of
a reclining human body, with
the head pointing to the west,
and the feet to the east. The feet
are represented by a five-tiered
gopuram, or entrance gate,
which is decorated with
intricately carved statues of
various Hindu deities. During an
extensive renovation of the
temple in the 1960s, gold and
precious stones as well as
Spanish and Italian tiles were
added to the *gopuram*.

Inside the temple are several
altars displaying images of
Hindu gods. The temple also
houses the ornate silver chariot
used in a procession during the
fascinating annual Thaipusam
festival *(see p35)*. The chariot is
brought out from the temple's
vault during the celebration,
when up to a million devotees
converge here and make their
way up to the Hindu shrine at
Batu Caves *(see p96)*. Visitors
must remove their shoes before
entering the temple.

Traditional tea shop at the Jalan Petaling street market

For hotels and restaurants see p278 and pp290–92

⑪ Chan See Shu Yuen Temple

172 Jalan Petaling. **Map** 4 F4.
Tel (03) 2078-1461. Ⓛ Pasar Seni.
Ⓜ Maharajalela. 🚌 B110.
Open 8am–5pm daily.

Built between 1897 and 1906, Chan See Shu Yuen Temple is said to be one of the finest examples of southern Chinese architecture in Malaysia. It features an elaborate pottery-tiled roof, undulating gables, and superbly sculpted green- and blue-glazed ceramic friezes depicting mythological scenes on the façade. Decorating the edges of the temple are blue ceramic vases. On either side of the main entrance are shrines to the female and male guardians of the doorway, with incense burning continually before them.

The temple is essentially a clan association, representing families bearing the related names of Chan, Chen, or Tan, and is dedicated to the family ancestors. Enshrined at the central altar of the temple are images of the clan founders, Chan Siow Ling, Chan Xin Xi, and Chan Zai Tian, while above the altar, to the right and left, are a series of black and white photographs of deceased clan members. Framing the central shrine are gilded wooden panels painted with scenes of warriors battling lions and mythical creatures. Devotees flock here during Buddhist festivals.

Detail of friezes carved on the façade of the Chan See Shu Yuen Temple

⑫ Kuala Lumpur Railway Station

Jalan Sultan Hishamuddin. **Map** 4 E4.
🚌 B109. ♿ 🛒 🚻 🛍

Among the best examples of colonial architecture in Malaysia, the ornate Kuala Lumpur Railway Station is a majestic, gleaming white building with Moorish arches, balustrades, minarets, and cupolas. Completed in 1911, it was designed by the British architect A B Hubbock, who is also known for the striking Masjid Jamek (see p68). Beneath the Islamic exterior, the building was constructed according to specifications for railroad stations in England and included an iron roof capable of withstanding up to 3 ft (1 m) of snow. The concrete structure was built to replace an *attap*, or thatched shed, which had served as the railroad terminal since 1886.

For 90 years it was the city's main intercity rail terminal, until it was replaced in 2001 by the state-of-the-art KL Sentral Station, a few streets south. Now only KTM Komuter trains pass through this historic station.

Opposite the station is the gleaming white Hotel Majestic (see p278). Built in the 1930s, it quickly became the city's most glamorous place to stay. The building fell into disrepair until it reopened in 2012 as a hotel once more, having been meticulously restored. You can enjoy afternoon tea in the splendid Orchid Room or have a cocktail in the gentlemen's clubrooms, the Smoke House.

Kapitan China

The office of Kapitan China, or headman of the Chinese community of Kuala Lumpur, was instituted in 1858 by Rajah Abdullah, Chief of Selangor state, as a way of imposing order on the fractious Chinese immigrants and their secret societies. In 1869, Yap Ah Loy, a fierce and ambitious immigrant from southern China, became the third Kapitan China. He soon found himself at the center of a bloody civil war between different Chinese groups and local Malays, but a major victory led by him in Kuala Lumpur in 1873, along with the arrival of the first British Resident in 1874 (see p47), put an end to the fighting. He remained headman until his death in 1885. Also credited with establishing the city as a major economic powerhouse, Yap Ah Loy is considered the founding father of modern Kuala Lumpur.

Kapitan China Yap Ah Loy

The magnificent edifice of the Kuala Lumpur Railway Station

The striking 18-pointed roof of Masjid Negara, the national mosque

⑬ Masjid Negara

Jalan Perdana. **Map** 4 D3.
Tel (03) 2693-7784. 🚉 KL Railway
Station. Ⓛ Pasar Seni. 🚌 B109.
Open 9am–noon, 3–4pm and 5:30–
6:30pm daily (pm only on Fri).

Built in 1965, Masjid Negara is
Malaysia's national mosque.
Set in sprawling gardens that
contain pools and fountains,
it is a vast modern building
with room for up to 15,000
worshipers. The main prayer
hall is open only to Muslims.
   The hall is covered with a
distinctive dome in the shape
of a stylized 18-point star,
representing the 13 states
of Malaysia and the five pillars
of Islam. Towering over the
mosque is a slender 240-ft (73-m)
high minaret. Visiting non-
Muslims are welcome to explore
the rest of the complex but must
be appropriately dressed;
headscarves are mandatory for
women. Shoes must be removed
before entering the building.

⑭ Islamic Arts Museum

See pp74–5.

⑮ National Museum

Jalan Damansara. **Map** 3 C4. **Tel** (03)
2282-6255. 🚉 KL Sentral, then a short
walk. Ⓛ KL Sentral, then a short walk.
🚌 B109. **Open** 9am–6pm daily.
📷♿🔲📱 🆆 **muziumnegara.
gov.my** KLTA Tourist Information
Center: **Tel** (03) 2287-1830.

Opened in 1963, the National
Museum, or Muzium Negara, is
built on the site of the old
Selangor Museum which
was destroyed by Allied
bombing during World
War II. It is housed in a
reproduction of a
traditional Malay palace
and its façade is adorned
with murals depicting
scenes from the
nation's history. Inside,
four themed galleries

provide an introduction to
Malaysia's ethnography and
natural history. Gallery A on
the first floor covers early
history, while Gallery B
describes the Malay Kingdoms
and trade routes. Upstairs,
Gallery C details the country's
colonial history and showcases
some fascinating photographs
and dioramas. Gallery D
recounts Malaysia's battle for
independence and other
recent history with exhibits
such as the pen used to sign
the independence agreement.
Outside, a collection of vehicles
includes trishaws, cars, and
even steam trains. A small
**KLTA Tourist Information
Center** is located within the
museum grounds.

⑯ Perdana Botanical Gardens

Jalan Perdana. **Map** 3 B3. 🚉 KL
Railway Station, then a short walk. Ⓛ
KL Sentral, then a short walk. 🚌 B115.
Open 7am–8pm daily. ♿🔲📱📷
🆆 **klbotanical garden.gov.my**
KL Bird Park: **Tel** (03) 2272-1010. **Open**
9am–6pm daily. 🐦 Bird feeding and
shows: check website for times.
🆆 **klbirdpark.com** Butterfly Park:
Tel (03) 2693- 4799. **Open**
9am–6pm daily. 🐦 National
Planetarium: **Tel** (03) 2273-
4303. **Open** 9am–6pm Tue–
Sun. 🐦 🆆 **angkasa.gov.my**
Lying on the western
edge of the city center are
the Perdana Botanical
Gardens, (Taman Tasik
Perdana in Malay). This
is a beautiful expanse
of greenery laid out in the late
19th century as a tranquil residential area for the governing
British elite. Today, it is the city's
biggest and most popular park,
with a large lake at its center
where boats can be hired, and
plenty of walking trails.
   Within the gardens are a
number of other attractions,
the highlight of which is the
KL Bird Park. Said to be the
world's largest walk-in free-
flight aviary, the park houses
around 3,000 tropical birds
including flamingos, hornbills,
and parrots. There is also a
Butterfly Park which is home

Chinese ceramic vase at
the National Museum

A gallery at the Muzium Negara, or National Museum

For hotels and restaurants see p278 and pp290–92

to over 6,000 butterflies of at least 120 different species. Close by is the **Orchid Garden**, which showcases over 800 species of Malay orchids, which are for sale during the weekend. On the southern edge is the **National Planetarium**, which stages various shows and screens IMAX movies. The 50-ft (15-m) high bronze **National Monument** which commemorates the defeat of the Communist insurgency dominates the northern end of the park. It was created in 1966 by Felix de Weldon, who was best known for the Iwo Jima monument in Washington, DC. Among the fine colonial mansions built here is **Carcosa Seri Negara**, which presides over the western boundary of the gardens. Smaller museums around the park are dedicated to the police, civil service, banking, and former political leaders. There is a popular food court on Jalan Cenderasari.

⑰ Carcosa Seri Negara

Lake Gardens. **Map** 3 B3. **Tel** (03) 2295-0888. 🚆 KL Railway Station, then taxi. Ⓛ KL Sentral, then taxi. ♿ 🖉 🖥 Ⓦ shr.my

This exquisite pair of colonial mansions set in their own grounds on the edge of the Perdana Botanical Gardens were built between 1896 and 1904. The first building, Carcosa,

Grand hallway of Carcosa Seri Negara, a luxury hotel

formerly known as The House on the Hill, was constructed as a home for Sir Frank Swettenham, the first British Resident-General of the Federation of Malay States (*see p47*), a function it continued to serve for subsequent British governors. The second building, Seri Negara, earlier known as the King's House, was the official home of the Governor of the Straits Settlements. After independence and until 1987, Carcosa was the official residence of the British High Commissioner while Seri Negara functioned as a state guesthouse for visiting foreign dignitaries. Today, the two buildings together form one of Kuala Lumpur's finest boutique hotels, and contain two award-winning restaurants including the elegant, colonial Drawing Room.

⑱ Thean Hou Temple

62 Persiaran Indah, off Jalan Syed Putra. **Tel** (03) 2274-7088. Ⓣ from KL Sentral. **Open** 8am–10pm; 6am–midnight during Chinese New Year. 🖥 📷 🖉 Chinese New Year (Jan/Feb).

Perched on a hill southwest of the city center, the Thean Hou Temple is a striking three-tier Chinese temple. Built in the 1980s, this is one of the biggest Chinese temples in Malaysia. It is dedicated to Thean Hou, or heavenly mother, the patron deity of sailors and fishermen. An image of the goddess, also known as Ma Zu, is enshrined in the main hall, flanked by statues of Sui Wei, goddess of the waterfront, and Kuan Yin, goddess of mercy. Statues of the Laughing Buddha and other Buddhist and Taoist images are also kept here.

The temple has a series of traditional Chinese-style roofs decorated with golden dragons, phoenix, and a canopy of red paper lanterns. Built on four levels, it has food outlets and shops on the ground level, while the main shrine is on the third floor. The temple also serves as a community center, and a hall on the second level forms the venue for social gatherings such as weddings. Outside the building stand twelve statues, which represent the twelve animals of the Chinese zodiac.

The extravagant Thean Hou Temple, with a series of tiled, Chinese-style roofs

⑭ Islamic Arts Museum

Situated on the eastern edge of the Perdana Botanical Gardens (see p72), the Islamic Arts Museum houses fascinating exhibits from the Muslim world. Opened in 1998, the museum has the largest collection of its kind in Southeast Asia with over 7,000 artifacts. The building itself is an impressive modern construction topped by turquoise domes, with Iranian tilework on columns at the entrance. Inside, five elegant domes created by Uzbek craftsmen decorate the ceilings. The emphasis of the exhibits here is on Asian arts in addition to those from Persia and the Middle East.

The magnificent dome at the Inverted Dome Pavilion

The state-of-the-art auditorium seats up to 250 people and is used for seminars and lectures.

The Inverted Dome Pavilion is an airy exhibition hall with its unique dome executed in white and gold, bearing extracts from the Koran.

The Architecture Gallery
The main focus of this gallery is the collection of scale models of mosques, including the Dome of the Rock, Taj Mahal, and the Al-Haram Mosque.

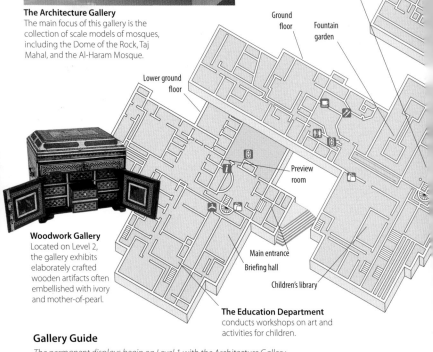

Ground floor

Fountain garden

Lower ground floor

Preview room

Woodwork Gallery
Located on Level 2, the gallery exhibits elaborately crafted wooden artifacts often embellished with ivory and mother-of-pearl.

Main entrance

Briefing hall

Children's library

The Education Department conducts workshops on art and activities for children.

Gallery Guide

The permanent displays begin on Level 1 with the Architecture Gallery, which has detailed scale models of mosques. Nearby is the Manuscript Gallery, a reconstructed Ottoman Room, and galleries dedicated to China, India, and Malaysia. Level 2 has the Jewelry, Arms and Armor, Coin and Seal, Metalwork, Woodwork, Ceramics, and Textile galleries. On the ground and lower ground floors are two galleries for temporary exhibitions. The non-exhibition area has facilities for research and education.

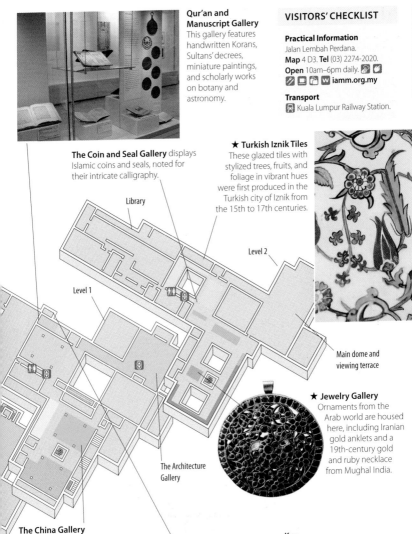

Qur'an and Manuscript Gallery
This gallery features handwritten Korans, Sultans' decrees, miniature paintings, and scholarly works on botany and astronomy.

VISITORS' CHECKLIST

Practical Information
Jalan Lembah Perdana.
Map 4 D3. **Tel** (03) 2274-2020.
Open 10am–6pm daily. 🔲 🔲
🔲 🔲 🔲 **w** iamm.org.my

Transport
🚉 Kuala Lumpur Railway Station.

The Coin and Seal Gallery displays Islamic coins and seals, noted for their intricate calligraphy.

Library

★ **Turkish Iznik Tiles**
These glazed tiles with stylized trees, fruits, and foliage in vibrant hues were first produced in the Turkish city of Iznik from the 15th to 17th centuries.

Level 2

Level 1

Main dome and viewing terrace

★ **Jewelry Gallery**
Ornaments from the Arab world are housed here, including Iranian gold anklets and a 19th-century gold and ruby necklace from Mughal India.

The Architecture Gallery

The China Gallery
displays Chinese manuscripts, a Koran, and blue and white porcelain with Arabic script.

Key

🔲 Jewelry Gallery
🔲 Arms and Armor Gallery
🔲 Textile Gallery
🔲 Woodwork Gallery
🔲 Coin and Seal Gallery
🔲 Metalwork Gallery
🔲 Ceramics and Glassware Gallery
🔲 Architecture Gallery
🔲 Qur'an and Manuscript Gallery
🔲 India Gallery
🔲 China Gallery
🔲 Malay World Gallery
🔲 Temporary exhibitions
🔲 Non-exhibition space

★ **Standard Chartered Ottoman Room**
This room once belonged to a lavish house built in Syria in 1820 and has now been restored to its original appearance. It is spectacularly decorated with painted wood paneling.

⓳ Jalan Alor

Jalan Alor. **Map** 5 C2. Ⓛ Bukit Bintang. ♿

The night market at Jalan Alor, near the neon-lit nightlife of Bukit Bintang, is now a popular spot with foodies. Hungry diners perch on rickety stools at stalls selling such delights as *char siew* (barbecued pork) and steaming plates of chili-fried squid. Stalls to look out for include Jalan Alor Nasi Lemak, at the road's junction with Changkat Bukit Bintang, where beef *rendang* is a specialty, and the Wong Ah Wah chicken stall at the end of the road.

⓴ Masjid India

Jalan Masjid India. **Map** 4 F1. Ⓛ Masjid Jamek. 🚌 B109. ♿

Originally built as a modest wooden structure in 1863, Masjid India has been rebuilt and upgraded over the years. The present building was completed in 1966, and designed in southern Indian style, with onion-domed cupolas and elegant arched windows. The three-story mosque is the main place of worship for Kuala Lumpur's Indian Muslims. It can accommodate up to 3,500 devotees, with separate floors for men and women.

㉑ Little India

Jalan Masjid India and environs. **Map** 1 B5. Ⓛ Masjid Jamek, Bandaraya. 🚌 B101 to Jalan Tuanku Abdul Rahman. 🎎 Deepavali (Oct).

Although tiny in comparison with the Indian enclaves of Singapore or even Georgetown in Penang, Kuala Lumpur's Little India is equally lively and colorful, steeped in the history and culture of the capital's Indian community.

Jalan Masjid India is the main street of this ethnic quarter, which takes its name from Masjid India. Rows of shops and stalls line the street, and are crammed with Indian merchandise such as saris, silk cloth and other fabric, jewelry,

Vibrant silk cloth and garments on sale at a Little India stall

flowers, and spices. There are also a number of hawker stalls that sell a variety of delicious and traditional Indian snacks such as *pakoras* and *samosas*.

At the end of Jalan Masjid India is Lorong Bunus, which marks the northern limit of Little India. It leads to Lorong Tuanku Abdul Rahman, a narrow lane that is the venue of another of the capital's popular *pasar malams,* or night markets, on Saturdays. An assortment of Indian goods are sold here, including household items and brassware, and it is also one of the best places in the city to sample authentic Indian street food. During the day, artisans, including garland makers, can be seen at work all along the street.

㉒ Jalan Tuanku Abdul Rahman

Map 1 B3. Ⓛ Bandaraya. 🚌 B101, B109. Coliseum Cinema: 96 Jalan Tuanku Abdul Rahman. **Tel** (03) 2692-5995.

Named for the first king of independent Malaysia, and commonly known as Jalan TAR, Jalan Tuanku Abdul Rahman is one of the busiest roads in Kuala Lumpur and is constantly choked with traffic. Stretching north from Merdeka Square to Little India, it is one of the city's most popular traditional shopping destinations, particularly known for silk shops such as the Globe Silk Store (*see p306*) as well as the small, bazaar-style carpet shops clustered around its southern end. The Japanese department store Sogo is also on this road.

Despite a lot of modern development, Jalan TAR has retained much of its historic architecture, revealed in many of the striking 19th- and early 20th-century façades that still exist above the gaudy shop signs. Among the most interesting and significant of these structures is the **Coliseum Cinema**. Barring a few years during World War II, the cinema has been in business since 1921, making it Kuala Lumpur's oldest running movie hall. These days, it screens Hindi and southern Indian Tamil films. Visitors are free to explore the building. Next door to the

Façade of the Coliseum Cinema, which dates back to the colonial era

cinema, and built around the same time, the **Coliseum Café** was once the favorite haunt of colonial planters and tin miners. It also counts English author Somerset Maugham among its early patrons.

The Coliseum Café still offers western meals, including its famous sizzling steak, and an authentic early 20th-century atmosphere that has changed little over the years.

㉓ Chow Kit Market

Jalan Haji Hussein. **Map** 1 B3. Chow Kit. B111. **Open** 10am–2am daily.

Strung out along the narrow lanes and alleys just to the east of Jalan Tuanku Abdul Rahman, Chow Kit Market is one of the city's biggest and most popular street markets. It is divided into various sections and is especially known for its fresh produce, which includes everything from exotic fruits and vegetables to live seafood, dried anchovies, and meat. Stall owners shout out their wares to vie for attention while porters busily ferry trays and carts laden with goods between the stalls. Although the smells can be overpowering and the narrow wooden walkways wet and slippery due to the extensive use of water to keep the produce fresh, the market offers an interesting glimpse of everyday life in Kuala Lumpur that few tourists see. Numerous other stalls sell household goods, shoes, and watches.

Most of Chow Kit Market, especially the fresh produce sections, closes before 6pm, which is when the night market takes over. A profusion of hawker stalls set up shop, offering a variety of Malay snacks, as well as inexpensive but substantial meals, cooked in the traditional way. Indian and Chinese food, authentically prepared, is also on offer. Some of these stalls also operate during the day. The market is always bustling, and often lasts into the early hours. As with other crowded areas, visitors should be vigilant of pickpockets, especially after dark.

Roadside vendor at Chow Kit Market, one of the city's largest day markets

㉔ National Art Gallery

Jalan Temerloh. **Map** 2 D1. **Tel** (03) 4026-7000. Titiwangsa or KLCC, then taxi. B104. **Open** 10am–6pm daily. 11am & 2:30pm Tue–Sun, 10:30am & 3pm Fri. **artgallery.gov.my**
National Theater: **Tel** (03) 4026-5000. **Open** box office: 10am–6pm Mon–Fri. **istanabudaya.gov.my**

Home to the city's finest permanent collection of contemporary Malaysian art, the National Art Gallery also hosts temporary exhibitions of Asian and international art. Since its establishment in 1958, it has acquired more than 4,300 works. The permanent exhibition on the first floor features a selection of works across different genres and periods. Highlights include Tan Wei Kheng's *Penan Hunter* (2008); Fadilah Karim's *Beautiful Tangle* (2013); Shia Yih Yiing's *Homage Couture* (2013); and Haslin Ismail's *Book Land* (2013), an installation that portrays the power of imagination derived from reading. The temporary shows of modern Asian art include photography, sculpture, and installation art.

Next door, the striking **National Theater**, designed in the shape of a Malay kite, hosts interesting cultural shows as well as national and international theater, and also features a traditional Malay theater costume gallery.

Contemporary art exhibits at the National Art Gallery

㉕ Titiwangsa Lake Gardens

Jalan Temerloh. Ⓛ Titiwangsa. Ⓡ Titiwangsa. B120. ♿ ✎ ▯

Located on the northern fringes of the city, these peaceful, manicured gardens are a great escape from the urban bustle and a popular recreational space. Laid out around a vast man-made lake, the lush gardens are a visual treat and offer a great view of the Petronas Towers. They are also a perfect place to relax, go jogging, or even go boating. There is a herb garden, a lotus pond, and a playground for children. Exercise enthusiasts can also hire bikes to explore the gardens.

㉖ Kampung Baru and Pasar Minggu Market

Jalan Raja Muda Musa. **Map** 2 D4. Ⓛ Kampung Baru. B102 & B103 to Jalan Raja Muda Abdul Aziz.

Established in 1899, the village of Kampung Baru is the oldest Malay residential area in Kuala Lumpur. Its traditional wooden houses, some on stilts, are still found throughout this small settlement which lies to the north of the Sungai Klang, roughly between Jalan Raja Muda Musa and Jalan Raja Muda Abdul Aziz, with Jalan Raja Abdullah and the incredibly busy Chow Kit area

Street food being prepared at Pasar Minggu

marking its western boundary. While the old-fashioned kampung-style houses and the 1920s Masjid Jamek on Jalan Raja Abdullah are worth a visit, the real highlight of Kampung Baru is the glimpse it offers of an older, more leisurely way of life that seems to be rapidly disappearing under the increasingly fast pace of modern Kuala Lumpur. Village elders have repeatedly turned down huge amounts of money to develop the land, said to be the most valuable in the city.

The area comes alive on Saturday nights for the locally popular Pasar Minggu, or Sunday Market. Stalls are set up along Jalan Raja Muda Musa and Jalan Raja Alang at about 6pm on Saturday evening, and stay open until 1am, or the early hours of Sunday morning. Plenty of food and fresh produce is available, as well as numerous hawker stalls tempting shoppers with delicious, traditional Malay street food. A few basic cafés offer visitors more substantial meal options.

Petronas Towers, the tallest twin structures in the world

Starfruit at Pasar Minggu

㉗ Petronas Towers

Jalan Ampang. **Map** 2E4. **Tel** (03) 2331-8080. Ⓛ KLCC. B103, B109. **Open** Skybridge: 9am–9pm Tue–Sun. **Closed** Mon, 1–2:30pm Fri. ⛩ ♿ 🏛 Ⓦ petronastwintowers.com.my

Soaring to a height of 1,483 ft (452 m), the 88-story Petronas Towers are an internationally recognized symbol of modern Malaysia. Designed by the famous Argentinian architect Cesar Pelli, who also designed the Canary Wharf Tower in London, the Petronas Towers were completed in 1998. Built with heat-reflecting stainless steel and laminated glass, and crowned by steel pinnacles, the towers resemble a pair of minarets. The eight-sided star of the floorplan and the overall architecture reflect Islamic principles of unity and harmony. One of the towers houses the national petroleum and oil company, Petronas. The skybridge, linking the towers at the 41st floor, offers a bird's-eye view of the city. Tickets can be bought ahead of time online through the website.

❷❽ Suria KLCC and KLCC Park

Jalan Ampang. **Map** 2 F5.
Tel (03) 2382-3326. Ⓛ KLCC.
🚌 B103, B105. **Open** 10am–10pm
daily. ♿ free hire inside Suria KLCC.
📷 📱 📧 Ⓦ **suriaklcc.com.my**
KLCC Park: **Open** 7am–10pm.
Galeri Petronas: **Tel** (03) 2051-7770.
Open Tue–Sun. ♿ 📷
Ⓦ **galeripetronas.com.my**
Petrosains: **Tel** (03) 2331-8181.
Open 9:30am–5:30pm Tue–Fri,
9:30am–6:30pm Sat & Sun. 📷 📱
Ⓦ **petrosains.com.my**

Spread out over six floors
below the Petronas Towers,
Suria KLCC is one of the city's
busiest shopping malls, with
numerous chain stores,
restaurants, coffee bars, and a
cinema, as well as banks, ATMs,
and a post office. A range of
giant international department
stores have branches here,
including Isetan and Parkson,
along with specialist retailers
and fast-food outlets.

On the third floor is the
Galeri Petronas, which hosts
rotating exhibitions of traditional and contemporary art,
both from Asia and farther
afield. **Petrosains**, on the
fourth floor, is an excellent
interactive science discovery
center. Young visitors can learn
about petroleum science and
technology through a range
of hands-on exhibits, and can
also visit a mock oil rig, try a
helicopter flight simulator,

The glitzy interior of the Suria KLCC
shopping mall

and learn about prehistory in
the geotime diorama. Highlights include a replica of
NASA's Mars space rover and
a singing dinosaur.

The lush KLCC Park that
sprawls in front of the complex
offers a welcome respite from
city traffic. The gardens are
laid out with benches and
shelters, a paddling pool, and a
children's playground. Planted
with over 1,900 native trees,
many bearing explanation
plaques, and centered on an
artificial lake with fountains
(which put on nightly
synchronized shows at 8pm),
the gardens are a cool and
pleasant place to wander
around in the evenings.

❷❾ Aquaria KLCC

Jalan Pinang. **Map** 2 F5. **Tel** (03) 2333-
1888. Ⓛ KLCC. 🚌 B105, B106.
Open 10:30am–8pm daily. 📷 ♿ 📷
Ⓦ **aquariaklcc.com**

Occupying two levels within the
Kuala Lumpur Convention Center,
a short walk from the Petronas
Towers, Aquaria KLCC is a visual
treat. This enormous state-of-
the-art aquarium is home to
over 5,000 creatures, both
aquatic and terrestrial, including
around 150 different species of
fish from across the world.

Conceptualized around the
route that water takes from the
mountains to the sea, the
aquarium recreates various
ecosystems. The journey begins
in the highlands and is
followed by a flooded forest
display where giant catfish can
be seen lurking among tree
roots. Other ecosystems
include mangroves, coral reefs,
and the spectacular open
ocean. A highlight is the 295-ft-
(90-m-) long moving walkway
underwater tunnel, which
offers views of a simulated
natural habitat and a shipwreck
colonized by reef inhabitants,
as well as close-up sightings of
stingrays, eels, and rare sand
tiger sharks.

Feeding times are spread
throughout the day, and a
touch pool lets children handle
aquatic creatures. Visitors who
have a diving qualification can
even dive with sharks.

Visitors observing a school of fish through the glass of a giant tank at the Aquaria KLCC

Malaysian Tourism Information Complex, housed in a colonial mansion

malls, including Lot 10 and Pavilion Kuala Lumpur. Adding local flavor are pavement reflexologists and Middle-Eastern cafés where locals puff hookahs, or tobacco pipes. Changkat Bukit Bintang is another street offering chic bars and restaurants. One of the country's biggest shopping malls, Berjaya Times Square, dominates Jalan Imbi while most of the top-end hotels lie on Jalan Sultan Ismail.

⓿ Malaysian Tourism Information Complex

109 Jalan Ampang. **Map** 2 E5.
Tel (03) 9235-4848. Ⓛ KLCC.
🚇 Bukit Nanas. 🚌 B106.
Open 8am–10pm daily.
♿ ▨ 📷 Ⓦ **matic.gov.my**

The largest tourist center in Kuala Lumpur, the Malaysian Tourism Information Complex is housed in an impressive colonial mansion. Built on the site of an old rambutan orchard in 1935, it was formerly the home of Eu Tong Seng, a wealthy Chinese tin and rubber businessman. Not long after its construction, World War II broke out and the house was taken over by the British military and used as their war office. It was subsequently captured by the Japanese army, who converted it into their headquarters in Malaysia for the remainder the war. After independence, the building housed several government agencies and also witnessed the coronation ceremonies of four successive Malaysian kings.

Today, the main building in the complex houses the Malaysia tourist information office, while annexes contain a tourist police office, restaurant, and a concert hall where regular cultural shows are performed *(see p309)*. Traditional games, such as top-spinning, are also hosted here on weekends and there is a daily dance performance at 3pm.

㉛ The Golden Triangle

Map 1 C5. 🚇 Bukit Bintang, Imbi.
🚌 B107, B108.

Spread over a large, roughly triangular area with its apex at Jalan Ampang in the north and its base formed by Jalan Imbi in the south, the Golden Triangle is Kuala Lumpur's main business, shopping, and nightlife district. Among the sea of glitzy high-rise buildings are most of the city's prominent shopping malls, along with countless bars, restaurants, cafés, and premier hotels, including the **Mandarin Oriental** *(see p278)*, which is located opposite the Petronas Towers. At the heart of the Golden Triangle is Jalan Bukit Bintang with its trendy bars, eateries, and the biggest concentration of shopping

Mandarin Oriental, a luxury hotel in the Golden Triangle

㉜ Menara KL and Bukit Nanas Forest Reserve

2 Jalan Punchak, off Jalan P Ramlee.
Map 5 A1. **Tel** (03) 2020-5444. 🚇 Bukit Nanas. **Open** 9am–10pm daily.
▨ ▨ 🖥 📷 Ⓦ **menarakl.com.my**
Bukit Nanas Forest Reserve:
Open 7am–6pm daily. 🚶 arranged by Menara KL. ♿

Built as a communications tower between 1991 and 1996, Menara KL, or KL tower, is among the five tallest tele-communications towers in the world. It stands at a height of 1,380 ft (421 m). Its lobby has several shops and a lift that whisks visitors up to the obser-vation deck for a panoramic view of the city. At a dizzying height of 905 ft (276 m), it is more than 328-ft (100-m) higher than the skybridge at the Petronas Towers. As well as a revolving restaurant, there is also an aquarium and a floor full of games simulators to explore. Each year, the tower hosts an official BASE jump event, which attracts around 100 participants.

At the base of the tower is Malaysia's oldest nature reserve, the **Bukit Nanas Forest Reserve**, gazetted in 1906. This legal status saved the 27-acre (11-ha) slice of rain forest from destruction when the tower was built, and even resulted in a reworking of the architectural plans to avoid the cutting down of a 100-year-old *jelutong* tree. The reserve is quite rundown but worth a visit to see a rich variety of wildlife, including monkeys and

Panorama of Kuala Lumpur from the Menara KL tower observation desk

squirrels, as well as numerous tropical trees. Be sure to bring mosquito repellent.

❸ Badan Warisan

2 Jalan Stonor. **Map** 6 E1.
Tel (03) 2144-9273. 🚇 Raja Chulan.
🚌 R108. **Open** 10am–5:30pm
Mon–Sat. **Closed** Sun. 🎨 🎫 11am &
3pm Mon–Sat. ♿ limited. 📷
🅦 badanwarisan.org.my

Founded in 1983 for the conservation of Malaysia's architectural heritage, Badan Warisan is a non-government organization that runs regular campaigns and projects to save historical buildings from neglect and destruction. In 1995, it renovated a colonial bungalow on Jalan Stonor and turned it into a heritage center, with exhibition facilities for art and craft shows as well as a resource center with books, drawings, slides, and photographs for those keen to learn more about the organization's conservation work. The highlight is **Rumuh Penghulu Abu Seman**, a traditional Malay wooden house dating from the 1920s. It was brought to this site in a state of serious disrepair from a village in Kedah. Since then, it has been expertly restored and now serves as a showpiece for modern conservation methods.

❸ Kompleks Budaya Kraf

63 Jalan Conlay. **Map** 6 E1. **Tel** (03)
2162-7459. 🇱 KLCC. 🚇 Raja Chulan.
🚌 R108. **Open** daily. 🎨 ♿ 🖥 📷
🅦 kraftangan.gov.my

Located on the eastern edge of the Golden Triangle, Kompleks Budaya Kraf is a handicrafts complex that showcases a wide range of traditional arts and crafts from the various states of Peninsular Malaysia and Malaysian Borneo. It is made up of four separate buildings that house shops and stalls, a museum, exhibition areas, and several workshops. The museum traces the history and development of age-old crafts and features dioramas

Earthenware at Budaya Kraf

of artisans creating their wares with displays of the various tools they would have used.

In the exhibition areas and workshops, craftspeople demonstrate ethnic art and craft skills, such as weaving, *batik*-printing, and silver and copperwork. Visitors are welcome to try their hand and can also receive lessons in a particular craft. The complex is one of the best places in Kuala Lumpur to buy these local handicrafts, with a number of shops and stalls selling pewter, silverwork, pottery, woodcarvings, hand-woven textiles, *batik*, and beadwork, alongside more unusual items such as rattan fishtraps, birdcages, and tribal blowpipes.

An array of traditional handicrafts on sale at the Kompleks Budaya Kraf

Sultan Salahuddin Abdul Aziz Shah Mosque in Shah Alam

③ FRIM

Kepong, 10 miles (16 km) NW of Kuala Lumpur. **Tel** (03) 6279-7575. ⊞ to Kepong, then taxi. **Open** park: 5am–7:30pm; canopy: 9:30am–2:30pm except Mon & Fri; museum: 8am–4:30pm. 🚗 for vehicles; canopy tours. 🎫 ♿ limited. 🖥 📷 ⛰ 🌐 **frim.gov.my**

Occupying 2 sq miles (5 sq km) of parkland within the Bukit Lagong Forest Reserve, the Forest Research Institute of Malaysia (FRIM) was founded in 1929 as a research and development center for tropical forests, with a special emphasis on sustainable forest management. An on-site museum explains the center's work. There are several arboreta of native trees, including the most comprehensive collection of dipterocarp (hardwood) species in the world. Also in the grounds is a traditional Malay house from Terengganu *(see p147)*. Among the highlights of a visit to FRIM is the 656-ft- (200-m-) long canopy walkway suspended 98 ft (30 m) above ground, which offers a fascinating close-up view of the treetops. There are also a number of easy walking trails, a more strenuous mountain bike trail, camping, bird-watching, and picnic areas.

FRIM logo

③ Shah Alam

11 miles (18 km) W of Kuala Lumpur. 🏛 319,600. ⊞ 🚌 ℹ Jalan Indah 14, (03) 5513-2000. 🎭 Bon Odori Festival (Jul). 🌐 **tourismselangor. gov.my** Museum Sultan Azlan Shah: Persian Bandaraya. **Tel** (03) 5519-0050. **Open** 9:30am–5:30pm Tue–Sun. **Closed** Mon, noon–2:45pm Fri. ♿ Galeri Shah Alam: Persiaran Tasik. **Tel** (03) 5510-5344. **Open** 8:30am–5:30pm daily. **Closed** 12:15–2:45pm Fri. Wet World Water Park: **Tel** (03) 5513-2020. **Open** 10am–6pm Thu–Tue. 🚗 🖥 🌐 **owg.com.my**

Designated the state capital of Selangor in 1978, Shah Alam is a well-planned modern city sprawled over a large area. It is essentially an industrial and administrative center, and is rarely visited by tourists. Still, the area's few sights of interest, most of which are within walking distance of each other, make it a pleasant day trip. Located in a park at the center of town is the city's main attraction, the **Sultan Salahuddin Abdul Aziz Shah Mosque**, more popularly known as the Blue Mosque owing to its large blue and silver aluminum dome. Its four 466-ft (142-m-) high minarets are said to be the tallest in the world. The mosque can accommodate up to 24,000 worshipers and is reputed to be one of the largest mosques in Southeast Asia and the largest in Malaysia.

Nearby is the **Museum Sultan Azlan Shah** with extensive displays covering the history of Selangor from prehistoric times to the present day. It also contains galleries dedicated to the state's wildlife as well as its sporting achievements. To the west of the museum is the attractively landscaped Lake Gardens, home to the **Galeri Shah Alam**, a modern art gallery located in a traditional Malay wooden building which hosts temporary exhibitions of modern art over three separate galleries. On the opposite side of the lake is Wet World Water Park, a water theme park with pools, slides, and rides.

③ Klang

18 miles (30 km) SW of Kuala Lumpur. 🏛 563,200. ⊞ 🚌 🌐 **mpklang. gov.my** Gedung Raja Abdullah: Jalan Raja Abdullah. **Tel** (03) 5519-0050. Closed for renovation.

The former royal capital of Selangor, the city of Klang, flourished during the 19th-century boom in the tin industry. However, in 1867, civil war erupted owing to the rivalry between the two local chieftains, Rajah Mahadi and Rajah Abdullah. The fighting was ended in 1874 when the British authorities intervened and installed the first Resident in the town. The discovery of new tin deposits in Kuala Lumpur in 1880 further diminished the

Inscribed mausoleum at Masjid Di Raja Sultan Suleiman in Klang

importance of Klang. Today, the city is a commercial center, with most sights of interest located in the old town, south of the Sungai Klang.

Built in 1857, **Gedung Raja Abdullah** was the former residence of Rajah Abdullah. Due to reopen following renovations (phone ahead to check), it houses the Tin Museum, which traces the history of the local mining industry through archived photographs and other artifacts. Nearby are the remains of Rajah Mahadi's fort. Also located in the old quarter is the attractive **Masjid Di Raja Sultan Suleiman**, the former state mosque, behind which is **Istana Alam Shah**, the royal palace of the Sultan of Selangor. Although closed to the public, visitors can view the pleasing façade of the palace, a blend of Islamic and modern architecture. **Port Klang**, or North Port, lies 5 miles (8 km) to the west, close to South Port, Malaysia's main seaport, and is the access point for Pulau Ketam.

❸ Pulau Ketam

34 miles (55 km) SW of Kuala Lumpur.
🏙 8,000. 🚢 from Port Klang.
Ⓦ pulauketam.com

First inhabited by Hainanese fishermen in the 1870s, Pulau Ketam, or Crab Island, remains largely populated by Chinese. The majority of the inhabitants still make their living by fishing. Although Pulau Ketam village is a simple settlement of stilt houses built over the water with narrow wooden walkways in place of roads, it contains a number of basic amenities including a bank and hospital. It is well known for its superb seafood restaurants, specializing in crab dishes, which make it a popular weekend dining venue for city residents. There are also ornate Chinese temples, such as the **Nang Thiam Keng Temple**, where locals host wedding feasts. The many floating fish farms offshore are worth visiting and can be reached by a short boat ride from the island jetty.

❸ Putrajaya

15 miles (25 km) SW of Kuala Lumpur.
🏙 45,000. 🚈 KLIA Transit from KL Sentral. 🚌 ℹ️ Precinct 1, (03) 8888-7272. Ⓦ ppj.gov.my
Botanic Garden: Precinct 1. **Open** 7am–7pm daily. 🚻 ♿ ✏️ 🖥 📷
Putrajaya Wetlands: Precinct 13. **Tel** (03) 8925-3817. **Open** 10am–6pm Tue–Fri, 7am–7pm Sat & Sun. 🚻 🖥 📷

Founded in 1995, Putrajaya is the new federal administrative capital of Malaysia. Lying at the heart of the Multimedia Super Corridor (MSC), an area designated to attract information technology companies, and with huge swathes of green spaces, it is a planned "intelligent" garden city. Putrajaya is built on cleared forest land and centered around a huge artificial lake. The city is designed to create a sense of vastness and with so much water around, great attention has been paid to building massive bridges. These include the Putra Bridge, inspired by the Khaju Bridge in Iran, and the 787-ft- (240-m-) long Seri Gemilang Bridge.

Government departments and ministries began the move here from Kuala Lumpur in 1999. These include the Prime Minister's office, known as **Perdana Putra**, built in a flamboyant Malay-Palladian style, and the equally grand **Palace of**

A close view of the pink granite edifice of the Putra Mosque

Justice, topped with a gigantic dome. The **Putra Mosque** with its 380-ft- (116-m-) high minaret looms over one edge of the lake and is one of the city's most impressive buildings, blending architectural styles from Iraq, Iran, and Morocco. Other sights worth exploring include the **Botanic Garden** with its collection of tropical flora, and the **Putrajaya Wetlands**, which were constructed to help cleanse river water. Paddleboats can be hired for trips on the wetlands and lake.

Lying on the outskirts of Putrajaya is its twin town, **Cyberjaya**. Conceived as a center for high-tech companies, more than 50,000 people work there every weekday.

Palace of Justice, Putrajaya, with its distinctive Islamic-style architecture

KUALA LUMPUR STREET FINDER

The key map below shows the area of Kuala Lumpur covered in this Street Finder. Map references given for sights, shops, and entertainment venues in the Kuala Lumpur section refer to the maps on the following pages. Map references are also provided for some of Kuala Lumpur's hotels and restaurants. An index of the street names and places of interest shown on the maps can be found on the facing page. The first figure in the map reference indicates which Street Finder map to turn to, and the letters and numbers that follow refer to the map's grid. The symbols used to represent sights and useful information on the Street Finder maps are listed in the key below. Common street designations have been abbreviated – Jalan to Jln. and Lorong to Lrg.

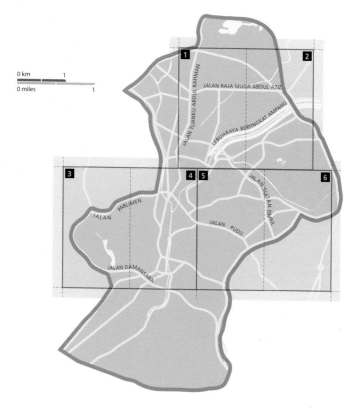

Key to Street Finder

- Major sight
- Place of interest
- Other buildings
- ⬛ LRT station
- ⬛ Railroad station
- ⬛ Bus station
- ⬛ Monorail
- ➕ Hospital
- ⬛ Police station

- ℹ️ Visitor information
- 🛕 Hindu temple
- ✝️ Church
- 🏯 Chinese temple
- ☪️ Mosque
- ═══ Railroad
- ═══ Expressway

Scale of Map Pages

0 meters 300
0 yards 300

Street Finder Index

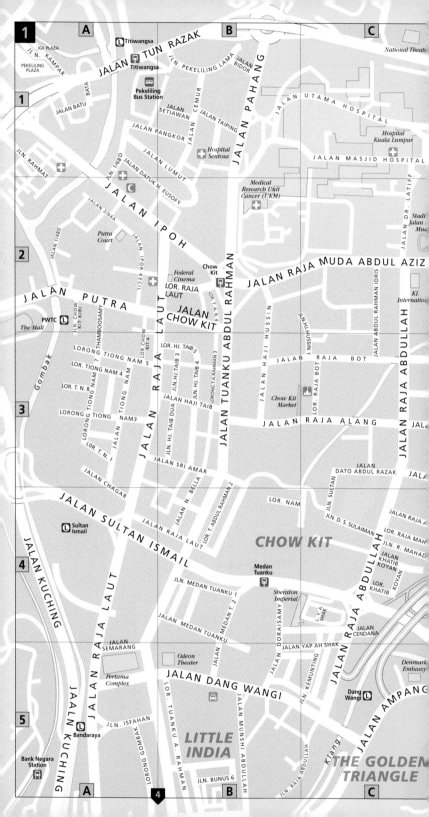

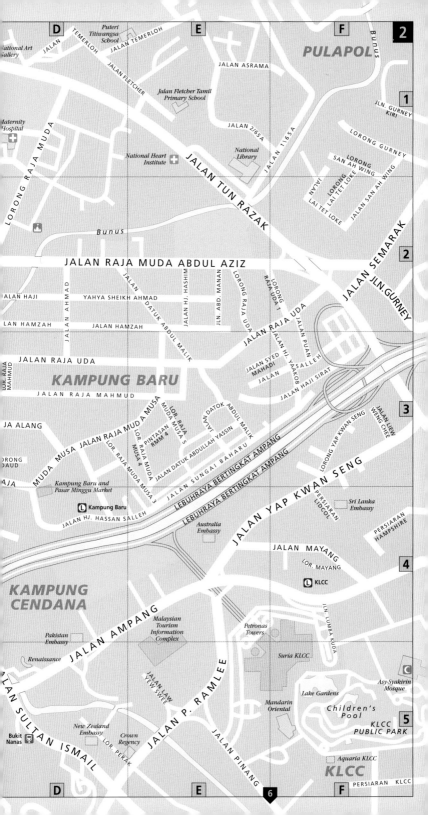

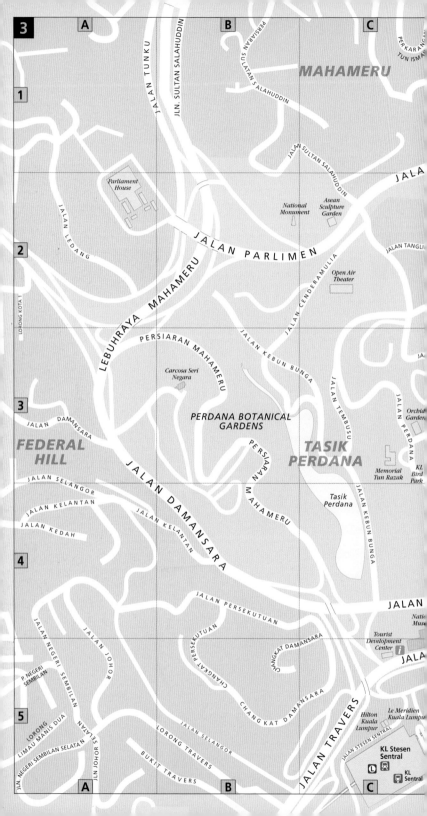

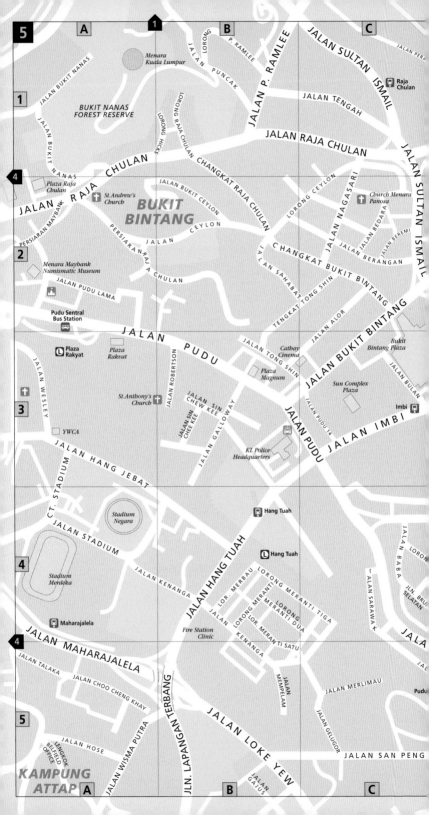

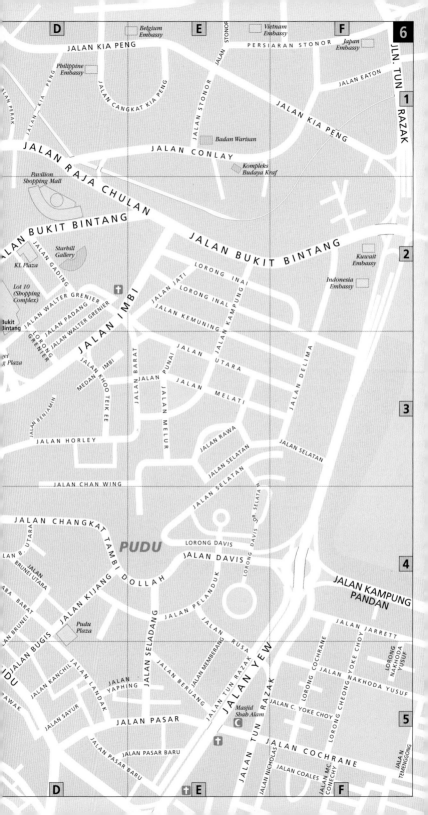

NORTHWEST PENINSULA

The northwestern states of Malaysia are among the most geographically diverse and historically significant in the country. The landscape encompasses everything from coastal plains and lushly forested mountains to jutting limestone cliffs and pristine islands. A long legacy of immigrants and rulers, attracted by the region's strategic geographical position and its natural wealth, has bequeathed a fascinating mix of cultures.

Archaeological remains found at the coastal site of Lembah Bujang provide evidence of a Hindu-Buddhist kingdom that dates back to the 4th century AD. In the 7th and 8th centuries, the region was ruled by the Srivijaya empire and later by Siam (now Thailand), while the 15th century saw the rise of the Sultanate of Malacca. With the beginning of the 17th century, a power struggle ensued between colonial powers in the area until the British finally gained control.

By the mid-19th century, the growing importance of tin mining in the states of Perak and Selangor brought with it far-reaching economic, political, and social repercussions. It fueled Malaysia's tremendous economic rise in the 20th century and also attracted a huge influx of Chinese immigrants. As a result of these varied early influences and economic developments, the Northwest Peninsula is more cosmopolitan and less culturally conservative than other parts of Malaysia. It is also one of the most developed and populous regions in the country, comprising not only ethnic Malays, Chinese, and Indians, but also indigenous groups such as the Orang Asli and the Orang Syam in the interior jungles and far north. The old royal capital of Kuala Kangsar and the vibrant, historic, and culturally diverse city of Georgetown in Penang are on the itinerary of most visitors to the Northwest Peninsula. More laid-back tourists head for the region's pristine beaches or the soothing environs of its tea plantations and cool hill stations.

The palm-fringed white sands of Pantai Cenang Beach, Langkawi

◀ The ornate tiered pagoda of the Kek Lok Si Temple in Penang

Exploring the Northwest Peninsula

Few regions in the country offer the range of attractions found in the Northwest Peninsula. The interiors feature cool hill stations, such as the celebrated Cameron Highlands, limestone cliffs riddled with cave temples, including the Batu Caves, and Chinese-dominated tin-rush towns such as Ipoh. The most popular destinations are along the coast, including Penang, which is an ideal base for exploring the region and a fascinating destination in itself, and the islands of Langkawi and Pangkor. The archaeologically important Lembah Bujang lies in Kedah which, together with Perlis, is carpeted with paddy fields.

Sights at a Glance

Towns and Cities

- ④ Kuala Selangor
- ⑦ Ipoh
- ⑪ Taiping
- ⑬ Kuala Kangsar
- ⑭ Georgetown *pp106–11*
- ㉔ Batu Maung
- ㉗ Alor Star
- ㉘ Kuala Kedah

Places of Worship

- ① Batu Caves
- ⑮ Dhammikarama Temple
- ⑯ Wat Chayamangkalaram
- ⑱ Kek Lok Si Temple
- ㉓ Snake Temple

Gardens and Themed Attractions

- ③ Genting Highlands
- ⑰ Penang Botanic Gardens

Museums and Galleries

- ② Museum JAKOA

Areas of Natural Beauty

- ⑤ Fraser's Hill
- ⑥ *Cameron Highlands pp98–9*
- ⑩ Kinta Valley
- ⑲ Penang Hill
- ㉒ Penang National Park
- ㉖ Gunung Jerai

Historical Sites and Buildings

- ⑧ Kellie's Castle
- ⑫ Lenggong Valley
- ㉕ Lembah Bujang

Islands and Beaches

- ⑨ Pulau Pangkor
- ⑳ Batu Ferringhi
- ㉑ Teluk Bahang
- ㉙ *Pulau Langkawi pp118–19*

0 kilometers   50
0 miles   50

Penang

0 kilometers   5
0 miles   5

Palm-fringed Pelangi Beach, Pulau Langkawi

For hotels and restaurants see p279 and pp292–3

Getting Around

A good domestic flight network covers Ipoh, Pulau Pangkor, Langkawi, Georgetown, and Alor Star. The North–South Highway and Route 1, the region's two major roads, and the national railroad (KTM) run almost parallel with each other, tracing the length of the west coast and linking the major towns. Driving is a good option; roads are safe and traffic is mainly law-abiding. Two bridges connect Penang to the mainland, as do car and passenger ferries. Lumut is the ferry point for Pulau Pangkor, while ferries to Pulau Langkawi are available at Kuala Kedah, Kuala Perlis, and Georgetown.

Kek Lok Si Temple in Penang, the largest Buddhist temple in Malaysia

Key

- ═══ Highway
- ── Major road
- ┄┄┄ Minor road
- ┅┅┅ Railroad
- ▬▬▬ International border
- ▪▪▪ State border
- △ Peak

For keys to symbols *see back flap*

Vibrant paintings of Hindu deities on the walls at one of the Batu Caves

❶ Batu Caves

8 miles (13 km) N of Kuala Lumpur on Middle Ring Road 2. **Tel** 1300-88-5050. Ⓛ Batu Caves. 🚇 **Open** 7am–6pm daily. 🚻 📷 🎎 Thaipusam Festival (Jan/Feb).

Set high in a range of rugged limestone cliffs, the Batu Caves are a vast cavern complex that has become one of the most popular attractions near the capital. Long known to the indigenous Orang Asli people, the caves only gained worldwide popularity when American naturalist William Hornaday came upon them in 1878. Deeply impressed by the largest cave, he compared it to a grand cathedral. In the 1890s, it was converted into a shrine dedicated to the Hindu deity Lord Murugan, and soon became the most important pilgrimage site for Malaysia's Hindus. During the annual Thaipusam festival, held in late January or early February, a spectacular scene unfolds here, when an estimated one million pilgrims visit the caves *(see p35)*.

Dominating the entrance to the caves is a 141-ft- (43-m-) tall golden statue of Lord Murugan. From here a steep flight of 272 steps leads up to the main cave. Also known as **Temple** or **Cathedral Cave**, it is 328 ft (100 m) high and is partially lit by shafts of light that stream through gaps in the roof. The cave walls are lined with statues of Lord Murugan, along with those of other Hindu gods, including Shiva, Ganesh, and Durga. The dome of the cave is richly painted with scenes from the Hindu scriptures. In a chamber behind the central shrine is the statue of another deity, Lord Rama.

The cave gets extremely busy so it's best to head there early in the morning. Another essential tip: do not feed the monkeys that congregate at the entrance.

❷ Museum JAKOA

Jalan Pahang, Gombak, 18 miles (30 km) N of Kuala Lumpur. **Tel** (03) 6189-2113. 🚇 **Open** 9am–5pm Sat–Thu. 💻 📷

Though visited by few people, Museum JAKOA, formerly known as the Orang Asli Museum, provides a superb introduction to the customs, traditions, and material culture of Malaysia's almost 100,000 Orang Asli people, the earliest known indigenous inhabitants of the peninsula. Run by the Orang Asli Affairs Department, the museum presents the history of the 18 distinct groups within the community along with their geographical distribution, musical instruments, ornaments, medicines, models of their dwellings, and a collection of traditional hunting weapons, such as blowpipes and poison spoons. Among the most impressive of these is the display of traditional handicrafts, which includes wooden head carvings with fierce facial expressions. Details of daily life, including wedding rites and religious practices, are also described.

❸ Genting Highlands

31 miles (50 km) NE of Kuala Lumpur. 🚇 from Kuala Lumpur, then cable car (optional). 🚻 📷 🌐 **rwgenting.com** Genting Skyway runs every 20 min; after midnight every hour.

Unlike most conventional hill-station retreats, the 6,562-ft (2,000-m-) high Genting Highlands, located in the Titiwangsa Mountain Range, is an extensive entertainment and gambling complex. The glitzy 24-hour **Casino de Genting**, one of the largest in the world, contains endless rows of Chinese and Western games tables, a computerized racetrack, and slot machines.

Replacing the older Genting Theme Park is the massive **Twentieth Century Fox World**, with more than 25 rides and attractions themed around

Genting Skyway, a cable car to Genting Highlands retreat

movies such as *Alien vs. Predator*, *Night at the Museum*, *Planet of the Apes*, *Titanic*, and *Ice Age*.

The resort, considered to be the largest in the world, has more than 10,000 rooms across 6 hotels, 100 restaurants and more than 80 shops, a golf course, and several concert halls that host international performing artists.

An attraction in itself is the Genting Skyway, one of the longest cable cars in Southeast Asia with the capacity to hold 100 gondolas and carry 1,600 passengers per hour on a 2-mile (3.4-km) distance from mid-hill at Gohtong Jaya to Maxims Hotel at the peak.

❹ Kuala Selangor

42 miles (67 km) NW of Kuala Lumpur on Hwy 4, then 5. 🚗 39,200. 🚌

The small and quiet district capital of Selangor, located at the mouth of the Sungai Selangor, was once the royal capital of the Sultanate of Selangor. It was conquered by the Dutch in 1784, and soon became the scene of a number of intense battles. During their invasion, the Dutch destroyed the sultan's fort and rebuilt it, naming it **Fort Atlingsburg** after their governor general. Perched atop Bukit Melawati, a hill overlooking the town, the fort was battled over repeatedly, and all that remains today are sections of the wall and cannons.

Directly below the fort lies the boundary of **Kuala Selangor Nature Park**, a mangrove forest, home to more than150 species of birds and a variety of wetland animals. This is the only area in Malaysia to record sightings of the spoonbill sandpiper. It is also home to a variety of fish and crabs, found in the mangroves along the park's coastline. Several artificial ponds are surrounded by nature trails, observation hides and towers.

Spoonbill sandpiper, Kuala Selangor Nature Park

A particular highlight of Kuala Selangor is the chance to see the dazzling *kelip kelip*, or fireflies, along the banks of the Sungai Selangor at **Kampung Kuantan**, 6 miles (10 km) east of the capital.

🏰 Fort Altingsburg
Bukit Melawati. **Open** daily.

🦅 Kuala Selangor Nature Park
Jalan Klinik. **Tel** (03) 2287-9422. **Open** 9am–6pm daily. 🌐 **mns.my**

❺ Fraser's Hill

62 miles (100 km) N of Kuala Lumpur. ℹ️ Tourism Malaysia Pahang, (09) 517-7111. 🌿 nature walks. 🖊️

A hill station sprawling across seven forested hills, the 4,921-ft (1,500-m) Fraser's Hill is named after British pioneer Louis James Fraser. A mule-train driver and tin-ore trader, he arrived here in the late 1890s, but then mysteriously disappeared around 1910. Shortly after, Fraser's Hill was developed as a refreshing retreat for the British expatriate community.

A picturesque journey leads to Fraser's Hill, passing through giant bamboo groves and tree ferns, and climbing steeply through the Gap, a mountain pass between Kuala Kubu Bharu and Raub. Traffic is heavily controlled because of the windy conditions on the road, so be prepared for your journey to take longer than expected.

Of all the hill stations set in the Titiwangsa mountains, Fraser's Hill retains the most distinct colonial ambience with Tudor-style buildings. There is no public transport, and just one road up and down. It can get busy on weekends and during the school vacations, but otherwise during the week it is usually quiet and relaxed, perfect for jungle strolls and afternoon teas.

At the center of town is a market square and a clock tower covered with creeper vines. There's an organic market garden next to the tiny Allan's Water lake, where you can pick your own strawberries. Paddle-boating is available on the lake. This small area is surrounded by dense woods, which contain several nature trails.

One of the hill station's main attractions is its abundant flora and fauna. Famous as a bird-watching destination, more than 265 species of birds have been recorded in the area. Every June, Fraser's Hill hosts the annual International Bird Race, in which teams of ornithologists compete to spot as many bird varieties as possible over a 24-hour period.

About 3 miles (5 km) northwest of the center is Jeriau Waterfall, which flows into a small stream.

Foliage-covered clock tower in the center of Fraser's Hill

❻ Cameron Highlands

The largest and most popular hill station in Malaysia, Cameron Highlands is located on the northwest corner of Pahang. It is named for the British surveyor William Cameron who charted the area in 1885. Dotted with lush tea plantations and farms, the region is renowned for its flowers and fresh produce. The temperature here rarely exceeds 22° C (72° F) and is accompanied by mists and light rainfall, which makes it a great getaway from the hot plains. It is also a popular destination for trekkers. Cameron Highlands retains a distinct colonial ambience, with its principal settlement located in Tanah Rata.

★ Smokehouse Hotel
A mock-Tudor building on the outskirts of Tanah Rata, the Smokehouse Hotel typifies the colonial architecture that adds to the appeal of Cameron Highlands. It is popular with visitors for its real Devonshire cream teas.

Key

=== Major road
=== Minor road
-- Trail
△ Peak

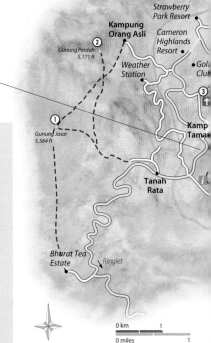

Jim Thompson

Jim Thompson shortly before his disappearance

In March 1967, James H W Thompson, a successful US-born Thai businessman, disappeared while on holiday in the Cameron Highlands. He simply walked out of the cottage where he was staying, and never came back. At the time, and for months afterwards, the media was filled with speculation about his fate. With his disappearance, he became a legendary figure, leaving behind him a resurrected and resilient Thai silk industry and a traditional teak home in Bangkok. Jim Thompson's home is now an exquisite museum of Southeast Asian art.

For hotels and restaurants see p279 and pp292–3

★ Sungai Palas Boh Tea Plantation
This stunning estate offers free daily tours. Visitors can purchase teas and enjoy fine views across the surrounding hills while sampling tea and cakes in the estate tearoom.

Butterfly Garden
Almost 300 species of butterfly are on show here, alongside scorpions, giant rhinoceros beetles, and camouflaged stick insects.

nung
nchang
45 ft

↗ *Ipoh*

Blue Valley Tea Estate

Kuala Terla

Rose Valley

cle Sam's Farm

Brinchang

Rose Garden
This garden has an immense appeal for locals as well as tourists who visit to see the exotic roses in bloom. The flowers flourish only in temperate hill areas such as the Cameron Highlands.

Gunung Beremban 6,037 ft

di Agricultural ion

binson ls

binson Falls wer Station

★ Sam Poh Temple
This ornate Chinese-Buddhist temple is situated on a hill overlooking the town of Brinchang. Protected by gilded lions and temple guardians, it serves as the main place of worship for the local Chinese.

KEY

① **Gunung Jasar**, at 5,564 ft (1,696 m), offers fine views across Cameron Highlands from its bald summit and is easily accessible by a carefully marked trail from Tanah Rata.

② **Gunung Perdah**, at 5,171 ft (1,576 m), rises above an Orang Asli village to the north of Tanah Rata and dominates the northwestern horizon.

③ **All Souls' Church**, erected in 1958, serves as a civilian church as well as the Anglican retreat center at Cameron Highlands.

Birch Memorial Clock Tower standing in Ipoh's Old Town

❼ Ipoh

128 miles (205 km) N of Kuala Lumpur on North–South Hwy. 🚇 625,000. ✈️ 🚉 🚌 ℹ️ 7–9 Jalan Medan Istana 3, (05) 255-2772. 🎨 International Orchid Festival (Jun/Aug). 🌐 **ipoh-online.com.my**

Nestled in the limestone cliffs of Kinta Valley, Ipoh is the state capital of Perak and Malaysia's third-largest city. It was built on profits from the valley's rich tin mines, which were developed by immigrant Chinese workers in the late 19th century. This influx of people bequeathed to the city some of the finest Peranakan architecture seen in the country.

The Kinta River divides Ipoh into two neat halves. Occupying the left bank is the **Old Town**, the most atmospheric part of the city. It boasts elegant Chinese mansions and shophouses, as well as grand colonial buildings. Built in 1917, Ipoh Railway Station is a blend of late Victorian and Moorish-Islamic styles. Directly opposite stands the Dewan Bandaran, or Town Hall, a dazzling white Neo-Classical structure. Other prominent landmarks near the station include the mock-Tudor Royal Ipoh Club with its half-timbered walls and mullioned windows, and the historical landmark Birch Memorial Clock Tower erected in memory of

James Birch, the first British Resident in Perak. A short distance from the Old Town center is **Darul Ridzuan Museum**. Set in a stately 1920s mansion, it briefly recounts the history of Ipoh and the rise of the tin-mining industry in Perak.

The **New Town**, on the right bank of the river, contains some splendid Chinese shophouses and most of the city's accommodations.

🏛️ **Darul Ridzuan Museum**
Jalan Panglima. **Tel** (05) 241-0048. **Open** 9am–5pm daily.

❽ Kellie's Castle

19 miles (30 km) S of Ipoh. **Tel** (05) 255-2772. 🚌 67 from Gopeng Station. **Open** 8:30am–7pm daily. 🚗 💻 🏛️

A unique fusion of Scottish castle and Moorish architecture, Kellie's Castle is an unfinished colonial structure. It was built by Scotsman William Kellie-Smith, who made a fortune in the rubber business in the 19th century. The mansion was envisioned as a spectacular edifice, complete with an elevator, and work began in 1915. However, Smith died of pneumonia in 1926, leaving his grand home incomplete. During World War II, the castle grounds were used as an execution site by the Japanese. Today, it is a crumbling attraction set in a park with fig and banyan trees. Also in the grounds is a Hindu temple built by Smith for his largely Tamil labor force. The temple was built after many Tamil workers were killed in an

epidemic of influenza during the mansion's construction. Grateful for this act, the workers added a small statue of Smith amid the Hindu deities on the temple roof.

❾ Pulau Pangkor

51 miles (83 km) SW of Ipoh. 🚇 25,000. ✈️ 🚌 from Kuala Lumpur. ⛴️ from Lumut. ℹ️ Jalan Titi Panjang, Lumut, (05) 683-4057. 🌐 **pulau-pangkor.com**

Endowed with a laid-back feel and some of the best beaches on the west coast of the peninsula, Pulau Pangkor is a popular destination. The island is inhabited by a thriving fishing community. Most of the local villages, including Pangkor Town, the main settlement, lie on its east coast, while the resorts, fishing villages, and stunning powder-white beaches are strung out on the west, around Teluk Nipah. The main beaches include Pasir Bogak, Coral Bay, and Pantai Puteri Dewi, which is privately owned and requires an entrance fee. The beach at Teluk Ketapang, or Turtle Bay, at the northern end of the island, is named for the increasingly rare sea turtles that come ashore here in the summer to lay their eggs.

Offering a change of scene from the beaches is the historical site of **Kota Belanda**, a 17th-century Dutch fort 2 miles (3 km) south of Pangkor Town. The fort was built mainly to protect Dutch interests in the tin trade from Malay pirates. Be warned, though, that very little of the fort remains. Pangkor's

Remains of the striking Kellie's Castle

The picturesque Lake Gardens in Taiping, near the foot of Bukit Larut

compact size makes it ideal for walking and cycling, although its densely forested interior remains largely inaccessible.

The resorts arrange fishing and snorkeling day trips to the small islands nearby. Among these is Pangkor Laut, home to Emerald Bay, one of Malaysia's most beautiful beaches, though access is restricted to residents of the island's exclusive resort.

⑩ Kinta Valley

9 miles (15 km) N of Ipoh, off North–South Hwy. 🚌 from Ipoh. ℹ (05) 255-2772. ▨

Once rich with tin ore, the magnificent jungle-topped limestone cliffs of Kinta Valley shelter a number of caves, which, over the years, have been converted into Buddhist temples and are now popular pilgrimage centers. The oldest and largest cave temple is **Sam Poh Tong**. Established by a Buddhist monk in the late 19th century, it features Chinese-style Mahayana Buddhist images. More impressive is **Perak Tong**, one of the largest Chinese temples in Malaysia, founded in 1926. Its interior walls are adorned with murals done by artists from across Southeast Asia. The main chamber contains over 40 Buddha statues and a huge bell believed to be more than a century old. A series of 400 steps leads up and through the

Bronze Buddha at Kek Lok Tong

cave to a balcony which offers splendid views across the valley. The temple also doubles as a Chinese art center. A more recent temple, **Kek Lok Tong**, is set in a two-tiered cavern and has a bronze Laughing Buddha.

⑪ Taiping

40 miles (70 km) N of Ipoh. 🏙 220,000. 🚉 from Ipoh. 🚌 ℹ 355 Jalan Kota; (05) 806-9487. 🎏 Taiping Festival Month (Sep). 🆆 **perak.gov.my/en**

Although the name Taiping means everlasting peace in Chinese, the old state capital of Perak traces its origins to a turbulent past, marked by bitter feuds between rival Chinese secret societies. The country's first tin-mining center and the most important town in Perak in the mid-19th century, it began to be overshadowed by Ipoh and Kinta Valley in the 1890s. Now a low-key town, with a distinctly Chinese feel, Taiping is best known for its vast, tranquil **Lake Gardens**, or Taman Tasik Taiping. A stroll around the town will reveal some attractive colonial architecture, best exemplified by the District Office. It is also home to **Perak Museum**, the oldest museum in the country, built in 1883. Housed in a grand colonial building, it is noted for its natural history and ethnological exhibits, as well as a fine collection of *keris,* or traditional Malay daggers. Next door to the museum is the colorful

Ling Nam Temple, the oldest Chinese temple in Perak, as well as **All Saints' Church**, the oldest church in Malaysia. Taiping also has a number of well-preserved Chinese shophouses.

🏛 Perak Museum
Tel (05) 242-6906. **Open** 9am–6pm daily. **Closed** 12:15–2:45pm Fri.

⑫ Lenggong Valley

62 miles (100 km) N of Ipoh on North–South Hwy. 🆆 **perak.gov.my/en**

Designated a UNESCO World Heritage Site in 2012, the Lenggong Valley is one of Malaysia's most important areas for archaeology. The valley has four archaeological sites in two clusters that span almost 2 million years. Lenggong is the oldest known site of human activity in Malaysia, and also the oldest outside the African continent.

Lenggong Valley features both open-air and cave sites with Paleolithic tool workshops, as well as evidence of early technological and cultural remains from the Paleolithic, Neolithic, and Metal ages. The valley's most famous find was the complete skeleton of Perak Man, which is more than 11,000 years old. It is currently on display at the National Museum in Kuala Lumpur (*see p72*). Other artifacts excavated in the area are displayed in the **Lenggong Archaeological Museum**.

Displays at Lenggong Archaeological Museum

⓭ Kuala Kangsar

31 miles (50 km) NW of Ipoh, off North–South Hwy. 🚗 40,000. 🚌 from Kuala Lumpur and Georgetown. 🚃 from Ipoh and Taiping. ℹ️ (05) 529-0894. 🎎 Sultan's Birthday (Apr 19). 🌐 **perak.gov.my/en**

Kuala Kangsar in Perak has been the royal capital of the sultans of Perak for the last 200 years. In the 1870s, it became the first foothold for the British in Malaysia, who initiated their control of the peninsula by installing Residents, or colonial officers, at the royal courts. During the same period, the town became the birthplace of Malaysia's rubber industry when Sir Hugh Low, then British Resident in Perak, planted the first seeds of rubber. By the 1890s, however, the town's prestige as an administrative and financial center was eclipsed by the tin-trading towns of Ipoh and Taiping.

Crafting *labu,* Sayong village

Today a tranquil town, Kuala Kangsar remains steeped in Malay tradition and is home to one of the most attractive royal districts in the country, as well as some fine colonial architecture and lovely gardens. All the main sights are within walking distance of each other and can be explored in half a day.

The small town center can be divided into old and new sections. The older part, close to the banks of the Sungai Perak, is a good place to buy traditional Malay handicrafts, such as *mengkuang* woven cloth, bamboo products, and the celebrated *labu,* or gourd-shaped earthenware pots. These are manufactured in the village of Sayong, which is located across the river and can be reached by boat. The new town is dominated by Chinese shophouses and modern buildings, including most of Kuala Kangsar's restaurants. Marking the center of town are two colonial-era structures, the distinctive clock tower and the **District Office**, whose grounds still contain one of the town's first rubber trees.

To the north of the town center is one of the most impressive colonial buildings in Kuala Kangsar, the **Malay College**. Opened in 1905 during the reign of Sultan Idris, it was the first Malay school to provide English education to the local elite who were hoping to join the colonial administrative service, and is now considered

The distinctive clock tower at the Kuala Kangsar town center

"the Eton of the East." Across the road from the Malay College stands **Pavilion Square Tower**. Built in 1930, this small wooden three-story structure, designed in colonial and Malay styles, enabled the royal family and British dignitaries to view polo matches and other sports events in privacy.

🅲 Masjid Ubudiah

Jalan Istana.

To the east of Kuala Kangsar, along the wide Sungai Perak, an ornamental gateway leads to Masjid Ubudiah, Perak's royal mosque and one of the finest examples of Islamic architecture in Malaysia. Gracing the slopes of the grassy Bukit Chandan, the striking mosque is built in Moorish style. Its magnificent golden onion-shaped dome is closely surrounded by four soaring white minarets, each crowned with its own small dome. Construction of the mosque began during the reign of Sultan Idris but was not completed until 1917, the first year of the reign of his successor, Sultan Abdul Jalil. The delays were partly due to World War I, and partly due to two royal elephants running amok and destroying the imported Italian marble floor.

Next to the mosque is the **Royal Mausoleum**, where rulers of Perak have been interred since the 18th century.

The interior of the mosque is officially closed to non-Muslims. However, visitors are free to explore the grounds of the mosque and are permitted to photograph the building.

The magnificent Masjid Ubudiah, Perak's royal mosque

For hotels and restaurants see p279 and pp292–3

⛫ Istana Iskandariah
Jalan Istana.

Perched at the summit of Bukit Chandan, overlooking the Sungai Perak and Masjid Ubudiah, the modern Istana Iskandariah was built in 1933 and is the official residence of the present royal family. Set amid rolling lawns, the imposing white marble palace, with its series of towers topped by golden domes, reflects a fusion of Moorish and 1930s colonial Art Deco styles. A less impressive annex was added on the southern side in 1984. Although the palace is not open to visitors, a stroll along the two small roads that form its boundary provides excellent views of the building and its lawns, especially from the riverside.

⛫ Istana Kenangan
Jalan Istana. **Open** 9:30am–5pm Sat–Thu. **Closed** 12:15–2:45pm Fri.

Just to the southwest of Istana Iskandariah stands the smaller but more captivating Istana Kenangan, or Palace of Memories. This palace was built in 1931 for Sultan Iskandar Shah (1876–1938) as a temporary royal residence while the Istana Iskandariah was being constructed. It is a superb example of traditional Malay architecture. The structure is built entirely of wood without the use of an architectural plan, nails, or steel, and is decorated with geometric-patterned bamboo

Façade of the grand Galeri Sultan Azlan Shah, a state museum

panels and intricate friezes. The roof features five ridges and is surmounted by a symbolic row of bananas. The ground floor of the palace features extensive verandas that allow cool breezes to flow through the entire space. The erstwhile palace now houses the **Perak Royal Museum**, popularly known as Muzium Di Raja, which traces the history of Perak and its royal family through images and artifacts.

⛫ Istana Hulu
Jalan Istana. **Open** 9:30am–5pm daily.

The beautiful Victorian-style Istana Hulu is another former palace that was built in 1903 for Sultan Idris, the 28th sultan of Perak. When the palace ceased to function as a royal residence, it became the location of the prestigious girls' college Sekolah Raja Perempuan Mazwin, or Mazwin School for Ladies, for several decades. The palace has now been converted into the **Galeri Sultan Azlan Shah**, or Sultan Azlan Shah Museum, a Perak state museum. Exhibits showcase traditional handicrafts of the state including a fine collection of traditional *keris*, or Malay daggers, and examples of *tekat* embroidery. Most significant, however, is the museum's extensive collection of royal gifts, photographs, and other personal effects belonging to Azlan Shah, the present Sultan of Perak, who has also served as the ninth Yang di-Pertaun Agong, or King of Malaysia, from 1984 to 1994, a rotating position held by sultans of the various states.

The beautiful Istana Kenangan, built in traditional Malay style, now housing the Perak Royal Museum

Old rickshaws at the Cheong Fatt Tze Mansion in Georgetown, Penang ▶

⑭ Georgetown

Located on the northeastern coast of Penang, and a UNESCO World Heritage Site since 2007, Georgetown is one of Malaysia's most visited cities. Founded in 1786 by Captain Francis Light as a base for the British East India Company in the Malay states, the town, which was named after the Prince of Wales, soon developed into the state's economic and cultural hub. An essentially Chinese city today, Georgetown has an authentic Straits Settlement atmosphere, enhanced by its well-preserved colonial architecture, traditional wooden shophouses, and the diverse cuisine developed by its Indian, Malay, Peranakan, Thai, and European communities.

⊞ Fort Cornwallis

Lebuh Light. ⊞ from Komtar on Cat **Tel** (04) 261-0262. **Open** 9am–7pm daily. 🎫 ▢

The spot where Sir Francis Light *(see p109)* stepped ashore in 1786, Fort Cornwallis, in the colonial core of Georgetown, is a great place to start an exploration of the city on foot, by bicycle, or by trishaw. The original fort was a simple palm-tree stockade, but in 1805 this was replaced by a star-shaped brick and mortar structure with a moat and crenellated walls to shelter cannon guarding the harbor. As the first headquarters of the British East India Company in Penang, Fort Cornwallis contained barracks, a signal station, administrative offices, and a Christian chapel. Today, little remains of the fort apart from its outer fortifications. The inner area is a park liberally scattered with cannon. The oldest of these, **Seri Rambai**,

Victoria Memorial Clock Tower

is of Dutch origin and dates back to 1603.

In a small traffic circle to the southeast of the fort stands the **Victoria Memorial Clock Tower**, an elegant colonial edifice crowned by a Moorish-style dome. Built in 1897 with funds donated by a Georgetown *towkay*, or Chinese businessman, it commemorates the diamond jubilee of Queen Victoria's reign. The memorial stands 60 ft (18 m) high in honor of the 60 years of the monarch's reign. To the west of the fort are the parklands of the **Padang Kota Lama**, or the Old City Green. Among the fine colonial buildings to the south and west are the Supreme Court, the Dewan Undangan Negeri, or State Legislative Building, and the grand **Dewan Bandaran**, or City Hall. To the north, facing the northern channel of the Strait of Malacca, runs the **Esplanade**, named Jalan Tun Syed Sheh Barakbah.

⊞ Weld Quay Clan Piers

Jalan Pengkalan Weld. ⊞ from Komtar. ⊞

South of Little India, along Weld Quay and projecting into the southern channel of the Strait of Malacca, stand long rows of jetties on which are built low houses, religious shrines, and shops. These are the clan jetties of Georgetown, dating back to the late 19th century. There are seven such jetties, all but one home to a different Chinese

clan, originally from the Tong An district of China's Fujian province. The oldest and largest is the Chew Jetty, founded in the 1870s, followed by the Lee, Tan, Yeoh, and Koay jetties. The most recent, the Mixed Clan and Peng Aun jetties, date from the 1960s. Six are home to Sino-Malaysian Buddhist clans, while the last, Koay Jetty, is Muslim, being home to around 30 Chinese Hui Muslim families. All the jetties except Koay terminate in small temples. The most important one, on Chew Jetty, is dedicated to the Jade Emperor.

The city skyline, with modern pavilions along the waterfront

One of the jetties at Weld Quay Clan Piers

🔲 Khoo Kongsi Temple

Medan Cannon. 🚌 from Komtar.
Open 9am–5pm daily. 🈂
🌐 khookongsi.com.my

Penang's greatest historical attraction, the gloriously ornate Khoo Kongsi Temple, was founded in 1835 by wealthy Hokkien merchants of the influential Khoo clan. The temple's full name, Leong San Tong Khoo Kongsi, or Dragon Mountain Hall, was chosen in honor of the merchants' ancestral village of Leong San in southern China.

clan took this as an indication of divine wrath at the building of a temple too grand for ancestor worship, so the temple was built again, but on a less lavish scale.

Rebuilt in Qing dynasty style, with elaborate wall carvings, detailed frescoes, and fine roof decorations, the building is adorned with painted dragons and other auspicious figures.

Altar at the Khoo Kongsi Temple, decorated with intricate carvings

Georgetown

1. Fort Cornwallis
2. Weld Quay Clan Piers
3. Khoo Kongsi Temple
4. Masjid Melayu
5. Syed Alatas Mansion
6. Masjid Kapitan Keling
7. Sri Mariamman Temple
8. Little India
9. Pinang Peranakan Mansion
10. Kuan Yin Temple
11. St. George's Church
12. Penang Museum and Art Gallery
13. Cathedral of the Assumption
14. 100 Cintra Street
15. Hainan Temple
16. Cheong Fatt Tze Mansion
17. E & O Hotel

Kongsis are designed to function as places of worship and community centers for members of the clan that built them. This *kongsi*, however, became a center not just for the Khoos, but for four other powerful Hokkien-speaking families, the Cheah, Lim, Tan, and Yeoh clans, who ran an influential secret society.

The original temple, thought too modest for the thriving Khoo clan, was demolished in 1894. A magnificent new temple was constructed over the next eight years, but it burned to the ground within a month of its completion. The

🟩 Masjid Melayu

Lebuh Aceh. 🚹 from Lebuh Chulia.
One of the oldest buildings in Georgetown, Masjid Melayu mosque was founded in 1808 by a prosperous Sumatran pepper merchant. It was originally built to serve the burgeoning Muslim community of Lebuh Aceh, Penang's first urban Malay village, and was a center of Hajj travel in the 19th century. The nearby **Masjid Kapitan Keling** was built by Indian-Muslim migrants in 1801 and has been added to over the centuries.

The mosque, a 5-minute walk from Lebuh Chulia, has an Egyptian-style minaret and an Achenese-style roof. The hole halfway up its minaret was the result of a cannonball fired in a clan riot in Penang.

For keys to symbols *see back flap*

The 19th-century Syed Alatas Mansion

🏛 Syed Alatas Mansion

128 Lebuh Armenian. 🚐

Syed Mohammed Alatas was a wealthy and influential 19th-century Achenese businessman and leader of Penang's Malay community. In the 1860s he built a magnificent *rumah besar*, or great house, on Armenian Street where he lived with his family until his death in the early 20th century. Set in a walled compound, the two-story Syed Alatas Mansion is an eclectic mix of Malay, Indian, and European architectural and cultural influences and is considered one of the finest examples of upper-class Malay Muslim residences in Penang.

☪ Masjid Kapitan Keling

Jalan Masjid Kapitan Keling.
Tel (04) 261-6663. 🚐 ℹ Islamic Information Center. **Open** 3–5pm Fri, 1–5pm Sat–Thu. **Closed** prayer times.

Masjid Kapitan Keling, the oldest and best-known historic mosque in Penang, was founded around 1800 by Caudeer Mohudeen. He was a prominent member of the island's Indian Muslim community and bore the title Kapitan Keling, or Captain of the Kelings. Keling was a term employed at that time to describe Tamil Muslims, also called Chulia, who formed the bulk of Penang's Indian Muslims. Mohudeen, officially named headman of the Chulias in 1801, died in 1834. His tomb is located at the nearby Kampung Kolam. The mosque has been restored and altered on several occasions, most notably in 1910 when it was given its present appearance with the addition of Indian-style copper domes, turrets, and a minaret. A *madrassa*, or religious school, was added in 1916. In 1935, the height of the central prayer hall was doubled, allowing more natural light and air into the interior. The most recent renovation took place in 2003, when Arabic calligraphy was added to the interior of the main dome and to the walls. Women entering the mosque are required to wear headscarves.

🛕 Sri Mariamman Temple

Jalan Masjid Kapitan Keling. 🚐
Open 6am–9pm daily. 🎉 Thaipusam (Jan/Feb), Navaratri (Oct/Nov).

On the opposite side of the street from Kapitan Keling Mosque is the Sri Mariamman Temple, a typical southern Indian temple with an elaborately carved and painted *gopuram*, or tiered entrance gateway of a Hindu temple. Dedicated to the deity Mariamman, or Great Powerful Mother, this is Penang's oldest Hindu temple.

Established by pious local Tamils as a simple shrine, it became a fully-fledged temple in 1833. Artisans were brought from Madras to create images of the goddess Mariamman in all her aspects. Subsequently, a 23-ft- (7-m-) high *gopuram* was added, with sculptures of about 38 Hindu deities. A statue of Lord Murugan, adorned with gold and diamonds, was also installed.

Several times a year, Sri Mariamman is taken out of the temple in a wooden chariot, and carried in procession through the streets of Little India. The most important occasion is Navaratri, a nine-night celebration in October or November when devotees worship female deities, such as Durga, Saraswati, Lakshmi, and Mariamman. Penang's annual Thaipusam *(see p35)* procession also begins here.

🏘 Little India

Lebuh Pasar. 🚐 🖊
🌐 tourism penang.gov.my

Penang's colorful and vibrant Little India, throbbing with antiquity and tradition, dates back to the early 19th century, when Indian migrants to Penang began to settle in and around Lebuh Pasar, then called Kadai Teru, or shop street. Since most of the early migrants were Tamils, the area was commonly known as Little Madras, but over the years other communities also moved in. Soon the enclave acquired a distinctive south Asian feel and gained its current sobriquet.

The ornate domes and graceful façade of Masjid Kapitan Keling

The narrow streets of Little India are lined with shops selling all kinds of south Asian produce, from saris and gold jewelry to flower garlands and images of Hindu deities. The wide range of shops and services includes astrologers, millers, grocers, fruit-sellers, herb dealers, and money changers. The aroma of spice, incense, and curry fills the air, while the bells of trishaw drivers and constant bustle of the crowds make the ambience quintessentially Indian.

Although Bahasa Malaysia and English are the main spoken languages of Penang, here, the rolling, fast-paced southern Indian tongues of Malayalam and Tamil predominate. With attractions that include mosques, Hindu temples, and Chinese clan enclaves, as well as a host of restaurants, Little India is now a great draw for food-lovers, heritage enthusiasts, and visitors who simply want to soak up the atmosphere.

Pinang Peranakan Mansion
29 Lebuh Gereja. **Tel** (04) 264 2929. **Open** 9:30am–5pm daily.

This private museum, a re-creation of an ornate Peranakan villa from the 19th century, is a fascinating glimpse into times past. Full of antique furniture and jewelry, it is well worth booking a tour guide to fully understand the exhibits on display, from beautiful Nyonya clothes to the ornate furniture that decorates every room.

Kuan Yin Temple
Jalan Masjid Kapitan Keling. **Open** 9am–6pm daily.

Dedicated to Kuan Yin, or the goddess of mercy, this temple was originally constructed as a shared Hokkien and Cantonese temple and community center. Its foundation stone was laid in 1800, making it one of the oldest Chinese temples in the province of Penang.

Kuan Yin is perhaps the most worshiped of Chinese deities, and also much revered by Buddhists and Taoists. Associated with peace, good

Ornate interior of the Pinang Peranakan Mansion

fortune, and fertility, she is portrayed with 18 arms. Feast days are held to honor Kuan Yin's birthday, initiation, and attainment of *nirvana*. Even today, the temple bustles with worshipers carrying ritual offerings of flowers, oil, and food, especially on temple days. These fall on the first and 15th day of every lunar month, and on the 19th day of the second, sixth, and ninth lunar months. Puppet shows and Chinese opera performances are held on these days to honor the goddess.

St. George's Church
Lebuh Farquhar. **Tel** (04) 261-2739. **Open** 8:30am–12:30pm & 1:30–4:30pm Tue–Sat, 8:30am–4:30pm Sun.

The oldest Anglican church in Southeast Asia, St. George's Church was constructed in 1818 to serve the growing Christian community of Penang. Designed by military engineer and painter Captain Robert Smith, it was built by the British East India Company using convict labor. In 1886, to mark the centenary of the founding of Penang and to honor Sir Francis Light, a small Greek-style domed pavilion was built on the church grounds. The tall octagonal steeple of the Neo-Classical church once dominated the town, although today the graceful structure is overshadowed by towering commercial buildings. Farther west on Lebuh Farquhar is the **Protestant Cemetery**, where Sir Francis Light is buried in a gazebo-like tomb shaded by frangipani trees.

St. George's Church with its Doric columns and octagonal steeple

Sir Francis Light

Born in Suffolk, England, in 1740, Francis Light joined the British East India Company in 1765. Directed to find a suitable island base for their commercial activities in Southeast Asia, he chose Pulau Penang, which he then acquired from the Sultan of Kedah in 1786. Having successfully established a colony, he served as its super-intendent until his death in 1794 of malaria. He was buried at the Protestant Cemetery at Lebuh Farquhar. As closely linked to Penang's growth as Sir Stamford Raffles is to Singapore's, Sir Francis Light is still honored as a founding father. His statue now stands at Georgetown's Fort Cornwallis.
Sir Francis Light

The stately gray exterior of the Cathedral of the Assumption

Penang Museum and Art Gallery

Lebuh Farquhar. **Tel** (04) 261-3144.
Open 9am–5pm daily.
W penangmuseum.gov.my

Located next to St. George's Church in the former Penang Free School, this small museum houses an excellent collection of maps, records, and displays charting the growth of Penang since the arrival of Sir Francis Light. The first floor showcases the various ethnic groups that constitute Penang's population, with exhibits of clothing, photographs, household items, and artifacts associated with the island's Peranakan, Malay, Chinese, and Indian communities. The second floor is devoted to Penang's history with special emphasis on the colonial era, the Japanese occupation, the Chinese and Indian settlements, and the gaining of independence. The art gallery features 19th-century paintings of Penang by Robert Smith, the architect of St. George's Church.

British East India Company insignia, Penang Museum and Art Gallery

Cathedral of the Assumption

Lebuh Farquhar.
The city's premier Catholic place of worship, the stately Cathedral of the Assumption was founded to serve the Eurasian Catholics who had moved to Penang following Sir Francis Light's establishment of a British colony here. The Eurasians, who were originally from Phuket, had fled to Kuala Kedah in 1781 with Bishop Garnault of Siam to escape religious persecution. In Kuala Kedah, they were joined by Catholics of Portuguese descent. The group, led by Garnault, arrived in Georgetown on the eve of the Feast of the Assumption in 1786. His mission was later relocated to Penang.

Although this imposing gray structure, built along classical lines, was not erected at Lebuh Farquhar until 1857, it was nonetheless named in memory of the arrival of these first parishioners. The cathedral houses Penang's only pipe organ. In 1955, it was elevated by Vatican decree to the status of Cathedral of the Diocese of Penang.

100 Cintra Street

100 Cintra Street. **Tel** (04) 261-3321.
Open 11am–6pm Tue–Sun.

Located in the heart of Chinatown, this is a Peranakan-influenced mansion that was built in 1897 by a local woman of Thai origin. Partially destroyed by fire in 1984, it was rebuilt using as much of the surviving structure as possible, and was reopened in 1999 as a shopping center specializing in antiques and artifacts. It also has a small tea shop.

Since then it has undergone several changes, and today the first floor of the three-story building functions as an antique and curio center offering a fascinating selection of 19th-century furniture, pictures, porcelain, brassware, calligraphy, paintings, and carpets. The second floor functions as a budget guesthouse, while the third floor has been converted into a folk museum, focusing on the history and culture of Penang, with special emphasis on the Peranakan, or Straits Chinese community. Indian and Malay items are also on display.

Hainan Temple

Lebuh Muntri. **Tel** (04) 262-0202.
Popularly known as the Hainan Temple, the bustling Thean Ho Keong, which means Temple of the Heavenly Queen, is dedicated to Mar Chor, the patron saint of seafarers. Commonly known as Matsu in China and Thien Hau in Vietnam,

Chinese worshiper praying at the colorful altar at Hainan Temple

Cheong Fatt Tze Mansion, now a luxurious hotel

the goddess is worshiped, in particular, wherever the Chinese settled throughout Southeast Asia. The temple was initially established as a clan house for overseas Chinese from Hainan Island in 1866, although the current building dates from 1895. During its centenary celebrations in 1995, the temple was carefully restored and a new frontage was added with ornate carvings and distinctive swirling dragon pillars.

Cheong Fatt Tze Mansion
14 Lebuh Leith. **Tel** (04) 262-0006. for tours. 11am, 1:30pm & 3pm daily. **w** cheongfatttze mansion.com

This spectacular mansion was built by Cheong Fatt Tze, a young Hakka Chinese entre-preneur who eventually became one of Southeast Asia's richest businessmen. Although he built several grand houses, this 1904 mansion is considered the most magnificent. Fatt Tze lived here with three of his favorite wives, raising eight sons. The house fell into disrepair after his death in 1916, but it has since been beautifully restored, winning the prestigious UNESCO Asia Pacific Heritage Award for authentic restoration in 2000. Said to be the largest traditional courtyard house in the region, the building conforms to the principles of geomancy, and blends Chinese and Western architectural concepts. Painted a deep blue, the mansion features Qing dynasty latticework and filigree ornamentation with

louvered and stained-glass windows in the Western style, cast-iron balusters, and geometric-patterned floor tiling. Today, the mansion operates as an opulent and unique homestay heritage hotel.

E & O Hotel
10 Lebuh Farquhar. **Tel** (04) 222-2000. **w** e-o-hotel.com

The grande dame of Penang's hotels, the Eastern & Oriental (see p279) is not just one of the most luxurious, but also one of the great historic hotels of Southeast Asia. Popularly called the E & O, it was established in 1884 by the Armenian Sarkies brothers, who went on to found Singapore's Raffles Hotel and Rangoon's famous Strand. A landmark in

colonial architecture, it boasts a 830-ft (253-m) seafront lawn – the longest in the world – and its suites overlook manicured lawns and lush gardens with a panoramic view across the Strait of Malacca. The Victory Annexe, opened in 2013, is very much in keeping with its surrounds.

Long a center of Penang's social life, the hotel has hosted eminent guests such as Noel Coward, Rudyard Kipling, Hermann Hesse, and Douglas Fairbanks. Somerset Maugham, another visitor, referred to the E & O in several of his writings. Today, it is a great place to eat a light tiffin lunch followed by afternoon tea, or to sip a cocktail at sunset under the rain trees on the hotel's private veranda.

Georgetown's historic Eastern & Oriental Hotel

Five Foot Ways

Originally used by builders from Guangdong in China, this style of Chinese shophouse has long been associated with the former Straits Settlements of Singapore, Penang, and Melaka. The widespread presence of Five Foot Ways in Singapore and urban Malaysia is attributed to Sir Stamford Raffles, who decreed that all shophouses should have verandas that form continuous and open passages.

Shop signs over a Five Foot Way

Characterized by load-bearing gable walls and massive roof beams that span the building, these shophouses extend over the narrow sidewalks forming a sort of covered walkway and providing shelter from the sun and the monsoon rains. The sidewalk can be further shaded by lowering split bamboo blinds.

⑮ Dhammikarama Temple

Burma Lane, off Jalan Burma, Pulau Tikus, 2 miles (3 km) NW of Georgetown. 🚌 **Open** daily. 🎎 Burmese New Year (Apr).

The 200-year-old Burmese enclave at Pulau Tikus is home to a spectacular Theravada Buddhist monastery, founded in 1803 and known originally as the Nandy Molah Burmese Temple. Now called the Dhammikarama Temple in honor of the *dhamma*, or corpus of Buddhist teachings, this is Penang's oldest Buddhist place of worship.

The temple gateway, well guarded by a pair of stucco elephants, leads to a compound shaded by a peepul tree and dotted with mythical figures and religious icons, among them myriad Buddhas, flying beings, and chimeras. The ornate red-tiled roof of the temple, embellished with gleaming gold filigree work, is Burmese in inspiration and visible from afar. The complex includes monks' quarters, a wishing pool where visitors toss coins that are later used towards temple maintenance, and a peaceful prayer hall housing a large Burmese-style image of the Buddha. Within the hall are rows of finely carved *arhats*, or spiritual practitioners who had attained nirvana, created by Burmese artisans. The temple also has a shrine to the Arahant

Upagutta, an *arhat* widely revered in Burma for his powers. A golden Pagoda Bell Tower opened in May 2011.

⑯ Wat Chaya-mangkalaram

Burma Lane, off Jalan Burma, Pulau Tikus, 2 miles (3 km) NW of Georgetown. 🚌 **Open** 6am–5:30pm daily. 🎎 Songkran (Apr).

Popularly known as the Temple of the Reclining Buddha, this is the largest Buddhist temple in Penang. The name means temple of auspicious victory. The building dates from 1845, when the Thai community asked the government for land on which to build a monastery. The land was granted by the then Governor of Penang, W L Butterworth. The temple houses a Reclining Buddha statue, constructed in 1958 to mark the 2,500th anniversary of the birth of Gautama Buddha. Called Phra Chaiya Mongkol, the statue measures an impressive 108 ft (33 m) in length and is said to be the third-longest Reclining Buddha in the world. Besides the main shrine hall, the temple includes a Thai-style gilded stupa, or *chedi*, and fierce temple guardians called *yaksas*. The whole complex is distinctively central Thai in style, down to the gold-painted pagodas. The temple is attended to by Thai

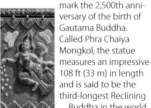

Detail on Wat Chayamangkalaram

monks and serves the small local Thai community, as well as both Theravada and Mahayana Buddhist devotees from across the island. Legend has it that the temple's first abbot, a monk named Phorthan Kuat, or honorable father Kuat, was fond of local *laksa* or spicy noodle soup, and even today devotees bring bowls of *laksa* to present as offerings at his shrine.

The manicured grounds of the Penang Botanic Gardens

⑰ Penang Botanic Gardens

5 miles (8 km) W on the outskirts of Georgetown. 🚌 ℹ️ (04) 227-0428. **Open** 5am–8pm daily. 📷 by prior arrangement. ♿ special walkways. 🍴 🎁 🎎 Flora Festival (Jun). 🌐 botanicalgardens.penang. gov.my

Established by the colonial administration in 1884 on the site of a disused quarry, the beautifully landscaped Penang Botanic Gardens are undoubtedly the finest botanical gardens in Peninsular Malaysia. Spread across 72 acres (29 ha) of land dominated by an attractive waterfall, rain forest-covered hills, and a small river, the gardens provide protected habitat for rare species of plant and also serve as a green lung for Georgetown and its people.

The gardens owe their beauty to the untiring work of Charles Curtis, who was the first to nurture and transform the former granite quarry into a lush tropical garden and nursery. In 1946, after World War II ended,

Ornate and colorful façade of the Buddhist Wat Chayamangkalaram

the Penang Botanic Gardens were separated from their parent establishment in Singapore and began functioning as an independent entity.

Besides their educational and preservational role, the gardens are a popular spot for locals to exercise, jog, or walk in the refreshingly unpolluted air. There are two paved trails, the shorter Lower Circle and the longer Upper Circle. Surrounding these are less accessible forested areas. Botanical attractions include the Aroid Walkway, featuring plants of the philodendron family, the ornamental plant house, the fern house, cactus house, and lily pool. Among the species of rare trees seen here are the cannonball tree, the candle tree, the baobab, ebony, and the argus pheasant tree. The gardens also house a nursery of commercial plants, such as pepper, cloves, and nutmeg.

The rich variety of fauna that blankets the Penang Hill

⑱ Kek Lok Si Temple

Ayer Itam, 5 miles (8 km) W of Georgetown. 🚌 ℹ️ (04) 828-3317. **Open** 8:30am–5:30pm daily. 🚫 📷 📹 👟 Loy Krathong (Nov).

The largest and most celebrated Buddhist temple in Malaysia, Kek Lok Si, or the temple of supreme bliss, is spread across a hilltop overlooking the district of Ayer Itam. Long sacred to the island's Chinese residents, the hills of Ayer Itam are believed by locals to be geomantically fortuitous and a suitable retreat for Taoist devotees seeking immortality.

The temple was initially envisioned by the head monk of the Kuan Yin Temple *(see p109)* on Jalan Masjid Kapitan Kling and supported by the Chinese consul in Penang. Later, the idea was backed by the Qing Emperor Guangxu, who gave its foundation an imperial tablet and 70,000 volumes of Buddhist sutras. Construction began in

1893 and took Burmese, Chinese, and Thai artisans more than two decades to complete.

Kek Lok Si's most celebrated feature is the magnificent seven-tier **Pagoda of King Rama VI**, completed in 1930 and named after the Thai monarch who laid the foundation stone. Also known as the pagoda of ten thousand Buddhas, it stands at a height of 100 ft (30 m). This impressive pagoda was designed in three different styles, with an octagonal Chinese-style base, middle tiers of Thai architecture, and a Burmese-style crown, symbolic of the unity of Mahayana and Theravada Buddhism. The temple grounds contain lovely gardens and sacred ponds, including the Sacred Turtle Pond where the devout release captive turtles as an act of spiritual liberation. Dominating all is a massive bronze statue of Kuan Yin, the goddess of mercy.

Bronze statue of Kuan Yin, Kek Lok Si Temple

⑲ Penang Hill

Ayer Itam. 🚋 Funicular Railway, 6:30am–10pm Mon–Fri, 6:30am–11pm Sat & Sun. 🚌 to Funicular Railway terminal. 👟

Malaysia's oldest hill station, Penang Hill, also known as Bukit Bendera or Flagstaff Hill, was first developed in 1897. Although only one hotel functions today, the 2,720-ft

(830-m) hill still offers a refreshing retreat from the tropical heat of Georgetown.

Sir Francis Light, the founder of Penang, is said to have ordered the construction of a horse track to the top of the hill in 1788. Today visitors can ride up the hill on the **Penang Hill Railway**, a steep funicular line built in 1923 and still in operation; the original wooden coaches can be seen on display. Enthusiastic walkers can opt for a 3-hour hike up a tarred track that begins at the quarry at the entrance of the Penang Botanic Gardens.

The hill is an area rich in biodiversity and has a number of rare endemic species. Dipterocarp and coniferous trees are common, as are tree ferns. The summit offers panoramic views across the nearby Strait of Malacca to Penang Bridge, the mainland, and Butterworth. Also on the summit are a colorful Hindu temple and a mosque.

The Penang Hill Funicular Railway, Malaysia

Boats and jet-skis off the beaches of Batu Ferringhi

⑳ Batu Ferringhi

9 miles (14 km) NW of Georgetown.
🚌 93 from Georgetown. 🏖️ 🏝️

Also known as Foreigner's Rock, Batu Ferringhi is Penang's premier beachside destination and one of the most developed beach strips anywhere in Malaysia. Facing northwest into the Strait of Malacca, the shore at Batu Ferringhi was once a delightful coconut-lined sandy strand and a popular destination for hippies in the 1970s.

However, over the past three decades, it has changed dramatically into a bustling coastal strip, lined with high-rise hotels and a wide range of restaurants and shops. Although the beach is clean, the sea is a little murky and filled with jellyfish. The waves are not high enough for surfing, but this is a good place to sunbathe and relax.

The beach was hit by the 2004 tsunami, but has since completely recovered. Today, Batu Ferringhi's easy accessibility from Georgetown means that it is popular with day visitors and usually busy, especially at weekends. Prices are especially low on weekdays and off-season months (Mar–Oct).

Just a mile (2 km) west of Batu Ferringhi is the **Tropical Spice Garden**, where visitors can view more than five hundred species of plants from Malaysia, Thailand, and Indonesia. Three specially designed garden trails lead to 11 separate gardens that feature special plant collections with signboards indicating their common and botanical names and their various uses.

🌿 **Tropical Spice Garden**
Open 9am–6pm daily. 🚻 free for children below 4 years. 🖥️ 📷

㉑ Teluk Bahang

12 miles (19 km) NW of Georgetown.
🚌 93 from Georgetown. ⚠️

At the western end of Penang's northern beaches sits the small fishing village of Teluk Bahang, or sunburned bay. The detritus of an active fishing industry litters the sand, and while the beach is not suitable for swimming, it is an excellent place to enjoy fresh seafood. Tracks lead westward from the village to the rocky promontory of **Muka Head**, passing the scenic Ailing and Duyong bays, heading southwest into the Pantai Aceh Forest Reserve and beyond to Kerachut Beach.

Just south of the bus station, **Craft Batik** is a handicraft workshop and showroom where visitors can observe *batik* being made and also shop for sarongs and *batik* paintings. Nearby is the **Penang Butterfly Farm**, where more than 100 species of butterflies, along with spiders and other insects, are on view amid attractive gardens with varied flora, waterfalls, and ponds. South of Teluk Bahang, the well-maintained **Forest Recreation Park** offers further good opportunities for trekking and camping in the lush jungle.

🦋 **Penang Butterfly Farm**
Tel (04) 805-1253. **Open** 9am–5pm Mon–Fri, 9am–5:30pm Sat & Sun. 🚻
🖥️ 🌐 **butterfly-insect.com**

Fishing boats moored along the shores of Teluk Bahang

㉒ Penang National Park

Jalan Hassan Abbas, Teluk Bahang, 12 miles (19 km) NW of Georgetown. **Tel** (04) 881-3530. 🚌 101 or 93 from Georgetown. **Open** 7am–5pm daily. 🐾 small fee to use canopy walk.

Located at the northwestern tip of the island, with its main entrance close to Teluk Bahang, Penang National Park was founded in April 2003. This is only the second national park located within the peninsula. Although fairly small and far less well known than Taman Negara, it offers an appealing contrast to the historical urban sights of Penang, with opportunities for jungle trekking and spotting marine turtles among other wildlife that includes flying squirrels, sea otters, monkeys, and more than 150 species of birds. There are also over 1,000 species of plants recorded, including wild orchids and insectivorous pitcher plants.

The park covers about 5 sq miles (13 sq km), offering a not-too-strenuous wilderness adventure. Basic but well-marked trails lead through lowland dipterocarp forest, mangrove, and sandy beach habitats. A canopy walk links two of the trails. An unusual feature is a meromictic lake, with a surface layer that does not mix with the water below.

The beaches here are quiet and unspoiled. Visitors can take a boat trip from Teluk Bahang to one of the most pleasant, Monkey Beach, named for its crab-eating macaques. There are no refreshment facilities in the park, so take snacks and plenty of water.

㉓ Snake Temple

Bayan Lepas, 7 miles (12 km) S of Georgetown. 🚌 66 from Komtar in Georgetown. **Open** 7am–7pm daily. 🎎 anniversary of the birth of Chor Soo Kong, 6th day of first lunar month (Jan/Feb).

Named Ban Kah Lan, meaning the temple of the azure clouds in the Hokkien dialect, this highly unusual temple was built in 1850 by Chinese migrants. It honors the memory of a venerated Chinese Buddhist monk named Chor Soo Kong who is said to have had healing powers. He was born in China's Fujian Province during the reign of the 11th-century Song Emperor Renzong. Chor Soo Kong later became an ascetic seeking spiritual enlightenment, which he attained under the guidance of Zen master Ming Song. Soon after he practiced as a doctor, catering to the needs of the poor. Chor Soo Kong retired to a monastery on Peng Lai Mountain, where he was sanctified after his death.

According to folklore, the statue of the deified Chor Soo Kong was brought to Penang by a monk from China in 1850, and was enshrined in a temple at Bayan Lepas. When the temple was complete, the pious monk allowed snakes from the surrounding jungle to take shelter there. The snakes were venomous Wagler's pit vipers called *ular kapak tokong* in Malay. Today, these vipers still inhabit the rundown temple, and are its main attraction, especially during the festival season. About 3 ft (1 m) long in maturity, they are dark green with yellow bands. Devotees regard them as harmless guardian angels of the temple. Although rarely fatal, the bite of the vipers is painful. Fortunately, they are sluggish during the day, perhaps dulled by the incense smoke, but are active at night, when they descend from their perches in the eaves to eat offerings left by the pious.

Offerings at the Sam Poh Footprint Temple at Batu Maung

㉔ Batu Maung

9 miles (15 km) S of Georgetown. 🍴 ♨ ✏ 🏪 📷

A Chinese fishing village in the southeast of Pulau Penang, Batu Maung is known for its fine fresh seafood restaurants and a small aquarium. It is also famous for the **Sam Poh Footprint Temple**, named for a strange footprint-shaped indentation in a rock. This footprint reportedly belongs to 15th-century Chinese Admiral Zheng He, who was locally known as Sam Poh.

He visited Pulau Penang during his exploration of Southeast Asia, the Indian Ocean, and the Red Sea. The footprint is said to mark the spot where he first stepped ashore. The rock is enshrined in the temple. Penang's second bridge connecting it to the mainland opened here in 2014.

A Buddhist monk praying at the Snake Temple

Archaeological remnants, main temple Candi Bukit Batu Pahat

㉕ Lembah Bujang

16 miles (26 km) NW of Sungai Petani.
🚌 📷 🌐 mykedah2.com

One of Peninsular Malaysia's most important archaeological sites, the Hindu-Buddhist remains at Lembah Bujang, or Bujang valley, reveal significant aspects of a major pre-Islamic civilization. First excavated by the British archaeologist H G Quaritch-Wales in 1936, this archaeological site stretches over a vast 87-sq-mile (225-sq-km) area extending from Gunung Jerai to Kuala Muda.

Bujang, which derives its name from a legendary winged dragon, was a notable kingdom and port in the 5th century AD. It had trade relations with India, Srivijaya (on Sumatra), and Cambodia, and was visited by the Chinese Buddhist monk I-Ching in AD 672. In the 7th century, it was absorbed into the Srivijaya Empire, and reached its zenith between the 9th and 10th centuries, before Islam gained a foothold on the peninsula.

Over 50 sites have been excavated in the valley. Among the finds, the most impressive are the *candi*, or two tomb-temples, which have been transported and reassembled at the **Lembah Bujang Archaeological Museum** in nearby Merbok. The 7th-century Candi Bukit Batu Pahat has a *vimana*, or inner sanctuary, with images of Hindu deities, and a *mandapa*, or open hall, with a stone roof supported by pillars. The *candi* performed the function of temples for Hindu or Buddhist religious activities, and honored the deceased rulers and members of the royal family.

The little-visited museum preserves, chronicles, and explains the various excavations as well as displaying collections of artifacts discovered at the site. These include Chinese porcelain, Shiva *lingas*, statues of the Hindu god Ganesh and goddess Durga, terra-cotta statues, and a bronze Buddhist image found here in 1976. It is possible to see the excavated sites through privately arranged guided tours from the museum. There was national uproar in 2013 when a developer destroyed some of the *candi* at the site. There are plans to reconstruct the damaged ruins.

Fragment of a stone lintel at Lembah Bujang

🏛 **Lembah Bujang Archaeological Museum**
Jalan Tanjung Dawai, Merbok.
Tel (04) 457-2005. **Open** 9am–5pm daily. **Closed** noon–2:45pm Fri (for prayers). 📷 🌐 jmm.gov.my

㉖ Gunung Jerai

19 miles (30 km) N of Sungai Petani.
Tel (04) 730-1957. 🚌 **Open** daily. 📷
🚻 🚲 ⛰

Rising sharply out of the surrounding Kedah plains is the imposing 3,993-ft (1,217-m) Gunung Jerai. Formerly known as Kedah Peak, this massive forest-clad limestone outcrop that is a part of the Titiwangsa Mountain Range is clearly visible from the sea. It adds a touch of variety to the scenic flat plains visible throughout the area. In the past, it acted as a navigation point for sailors, and was considered sacred by the Hindu kingdom of Bujang. It marked the start of a cross-peninsula portage route between the Indian Ocean and the South China Sea that avoided the long voyage around the Strait of Malacca. Today, the peak is visited for its pristine splendor and panoramic forest views. On the summit is a dilapidated 6th-century Hindu shrine and bath called **Candi Telaga Sembilan**, or nine pool temple, which was discovered in 1884.

Another attraction on the mountain is the Muzium Perhutanan, or **Forestry Museum**, which is saturated with fragrances from various types of coniferous and oak trees. Run by the Malaysian Forestry Commission, the museum has exhibits on trees of the surrounding **Sungai Teroi Forest Recreation Park**, which houses rare orchids and wildlife.

🏛 **Forestry Museum**
Gunung Jerai. **Tel** (04) 731-2322.

🏞 **Sungai Teroi Forest Recreation Park**
Gunung Jerai. 🚻 📷 compulsory.

Misty view above the treetops at Gunung Jerai

The elegant Masjid Zahir, or state mosque, in Alor Star

㉗ Alor Star

59 miles (95 km) N of Georgetown.
㉒ 205,000. ✈ ℹ 179B Kompleks
Alor Star, Lebuhraya Darul Aman,
(04) 730-1322. ⓦ **tourism.gov.my**

Kedah's state capital, Alor Star (also known as Alor Setar), is mainly a transit point to Thailand and a junction for the road west to Kuala Kedah, the ferry port for Pulau Langkawi. However, the city itself, proud birthplace of Malaysia's first and fourth prime ministers, has several attractions. Among these is the **padang**, a lovely old colonial town square surrounded by a number of royal and religious buildings. Look out for the **Balai Besar**, or the royal audience hall, which stands on tall pillars embellished with Victorian iron lacework. The unique **Balai Nobat**, or drum hall, is an eight-sided tower topped by an onion-shaped dome. The building houses the Kedah Royal Orchestra. **Masjid Zahir**, or state mosque, incorporates elegant Moorish designs in its five black domes and slender minarets. Built in 1912, this is one of the oldest mosques in Malaysia. The mosque welcomes non-Muslim visitors who are dressed appropriately.

More interesting is the Muzium Negeri, or the **State Museum**, located a mile (2 km) north of the padang. It displays exhibits dating back to the 19th century when Kedah was a tributary of neighboring Siam (now known as Thailand). Look out for the *pokok bunga emas*, a beautiful, intricately wrought little tree made of gold,

produced as an offering to the Thais in return for their protection. Another reminder of the state's Siamese connections is **Wat Syam Nikrodharam**, a Theravada Buddhist temple built in the unmistakable Thai style, located at Kampung Telok Sena. Today, the city's considerable Chinese Buddhist population worships here.

🅲 Masjid Zahir
Jalan Sultan Muhamad Jiwa.
Open daily. **Closed** noon–3pm Fri (for prayers).

🏛 State Museum
Lebuhraya Darul Aman. **Tel** (04) 733-1162. **Open** Sat–Thu. **Closed** noon–3pm Fri (for prayers).

㉘ Kuala Kedah

7 miles (12 km) W of Alor Star. ㉒
220,000. 🚌 🚢

As Kuala means river mouth in Malay, Kuala Kedah is an aptly named fishing port that is located at the northern bank of its namesake river. This small town serves as the convenient southern ferry point for travelers sailing to Pulau Langkawi. The crowning glory of the town is the atmospheric **Kota Kuala Kedah**, a fort dating to the mid-18th century standing on the right bank of Sungai Kedah. The structure was originally built to protect the kingdom against naval attacks by Siam (Thailand). However, the Thais invaded and captured the fort in the early 19th century. The town is guarded by thick walls and a moat, and comprises a number of buildings including the Royal Audience Hall. Six of the 19th-century British cannons are on display, resting on the crumbling walls, facing the river estuary. Today, Kuala Kedah is famous for the variety of delectable seafood, especially *laksa*, served at the numerous restaurants all over town.

Orang Syam

Malaysians of Thai ethnic origin, known in Malay as *Orang Syam*, have lived in northern Malaysia for centuries. When and how they came to settle in this predominantly Malay-speaking region remains unclear. Their dialect suggests that their roots go back at least four centuries to the Narathiwat province which neighbors Thailand. The *Orang Syam* are recognized as *bumiputras*, or indigenous Malaysians, having the same rights and status as Muslim Malays. They settled primarily in prosperous *kampung syams*, or Siamese villages in Kedah, Kelantan, Perak, Penang, and Perlis, dwelling harmoniously with their Muslim neighbors. One easy way to identify a *kampung syam* is the presence of elaborately sited Buddhist temples. They have quintessentially Thai curved roofs, lavishly gilded pagodas, tinkling wind-chimes, and edifices of the Buddha in various postures. The five-centuries-old temple at Kampung Jubakar claims to have the largest Seated Buddha image in Southeast Asia.

Orang Syam people working in the fields

㉙ Pulau Langkawi

Set in the heart of an archipelago of some 100 islands and islets in the Andaman Sea, Pulau Langkawi is one of Malaysia's most popular destinations. Fringed with sandy beaches and forested hills in the interior, it is also one of the most beautiful. A number of idyllic resorts and spas offer soothing retreats, while a range of sporting activities, such as waterskiing, diving, and trekking, attract adventurous visitors. Kuah, the small bustling capital, is a good jumping-off point for Langkawi's other sights.

Langkawi Sky Bridge
This suspended walkway at the top station of the Langkawi Cable Car affords magnificent views.

Telega Tujuh Falls
Literally meaning seven wells, Telega Tujuh is a cascading waterfall – an ideal site for bathing and picnics.

★ **Pantai Cenang**
This long strip of sandy beach has numerous beach chalets and a fine selection of restaurants and bars.

The Datai
Pantai Datai
Tasik Datai
Pasir Tengorak
Els Club
Teluk Datai
Gunung Machinchang 2,315 ft
Langkawi Crocodile Farm
Telaga Harbor Park
Pantai Kok
Kuala Teriang
Beras Terbakar
Padang Matsirat
Langkawi International Airport
Bon Ton
Kedawang
Pulau Rebak
Pantai Cenang
Underwater World
Temonyon
Pantai Tengah
Pulau Tepor
Star Cruise Jetty
Pulau Payar 20 miles (32 km)
Petar

0 km   5
0 miles   5

The Legend of Tasik Dayang Bunting

Tasik Dayang Bunting, or lake of the pregnant maiden, is a freshwater lake set amid the limestone cliffs and dense forests of Pulau Dayang Bunting, the second-largest island in the archipelago. A legend revolves around the tragic tale of Princess Mahsuri who claimed she became pregnant by drinking from the lake. She was then falsely accused of adultery and executed. The legendary crocodile which inhabits the lake is said to be Mahsuri's child. Local women still come here to pray for children.

A boat on Tasik Dayang Buntin

The Langkawi Birds Paradise
Located at Belanga Pecah, this lush tropical garden is home to at least 150 species of birds, including hornbills, toucans, and flamingos.

The Durian Perangin Waterfall cascades through 14 levels and is a popular picnic spot.

★ **Gunung Raya**
Literally the great mountain, Gunung Raya is the highest peak in the archipelago. Its summit offers fine views across the Andaman Sea.

Masjid al-Hana
The largest mosque on Pulau Langkawi, the golden domes of Masjid al-Hana tower over Kuah, the island's capital.

★ **Tomb of Mahsuri**
This quiet shrine was built in memory of Princess Mahsuri who was executed at this spot after being unjustly accused of adultery.

Key
= Major road
= Minor road
- - - Ferry route
⊢⊣⊢⊣ Cable car route
△ Peak

For keys to symbols see back flap

Exploring Pulau Langkawi

The largest among a cluster of tropical islands, Pulau Langkawi is a mountainous, palm-fringed island peppered with paddy fields and sandy coves. In the 1980s, Pulau Langkawi was transformed from an isolated, overwhelmingly Malay rural area, into a duty-free zone in a successful attempt to make it a holiday destination, wooing backpackers and upmarket visitors alike. Access to the archipelago by air and ferry has never been easier, and Langkawi's excellent road network makes exploring the island convenient. Once-sleepy Kuah, Langkawi's capital, now boasts a slew of shopping centers, supermarkets, resorts, and luxury hotels catering to rising tourist demands.

Main street in Kuah lined with shops and cafés

Kuah

SE Pulau Langkawi. 94,000. Jalan Persiaran Putra, (04) 966-7789. Wed & Sat. Taman Legenda: Jalan Persiaran Putra, near Kuah Jetty. **Tel** (04) 966-4223. **Open** 8am–11pm daily.

Skirting a large bay on the southeastern tip of the island, Kuah is Langkawi's main town and travel hub. Originally a small fishing village, Kuah is undergoing rapid development as a result of the island's growing tourism industry.

The most distinguished building in town is the Friday Congregational Mosque, **Masjid al-Hana**, located next to the tourist office. Built in 1959, the mosque incorporates Uzbek and Moorish elements along with traditional Malay design. **Taman Legenda**, a theme park by the seafront, features sculptures and exhibits that recount the archipelago's history. The garden overlooks Dataran Lang, a landscaped square with a prominent statue of an eagle. Kuah is the best place on Langkawi to shop, change money, and rent vehicles for sightseeing. It also has a vibrant *pasar malam*, or night market. For those arriving by sea, Kuah is a useful transit point to Kuala Perlis, Kuala Kedah, Penang, Alor Star, and Satun in Thailand.

Tomb of Mahsuri

7 miles (12 km) W of Kuah. **Open** tomb: 7:30am–6pm daily; show: 11am.

Dedicated to the memory of a Malay princess, the tomb of Mahsuri is a simple white structure. According to legend, Mahsuri was unjustly accused of adultery and sentenced to death. Mahsuri was stabbed by the executioner with her own *keris*. Her blood flowed white as an indication of her purity, and with her dying breath she cursed the island to seven generations of bad luck. A tomb of fine marble was built on the spot where she was killed. Today, this is honored as a shrine by the islanders. There is also a small museum and some traditional Malay houses to walk around.

Langkawi Canopy Adventures

9 miles (15 km) NW of Kuah. 12-466-8027. langkawi.travel

One of Malaysia's most exhilarating outdoor activities is offered by Langkawi Canopy Adventures, where visitors pass high above the rain forest floor on the Gunung Raya mountainside. This adrenalin-charged experience features a 492-ft (150-m) slide along metal cables and a 98-ft (30-m) vertical rappel. Pre-activity training is provided on site. They also offer kayaking.

Pantai Cenang

10 miles (16 km) W of Kuah. Underwater World: **Tel** (04) 955-6100. **Open** 10am–6pm daily. underwaterworldlangkawi.com.my

A sweep of dazzling white sand, Pantai Cenang is the most popular and developed beach on Pulau Langkawi. Although much has changed here since the early 2000s, the beach is not totally spoilt. At its southern end

Plaque narrating the story of Princess Mahsuri at the site of her death

Visitors taking a closer look at marine life at Underwater World

are a number of entertainment projects, including the vast **Underwater World**. This spectacular aquarium is among the largest in Malaysia, with over 5,000 marine species on display. The aquarium also boasts a walk-through tunnel and 3D cinema.

Pantai Cenang's night market is well worth a visit. Markets open in different Langkawi locations every evening, with Thursday being market night in Pantai Cenang. From 5:30pm to 10pm the street opposite Bon Ton Resort is transformed by a lively mix of hawker food stalls, souvenir shops, and local farmers selling produce. Nearby, **Pantai Tengah** beach is a southward continuation of Cenang, with a harbour, hotels, and a nightclub.

🐾 Telaga Tujuh Falls

14 miles (22 km) W of Kuah. Langkawi Cable Car: **Open** 10am–7pm daily. 🐾

Basketwork at Kompleks Budaya Kraf

Set in an attractive spot on the west coast of Langkawi, Telaga Tujuh or seven wells, is ideal for freshwater bathing and picnics. Located west of Pantai Kok, it is a 30-minute walk to the seven waterfalls, which are joined by smooth, slippery stone sills that bathers can slide down. Look out for the brazen monkeys along the way, and keep your bag firmly closed as they may try to steal any food you have.

In the vicinity is the **Langkawi Cable Car**, which carries passengers over ancient rain forests to the summit of Gunung Machinchang, at 2,315 ft (706 m), for fabulous views across the island to the sea and neighboring Thailand. At an incline of 42 degrees, with a vertical rise of 2,231 ft (680 m), the ride is among the steepest in the world. There are two stops, Middle and Top stations, where visitors can alight.

The rocks here are some of Malaysia's most ancient, at 450 million years old. Since 2007 the whole of Langkawi has been designated as a UNESCO Geopark, a designation given to areas of global geological significance. Langkawi's was the first Geopark listing in Southeast Asia, and while the designation extends over the entire Langkawi archipelago, which comprises some 100 islands, it identifies three primary hotspots: the Machinchang Cambrian, Kilim Karst and Dayang Bunting Marble geoforest parks.

🐾 Teluk Datai

22 miles (35 km) NW of Kuah. 🖼️ 🖼️ Ibrahim Hussein Museum: Pasir Tengkorak. **Tel** (04) 959-4669. **Open** daily. 🖼️ Kompleks Budaya Kraf: Teluk Yu. **Tel** (04) 959-1917 **Open** daily. 📷

Teluk Datai on the island's north coast offers the most stunning vistas on the island, with several beautiful beaches scattered along the shore. The lovely bay is home to exclusive resorts and Els Club, a famous golf course. Along the coast, the **Kompleks Budaya Kraf**, or craft cultural complex, showcases Malay handicrafts, such as *batik, ikat*, pottery, paintings, and woodcarvings.

⛴️ Pulau Payar Marine Park

20 miles (32 km) S of Langkawi. ⛴️
An hour's boat ride from Kuah, the tropical island of Pulau Payar is popular with keen divers and snorkelers. Payar and the smaller islands of Lembu, Segantang, and Kaca cluster around coral reefs that teem with marine life, such as moray eels, large groupers, and black-tipped reef sharks.

The **Coral Garden** in the sheltered, clear waters off Pulau Payar is enduringly popular and is said to have the largest number of coral species in Malaysia. Here visitors can also feed baby sharks under the supervision of experts. To visit, it is best to book a day in advance with a tour group.

🐾 Pulau Dayang Bunting

3 miles (5 km) S of Kuah. ⛴️ 🖼️ 🖼️
Lying across the Kuah Straits, Dayang Bunting is the second-largest island in the Langkawi archipelago. Covered with rain forest and mangroves, the island boasts over 90 species of birds, including hornbills, kingfishers, and woodpeckers. The highlight here is the freshwater Tasik Dayang Bunting, or lake of the pregnant maiden, surrounded by limestone cliffs and dense forests. A legend holds that the waters of the lake bestow fertility, and local women who want to conceive come here to bathe. Visitors can swim in the lake, explore it by pedalo, or simply picnic by its shores.

Boats anchored in the waters off Pulau Dayang Bunting

SOUTHERN PENINSULA

The southern tip of Peninsular Malaysia is also the southernmost extremity of continental Asia, encompassing Johor and
the often overlooked state of Negeri Sembilan, stronghold of
the Minangkabau culture. Cosmopolitan Melaka, the capital of the
historically significant state of the same name, is on every tourist's
itinerary, while on the east coast, the sandy beaches and colorful reefs
of Pulau Tioman are a magnet for visitors from around the world.

With only the narrow Strait of Malacca
dividing this side of Malaysia from Sumatra,
there have always been close relations
between the two cultures. Negeri Sembilan
was settled by the Minangkabau people
from Sumatra in the 15th century and
their unique style of architecture, with
upswept roofs imitating buffalo horns,
is still seen across the state.

Melaka, too, was founded by an exiled
Sumatran prince who introduced Islam to
the peninsula in the 15th century. The
city's strategic location on the busy trade
routes between China and India made
it phenomenally wealthy, as everything
from tea, silks, and spices to gold, opium,
and slaves was bought and sold here.
Such riches attracted the attention of the
Portuguese, who captured the city in 1511.

They were followed by Dutch and then
British colonists, alongside Chinese and
Indian ethnic groups who intermarried
with Malays to create the distinct
Baba-Nyonya and Chitty communities.
Melaka is famous today for its colonial
architecture and an eclectic cuisine that
draws on its multicultural influences.

After the fall of Melaka to the
Portuguese, Johor became the most
powerful state on the peninsula. Facing
threats from the Minangkabau, Johor was
forced to cede Singapore to Sir Stamford
Raffles in 1819. Today, the hectic state
capital, Johor Bahru, is Malaysia's second-
largest city, but the islands of the Seribuat
Archipelago hold more appeal, offering
some of the very best diving and
snorkeling in the country.

Colorful trishaws decorated with flowers outside Christ Church, Melaka

◀ Brightly painted verandas at Salang Bay on the idyllic island of Pulau Tioman

Exploring the Southern Peninsula

Bounded on the west by one of the world's busiest shipping lanes, the Strait of Malacca, on the east by the open South China Sea, and on the south by the island city-state of Singapore, the Southern Peninsula offers everything from bustling cities to great tracts of jungle, lazy seaside resorts, and deserted islands. The top draw is historic Melaka, home to some of Malaysia's best museums, most varied cuisine, and earliest European buildings. The beautiful old palace, Istana Lama, in Sri Menanti is a prime example of Minangkabau craftsmanship, while Seremban, the capital of Negeri Sembilan, makes the ideal base for exploring the state. Johor's main attractions are its beach resorts and the beautiful islands of the Seribuat Archipelago off the east coast.

Inside the royal throne room at Istana Lama, Sri Menanti

Sights at a Glance

1. Seremban
2. Sri Menanti
3. Kuala Pilah
4. *Melaka pp128–33*
5. Muar
6. Kukup
7. Johor Bahru
8. Desaru Beach
9. Mersing

Islands

10. Seribuat Archipelago
11. *Pulau Tioman pp136–7*

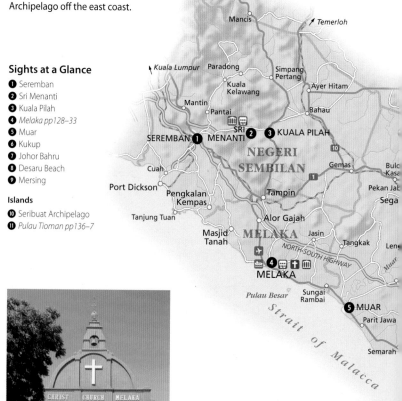

The bright façade of Christ Church, Melaka

Getting Around

A train line runs between Kuala Lumpur and Johor Bahru, and then on to Singapore. Seremban lies at the end of the KTM line from the capital. However, the quickest and easiest way of getting around the region is by car or bus and there are regular services between all the main urban centers. Smaller towns, such as Kukup, are best reached by taxi while Pulau Tioman can be reached by ferry from Mersing.

Key

≡≡≡ Highway
─── Major road
····· Minor road
╌╌╌ Railroad
▨▨▨ International border
▨▨▨ State border
△ Peak

0 kilometers 40
0 miles 40

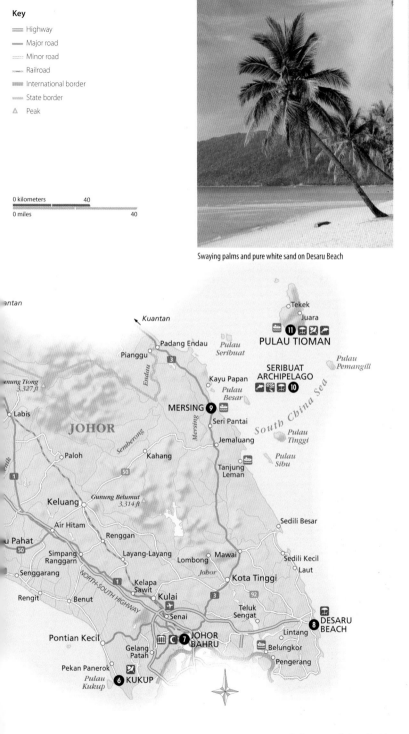

Swaying palms and pure white sand on Desaru Beach

Kuantan

antan

Kuantan

Padang Endau

Pianggu

3

Pulau Seribuat

Endau

Kayu Papan

Pulau Besar

PULAU TIOMAN

Tekek

Juara

11

Pulau Pemanggil

SERIBUAT ARCHIPELAGO

10

South China Sea

MERSING **9**

Seri Pantai

Jemaluang

Mersing

Sembrong

Pulau Tinggi

JOHOR

unung Tiong 3,327 ft

Labis

Paloh

Kahang

Tanjung Leman

Pulau Sibu

50

Keluang

Gunung Belumut 3,314 ft

Air Hitam

Renggan

Sedili Besar

u Pahat

50

Simpang Ranggarn

Layang-Layang

Lombong

Mawai

Johor

Sedili Kecil

Laut

Senggarang

Kelapa Sawit

Kota Tinggi

Rengit

Benut

NORTH-SOUTH HIGHWAY

1

Kulai

Senai

3

92

Teluk Sengat

Lintang

DESARU BEACH

8

Pontian Kecil

Gelang Patah

JOHOR BAHRU

7

Belungkor

Pekan Panerok

Pulau Kukup

KUKUP

6

Pengerang

The peaceful Lake Gardens in Seremban

❶ Seremban

42 miles (67 km) S of Kuala Lumpur.
🏛 700,000. 🚉 KTM Seremban.
🚌 from Kuala Lumpur and Melaka.
🎭 Negeri Sembilan Cultural Carnival
(Jun). 🌐 **tourism.gov.my**

The capital of Negeri Sembilan
state, Seremban is a busy and
largely modern town that at
first glance seems much like
any other provincial Malaysian
city. Although low on sights,
Seremban is a center for the
unique Minangkabau culture. The
most obvious expression of this
is found in the local architecture,
such as the **State Secretariat
Building** with its striking,
traditional pointed roof made
to resemble a pair of buffalo
horns. Some original, relocated
Minangkabau buildings are on
show at the **State Museum**.
These include the Istana Ampang
Tinggi, with its beautiful carvings,
built for a sultan's daughter in the
1860s, and the less ornate Rumah
Negeri Sembilan. The State
Museum also hosts exhibitions of
costumes, musical instruments,
weaponry, and stamps.

East of the town center are
the attractively landscaped
Lake Gardens and the circular
State Mosque.

Environs
Port Dickson is a small port town
20 miles (32 km) southwest of
Seremban. It is the main base for
the 11-mile (18-km) beach strip
running south to **Tanjung Tuan**,
also known as Cape Rachado. As
the nearest beach resort to Kuala
Lumpur, it is hugely popular with
locals at weekends so the

beaches can get crowded.
The water quality in the Strait of
Malacca is not great, but there's
always something going on.
There is also an Army Museum,
providing a change of pace
from the beach.

🏛 **State Museum**
Cultural Handicrafts Complex,
Jalan Sungei Ujong. **Tel** (06) 763-
1149. **Open** 10am–6pm daily.
Closed noon–2:45pm Fri.
♿ grounds only. 📷 🎥

❷ Sri Menanti

19 miles (30 km) E of Seremban.
🏛 6,000. 🚌 from Seremban.
🎭 Sultan's Birthday Celebrations (Jul).

The old royal capital of Negeri
Sembilan, Sri Menanti is today
little more than a rustic village.
The Old Palace, or **Istana
Lama**, was used as the royal
residence until 1931 and is a
fine example of Minangkabau
architecture. Now a museum,
this magnificent wooden edifice was completed in 1908
without the use of a single nail.

The palace stands upon 99
pillars representing the royal
warriors, while the façade is
decorated with elegant
carvings of foliage and animals.
The royal bedchambers and
banquet hall can be viewed
inside, along with displays of
costumes and photographs.
Balconies on the upper floors
offer panoramic views over the
neat palace gardens.

🏛 **Istana Lama**
Tel (06) 497-0242. **Closed** for
renovation; due to reopen end 2016.

❸ Kuala Pilah

25 miles (40 km) E of Seremban. 🏛
154,000. 🚌 🚕

In the heart of Minangkabau
territory, Kuala Pilah is a small
provincial center with little
to interest tourists, but it has
an attractive collection of
1930s shophouses and a
handful of minor sights. Among
the most interesting is the
Martin Lister Memorial Arch
located just behind the bus
station. This grandiose classical
arch, topped with a Chinese
roof, commemorates the state's
first British Resident, Martin
Lister, and dates from 1897.
Nearby is the blue clapboard
St. Joseph's Catholic Church.

The center of town hosts
a number of temples that
include the multicolored **Sri
Kanthaswamy Hindu Temple**,
filled with ornate statues of
various deities.

🏛 **Sri Kanthaswamy
Hindu Temple**
Jln Melang. **Open** 6am–7pm daily. ♿

Detail of a frieze at the Sri Kanthaswamy Hindu Temple in Kuala Pilah

Minangkabau Architecture

Negeri Sembilan is a stronghold of the Minangkabau people who originally came from the highlands of western Sumatra and settled here in the 15th century. Their name comes from *minang* and *kerbau*, translating as victorious buffalo, and according to legend derives from a war with the Javanese in which the final battle was decided by a fight between two water buffalos. The Minangkabau won and adopted the buffalo horns as their national symbol. These stylized horns are used in traditional female headwear and, more notably, in their houses, which are supported on pillars and are always topped with an elaborate roof with pointed, upswept gables reminiscent of a pair of horns. These family homes are known as *rumah gadang*, or big house, and, as the Minangkabau are a matrilineal society, belong to the women and are passed down the female line.

The central tower once held the royal records and functioned as a look-out post. It is reached via steep wooden stairs.

Roof tiles are made from expensive, and now scarce, ironwood specially imported from Sarawak.

Istana Lama, Sri Menanti

The Old Palace is the most impressive example of Minangkabau architecture in Malaysia. Built between 1902 and 1908, it remained the royal residence until 1931 and has been a museum since 1992.

The palace is supported on 99 pillars, each hewn from a *cengal* tree trunk. Many are carved with elaborate designs.

The dramatic upswept gables of the State Museum in Seremban, erected in 1984, are typical of Minangkabau architecture. Older reconstructed houses can also be seen within the grounds.

Istana Ampang Tinggi, with its *attap* (thatched) roof, was built for a local 19th-century princess. It originally stood near Sri Menanti but is now at Seremban's State Museum.

The magnificent gateway straddling the main road into Sri Menanti has dramatic horn-shaped pillars.

❶ Melaka

With its colorful, cosmopolitan heritage, the town of Melaka (also known as Malacca) is one of Malaysia's biggest tourist draws. According to legend, it was founded by the Sumatran Prince Parameswara in 1400 and named by him for the local melaka tree. The city grew quickly and by the 15th century it was one of the richest trading empires in the East. In 1511, it fell to the Portuguese, who in turn gave way to the Dutch in 1641 and the British in 1795. The influences of all the city's rulers can still be seen in its historic core around St. Paul's Hill. The city is known for its multicultural population, including Portuguese Eurasians and, most notably, the Baba-Nyonya who are descendants of early merchants from China who intermarried with local Malay women.

Stadthuys, the former hub of Dutch colonial administration

🏛 Stadthuys

Town Square. **Tel** (06) 284-1934. **Closed** for renovation until end 2016; phone ahead for times. 🅿 ♿

This magnificent, sturdy old building looming over the town square was built by the Dutch in the 1650s as the seat of colonial administration.

The interior, which reopens at the end of 2016 after renovations, houses the **Museum of History and Ethnography**. Exhibits include Nyonya tableware, Ming ceramics, Dutch furniture, pistols, and swords, alongside dioramas illustrating wedding ceremonies of local ethnic groups and a full-size replica of a traditional wooden Malay house.

Behind the Stadthuys, and included in the same entry ticket, are a number of small museums including the **Museum of Literature**, dedicated to Malaysian writers and historical manuscripts, and the **Democratic Government Museum**, hosting displays on the political history of post-independence Malaysia. Also included is the **Seri Melaka**, an impressive colonial mansion, which was the official residence of Dutch and British colonial governors and, until 1996, was the home of local chief ministers.

🏛 St. Paul's Hill

Occupying a commanding site in the heart of town overlooking the sea, St. Paul's Hill was the site of the now almost entirely vanished Portuguese **A'Famosa** fortress. Its last remnant, Porta de Santiago, stands sentinel at the bottom of the mount.

At the summit of the hill is **St. Paul's Church**, originally erected in 1521 and then known as Nossa Senhora da Annunciada, or Our Lady of the Annunciation. Under Dutch rule the church was renamed St. Paul's, but was abandoned after Christ Church was built. Sadly, St. Paul's Church is now a ruin, but it still holds a fascinating collection of elaborate 17th-century Dutch tombstones, as well as the empty tomb of St. Francis Xavier, the co-founder of the Jesuit order in the 16th century.

Outside the main entrance is an abandoned 19th-century lighthouse and a marble statue of St. Francis Xavier, erected in 1952. From here, a path leads down to the Dutch Cemetery at the bottom of the hill. Only five of the 38 tombs here belong to 17th-century Dutchmen; the rest are 19th-century British residents. Most are in a bad state of disrepair but an information board at the entrance lists the names of those who lie here.

🏯 Porta de Santiago

Jalan Kota.

One of four main gateways into the Portuguese A'Famosa fortress, the Porta de Santiago is the sole surviving remnant of those once massive defenses. It was built in 1512 by Alfonso de Albuquerque, the Portuguese viceroy, and the fortress was reused and redeveloped by the Dutch in the 17th century. The squat stone archway, now standing in isolation at the bottom of St. Paul's Hill, bears the coat of arms of the Dutch East India Company on both sides and there are several Dutch cannons on display in front.

The fortress, with its 10-ft (3-m-) thick walls, was demolished by the British in 1807 in case the city fell into the hands of the French. It was only the intervention of Sir Stamford Raffles (see p44), the founding father of Singapore, that saved this small section for posterity.

The ruins of Porta de Santiago, all that remains of A'Famosa fortress

Plinth and gardens in front of the Istana Kesultanan Melaka, a replica Malay palace

Istana Kesultanan Melaka

Jalan Kota. **Tel** (06) 282-6526.
Open 9am–5:30pm daily.
free admission to the garden.
W perzim.gov.my

At the base of St. Paul's Hill is the Istana Kesultanan Melaka, an impressive re-creation of a traditional Malay palace based closely on descriptions of the original 15th-century Melaka Sultanate Palace that once stood in this area. It houses the **Muzium Di Melaka**, which displays life-sized dioramas of the sultan's court in session and the *nobat*, or royal orchestra. Also on show are scale models of other royal palaces from across Malaysia and displays of costumes and weaponry, including the fearsome *tombak* spears.

Upstairs is the sultan's bedchamber and another flight of stairs leads to a small room housing a display of *keris*, or curved Malay daggers.

In front of the palace is the so-called Forbidden Garden, a pleasant, formal space, laid out with fountains and pools, and shaded by bamboo, palm trees, and magnolia trees.

Christ Church

Town Square. **Tel** (06) 284-8804.
17. **Open** daily. 8:30am
English Eucharist.

This striking, bright red church is one of the iconic symbols of Melaka. It was built by the Dutch in 1753 to celebrate the centenary of their rule over the city, and consecrated for Anglican worship in 1838. Built of local red laterite stone, the building is now painted red and the color scheme continues on the neighboring Stadthuys and Clock Tower. A three-arched porch runs along the front of the church, while inside there are numerous Dutch and British tombstones. Look out too for the gigantic ceiling beams, each cut from a single tree trunk, the hand-carved pews, and the frieze of the Last Supper over the altar.

Melaka

① Stadthuys
② St. Paul's Hill
③ Porta de Santiago
④ Istana Kesultanan Melaka
⑤ Christ Church
⑥ Sri Poyyatha Vinayagar Moorthi Temple
⑦ Kampung Kling Mosque
⑧ Cheng Hoon Teng Temple
⑨ Jalan Hang Jebat
⑩ Jalan Tun Tan Cheng Lock
⑪ Baba-Nyonya Heritage Museum
⑫ Maritime Museum

| 0 meters | 200 |
| 0 yards | 200 |

For keys to symbols *see back flap*

Sri Poyyatha Vinayagar Moorthi Temple

5–11 Jalan Tukang Emas.
Tel (06) 288-3599.

This unassuming structure is the oldest surviving Hindu temple in Malaysia. It was built in 1781 on the site of the city's first Chitty, or Indian Peranakan, settlement. The temple is dedicated to the deity Vinayagar, also known as Ganesh, the elephant-headed god of wisdom. An image of Vinayagar stands on the main altar in the back of the temple, and his younger brother, Lord Murugan, appears at a side altar. The temple is crowded during Thaipusam (Jan/Feb).

Sri Poyyatha Vinayagar Moorthi Temple

Kampung Kling Mosque

Jalan Tukang Emas.
Tel (06) 283-7416.

Founded in 1748, this is one of the oldest mosques in the country, although the present buildings date largely from 1872 when the old wooden structure was replaced with brick in the original design.

Like Melaka itself, the mosque draws influences from other cultures and its unique architectural features are based on Sumatran, Chinese, Malay, and European styles. The unusual pyramidal roof with its green tiling shows a strong Hindu influence, while the striking pagoda-like minaret has recognizably Chinese and Moorish origins. The main prayer hall, which is closed to non-Muslims, is surrounded by Ionic columns, ironwork, and English ceramic tiles.

Cheng Hoon Teng Temple

Jalan Tokong 25. **Tel** (06) 282-9343.
Open 7am–7pm daily.
W chenghoonteng.org.my

Also known as the temple of the green clouds and Kuan Yin Teng, this venerable building is the oldest Chinese temple in Malaysia. Founded in the mid-17th century and dedicated to Kuan Yin, the goddess of mercy, it is a superb example of southern Chinese architecture, and is still a vital focus for the local Chinese community. Taoism, Confucianism, and Chinese Buddhism are given equal status within the temple.

Restoration work on the main complex led to the temple receiving a UNESCO award for outstanding architectural restoration. The main hall is richly adorned with beautiful paintings and symbolic carvings, with lions, golden phoenix, and other mythical creatures gracing the interior. There are also scenes from Chinese legend and literature including a prayer screen depicting the life of the Buddha, and a watercolor of Lao Tzu, the Chinese philosopher and founder of Taoism. Religious ceremonies take place here every day, and visitors are welcome to come in and watch.

Mausoleum of Hang Kasturi on Jalan Hang Jebat

Jalan Hang Jebat

Tamil Methodist Church: 9:30am Sun (English service). Jonker Walk Night Market: **Open** Fri–Sun evenings.

Better known by its old name of Jonkers Street, busy Jalan Hang Jebat is the main thoroughfare of Melaka's Chinatown. It is famous for its many antique and curio shops, bars, and restaurants, although prices here tend to be higher than elsewhere. The street is especially lively on weekend evenings when the **Jonker Walk Night Market** gets going. There are stalls selling Chinese food, clothes, and souvenirs, while Chinese opera takes place on outdoor stages. Unfortunately, rapid tourist-oriented development has forced many traditional businesses out and historic buildings have been demolished. There are still some points of interest, including the **Mausoleum of Hang Kasturi**, dedicated to a local 15th-century hero, and the **Tamil Methodist Church** dating from 1908.

Detail from an intricately carved frieze at the Cheng Hoon Teng Temple

🚪 Jalan Tun Tan Cheng Lock

8 Heeren Street: 8 Jalan Tun Tan
Cheng Lock. **Tel** (06) 281-1507. **Open**
11am–4pm Tue–Sat. 🎴10:30am Tue
& Thu. 🔳 **badanwarisan.org.my**
Tham Siew Inn Artist Gallery: 49 Jalan
Tun Tan Cheng Lock. **Tel** (06) 281-
2112. **Open** Tue–Sun. 🏠 ♿
Malaqa House: 70 Jalan Tun Tan
Cheng Lock. **Tel** (06) 281-4770.
Open daily. 🏠 ♿

Formerly known as Heeren Street,
and still referred to as such by
many locals, Jalan Tun Tan Cheng
Lock has retained much more of
its original character than nearby
Jalan Hang Jebat. The long,
narrow street is now lined with
shops, cafés, hotels, restaurants,
and several art galleries.

The townhouses here date
from the 18th century, and the
narrow façades are a result of
the tax on house widths that
was imposed by the Dutch
colonial authorities at that time.
To make up for this, they also
tend to have very deep interiors.
The houses, with their colorful
tiles, stucco work, and painted
plaster, were once the homes of
rich Baba-Nyonya families and
most are still in private hands.

A few of the historic buildings
along this road are in a very poor
state of repair. However, one of
these townhouses, known as
8 Heeren Street, has been
restored and now functions as a
resource center. In the few rooms
on show here, there are displays
that explain the conservation

The decorated façade of a townhouse on Jalan Tun Tan Cheng Lock

and restoration processes, and
document the traditional techniques and materials used by the
artisans who worked on the
project. Local architects
sometimes give tours.

Farther along Jalan Tun Tan
Cheng Lock is the Baba-Nyonya
Heritage Museum *(see pp132–3)*,
a preserved townhouse that
provides a glimpse into a
wealthy Melakan home. One of
the street's best art galleries is
the **Tham Siew Inn Artist
Gallery**, which displays beautiful watercolors by local artist
Tham Siew Inn. Another gallery
worth visiting is **Malaqa House**,
a grand Baba-Nyonya mansion
with large rooms filled with
Oriental furniture, carvings,
paintings, and bric-a-brac.

🏛 Baba-Nyonya Heritage Museum

See pp132–3.

🏛 Maritime Museum

Jalan Quayside. **Tel** (06) 283-0926.
Open 9am–5:30pm daily. 📷
♿ modern building only. Melaka
River Cruise: Quayside Heritage Center.
Tel (06) 281-4322. **Open** 9am–
11:30pm daily. 📷 ♿

The Maritime Museum is
Melaka's most visually arresting
museum, located on board an
impressive, full-scale replica of
the 16th-century Portuguese
galleon *Flora de la Mar*, which
sank in the Strait of Malacca
overburdened with looted
treasure. Displays recount the
city's seafaring past from the
time of the 15th-century Melaka
Sultanate through the ensuing
Portuguese, Dutch, and British
colonial periods. Exhibits
include dioramas depicting
bustling dock scenes, cases
containing scale-model ships
and weapons, maps, and other
nautical artifacts.

Around a 5-minute walk from
the museum is the Quayside
Heritage Centre; the jetty in front
of the building is the boarding
point for cruise boat tours of the
Melaka River. Once the meeting
point between East and West,
the river was the main trade
artery during the city's heyday.
There are two cruise options
available – the first includes
an on-board tour guide, while
the other has a recorded
commentary. Passengers are
also serenaded with traditional
songs. Both tours leave every
30 minutes and last 45 minutes.
The cruise takes in historic
Kampung buildings, beautiful
riverside gardens, and the Eye on
Malaysia Ferris wheel. The tour is
particularly atmospheric at night.

Betel, "The Nut of Love"

Betel nuts, the dried seeds of the areca or Pinang palm tree, are prized
for their mildly narcotic and supposed aphrodisiac qualities. The ritual

Betel nuts, thought to be an
aphrodisiac, growing in the wild

chewing of this nut was once
common across Malaysia but the
practice is now mainly confined
to rural areas. The nut is prepared
during courtship rituals by
combining it with herbs, cloves,
tobacco, and ground lime, which
are then wrapped in betel leaves.
Chewing releases a sticky substance
said to freshen the breath, relax
the mind, and stimulate passion.
In the past, brides would chew
betel nut to blacken their teeth,
considered an attractive sign of
status. Today, a betel-nut decoration is still presented as a gift
at weddings and festivals.

Melaka: Baba-Nyonya Heritage Museum

This absorbing museum is dedicated to the unique culture of Melaka's Baba-Nyonya, also known as Straits Chinese or Peranakan, community, who were born through the intermarriage of Chinese traders and local Malay women. The house dates from 1896 when three older houses were combined to create a grand home for a wealthy Baba-Nyonya family. Opulent decor with gold leaf, mother-of-pearl, and exotic hardwoods is used throughout the house. The eclectic design incorporates traditional Chinese wall-hangings and woodcarvings alongside English tilework, heavy Dutch furniture, Italian marble, and colorful Baba-Nyonya porcelain.

Hand-painted lantern, a typical decoration in Chinese homes

Bedroom
The four-poster bed in the master bedroom is decorated with elaborate gilded carvings of foliage and mythological scenes. A hidden peephole in the floor overlooks the guest hall.

Second floor

The atrium allows natural light and cool air into the house.

First floor

House no. 52

House no. 50 (entrance)

House no. 48

★ Glass Partition
This screen allowed young unmarried women, hiding in the Dark Chamber, to peer through the etched panels at male visitors in the Guest Hall without being seen themselves.

★ Wooden Staircase
This highly ornate wooden staircase, constructed without the use of a single nail, is decorated with gilded carvings and is the only one of its kind in Melaka.

For hotels and restaurants see pp279–80 and pp294–5

Baba-Nyonya Shutters
These elegant louvered shutters, made of overlapping movable wooden slats, draw on European design and are a common feature of 19th-century Baba-Nyonya architecture.

Baba-Nyonya Porcelain
This distinctive pink and green porcelain, decorated with floral motifs and Buddhist symbols, was made to order in China for wealthy Baba-Nyonya customers.

Museum Guide
After walking through the impressive Guest Hall, continue beyond the glass partition into the living area. Take the stairs to the master bedroom and the funerary room on the first floor. Descend at the rear of the building to the kitchen area and return to the main entrance passing the ancestral altar en route.

Key
- ☐ Bedroom
- ☐ Kitchen
- ☐ Ancestor worship
- ☐ Guest hall
- ☐ Dark chamber
- ☐ Funerary room
- ☐ Bathroom
- ☐ Exhibition space
- ☐ Non-exhibition space

The kitchen is perfectly preserved and stocked with traditional objects, including a noodle press.

★ Ancestral Altar
A common feature of Chinese homes, this family altar has Ming dynasty-style carvings of dragons and bats. The bronze cherub lamps show a strong European influence.

Façade
The façade is typical of the ornate and eclectic styles favored by the 19th-century Baba-Nyonya. It incorporates Chinese style with elements of European design, such as stucco pilasters, Rococo plasterwork, and louvered windows.

Boats moored at jetties in the old port town of Muar

❺ Muar

28 miles (45 km) SE of Melaka.
🏙 329,000. 🚌 from Melaka and
Kuala Lumpur. ⛴ from Dumai,
Sumatra. 🎿 Water Sports
Festival (Sep).

The bustling riverside town of
Muar, also known as Bandar
Maharani or Empress Town, is
bypassed by most tourists, but
its colorful history and elegant
colonial architecture make it a
pleasant stopover.

The town was once a major
trading port, and its former status
can be seen in the collection of
impressive colonial buildings
standing close to the waterfront
on Jalan Maharani, including
the grand **Royal Customs and
Excise Building**, dating from
1909. Also here is a row of
early 20th-century shophouses,
and nearby is the magnificent
Sultan Ibrahim Mosque, with
its soaring four-story minaret,
completed in 1930.

Muar is renowned as a center
of Malay culture. However,
it is best known for its food,
in particular the popular
mee bandung Muar, a tasty
concoction of noodles, eggs,
prawns, and chili in beef broth,
and *ikan asam pedas*, a sour
and spicy fish dish.

❻ Kukup

25 miles (40 km) SW of Johor Bahru.
🏙 3,000. 🚌 from Johor Bahru
to Pontian Kecil, then taxi.
ℹ (07) 223-4935.

Sitting on the southwestern tip
of Johor close to the southernmost point of continental Asia,

Kukup is a traditional fishing
village, complete with old-
fashioned kampung-style
wooden houses on stilts.

The village is famous for its
seafood, with chili crabs being
the local specialty, and the
many seafront restaurants do a
roaring trade with weekend
visitors, many coming from
Singapore. Offshore lies **Pulau
Kukup**, one of the world's
largest uninhabited mangrove
islands. Once the haunt of
pirates, it has been declared a
national park and wetland area
of international importance.
A regular ferry service to the
island allows visitors a glimpse
of this fascinating protected
ecosystem. Its wildlife includes
wild pigs, crabs, and numerous
species of birds.

☒ Pulau Kukup
🚤 from Kukup jetty. ℹ Pulau Kukup
Johor National Park, 1319 Mukim
Air Masin, (07) 696-9355.
Ⓦ johorparks.blogspot.hk

❼ Johor Bahru

2 miles (3 km) N of Singapore;
124 miles (200 km) SE of Melaka.
🏙 1,065,000. ✈ Senai. 🚆 🚌 ⛴
🚌 ℹ 2 Jalan Air Molek, (07) 223-
4935. 🎎 Johor Cultural Festival (Jul).
Ⓦ johortourism.com

The capital city of Johor state,
commonly known as JB,
sprawls across the southern
tip of the peninsula facing
Singapore over the narrow
strait. The planned special
economic zone of Iskandar
Malaysia encompasses JB,
and the government is
investing a vast amount of
money into its creation.

Aside from the excitement
over the development of
the region, Johor Bahru has a
number of sights worth visiting.
The **Royal Sultan Abu Bakar
Museum**, housed in the
sparkling white Victorian Istana
Besar, or Great Palace, west of
the city center. Built in 1866, it
is one of the oldest buildings
in Johor Bahru and is set in
extensive landscaped grounds
overlooking the Strait of
Singapore. The palace is

Fountain in the Royal Sultan Abu Bakar Mosque, Johor Bahru

now a museum devoted to the royal family and is still used for occasional official ceremonies. Photographs, costumes, weapons, and other royal mementos are on show in the lavishly furnished rooms, such as the Hunting Room featuring stuffed tigers, elephant-foot umbrella stands, and suchlike.

LEGOLAND® Malaysia has more than 40 rides, shows, and attractions and is a popular attraction. The centerpiece is Miniland, where Asian landmarks have been recreated using more than 30 million LEGO bricks.

Also of interest nearby is the **Sultan Abu Bakar Mosque**, an Anglo-Malay edifice that was erected in 1893 and can hold up to 2,000 worshipers. The **Sultan Ibrahim Building** with its 210-ft (64-m-) high Mughal-style tower dominates the skyline. During World War II, it was used by the Japanese but today houses state government offices.

🏛 Royal Sultan Abu Bakar Museum
Jalan Ibrahim. **Tel** (07) 223-0555. **Open** 8am–5pm Sat–Thu. 🚫 🚹 limited.

🎡 LEGOLAND® Malaysia
7 Jalan Legoland, Iskandar Malaysia, JB. 🚌 from JB, Singapore. **Tel** (07) 597-8888. **Open** 10am–8pm daily. 🚫
W legoland.com.my

❽ Desaru Beach

55 miles (88 km) E of Johor Bahru.
🚌 from Johor Bahru to Kota Tinggi, then taxi. 🚢 from Singapore to Tanjung Belungkor, then bus.
W desaru.com.my

The seaside resort of Desaru boasts over 15 miles (25 km) of fine, white sandy beaches fringed with casuarinas. It attracts more than one million visitors every year, and is particularly popular with weekend trippers from nearby Singapore. The government has invested money into developing Desaru into a popular tourist destination, and the small hotels and quiet beaches have been replaced with luxury resorts, golf courses, and theme parks.

Luxurious swimming pool at one of Desaru Beach's hotel resorts

❾ Mersing

124 miles (200 km) N of Johor Bahru.
🚶 68,000. 🚌 from Kuala Lumpur and Singapore. 🚢 to Pulau Tioman.
i Jalan Abu Bakar, (07) 799-5212.

This fishing town is the main access point for Pulau Tioman *(see pp136–7)* and the islands of the Seribuat Archipelago. Many people spend a night here en route but there is not a great deal to do in this slow-paced town except to enjoy its unspoilt nature and watch the boats set sail.

❿ Seribuat Archipelago

59 miles (95 km) S of Kuantan. 🚢 from Mersing; each of the private resorts runs a ferry service for guests.

Off the east coast of Johor lies the Seribuat Archipelago, made up of 64 volcanic islands, the largest being Pulau Tioman *(see pp136–7)*. Most are tiny and uninhabited and can only be reached by chartering a private boat, but they are among the most beautiful islands in Malaysia.

Just a handful of the islands are big enough to support tiny villages and some secluded beach resorts, which range from simple beach huts to smart hotels with restaurants and swimming pools. The larger and more developed islands are Pulau Besar, Sibu, and Tinggi, renowned for their fine sandy beaches and excellent snorkeling and diving opportunities among the abundant coral reefs. Smaller islands provide a more sedate experience, such as Pulau Rawa, which has two acccommodation options. The remote islands, including Pulau Pemanggil, Dayang, and Aur, have basic facilities, but are rich in marine life and popular with more intrepid divers.

Tour operators in Mersing run island-hopping trips stopping off at a few of the islands, but otherwise access is restricted to guests at the private resorts. Ferries to Pulau Sibu depart from Tanjung Leman, 37 miles (60 km) south of Mersing, and take about an hour to reach the island.

⑪ Pulau Tioman

The largest of Malaysia's east coast islands, Tioman is famed for its soft, sandy beaches, warm waters, and coral reef. Its past is shrouded in myth – it is said that a dragon princess stopped here to break a long journey. She loved it so much that she stayed and her body was transformed into Pulau Tioman. Most of the resorts are strung out on isolated bays along the western coast. Diving and snorkeling opportunities in the protected marine park are superb, but jungle hiking and sunbathing are also popular activities. The island is a haven for wildlife – more than 140 different bird species live here. Monitor lizards, snakes, monkeys, and porcupines thrive in the jungle interior thanks to the absence of large predators, while the sea teems with countless varieties of tropical fish.

★ **Snorkeling**
Easy to arrange either alone or on organized trips, snorkeling is a captivating way to observe coral life.

Twin Peaks
The twin peaks of Bukit Nenek Semukut are often shrouded in mist. Legend has it they are the horns of the dragon princess.

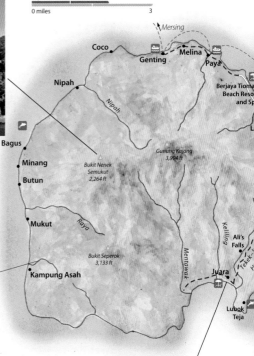

Twin Peaks

Asah Waterfall

Juara

0 km ——— 3
0 miles ——— 3

Mersing

Coco
Genting   Melina
Paya
Berjaya Tioma
Beach Reso
and Sp
Nipah
Nipah
Bagus
Minang
Butun
Bukit Nenek
Semukut
2,264 ft
Gunung Kajang
3,994 ft
Mukut
Raya
Bukit Seperok
3,133 ft
Kampung Asah
Mentawak
Keliling
Ali's
Falls
Juara
Lubok
Teja

★ **Asah Waterfall**
A short walk from Kampung Asah is this picturesque waterfall, which was once used as a backdrop in the 1958 film *South Pacific*.

Juara
Home to a large resort, secluded Juara is located in a beautiful curving bay on the east coast. It has the finest white-sand beach on Tioman but the sea can be rough.

For hotels and restaurants see pp279–80 and pp294–5

★ **Tekek–Juara Hiking Trail**
This sometimes challenging 5-mile (8-km) trail cuts across the island through jungle that is full of wildlife, streams, and waterfalls. It takes about three hours to reach Juara from Tekek.

Pulau Tulai ②

① 🏠 🌄

Air Batang 🏠 Panuba 🏖 Salang 🏖

Tekek 🚢

Salang Beach
Tioman's most northerly resort, Salang has a short, sandy beach and shallow waters. There are plenty of budget accommodations and seafront bars providing low-key nightlife.

Key

═══ Minor road
– – Trail
– – Ferry route
△ Peak

Air Batang
Popularly known as ABC, this lively resort is a favorite backpacker hangout, although better beaches can be found elsewhere.

KEY

① **Monkey Beach** is a secluded cove with deep, clear water – ideal for diving.

② **Pulau Tulai** has reefs that are popular with snorkelers and divers.

Coral Reef
With more than 180 coral species, Tioman's waters offer some of the most rewarding diving in Malaysia.

For keys to symbols *see back flap*

EASTERN AND CENTRAL PENINSULA

The Eastern and Central Peninsula is blessed with some of the most beautiful natural features in Malaysia. Rising in the west are the lush forested Titiwangsa mountains, to the east of which lie Kelantan, Pahang, and Terengganu. Dominated by a vast rain forest and flanked by an unbroken coastline with delightful beaches and islands, the region is considered the heartland of Muslim Malay culture.

The three states of this region share a similar early history, having been vassals of Siam (now Thailand) and under the rule of the Sultanate of Melaka in the 14th and 15th centuries. Thereafter, Pahang was ruled by the sultans of Johor until the British took control and made it one of the Federated Malay States. Terengganu and Kelantan continued to be under Siamese rule through the 19th century. In 1909, they became part of the Unfederated Malay States. In 1963, all three states were incorporated into the Federation of Malaysia.

Physically cut off from the west coast by the jungle interior, and free from British control until the 19th century, the eastern and central states developed at a different pace, commercially and culturally. Separated from the tin and rubber boom of the 19th century, which attracted Asian immigrants, they retained a rural and predominantly Malay character. These states are still considered the conservative Malay Muslim heartland of the country. The interior regions are inhabited by Orang Asli and Orang Syam people.

The east coast possesses a rural tranquility and offers spectacular natural scenery. Pahang is home to Taman Negara, the country's premier national park, as well as a host of offshore islands and some of Malaysia's best beaches. While the towns and villages of Terengganu are centers for Malay handicrafts, those of Kelantan are the best places to see traditional activities, such as fishing. Trips along the east coast may become difficult during the rainy season, between November and March.

The colorful fishing boats on Sabak Beach, Kelantan

◄ An Orang Asli boy climbing a tree in Taman Negara

Exploring the Eastern and Central Peninsula

This region offers spectacular natural beauty with the magnificent Taman Negara and Endau-Rompin national parks located in its forested interiors and an endless coastline of white-sand beaches and stunning offshore islands. Pulau Redang, Pulau Tenggol, and the Perhentian Islands are home to a fascinating underwater world and offer some of Malaysia's top diving and snorkeling. While Kuantan, the capital of Pahang, is a transport hub for the region and used mostly as a transit point, especially for nearby beaches and the picturesque Tasik Chini, the two other state capitals, Kuala Terengganu and Kota Bharu, are rich in Malay culture.

Sights at a Glance

Towns and Cities

- **1** Kuantan
- **4** Pekan
- **5** Cherating
- **11** Kuala Terengganu
- **14** Kota Bharu pp152–3
- **15** Tumpat

Parks and Preserves

- **6** Endau-Rompin National Park
- **7** Taman Negara pp144–5

Places of Worship

- **17** Wat Phothivihan
- **18** Wat Machimmaram

Areas of Natural Beauty

- **2** Gua Charas
- **3** Tasik Chini
- **10** Tasik Kenyir

Islands and Beaches

- **8** Pulau Tenggol
- **9** Pulau Kapas
- **12** Pulau Redang
- **13** Perhentian Islands
- **16** Pantai Dasar Sabak

Tour

- **19** The Jungle Railway p155

0 km | 25

0 miles | 25

Fishermen and women drying their catch by the sea in Kuantan

For hotels and restaurants see pp280–81 and pp295–6

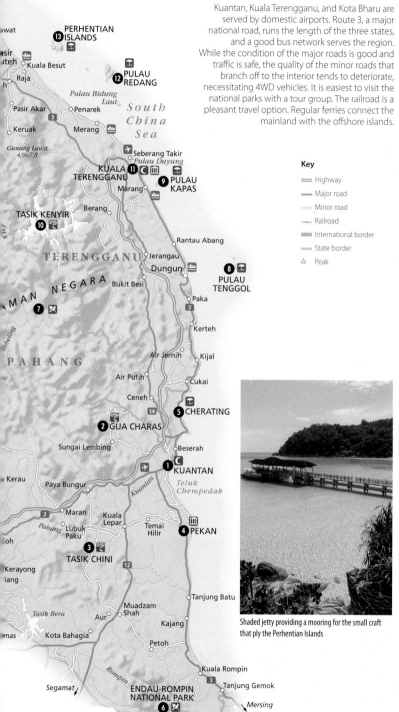

Getting Around

Kuantan, Kuala Terengganu, and Kota Bharu are served by domestic airports. Route 3, a major national road, runs the length of the three states, and a good bus network serves the region. While the condition of the major roads is good and traffic is safe, the quality of the minor roads that branch off to the interior tends to deteriorate, necessitating 4WD vehicles. It is easiest to visit the national parks with a tour group. The railroad is a pleasant travel option. Regular ferries connect the mainland with the offshore islands.

Key

— Highway
— Major road
···· Minor road
⌐ Railroad
▬ International border
▬ State border
△ Peak

Shaded jetty providing a mooring for the small craft that ply the Perhentian Islands

For keys to symbols see back flap

Ferries docked in Kuantan, capital of Pahang

❶ Kuantan

160 miles (259 km) E of Kuala Lumpur. 🚇 315,000. ✈ 🚌 ⛴ 𝑖 Jalan Makhota, (09) 517-7111.
🌐 **pahangtourism.com.my**

The capital of Pahang, Kuantan is a commercial town and a major transport hub, located at the mouth of Sungai Kuantan. The town has a few sites of interest and is visited mostly by travelers en route to the attractive beaches and riverside villages nearby.

Overlooking the padang at the heart of town is the stunning Moorish-style **Masjid Negeri**, or state mosque. It is crowned with a blue and white dome and is surrounded by four Ottoman-style minarets. It also features stained-glass windows, a rare feature in Malaysian Islamic architecture. The mosque is illuminated every night. The redeveloped riverfront of Kuantan offers pleasant views and has shops that sell excellent local handicrafts. From the jetty, boat trips take visitors to the nearby fishing village of **Tanjung Lumpur** as well as to a mangrove forest reserve.

Environs
Just 3 miles (5 km) east of the capital, **Teluk Chempedak**, or jackfruit bay, is Kuantan's main attraction. It marks the beginning of the splendid beaches on the east coast and is famous locally for its sands and waves. Besides an array of watersports, there are several walking trails. Located 20 miles (35 km) southeast of Kuantan is **Bukit Gambang Resort City**. The resort has many attractions including a vast water park, a zoo safari, and a man-made lake, making it popular with families. There are several hotels on-site.

🏨 Bukit Gambang Resort City
Jalan Bukit Gambang Utama.
Tel (09) 548-8000. 🚗 🚕
Water park: **Open** 10:30am–6:30pm Mon, Wed & Thu; 9:30am–6:30pm Fri–Sun. 🌐 **bgrc.com.my**

❷ Gua Charas

15 miles (25 km) NW of Kuantan. 🚌 from Kuantan.

Near the small settlement of Panching, Gua Charas is a series of deep caves set dramatically in a massive limestone karst outcrop. In 1954, the Sultan of Pahang granted permission to a Thai Buddhist monk to convert the main cave into a Buddhist shrine. A steep ascent up 200 steps leads to this enormous cave, which contains several religious images carved out of stone. Dominating the cave is a 30-ft- (9-m-) long Sleeping Buddha. Next to it are shrines dedicated to Kuan Yin, the Chinese goddess of mercy, and to several bodhisattvas.

❸ Tasik Chini

85 miles (138 km) SW of Kuantan on Federal Hwy 82. 🚌 to Felda Chini – 3.1 miles (5 km) S of Tasik Chini, then taxi; to Maran, then taxi to Kampung Belimbing, then boat. 🚤

Nestled in the hills, deep in Malaysia's forested interior, Tasik Chini is a collection of beautiful lakes connected by waterways teeming with fish and birds and framed by giant trees. The best time to visit is between June and September when the lakes are covered with red and white lotus blooms. Around the shores live the indigenous Jakun people, belonging to the Orang Asli community. Sadly, these people are struggling to protect their traditional way of life and fight pollution of this lovely environment by the mining and logging industries. **Kampung Gumum** is a small Orang Asli settlement at the northern end of the lakes, where friendly locals show visitors around their homes and display their traditional handicrafts. At the village, accommodation is also available.

Although public transport to the lakes is not conveniently accessible, once there, the entire lake system can be explored by boat, organized by the resort and the village. Several trails of varying lengths weave through the area. Day tours to Tasik Chini can be arranged from Kuantan and Cherating.

The enormous Sleeping Buddha enshrined at Gua Charas

The impressive Buaya Sangkut cascades at Endau-Rompin National Park

❹ Pekan

27 miles (44 km) S of Kuantan on Federal Hwy 3. 30,000. from Kuantan. **pekan.my**

Located on the south bank of Sungai Pahang, the longest river in Malaysia, is the town of Pekan, the former royal capital of Pahang.

Scattered along the busy riverfront street at the town's northern edge are many of its attractions, including a row of beautiful Chinese shophouses with jack roofs, many of which are antiques shops, and the **Sultan Abu Bakar Museum**. Housed in a Victorian palace, once the residence of the Johor royal family, this interactive museum exhibits a collection of royal regalia, weapons, and Chinese porcelain, some of which were salvaged from a wrecked junk (Asian shipping vessel). Visitors can stroll around the attractive gardens for free. Nearby are two white marble mosques, the blue-domed **Masjid Abdullah**, which dates back to the 1920s, and the newer **Masjid Abu Bakar**, with its more conventional golden domes. Farther away from the river is the royal quarter, with its lavish **Istana Abu Bakar**, or royal palace, overlooking a polo ground. **The Kedah Royal Mausoleum**, dating back to 1778, is also nearby.

Sultan Abu Bakar Museum
Jalan Sultan Ahmad. **Tel** (09) 422-1371. **Open** 9am–5pm Tue–Sun (9am–noon, 2:40–5pm Fri).

❺ Cherating

29 miles (47 km) N of Kuantan on Federal Hwy 3. 2,000. from Kuantan, Kota Bharu, Kuala Terengganu.

Occupying a windswept bay facing the South China Sea, the palm-fringed fishing village of Cherating is one of the best beaches on Malaysia's lovely east coast. Well provided with accommodation of all types, from budget guesthouses to high-end resorts, Cherating is a very popular destination. The waters here are ideal for surfing, especially during November and December. Another area of interest, around 6 miles (10 km) from Cherating, is **Chendor Beach**. Visitors come here for sightings of green turtles and, occasionally, giant leatherbacks, which come ashore to lay their eggs between April and September, the nesting period. There are also some secluded bathing spots. The **Chendor Turtle Sanctuary** is worth a visit, especially at nesting time.

❻ Endau-Rompin National Park

35 miles (57 km) S of Kuantan. to Kahang, then 4WD for Peta; or to Bekok, then 4WD for Selai. (07) 223-7471. **Closed** during monsoon season (Nov–Mar). guides mandatory. **johorparks.blogspot.hk**

Named for the two rivers that bound it, the 336-sq-mile (870-sq-km) Endau-Rompin National Park is among the last remaining stretches of lowland forest in Malaysia. It nurtures a splendid variety of flora and fauna and is one of the few habitats of the Sumatran rhinoceros. The park's varied landscape allows for a variety of activities, such as trekking, rafting, climbing, and abseiling. There are entrances at Peta, near Mersing, and, less accessibly, at Selai.

At the confluence of Sungai Endau and Sungai Jasir is the base camp, **Kuala Jasin**, 9 miles (15 km) from the park headquarters. From here, a 4-hour trail leads to **Janing Barat Plateau** while two other routes trace the Sungai Jasin leading to the park's most spectacular waterfall, **Buaya Sangkut**. Visitors are also welcome at the Orang Asli villages that dot the area.

All visitors must carry entry permits, which can be obtained for free from Kuala Rompin or the park headquarters, or for a fee from Johor Bahru. An organized tour is the best way to explore the park, either through the Johor Parks Corporation or a travel agency; accommodations are limited, and ideally three days are needed to cover the park.

The sky-blue-domed Masjid Abdullah at the former royal capital of Pekan

❼ Taman Negara

Established in 1938, Taman Negara is Malaysia's oldest and largest national park. Extending across 1,660 sq miles (4,300 sq km) of pristine rain forest, the park encompasses parts of three states: Pahang, Kelantan, and Terengganu. A profusion of birdlife can be spotted here, along with rare animals such as the Indochinese tiger, Sumatran rhinoceros, Malayan gaur, and Asian elephant. Access to the park is spectacular, involving a 37-mile (60-km) boat journey along the lovely Sungai Tembeling, passing Orang Asli villages en route. Be aware, however, that during the rainy season the park may be inaccessible.

KELANTAN   TERENGGANU

Area of map Illustrated   PAHANG

Kuala Tahan

★ **Gunung Tahan**
The 7,175-ft- (2,187-m-) high Gunung Tahan is the highest peak in Peninsular Malaysia. The long trek to the summit is very demanding with the route passing rivers and undulating ridges before finally reaching the peak.

Four Steps Waterfall

Gunung Tahan 7,152 ft   **Padang**

Gunung Gedong 6,752 ft

Kuala Teku

Gunung Tahan Trail

Kuala Put

Boat Trips
At the Mutiara Taman Negara Resort park headquarters, boats can be hired for trips to the Lata Berkoh rapids, as well as for fishing trips to the Tahan and Kenyam rivers.

Tenor

Ken-

① Bukit Gen 1,8

KEY

① **Bukit Guling Gendang**, at a height of 1,864 ft (568 m), offers panoramic views across virgin rain forest from its summit.

② **Gua Telinga**, a limestone cave, is one of the most easily accessible in the park. Guided by a rope, visitors can follow a stream through the cavern.

Atok

Hornbills
For many the main attraction of Taman Negara is its abundant birdlife. The park is home to rare hornbills, including the wreathed hornbill, great hornbill, Indian pied hornbill, and the rhinoceros hornbill.

Asian Elephants
Taman Negara is a haven for endangered species such as the Asian elephant. Wild elephants are often relocated here from the surrounding region.

VISITORS' CHECKLIST

Practical Information
106 miles (170 km) W of Kuantan.
🛈 Kuala Tahan, (09) 266-1122.
Permits: available at Department of Wildlife and National Parks.
🌐 taman-negara.com

Transport
🚌 to Kuala Tembeling, then boat to Kuala Tahan.

★ Bukit Teresek
The climb up to the summit of Bukit Teresek along a muddy track takes over an hour but is well worth the effort for the great views across the valley to Gunung Tahan and Gunung Perlis.

Perkai Lodge

Kuala Keniam

Key

\--- Trail

— Park boundary

Exploring the Park

All trails start from or near park headquarters and have been marked or signposted. The two main trails in the park are the 9-day, 34-mile (55-km) trek to Gunung Tahan and the 4-day, 10-mile (16-km) Rentis Tenor loop trail. However, the most heavily used trail in the park is the short 1.6-mile (2-km) route to Bukit Teresek, which also leads on to Bukit Indah. Guides are compulsory for the longer, more strenuous treks.

Lata Berkoh Kenyam
la ai
Kuala Terenggan
Bukit Teresek 1,122 ft
utiara Taman egara Resort
Kuala Tahan
Sungei Tiang Airstrip
Kuala Tembeling

★ Canopy Walkway
A 1,673-ft (510-m) walkway, one of the world's longest, runs through the canopy at Kuala Tahan. Suspended 147 ft (45 m) above the ground, it enables visitors to explore the rain forest from a novel perspective.

For keys to symbols *see back flap*

Clear blue waters lapping the pristine shore of Pulau Tenggol

❽ Pulau Tenggol

8 miles (13 km) E of Kuala Dungun. 🚌 from Kuala Dungun. 🛥️

Part of a group of 12 small and remote islands, Pulau Tenggol is a renowned diving destination on the east coast of Malaysia. Uninhabited until the 1970s, the island was developed into a dive site *(see p314)* and is now part of the Terengganu Marine Park.

The blue waters around the densely forested islands harbor spectacular underwater cliffs, boulders, and coral reefs that shelter a variety of colorful marine life. A ban on fishing, spear-fishing, and any other form of marine life harvesting ensures a rewarding underwater diving experience. There are at least ten dive sites in this group of islands, but most of them are deepwater and suitable only for divers with prior experience.

❾ Pulau Kapas

4 miles (6 km) E of Marang. 🚌 from Marang. 🏊 🏨 🍴 🛥️

A small, beautiful island with white-sand beaches and dazzling waters, Pulau Kapas, or cotton island, is a designated marine park and promoted as a diving and snorkeling paradise. Located to the north is the much smaller islet of **Pulau Gemia**, which can only be visited by guests of its resort.

The best sites for snorkeling on Pulau Kapas are found around its northern shore as well as around Pulau Gemia. North of Gemia, a sunken World War II shipwreck is one of the most popular sites. All the resorts on Kapas can arrange diving trips. There is also a professional scuba-diving center that offers training programs. The island is an excellent place for swimming, windsurfing, and sea kayaking or just relaxing under the palm trees. A walking track that cuts across the island to its isolated eastern shore offers panoramic views.

❿ Tasik Kenyir

34 miles (55 km) SW of Kuala Terengganu. 🚌 from Kuala Lumpur. 🚆 from Kuala Terengganu. 🛥️ boat tours. 🛥️ 🌐 kenyirlake.com

Extending over 100 sq miles (260 sq km) and containing around 350 small islands, Tasik Kenyir is the largest man-made lake in Southeast Asia. It was created by the construction of a dam on the Sungai Kenyir in 1985. Surrounded by lush tropical jungle, which is home to a number of wildlife species, including thousands of hornbills, Tasik Kenyir has been developed as an ecotourism destination, and is also a duty-free zone. Today, there are some 15 resorts around the lake. Among the highlights of the lake are 14 picturesque waterfalls, which cascade into natural pools. These can be reached by boat from the lake's main jetty. Boat trips can also be taken to the limestone Bewah Caves at the southern end of the lake. There is an elephant sanctuary and a canopy walk along the water's edge. The best time to visit is between February and June when the water level is high due to the monsoon season.

A trained monkey selecting a ripe coconut

Coconut-Collecting Monkeys

It is common practice in Peninsular Malaysia to train monkeys to shin up palm trees, twist off the coconuts, and throw them to the ground where they are gathered up by the tree's owner. It has been estimated that after about three months' training, monkeys can harvest at least five times as many coconuts per day than a human collector, chiefly due to their speed, agility, and ease with heights. **Kampung Jenang**, near Marang in Terengganu, has made a thriving business out of this technique. A monkey-training school established by Muda Mamat, a local villager, now even tutors monkeys belonging to coconut plantation owners from neighboring states for a steep fee.

One of the 14 beautiful waterfalls at Tasik Kenyir

Exquisite traditional Malay houses in the grounds of Terengganu State Museum Complex

⓪ Kuala Terengganu

138 miles (220 km) N of Kuantan. 🖼 275,000. ✈ 🚌 🚆 🏨 *i* Plaza Padang Negara, (09) 623-1553. 🌐 **tourism. terengganu.gov.my**

The state capital and the seat of the sultans of Terengganu, Kuala Terengganu is a former fishing village that was transformed into an affluent city from the revenue of its South China Sea oilfields.

The city remains a stronghold of Malay culture, with colorful markets and vibrant traditional handicraft workshops where visitors can buy *batik*, brocade, *songket*, brassware, and basketware. The busiest spot in town is the **Pasar Payang**, or central market. All kinds of foods including fresh fish, fruit, and vegetables are available here. The nearby Waterfront Heritage Bazaar is another good place to browse. South of the market is the compact **Chinatown**. Its crescent-shaped street is lined with restored shophouses and restaurants, as well as a Buddhist temple.

Just a short walk away from the market, in the opposite direction, is the colonial-style, apricot-colored **Istana Maziah**, which is the sultan's palace. It is closed to the public except for some ceremonial occasions. Nearby is the beautiful **Masjid**

Zainal Abidin, with golden domes and a single, towering minaret. A number of fascinating sights are within easy reach of the capital, including the **Terengganu State Museum Complex**, the **Masjid Tengku Tengah Zaharah**, and the island of Pulau Duyung *(see p149)*, which is host to the prestigious Monsoon Cup yachting race.

🏛 Terengganu State Museum Complex

Losong, 2 miles (3 km) SW of Kuala Terengganu. **Tel** (09) 622-1444. **Open** 9am–5pm daily. **Closed** noon–3pm Fri. 🎫

One of the largest museums in Southeast Asia, Muzium Negeri Terengganu, or Terengganu State Museum Complex, consists of several buildings sprawled across landscaped gardens. The main building, which is a reproduction of a

traditional Malay stilt house, contains displays of textiles, handicrafts, Islamic artifacts, and a gallery dedicated to the state's petroleum industry. Within the grounds are several traditional Malay boats and houses as well as a maritime museum. The highlight of the complex, however, is the **Istana Tengku Long**, a wooden palace that dates back to 1880, with exhibits of royal artifacts.

🕌 Masjid Tengku Tengah Zaharah

3 miles (5 km) SE of Kuala Terengganu. Owing to its location by the water, Masjid Tengku Tengah Zaharah is also referred to as the Floating Mosque. This sparkling white mosque is set in a park and combines modern and traditional Moorish architecture. The mosque is closed to non-Muslims.

Fresh vegetables at the Pasar Payang in Kuala Terengganu

Holidaymakers relaxing on one of the quiet, beautiful beaches of Pulau Perhentian Besar

⓬ Pulau Redang

38 miles (62 km) N of Kuala Terengganu. from Merang and Kuala Terengganu.
redang.org

One of the largest and most beautiful of the east coast islands, Pulau Redang is also the most developed. It is set at the center of the Redang Archipelago, a group of nine islands that together constitute a protected marine park. With crystal-clear waters and a wealth of marine life sustained by some of Malaysia's best coral reefs, the island offers excellent diving and snorkeling opportunities. Sadly, silt and building waste have damaged the coral, but active efforts are being made to prevent further damage and even snorkeling has been restricted to certain parts of the reef. The permitted areas do, however, offer superb opportunities for underwater exploration. The waters also contain the historic wrecks of two British warships, HMS *Repulse* and HMS *Prince of Wales*, which were sunk off Pulau Redang by the Japanese during World War II.

The island's beaches are set against a backdrop of verdant jungle-clad hills. **Pasir Panjang** and **Teluk Dalam Kecil**, two of the best beaches, occupy the eastern coast and have most of the resorts. Kampung Air, Pulau Redang's main village, sits at the center of the island.

Most travelers visit the island on a package tour but dive trips can also be arranged from the Perhentian Islands.

⓭ Perhentian Islands

12 miles (20 km) NW of Kuala Terengganu. from Kuala Besut.

Located off the Terengganu coast, **Pulau Perhentian Besar** and **Pulau Perhentian Kecil** together comprise the Perhentian Islands, which means stopping-place islands. Breathtakingly beautiful, the islands have inevitably attracted a great deal of development but still retain their appeal. Both islands feature white-sand beaches and an aquamarine sea that is home to spectacular coral reefs teeming with an astounding variety of marine life. Besides diving and snorkeling, other activities available on the islands include sailing, windsurfing, and jungle walks.

Among the beaches on Pulau Perhentian Besar is the exquisite **Three Coves Bay**, a group of three beaches separated by rocky outcrops. This sheltered spot is where green and hawksbill turtles lay their eggs between May and September, when the bay is closed to visitors.

Snorkeling in the crystal-clear waters off the east coast islands

Pulau Perhentian Kecil is smaller than Pulau Perhentian Besar, but is otherwise an exact replica of it, with beautiful beaches, coconut palms, and azure waters. A small village on its southeastern coast is inhabited by people originally from Sulawesi in Indonesia. The island's main attraction is the east-facing **Pasir Panjang**, or Long Beach.

Of the two islands, the more expensive accommodations, with quieter ambience, are available in Perhentian Besar. Dozens of resorts and guesthouses are clustered around the southwestern shore. With the vast abundance of cheaper hotels and restaurants, Perhentian Kecil is attractive to backpackers.

The islands are usually packed during the peak season between late May and September, and finding accommodation is difficult. It is worth exploring options on both islands since the narrow strait separating them is easily crossed by boat. Getting around the islands is simple. There are some good walking trails but the best way to hop between beaches is by boat, which can be arranged by most resort and chalet owners.

Northwest of these islands lie the smaller, uninhabited **Pulau Susu** group covered in virgin forests. They provide one of the best diving sites in the region.

For hotels and restaurants see pp280–81 and pp295–6

Boatbuilders of Pulau Duyung

Just off the western waterfront of Kuala Terengganu lies Pulau Duyung where an ancient tradition of boatbuilding still thrives. Decorated vessels, called *bangau*, were once made all along the east coast, from Kota Bharu to Kuantan and beyond. Primarily used as fishing boats, these wooden craft are constructed by master boatbuilders using techniques passed down through many generations and it is believed that they are built entirely from memory. Each boat is painted in bright colors and painstakingly decorated with individual designs, making them unique. The island is accessible via a causeway from Kuala Terengganu and by ferry from a jetty near the Seri Malaysia Hotel.

Local shipyards and workshops are scattered throughout the island and visitors are usually welcome to see the boatbuilders at work. Most of the boats are used by local fishermen, but their exquisite craftsmanship has won them international acclaim.

Boat Design

Most boat designs feature representational characters, often derived from Hindu mythology. However, these are becoming rarer as boat designers are increasingly turning to non-representational Islamic art such as the elaborate geometric arabesque pattern.

Stylized prows are carved and painted to represent shadow puppets, birds, and Garuda, a bird from Hindu mythology.

Rows of vibrant fishing boats line the beaches of Pulau Duyung. Originally propelled by oars or sails, many of the boats today are fitted with removable motor engines, both for convenience as well as modernity.

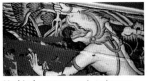

Mythical creatures, such as dragons and demons, appear to be derived from Hindu epics such as the *Ramayana*.

The boats need to be brought ashore every day, far away from treacherous waves and close to the tree line. Therefore, they are created with an expert blend of functionality and aesthetics: sturdy in order to withstand the strongest of storms, yet light enough to be easily pulled out of the water.

⑭ Kota Bharu

Situated in the northeast corner of the peninsula, near the mouth of Sungai Kelantan, Kota Bharu, or new fort in Malay, is the state capital of Kelantan, and perhaps the most traditional Malay and predominantly Muslim city in the country. A modern city on the surface, Kota Bharu is a repository of culture, crafts, and religion. It is rich in palaces, museums, and mosques, and offers a fine regional cuisine. Traditional skills and customs such as kite-flying, silver-working, and weaving thrive here. Prayer times are rigorously observed, when all activity comes to a standstill, especially on Fridays, the Muslim holy day. Most of the city's attractions lie in its northeast section, at the heart of which is the Pasar Besar, one of the most vibrant markets in the country. Kota Bharu is also a good base to explore the surrounding region.

Elegantly furnished dining room at Istana Batu, now the Royal Museum

🏛 Istana Batu

Jalan Istana. **Tel** (09) 748-2266.
Open 8:30am–4:45pm Sat–Thu. 🖼
The sky-blue Istana Batu, or stone palace, completed in 1939 by Sultan Ismail, was given by him as a wedding gift to his nephew Sultan Yahya. Once used as a guesthouse for visiting royalty and a wedding venue for the sultan's family, it has been made into the Royal Museum. Rooms preserved in their original state display royal artifacts such as old family pictures and glassware.

🏛 Istana Balai Besar

Jalan Tengku Seri Akar.
Closed to public.
Standing at the very center of town, surrounded by a wooden fort, Istana Balai Besar is a traditional Kelantan palace. Built in 1844 by Sultan Muhammad II, it served as the official residence of the royal family of Kelantan for

many years. This unique Malay palace has Thai architectural influences in its design. The throne room and the audience hall are used on important royal occasions and official state functions. The palace is closed to the public but visitors can view the beautiful façade.

🏛 Istana Jahar

Jalan Sultan. **Tel** (09) 744-4666.
Open 8:30am–5:45pm Sat–Thu. 🖼
Built by Sultan Ahmad in 1887 for his son Long Kundur, Istana Jahar remains an outstanding example of traditional Kelantan wooden architecture, with delicately carved beams, panels, and iron grilles. It is now the **Museum of Royal Traditions and Custom**. Its collections include textiles, brass and silverware, and artifacts related to various royal rituals and ceremonies, such as weddings and births. The Weapons Gallery displays spears, old *keris*, and other weapons. Perhaps the most impressive among all the

exhibits is the *singakerti*, an impressive royal carriage shaped in the form of a mythical beast.

The towering Muhammadi Mosque, northwest of the city center

⬛ Muhammadi Mosque

Jalan Sultanah Zainab.
Near the palaces, which are clustered near Padang Merdeka, the imposing Muhammadi Mosque was built in 1926 during the reign of Sultan Ismail IV. Known locally as the Brick Mosque, it serves as the center for Muslim *dawah*, or missionary activity in Kelantan. Visitors should dress conservatively, ensuring that their arms and legs are covered. Non-Muslims are not allowed to enter during prayer times.

🏛 Islamic Museum

Jalan Sultan. **Tel** (09) 744-0102.
Open 10:30am–5:45pm Sat–Thu. 🖼
Close to the Muhammadi Mosque is the beautiful old wooden building of the Islamic Museum, decorated with fine carvings. Formerly known as the Serambi Makkah, or veranda to Mecca, it functioned as a religious college, the first of its kind in Kelantan. It also

The green and white façade of the Islamic Museum

symbolized the prominence of Islam in the state. The museum now houses a display of photographs and artifacts that give an account of the history of Islam in the state.

🏛 World War II Memorial Museum

Jalan Sultan. **Open** 8:30am–4:45pm Sat–Thu. 🖼

Located in the old Bank Kerapu, the World War II Memorial Museum contains more than 1,000 exhibits, pictures, and guns that document the Japanese occupation of Kelantan during the Second World War. Kota Bharu was the landing point for the Japanese forces in Malaysia, on December 8, 1941. During the invasion the bank also functioned as the headquarters of the Japanese secret police, or *kempetai*. Another display of photographs and arms dates from the years of the Emergency, when British and Malay troops fought a long-running struggle against the Chinese Communist Party of Malaya between 1948 and 1960. An upstairs gallery describes the history of prewar Kelantan.

🏛 Gelanggang Seni

Jalan Mahmood. **Tel** (09) 744-3124. **Open** timings vary, call to confirm; free shows Mon, Wed, Fri afternoons

and evenings Mar–Oct, except during the Ramadan period.

The city's premier cultural center, Gelanggang Seni organizes cultural shows and exhibitions to showcase a wide variety of traditional Kelantan arts and sports, many of which are in danger of dying out. There are free performances of *silat*, a Malay martial art form, and *mak yong* and *manohra*, traditional dance-dramas accompanied by *gamelan* music. Drummers perform on huge *rebana*, drums made out of hollowed logs, and *kertok*, smaller coconut drums. The center presents displays of *gasing*, the traditional game of wooden top-spinning, and

kite-flying using huge Kelantan moon kites called *wau bulan*. There are also performances of spellbinding shadow-puppet plays called *wayang kulit*, using characters and stories from the fascinating Hindu epics of the *Ramayana* and the *Mahabharata*.

A traditional kite-maker surrounded by colorful kites in Kota Bharu

Kota Bharu City Center

① Istana Batu
② Istana Balai Besar
③ Istana Jahar
④ Muhammadi Mosque
⑤ Islamic Museum
⑥ World War II Memorial Museum
⑦ Gelanggang Seni

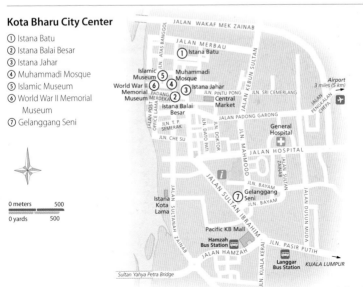

| 0 meters | 500 |
| 0 yards | 500 |

For keys to symbols *see back flap*

The elaborate temple roof of Wat Phothivihan

⑮ Tumpat

9 miles (15 km) NW of Kota Bharu.
🚌 🚊 from Kota Bharu.

Located in a predominantly agricultural region, the little town of Tumpat in Kelantan is a center of the Orang Syam people. It is also an important transport hub for southbound travelers on the Jungle Railway track or northbound travelers to nearby Thailand.

Tumpat is a good place to start exploring the region's numerous Thai Buddhist temples, always a surprising and colorful sight in the otherwise strictly Islamic Kelantan.

⑯ Pantai Dasar Sabak

8 miles (13 km) NE of Kota Bharu.
🚊 from Kota Bharu.

To the north and east of Kota Bharu are several attractive beaches overlooking the South China Sea. One of the most easily accessible is Pantai Dasar Sabak. Situated near the Malay fishing village of Sering, it is a dazzling stretch of palm-lined beach and has a significant history. On December 8, 1941, the Imperial Japanese Navy troops landed here in one of Japan's first acts of aggression during World War II.

It is possible to combine an excursion to the beach with an opportunity to watch the return of the local fishing fleet in the afternoon, and perhaps to buy some fresh seafood for

cooking on the spot. Visitors should bear in mind that the east coast of Kelantan is predominantly Malay Muslim, and dressing modestly is advisable.

⑰ Wat Phothivihan

2 miles (3 km) S of Chabang Empat, near Tumpat. 🚊 from Kota Bharu or Tumpat. 🕐 7am–5pm daily.
🎎 Vesak Day (Apr/May).

Within Kelantan, the lives of Thai Buddhists are organized around 20 or so monasteries. One of the most interesting of these, Wat Phothivihan is worth visiting for its elaborate temple roof and saffron-clad monks, both of which form a marked contrast to the surrounding Muslim villages.

Built in 1973 by chief abbot Phra Krurasapia Chakorn, the monastery attracts thousands of Thai pilgrims every year. As with most Thai temples, the

buildings and grounds are large and imposing. The main attraction here is a 131-ft- (40-m-) long *phra non*, or Reclining Buddha that was built in 1975.

Wat Phothivihan is a social, cultural, and spiritual center for Thai, Chinese, and Indian worshipers. Its monks are always eager to show vistors around. The temples and groves also elicit the secular interest of Muslims who view it as a tourist attraction.

⑱ Wat Machimmaram

Kampung Jubakar, near Tumpat.
🚊 from Kota Bharu or Tumpat.
🕐 7am–5pm daily. 🎎 Vesak Day (Apr/May).

One of the many Buddhist temples in the Thai villages of Kelantan, Wat Machimmaram is located in the village of Kampung Jubakar on the main road between Kota Bharu and the Thai border. As in neighboring Thailand, the *ketek*, or temple, has familiar lotus-shaped corner stones, gilded spires of venerable *chedi*, or stupas, lacquered doors, and shuttered windows. Its most outstanding feature is a statue of the Seated Buddha, constructed by local Thai Buddhists and said to be the largest in Southeast Asia. At about 105 ft (32 m), the statue towers over the surrounding Kelantan plains, making a definite statement about the presence of Theravada Buddhism in this predominantly Islamic state.

A golden seated Buddha and ornate pillars at Wat Machimmaram

⑲ The Jungle Railway

One of the most delightful ways of exploring the wild interior of Peninsular Malaysia is by the Jungle Railway, officially called the East Coast Line. Considered an engineering marvel when it was completed in 1931, it created links between the east coast state of Kelantan with the west coast states of Kedah, Perak, and Penang. This line winds its way south from Kelantan through the spectacular jungle gorges of Kuala Lipis to join the main line from Singapore to Kuala Lumpur at Gemas.

Tips for Travelers

Starting point: Tumpat, 9 miles (15 km) from Kota Bharu.
Getting there: by taxi, or by bus no. 27, 27A, and 43 from Central Bus Station, Kota Bharu.
Duration: 15 hours by daytime slow train from Tumpat to Gemas; 10 hours by overnight express train.

② Kuala Krai
The Railway passes by the banks of the Sungai Kelantan near the settlement of Kuala Krai, which is surrounded by rubber plantations and dense rain forest.

④ Kuala Lipis
Located at the confluence of Jelai and Lipis rivers, this former gold-mining town is known for its tranquility and lovely colonial architecture.

① Tumpat
The line starts at Tumpat in the north, a small agricultural town in rural Kelantan that is chiefly noted for the several Thai temples in its vicinity.

③ Gua Musang
An isolated town, Gua Masang is known for its caves and trekking opportunities, but is dependent on timber for its economic survival.

⑤ Jerantut
A popular gateway to Taman Negara (see pp144–5), this small town has several restaurants and accommodation options.

⑥ Gemas
The Jungle Railway ends at Gemas, a busy junction town with excellent road and rail links to Kuala Lumpur and Johor Bahru.

Key

═══ Minor road
─·─ Railroad
▬·▬ International border
─·─ State border
△ Peak

0 km — 50
0 miles — 50

For keys to symbols *see back flap*

SARAWAK

Teeming with natural wonders, including precipitous mountains, lush rain forests, abundant wildlife, and some of the world's largest caves, Sarawak is nicknamed the Land of the Hornbill. This diversity of flora and fauna, along with Sarawak's swashbuckling history and the cultural heritage of its indigenous people, attracts increasing numbers of visitors to the state.

Sarawak's first inhabitants were cave-dwelling hunter-gatherers who lived here about 40,000 years ago. Evidence of the existence of early settlements was discovered in 1958 at Niah Caves in the northeast of the state, testifying to Sarawak's long, although largely unwritten, history of human habitation.

Until the mid-19th century, the region was governed by the Sultan of Brunei whose imposition of heavy taxes led to frequent rebellions by local indigenous groups. During one such outbreak in 1839, the English adventurer James Brooke entered the service of the Sultan and subdued the rebels. For this, he was rewarded with the title of Rajah, becoming the first of the White Rajahs *(see p163)* who ruled an area the size of Britain as their private kingdom for over a century. Sarawak joined the Federation of Malaysia in 1963.

The state is blessed with an abundance of natural resources, and petroleum and forestry became the mainstay of Sarawak's economy in the 20th century. Sarawak's population of 2.4 million largely comprises the indigenous people known collectively as Dayaks, while the remaining minority are the Orang Ulu.

Most people live in the southwest of the province, in and around the historic capital of Kuching. The city is an excellent base for visiting the traditional Dayak longhouses, wildlife reserves, and national parks scattered throughout the province. The breathtaking ancient limestone pinnacles at Mulu National Park are excellent for trekking and rock climbing. These, together with Niah Caves and Bako National Park – one of Sarawak's oldest national parks – are the highlights of a visit to the state.

Mother and baby orangutan moving through the trees at Semenggoh Nature Reserve

◀ Trekking to the giant caves of Mulu National Park

Exploring Sarawak

Located in northwest Borneo, Sarawak is the largest state in Malaysia and is famous for its diversity of flora and fauna. Within easy reach of its capital, Kuching, are beautiful national parks and scenic beaches. Flanked by longhouse settlements of the Dayaks, the Batang Rajang meanders through the heart of the state as the main channel of communication with the towns of Sibu, Kapit, and Belaga. In the northeast of the state, the Niah Caves are a site of archaeological significance, while the limestone outcrops at Mulu National Park are a climber's dream. Brunei, one of the world's smallest countries, is situated on the northern coast.

The opulent façade of Masjid Jamek, or Friday Mosque, Brunei

Sights at a Glance

Towns, Cities, and Regions
1 Kuching pp160–63
3 Santubong
7 Sematan
14 Sibu
15 Kapit
16 Belaga
17 Mukah
18 Bintulu
20 Miri
26 Brunei pp178–9

Parks and Preserves
6 Kubah National Park and Matang Wildlife Center
8 Tanjung Datu National Park

9 Gunung Gading National Park
11 Semenggoh Wildlife Centre
12 Bako National Park pp168–9
19 Similajau National Park
21 Niah Caves National Park
22 Lambir Hills National Park
23 Loagan Bunut National Park
25 Mulu National Park pp176–7

Rivers
2 Sungai Santubong
13 Batang Rajang

Areas of Natural Beauty
10 Wind Cave and Fairy Cave
24 Kelabit Highlands

Themed Attractions
5 Sarawak Cultural Village

Islands and Beaches
4 Damai Beach

South China Sea

MUKAH 🔲 17

Baling

Sirik
Matu Kut
Daro
Narub
Nanga Tamin
Ru Cha
Mar
Sekuau

🔲 14 SIBU

BAT. RAJ.

Belawai
Binatang *Rajang*
Sarikei
Grigat
Julau Kanowit
Roban Pakan
Saratok Uka
Kabong Rumah
Penom Rumah Layang Rumah Tungk.
Beladin Pusa
Debak
Layar

TANJUNG DATU NATIONAL PARK 8

SEMATAN 7
SARAWAK CULTURAL VILLAGE
GUNUNG GADING NP 9
DAMAI BEACH
BAKO NATIONAL PARK
5 4 3 12
SANTUBONG
2 SUNGAI SANTUBONG
KUBAH NP 6
WIND CAVE AND FAIRY CAVE 10
Bau
1 KUCHING
Siburan
SEMENGGOH WILDLIFE CENTRE 11
Gedong
Simunjan
Lupar
Betong
Bandar Sri Aman
Engkilili
Batang Ai Reservoir
Ensabang
Lubok Antu

0 kilometers 50
0 miles 50

Key

═══ Highway

──── Major road

┄┄┄ Minor road

▬▬▬ International border

▬▬▬ State border

△ Peak

Getting Around

Domestic flights connect most towns in Sarawak and are ideal for visitors with limited time. For those with a more leisurely schedule, boat rides are an exciting way of getting to the remote villages and national parks and are the most common mode of local transport. There are speedy passenger *ekspres* boats as well as longboats for long- and short-haul journeys. Because of the rugged terrain, the road network in Sarawak is limited to a highway between Kuching and the Brunei border, plus a few short routes from Kuching to places such as Bako and Semantan.

Aerial view of mangrove forests surrounding Sungai Sarawak

For keys to symbols *see back flap*

● Kuching

The capital of Sarawak, Kuching is one of Malaysia's most attractive cities with historic buildings juxtaposed against modern high-rises and restaurants. It became the capital of Rajah James Brooke's empire in the mid-19th century and was known as Sarawak until 1872 when its name was officially changed to Kuching. Long a confluence of Malay, Chinese, Indian, and indigenous people, such as the Iban and Bidayuh, Kuching reflects its varied cultural influences. Although the city sprawls both to the north and south of Sungai Sarawak, the main sights of interest, such as the waterfront, colonial buildings, and ethnic souvenir shops, are all concentrated around the south bank of the Kuching waterfront.

Sungai Sarawak meandering through the city of Kuching

🏛 Sarawak Museum

Jalan Tun Haji Openg. **Tel** (082) 244-232. **Open** 9am–4:45pm Mon–Fri, 10am–4pm Sat, Sun & public hols. 📷 🔲 **museum.sarawak.gov.my**

Perhaps one of Malaysia's finest museums, the Sarawak Museum provides an overview of the province's history and ethnography. The artifacts of the museum are housed in two buildings. The Ethnology Museum is set in a colonial mansion opened in 1891 at the suggestion of naturalist Alfred Wallace who discovered many of Sarawak's endemic species of flora and fauna. The natural science section, on the first floor, has stuffed specimens of many of Sarawak's best-known species, such as rhinoceros hornbills, hawksbill turtles, and proboscis monkeys. On the upper floor is an introduction to the traditional lifestyles of Sarawak's main indigenous groups, with displays of handicrafts, traditional

Detail of a burial pole at Sarawak Museum

dress, ceremonial artifacts, musical instruments, and various tools such as the three-pronged pricker that is used by the Iban to create tattoos. Among the highlights on display are a replica of an Iban longhouse, Iban war totems, and early 20th-century Chinese glazed jars. Rotating art exhibitions are held in the Tun Abdul Razak Hall, which is accessible by a footbridge. There is also an aquarium.

🏛 Islamic Heritage Museum

Jalan P. Ramlee. **Tel** (082) 244-232. **Open** 9am–4:45pm Mon–Fri, 10am–4pm Sat, Sun & public hols. 📷 🔲 **museum.sarawak.gov.my**

Housed in a restored colonial building that was constructed in 1930 and once functioned as a school to train Malay teachers, the Islamic Heritage Museum presents the history of Islam and its spread in Sarawak as well as the rest of the Malay-Indonesian archipelago. Its seven galleries, each with a different theme, contain displays on traditional Islamic design, architecture, costumes, coins, jewelry, decorative arts, weapons, ceramics, domestic utensils, and weights and measures. The diverse artifacts have been very well preserved and the displays here are some of the best of any museum in Malaysia.

🏛 Textile Museum

Jalan Tun Haji Openg. **Open** 9am–4:30pm daily. 📷 🔲 **museum.sarawak.gov.my**

Located in the heart of the city, it is hard to miss the Pavilion, a building decorated with ornate ironwork. Built in 1907 as a hospital, it was used as a propaganda center by the invading Japanese army during World War II. Today, the Pavilion is home to the Textile Museum. Its two floors contain exhibits of everyday clothes worn by the various indigenous groups of Sarawak, as well as costumes worn for weddings and other ceremonies. There are also models of women engaged in cloth spinning, weaving, and dyeing. Traditional *songket* and *ikat* are also on display.

🏛 Tun Jugah Gallery

Level 4, Tun Jugah, 18 Jalan Tunku Abdul Rahman. **Tel** (082) 239-672. 🔲 **tunjugahfoundation.org.my**

Vivid and fascinating textiles can also be seen at the Tun Jugah Gallery. Here, local people are reviving the art of making Iban cloths, which use especially intricate weaving patterns, and are growing the traditional plants used to dye them.

🏛 Round Tower

Jalan Tun Haji Openg. **Tel** (082) 245-652. **Open** 8:30am–12:30pm & 2–5pm Mon–Fri; 8:30am–noon Sat & Sun.

Built in the 1880s, the Round Tower was originally intended to be a fort, as a defence against the arrival of pirates, but functioned instead as a dispensary in its early days. It now houses the **Sarawak Crafts Council**, which has showrooms that feature some of the province's finest handicrafts, with regular demonstrations.

Colonial buildings with ironwood roofs in the Courthouse Complex

Jalan India

Near the waterfront. Masjid Bandaraya:
Open 9am–3pm Sat–Thu. **Closed** Fri.

On the western edge of the city center, near the main produce market on Jalan Gambier, the pedestrianized Jalan India is one of Kuching's most popular shopping streets. Most of the shops are fronted by colonial-style arches and sell textiles, shoes, brassware, souvenirs and household goods. Dominating the western end of the street is the large and impressive **Masjid Bandaraya**, or City Mosque, topped with gilded cupolas. Built in 1968 to replace an old wooden mosque, it quickly became one of the city's most distinctive landmarks. Non-Muslims, dressed appropriately, are allowed to enter except at prayer times. The mosque has now been superseded in size by the **State Mosque** across the river at Petrajaya, which can accommodate 14,000 worshipers.

Courthouse Complex

Junction of Main Bazaar and Jalan Tun
Haji Openg. **Closed** Mon.

A splendid example of Kuching's colonial heritage, the Courthouse Complex is a cluster of buildings covered with ironwood roofs that are supported by Romanesque and regal columns. It was built in 1871 as the seat of Sarawak's government, which remained its function until 1973. The state's law courts continue to operate from here, and the main court chamber, with walls and ceiling covered with murals depicting rural life in Sarawak, is worth visiting. The **Clock Tower** at the front of the complex was added in 1883 and the granite **Charles Brooke Memorial** in 1925. At the four corners of the memorial are stone figures representing the principal ethnic groups of Sarawak – the Dayaks, Malays, Chinese, and Orang Ulu. The complex houses a café and the Sarawak Tourism Board's **Visitor Information Center**.

Kuching City Center

1. Sarawak Museum
2. Islamic Heritage Museum
3. Textile Museum
4. Tun Jugah Gallery
5. Round Tower
6. Jalan India
7. Courthouse Complex
8. Square Tower
9. Kuching Waterfront
10. Tua Pek Kong
11. Fort Margherita

For keys to symbols *see back flap*

The historic Square Tower, a reminder of the Brooke era

🏚 Square Tower

Main Bazaar. **Tel** (082) 426-093.
Open 10am–4pm daily.

In 1879, the Square Tower was built by Rajah Charles Brooke just north of the Courthouse to replace a wooden fort that had been burnt down by Chinese gold miners during a rebellion in 1857. However, the tower was never again needed as a defensive structure and over the years it was put to other uses, including a brief role as a prison and later even as a ballroom. The tower is one of the few buildings that remain from the Brooke era.

🏚 Kuching Waterfront

Between Square Tower and Hilton Hotel. 🛍 🍴 stalls in the evening.
Sarawak Steamship Building:
Main Bazaar. **Open** daily.
Chinese History Museum: Main Bazaar. **Tel** (082) 231-520.
Open 9am–6pm Sat–Thu.

A stroll along the Kuching waterfront is one of the highlights of a visit to the city. In the mid-1990s, several dilapidated warehouses along the waterfront were demolished and an extensive renovation project transformed this stretch into a lovely riverside promenade. Landscaped gardens, sculptures, cafés, food stalls, and benches now embellish this strip. Several plaques along the path mark historical spots. It also offers spectacular views of the Astana and Fort Margherita on the north bank of Sungai Sarawak,

and has rapidly grown into one of the city's most popular spots for jogging, dining, strolling, and enjoying a spectacular sunset over the river. Sampan (boat) rides are available to cross the river or for longer cruises.

Set back a little from the waterfront, the Main Bazaar is the city's oldest street and is packed with shops. Two of the most significant buildings on this street, both carefully restored, are the **Sarawak Steamship Building** and **Chinese History Museum**. The former, built in 1930, is now home to the Kuching Waterfront Bazaar, which has several souvenir and handicrafts stalls. The museum was built by Rajah Charles Brooke in 1911 and once functioned as the Chinese Chamber of Commerce. Today, however, the museum provides an

overview of the evolution of the Chinese community in Sarawak through photographs, artifacts, documents such as maps of early trade routes, and information about their traditional trading activities.

🏯 Tua Pek Kong

Jalan Tunku Abdul Rahman.
Open 6am–10pm daily.
🎎 Chinese New Year (Feb).

Located opposite the Chinese History Museum and overlooking the river, Tua Pek Kong is the oldest Taoist temple in Kuching, dating back to 1876. It is thought that the current structure was preceded by a Chinese temple that existed here in the late 18th century. Vibrantly colored and intricately decorated, the temple is dedicated to Tua Pek Kong, the patron saint of merchants, and is always very busy. It is built on a site carefully chosen for its geomancy, according to Chinese tradition. The Wang Kang festival to commemorate the dead is also held here.

🏰 Fort Margherita

North bank of Sungai Sarawak.
🚤 from the jetty near the Square Tower. **Closed** to the public.

Close to the Astana, along the riverbank to the east, is Fort Margherita, with crenellated, whitewashed walls and large cannons. This structure, built in 1879 by Rajah Charles Brooke and named for his wife, was the second fort to be built on the site. The first, built by his uncle,

An early morning view of the Kuching waterfront

James Brooke, was burnt to the ground by rebel Chinese gold miners in 1857. Commanding a sweeping view of Sungai Sarawak, Fort Margherita was built to protect Kuching against attack from pirates and other enemies approaching the town by the river route. However, it never fulfilled its intended purpose as Kuching did not come under attack until World War II when the Japanese took control of the entire city.

The stately Astana on the north bank of Sungai Sarawak

An imposing watch tower at Fort Margherita in Kuching

The White Rajahs

In 1839, British explorer James Brooke found Sarawak in the grip of a rebellion by the local Dayaks against the rule of the Sultan of Brunei. After his success in quelling the uprising, he was granted the title of Rajah of Sarawak in 1841, establishing an empire that was to last for over a century. At the time of James Brooke's death in 1868, his territory only covered what is now the southwest corner of Sarawak – the area around Kuching. It was his successor and nephew, Charles Brooke, who was responsible for expanding Sarawak to the current size, and also for commissioning

Sir James Brooke

most of the town's colonial buildings. A stickler for detail, he made frequent unannounced inspections of his officers, and any slack conduct was severely punished. Upon his death in 1917, Charles was succeeded by his son, Charles Vyner Brooke, and for a while Sarawak was run as a personal fiefdom. This ended with the Japanese invasion in 1941. After World War II, Vyner Brooke ceded the territory to Britain, and in 1963 it became part of the Federation of Malaysia.

Unfortunately, the fort has been very poorly maintained and is closed to the public.

Astana

North bank of Sungai Sarawak. 🚤 from the jetty near the Square Tower.

On the river's north bank lies Kuching's most important historical building, the impressive Astana. The name is a local version of the Malay word *istana*, meaning palace. The Astana was built in 1870 by Rajah Charles Brooke as a gift to his bride, Margaret. She later reminisced about her time here in her 1913 memoir, *My Life in Sarawak*.

Set among manicured lawns and offering a lovely view of the Courthouse on the south bank, the palace consists of three elegant bungalows with wooden shingle roofs. Charles Brooke is said to have grown betel nut on the palace grounds so that he could offer it to visiting Dayak chiefs. The Astana still functions as the official residence of the governor of Sarawak, and is not open to the public.

Cat Statues

Kuching means cat in Malay and although the origin of the city's name is uncertain, there are several statues of cats in the town, giving it a unique identity. They are all on the south bank of Sungai Sarawak, and include a small statue on the waterfront just east of the Chinese History Museum, a larger one opposite the Hilton Kuching on Jalan Tun Abdul Rahman, and a third at the base of a pillar farther east along Jalan Pandungan. The biggest statue, the 5-ft- (1.5-m-) tall Great Cat of Kuching, is at the junction of Jalan Padungan and Jalan Central.

Cat Museum

North of Kuching City Hall. **Tel** (082) 446-688. 🚌 Petra Jaya bus 2C or 2D. **Open** 9am–5pm Tue–Sun. **Closed** Mon & public hols. 📷 RM3 for use of camera, RM5 for use of video.

Located in the new town of Petra Jaya, on the north bank of the river, the rather kitsch Cat Museum claims to be one of the few such museums in the world dedicated exclusively to cats. It covers everything to do with cats, and the exhibits include cat-related art, stamps, photographs, music, movies, and even Garfield comic strips.

❷ Sungai Santubong

12 miles (20 km) N of Kuching.
🚌 tour bus to Santubong jetty.
🚤 tour boats between 4 and 5pm.
🚗 from Kuching.

After meandering through the plains around Kuching, Sungai Santubong flows through Sarawak into the South China Sea. During the dry season, between March and October, groups of the rare Irrawaddy dolphin are sometimes seen feeding and playing around the mouth of the river. These small, snub-nosed dolphins are often difficult to spot as they do not leap out of the water like their seafaring cousins. Nevertheless, the experience of watching these unusual creatures is a major draw on the popular boat trips.

Some cruises continue down the adjoining Sungai Salak to **Kuching Wetlands National Park**. Covering a vast expanse of saline mangrove swamps and patches of scrubland, the wetlands also include a network of small water channels and tidal creeks. The swamps are inhabited by a variety of wildlife, including crocodiles, proboscis monkeys, lorises, and colorful birds. In the evenings, large groups of fireflies illuminate the riverside trees. River cruises are the only way to explore the wetlands, and a number of tour operators in Kuching offer trips.

🗺 Kuching Wetlands National Park

9 miles (15 km) N of Kuching.
🚤 🚫 🚗

Lagoon-style pool at the Holiday Inn Resort at Damai Beach

❸ Santubong

19 miles (32 km) N of Kuching.
🚐 800. 🚌 Petra Jaya bus 2B.

This fishing village sits near Sungai Santubong in the shadow of the 2,657-ft (810-m) Gunung Santubong. During the Tang and Sung dynasties, which lasted from the 9th century to the 13th century, Santubong was an important trading center. Today, it is merely a small village but it is worth visiting for the colorful wooden houses built on stilts and fishing boats on the beach, which are very photogenic. The morning is the liveliest time in Santubong when the fishermen sell their daily catch at the quay. The cafés nearby are well known for their excellent seafood.

From the main road into Santubong is a small, easy-to-miss turning which leads to **Sungai Jaong**, one of the most important archaeological sites in Sarawak. Among its artifacts are ancient Buddhist and Hindu rock carvings, thought to be about 1,000 years old. A reclining human figure is still well defined, but many other carvings have eroded.

❹ Damai Beach

21 miles (35 km) N of Kuching.
🚌 Petra Jaya bus 2B. 🏄 🚣 🏕 ⛰

On the west coast of the Santubong Peninsula, Damai is one of Sarawak's prettiest beaches. Only a short journey from Kuching, and featuring some beautifully designed resorts, the beach is a popular tourist destination and can get quite crowded on weekends. There is a wide selection of watersports on offer, including sailing, snorkeling, and windsurfing, as well as other activities such as mountain biking and golf. Cafés and restaurants here have gained a reputation for their superb fresh seafood dishes.

Picturesque trails around Gunung Santubong begin here and trekking is a popular activity for visitors to Damai Beach. The Santubong Jungle Trek, with blue trail markers, is an easy, circular 1-mile (1.6-km) walk that starts at the Damai Beach Resort. A more challenging route that also begins here is the Gunung Santubong Summit Trek, winding up to the top. The trail, with red markers, takes 5 to 7 hours to complete. It also requires a good level of fitness, sturdy hiking shoes, and plenty of drinking water. The resorts at Damai can arrange for guides.

Gunung Santubong towering over Sungai Santubong

❺ Sarawak Cultural Village

21 miles (35 km) N of Kuching. **Tel**
(082) 846-411. 🚌 tour bus and Petra
Jaya bus 2B, 15. **Open** 9am– 5:15pm
daily; cultural shows at 11:30am and
4pm daily. 🖼 📷 🖼 Harvest
Festival (May), Rainforest World Music
Festival (Jul). 🆆 scv.com.my

Located at the foot of Gunung
Santubong, Sarawak Cultural
Village serves as an excellent
introduction to the cultural
traditions of Sarawak. Erected
by the Sarawak Development
Corporation in the early 1990s
to give visitors a taste of indigenous lifestyles, the village
comprises seven houses
clustered around a lake, each
a good example of the traditional dwellings built by the
main indigenous groups.
Iban, Bidayuh, and Orang Ulu
longhouses sit side by side
with a Melanau tall-house, a
Penan hut, a Chinese farm-
house and a Malay house.
Women and men of respective
groups live in these dwellings
and also demonstrate art
and craft skills, such as woodcarving, textile and basket-
weaving, sword-making,
and beadwork. Outside the
Melanau tall-house is a
demonstration of a traditional
sago press, while the process of
blowpipe-making can be seen
at the Penan hut. Visitors can
take part in 3- to 4-day courses
to learn a particular skill or
craft. A cultural show featuring
traditional music and dancers

Rainforest World Music Festival

In August each year, Sarawak Cultural Village hosts this festival, which
celebrates music from around the world. This 3-day event, which has
been held every year since 1998, previously featured musicians from as
far away as Mali, Mongolia, and Madagascar. The festival now also
provides a rare opportunity to hear
indigenous musicians from various
regions of Malaysia. Seminars and
workshops are held during the day,
spontaneous jam sessions take place
in the longhouses, and artistes
perform on outdoor stages in the
evenings. The exotic setting around a
lake against the backdrop of Gunung
Santubong makes for an electric
atmosphere. Accommodation is
available at the resorts on Damai
Beach, and frequent buses run from
Kuching for those who prefer to stay
in town. It is advisable to check the
official website (www.rwmf.net) for
information on events.

Jerry Kamit, a *sape* (lute-like
instrument) virtuoso

in elaborate costumes is held
daily at the village's indoor
theater. There is a well-regarded
restaurant at the village, too.

❻ Kubah National Park and Matang Wildlife Center

12 miles (20 km) W of Kuching.
Tel (082) 248-088. 🚌 from Kuching.
Open 8am–5:15pm daily. 🖼 🖼 ⚠
🆆 sarawakforestry.com

Encompassing 9 sq miles (22 sq
km), Kubah National Park is one
of the smallest and most
accessible parks in Sarawak. A
sandstone plateau and three
peaks – the 2,990-ft (911-m)
Gunung Serapi and the smaller

Gunung Selang and Gunung
Sendok – form the backdrop to
this wildlife haven. Among the
dipterocarp (hardwood) forests
and gentle waterfalls and
streams are more than 90
species of palms and a wide
variety of orchids. Although
there are bearded pigs, mouse
deer, and other wildlife, these
are rarely seen. Visitors are more
likely to spot birds such as the
maroon woodpecker or the
rufus-collared kingfisher.
    Several trails crisscross the
park and the mountains including the beautiful Waterfall Trail
that leads through split-level
falls and a 2- to 3-hour hike to
the mist-shrouded peak of
Gunung Serapi. **Matang Wildlife
Center** is nearby, but gains
mixed reviews for its care of
endangered species such as
orangutans, sambar deer,
hornbills, and proboscis
monkeys. Along the Pitcher Trail
are several varieties of the
carnivorous pitcher plant.
Accommodation for the parks
may be booked in advance at
the Visitor Information Center in
Kuching (see p161) or online at
www.ebooking.gov.my.

🗺 **Matang Wildlife Center**
8 miles (13 km) N of Kubah. **Tel** (082)
225-012. 🚌 to Kubah or Matang
Polytechnic, then local minibus. 🖼
🖼 🖼 ⚠

A Bidayuh woman weaving rattan baskets at the Sarawak Cultural Village

❼ Sematan

100 km (62 miles) W of Kuching.
🚹 2,300. 🚌 from Kuching to Lundu,
STC 17 from Lundu.

The coastal village of Sematan is a popular weekend retreat for Kuching residents. There is a long, quiet beach lined with coconut palms and colorful fishing boats are harbored in the bay. The village itself is small, consisting of a few rows of shophouses, a local market with food stalls that serve delicious fish dishes, and a jetty. The tides mean that swimming is not always advisable. Boats go from Sematan to Teluk Melano, a Malay fishing village nestled in a pretty bay on the Datu Peninsula. The village has a homestay program that is organized by the Malaysian Fisheries Board, which enables visitors to stay with local families. Boat trips are not possible in the monsoon season, from October to March. There is also an attractive hotel called Sematan Palm Beach Resort which is a popular place to stay. For a small fee non-residents can spend the day here and make use of the facilities, which include a swimming pool and bicycle and canoe hire.

Flowers at Tanjung Datu

❽ Tanjung Datu National Park

14 miles (23 km) from Sematan. 🚤 chartered from Sematan or Teluk Melano. **Open** Apr–Sep: 8am–5:15pm daily. 🅿 🅆 **sarawakforestry.com**

Occupying just 14 sq km (5 sq miles) on the westernmost tip of the state, Tanjung Datu is one of Sarawak's smaller, but most beautiful, national parks. It has two stunning beaches, Pasir Antu and Pasir Berunpu, backed by towering peaks. The real highlight of the park are the beautiful coral reefs, visible in the crystal-clear water and close enough to the shore to walk around. Artificial reefs farther out in the sea are accessible by boat. The park's lush rain forest is home to varied wildlife, so visitors are likely to hear gibbon-cries and may even spot dolphins and turtles near the shore. Tanjung Datu has four trails of varying lengths leading through an unspoilt forest and coastline. There are no facilities for visitors at the park, but given its natural beauty and the idyllic landscape, a day trip to the park is worth the effort. Permits for the park and entry tickets

Trekking through a lush trail at Gunung Gading National Park

should be obtained from the Visitor Information Center in Kuching (see p161).

❾ Gunung Gading National Park

50 miles (80 km) W of Kuching.
🚌 STC 17 from Lundu. ℹ **Tel** (082) 735-714 (Park HQ). **Open** 8:30am–5:15pm daily. 🅿 🏕 🛶 🅆 **sarawakforestry.com**

In 1983, Gunung Gading National Park was established as a conservation area for the world's largest flower, the rafflesia. Visitors can view the flowers from walkways which have been designed to prevent people from treading on the fragile young buds that sprout inconspicuously. The bud grows into a foul-smelling red flower with white specks, and reaches a width of up to 3 ft (1 m). This rare parasitic plant blooms at unpredictable times and lasts only a few days, therefore it is advisable to call the park ahead to check if one is in bloom. Visitors can also see *Amorphophallus*, a gigantic herbaceous plant of the aroid family.

The park sprawls across four jungle-clad mountains, Gunung Gading, Gunung Perigi, Gunung Lundu, and Gunung Sebuloh. Color-coded trails of varying levels of difficulty crisscross the park. The easiest is the Waterfall Trail which passes through seven cataracts. The challenging

Fishing boats docked at the Sematan jetty

Gunung Gading Trail leads up to the summit of the 2,985-ft (910-m) hill. Visitors will also find a natural pool near the Park Headquarters.

⑩ Wind Cave and Fairy Cave

31 miles (50 km) SW of Kuching. 🚌 STC 2 to Bau from Kuching, then taxi. **Tel** (082) 765-490. **Open** 8am–5:15pm daily. 🚗 from Kuching. 🆆 sarawakforestry.com

Two caves formed in a range of limestone cliffs located near the former gold-mining town of Bau make an interesting day trip from Kuching. Wind Cave, 2 miles (3 km) west of Bau, is made up of a network of underground streams that pass through the cave before joining Sungai Kayan. The cave's interior is filled with stalagmite and stalactite pillars. A boardwalk passes through the cave to the river at the other end, which is a popular spot for picnics and swimming. To protect the cave and its surrounding limestone forest, which is home to a number of rare plant species, including some types of palms, Wind Cave has been designated as a nature reserve.

Fairy Cave, 3 miles (5 km) farther south, is larger and accessed by a flight of steps leading up to the cave mouth. Its main chamber also contains stalagmite formations. One, thought to resemble Kuan Yin, the Chinese goddess of mercy, has transformed the chamber

Mother and baby orangutans at Semenggoh Wildlife Centre

into a popular shrine. Neither of the two caves is illuminated and flashlights are essential. Be aware than in the rainy season, the caves may be closed.

⑪ Semenggoh Wildlife Centre

15 miles (24 km) SW of Kuching. **Tel** (082) 618-325. 🚌 STC 6 from Kuching. **Open** 9–11am & 2–4pm daily. 🚗 🆆 sarawakforestry.com

This wildlife center functions as a rehabilitation center for honey bears, orangutans, crocodiles, monkeys, gibbons, hornbills, and porcupines, all of which were either orphaned due to hunting or rescued from cages where they were kept illegally as pets. Reintroducing orangutans to their natural habitat is the primary aim of this center and its orangutan rehabilitation program has been particularly successful, resulting in a thriving population of semi-wild orangutans inhabiting the surrounding forest. With the forest having reached its capacity to hold the primates, the program has now been transferred to the Matang Wildlife Center (see p165). Since the orangutans roam freely, spotting them is not guaranteed. The best chance to see them is feeding time, around 9am and 3pm.

There are also pleasant walking trails around the reserve. A Botanical Research Center here is dedicated to analyzing jungle plants with medicinal properties.

The Bidayuh

The Bidayuh are one of the largest indigenous Dayak groups living in Sarawak and have traditionally been farmers and hunters. Concentrated in the area west of Kuching, their longhouses dot the slopes of Anna Rais. Unlike other Dayak groups of Sarawak, they build their longhouses at the foot of hills rather than on riverbanks. The British referred to them as "Land Dayaks" to distinguish them from the "Sea Dayaks" – such as the Iban – who traveled everywhere by boat. The Bidayuh are particularly skilled at bamboo-carving, basket-weaving, and beadwork. Women can be seen sitting on the *ruai*, or communal veranda, making bead-covered hats that are used for special occasions. Among these is the Gawai Padi festival, held in early June, when Bidayuhs give thanks to the rice goddess for a bountiful harvest. The celebration involves singing, dancing, and drinking.

The terrace, *ruai*, of a Bidayuh longhouse

⑫ Bako National Park

Established in 1957, Bako was Sarawak's first national park. Spread across 10 sq miles (27 sq km), it nurtures vegetation that ranges from rain forest to swampland and mangrove forests to *kerangas*, or scrubland. With steep rocky cliffs punctuated by deep bays, white sandy beaches, and a mangrove-fringed coastline, Bako is a nature-lover's paradise. It is also one of the best parks in Malaysia for spotting rare animals, such as proboscis monkeys, bearded pigs, sambar deer, and macaques, which makes it a popular destination for wildlife enthusiasts. Though the park can be visited on a day trip, the chances of wildlife sightings are higher in the early morning and in the evening, so an overnight stay is recommended.

South China Sea

Area of map illustrated

0 kilometers   1

0 miles

Teluk Pandan Kecil

Teluk Batu Belah

Teluk Paku

Kampung Bako

Teluk Assam

Bako Park Headquarters

Tanjung Sapi

Teluk Delima ②

Ulu Assam

Serait Trail

Lintang Trail ①

Teluk Pandan Besar

Bukit Tambi

★ Sea Stacks

These towering rock formations are a peculiar characteristic of Bako's coastline. They were formed by the action of the sea on the softer sandstone at the base of the cliffs, which eroded, leaving behind pillars of harder limestone.

★ Bako's Wildlife

Bako offers opportunities to spot a diverse range of wildlife, including flying lemurs, monitor lizards, and 150 species of birds. However, the stars of the park are the endangered proboscis monkeys, named for their prominent nose, who forage in groups for mangrove leaves.

KEY

① **Lintang Trail** is a 3-mile- (5-km-) long loop route that climbs to a sandstone plateau before plunging down to the coast.

② **Teluk Delima Trail** is one of the best trails in Bako for spotting proboscis monkeys.

③ **Tajor Trail**, 2 miles (3 km) long, includes a brisk climb up to *kerangas* scrubland before descending into a shady forest.

For hotels and restaurants see pp281–2 and pp296–8

Sundew Plant
With much of the soil in Bako lacking nutrients, carnivorous plants such as the pitcher and sundew plants must attract and trap insects to derive sustenance from their victims.

Exploring the Park
There are 18 trails in the park, and each one is color-coded with splashes of paint on trees, making it easy to explore without a guide. Viewpoints along the trails offer great views. There are lodges and a campsite near the Park Headquarters but bookings should be made well in advance.

Key
- - - Trail
— Park boundary
△ Peak

★ **Tajor Waterfall**
A popular picnic spot, Tajor Waterfall is 2 miles (4 km) down the Tajor Trail. The waterfall is quite small and has a dip pool. The best time to visit is after a heavy rainfall. It takes about two hours to get to the waterfall from the Park Headquarters.

Monkey Business in Bako

Relatively accustomed to the presence of visitors, long-tailed macaques are easy to spot as they scavenge for food near the Park Headquarters. While a close sighting can initially be thrilling, macaques can be intimidating and are likely to snatch bags or possessions left unguarded for a moment. Even the garbage disposal system has had to be specially designed to keep the macaques out.

A female macaque carrying an infant

Colorful longboats moored on the banks of the Batang Rajang

⑬ Batang Rajang

From Kuching. 🚍 Bintawa Wharf, daily boat from Kuching to Sibu at 8:30am (takes 4 hours). 🛥 daily. 🎏 Gawai Padi Festival (May–Jun).

Flowing 348 miles (560 km) through the heart of Sarawak, the vast Batang Rajang is Sarawak's longest river and the main artery of trade for towns in the central and southern parts of the province. The upper reaches are the heartland of the timber industry, and the river is often muddy with topsoil and littered with debris from various logging operations.

This region is populated largely by the indigenous people, and the banks of the river and its tributaries are scattered with longhouses. The lower reaches of the river are inhabited predominantly by the Iban people, while the upper section mostly contains the dwellings of the Kayan and Kenyah. Trips up the river to these longhouses can be arranged through tour operators in Kuching, Sibu, and Kapit. Independent travel is also possible, but it is essential that visitors wait to be invited in before entering a traditional longhouse.

Boats are a major form of transportation between the towns that flank the Batang Rajang. The jetties of all the towns teem with huge *ekspres* boats as well as the smaller, motorized longboats. It is possible to travel the entire distance from Kuching to Belaga by boat. The first leg of this journey is up to the town of Sibu, the principal transport hub on the Batang Rajang. The jetties are divided between upriver and downriver traffic, which provides easy access to Kanowit and Kapit.

The journey from Kapit to the town of Belaga, a further six hours away, passes through the treach-erous Pelagus Rapids, a 1.5-mile (2.5-km) stretch of cataracts and whirl-pools caused by a sudden drop in the riverbed. Boats may not run at all on this stretch when the water level in the rapids is dangerously low, usually between May and August. Beyond Belaga, the Rajang divides into Sungai Belaga and Batang Balui.

The best time for a trip up the Batang Rajang is between late May and early June to coincide with the Gawai Padi (*see p57*) festival celebrated by the Dayak people in their longhouses.

⑭ Sibu

120 miles (193 km) NE of Kuching. 🏙 260,000. ✈ 🚌 Sungei Antu. 🚍 Jalan Khoo Peng Loong. 🛈 32 Jalan Cross, (084) 340-980. 🛥 daily.

The capital of Sarawak's largest district, Sibu is also the major port of the province and an important economic center, managing trade between the coast and the hinterland. The town's early growth was funded by the rubber industry, run mostly by Chinese merchants who were encouraged by Rajah Charles Brooke to set up businesses here. Later, they also established a thriving timber trade.

Among the sights of Sibu is the 100-year-old temple dedicated to Tua Pek Kong, the patron saint of merchants. Located on the western end of the waterfront, the temple has a beautiful seven-story pagoda with fantastic views.

Set in the former municipal council building, the **Sibu Civic Center Heritage Museum** traces the town's history through old photographs and artifacts, including some skulls from from the era of head-hunting tribes. The museum

Temple guardian, Tua Pek Kong Temple

also has a rich collection of white ceramics that dates back to the 10th and 12th centuries.

Environs
About 40 miles (65 km) upriver of Sibu, **Kanowit** is a small place with few sights of interest. The main highlight is Fort Emma, built by Rajah James Brooke in 1859 and named after his sister. Constructed of bamboo and timber, it was an attempt to prevent Iban raids on Melanau tribes on the Batang Rajang. Eventually, it became key to the success of the Rajahs' rule. The fort is not open to the public.

🏛 **Sibu Civic Center Heritage Museum**
Jalan Sentral. **Tel** (082) 240-620.
Open 9am–5pm Tue–Sun.

⓯ Kapit

124 miles (200 km) E of Sibu.
🚐 99,840. ✈ 🚌 from Sibu.
ℹ (084) 796-445.

Kapit is a small but bustling riverside town, with an attractive waterfront lined with trees and plants. The town's main landmark is the historic **Fort Sylvia**, a whitewashed ironwood structure named after the wife of Vyner Brooke, the third of the White Rajahs. It was built in 1880 in an effort to control Iban head-hunting parties in the region. In 1997 the fort was listed as a historical monument, and now houses a museum and a training center

Vegetable vendor at the daily market in Kapit

for artisans. There is also an interesting museum at the town's civic center, which has displays of Iban and Orang Ulu longhouses as well as photographs of the early days.

Kapit is also a trading center for the indigenous people that inhabit the upriver areas. A lively market sets up daily, near the center of town, packed with vendors selling jungle produce, such as vegetables, tropical fruits, and beeswax. A major draw for most visitors is a chance to visit the remote longhouses along the upper tributaries of the mighty Batang Rajang.

Environs
Located just 6 miles (10 km) from Kapit, **Rumah Bundong** is an authentic Iban longhouse that is the home to about 40 families. The best time to visit is in the late afternoon, as most longhouse residents work in the fields through the day. Guests are usually shown around and often offered a glass of *tuak,* the potent rice wine. An overnight stay can be arranged.

🏛 **Fort Sylvia**
Jalan Kubu. **Open** 10am–noon, 2–5pm Tue–Sun.

🏛 **Rumah Bundong**
🚌 irregular service from Jalan Airport, Kapit.

⓰ Belaga

93 miles (150 km) NE of Kapit.
🚐 25,300. ✈ to Bintulu. 🚌 from Kapit. 🚢 daily. Belaga Hotel: 14 Belaga Bazaar. **Tel** (086) 461-244.

The last settlement of any significant size on the Batang Rajang, Belaga has a wider mix of ethnic groups than any other town in Sarawak. Apart from Iban, Kayan, Kenyah, and Penan people, who bring their jungle produce to sell at the Belaga bazaar, the town is also visited by seasonal collectors of wild honey from Kalimantan. Few foreign visitors make it so deep into Sarawak, but if they do, it is one of the best places to arrange visits to Kenyah and Kayan longhouses, common to this section of the river. These longhouses feature *salong,* or intricately carved tomb markers, which can be seen from a distance. Arrangements for a longhouse visit can be made at the **Belaga Hotel**.

The whitewashed exterior of Fort Sylvia on the Kapit waterfront

⑰ Mukah

112 miles (180 km) NE of Kuching.
🗺 55,000. ✈ from Kuching only.
🚌 🚢 Pesta Kaul (2nd week of Apr).

Located on the coast north of Sibu *(see p170)*, Mukah is a quiet fishing town that offers a glimpse into the lifestyle of the Melanau, the indigenous group that predominates in this region. A few of their traditional tall-houses can still be seen in the area, although most Melanau prefer simple Malay dwellings now. The majority of the town's sights are clustered along the south bank of Sungai Mukah, and include the market and Tua Pek Kong Temple, whose walls are adorned with well-executed murals of Buddhist and Taoist deities.

Mukah springs to life in mid-April to celebrate the Pesta Kaul *(see p57)* festival, held annually to appease the sea spirits and mark the beginning of a new fishing season. As part of the festivities, the Melanau dance to folk rhythms on the beach and sway back and forth on a *tibau*, a tall swing used as part of a fertility rite.

A short distance from town is Kampung Tellian, a fishing village with winding lanes and narrow bridges. Here, the **Lamin Dana Cultural Boutique** is a cultural center and guesthouse dedicated to the preservation of Melanau culture, with exhibits of textiles, betel nut boxes, and rattan baskets. As well as accommodation, it also has a restaurant.

🏛 **Lamin Dana Cultural Boutique**
Kampung Tellian. 📍 (082) 241-735.

⑱ Bintulu

372 miles (600 km) NE of Kuching. 🗺 100,000. ✈ 🚌 🚢 🌐 bintulu.org

Originally a fishing and farming center on Sungai Kemena, Bintulu experienced a period of intense development in the late 1970s when Malaysia's largest natural gas reserves were found just offshore. This led to the construction of an oil terminal

A boardwalk across a small stream in Similajau National Park

and Bintulu Port, Malaysia's second-largest deep-sea port. Among the prominent buildings in town is a tower called the **Council Negeri Monument**. Located in the western part of town near the river, the monument commemorates the first meeting of the Legislative Council of Sarawak during September 1867. Also worth visiting are **Masjid Assyakirin**, a Moorish-style mosque bearing a distinctive blue dome and set in landscaped grounds, and **Kuan Yin Tong Temple**, which features a beautiful rock garden and an artificial waterfall.

Across the river, Kampung Jepak features Melanau stilt houses and is famous for its *belacan*, a pungent shrimp paste used in Malay cooking. **Taman Tumbina**, a short distance north of town, is a compact recreational park with a zoo, the ideal place to escape the bustle of town.

Monument marking the founding of the Sarawak Legislative Council

⑲ Similajau National Park

19 miles (30 km) NE of Bintulu.
Tel (086) 391-284. 🚌 🚢 speedboat from Bintulu. **Open** 8am–12:30pm & 1:30–5:15pm daily. 🏞 🚢 ⚠
🌐 sarawakforestry.com

Occupying just 27 sq miles (70 sq km), Similajau National Park was established in 1976 to create a protected habitat for the green turtles that nest on its beaches each year. Similajau is one of Sarawak's least-visited parks.

A 19-mile (31-km) strip of coastline lined by trees and punctuated by rocky headlands offers visitors some of the country's best beaches. The park's main walking trail is well marked and follows the coast. Interesting routes branch off from it, including the **Viewpoint** and the **Selansur Rapids trails**. The path ends at Golden Beach, which is great for swimming. Walkers can look out for gibbons and banded langurs, as well as flying foxes, which are under threat elsewhere due to excessive hunting. The park supports over 180 bird species, including the hook-billed bulbul and the wrinkled hornbill. Saltwater crocodiles live in some of the larger rivers and signs warn against swimming here.

Dolphins and porpoises are occasionally found swimming in the area. One of the best ways to enjoy the park is to hire a boat to explore its waterways and the coastline. Ask about this at the park HQ.

Iban Longhouses

Traditionally, all indigenous groups of Sarawak lived in communal longhouses that reflected the tight-knit nature of tribal culture. One of the largest Dayak groups, the Iban migrated to Sarawak from Kalimantan's Kapual River basin (now in Indonesia) between the 16th and 18th centuries. Most Iban longhouses, called *rumah panjang*, or *rumah panjai*, are located in the Skrang, Lemanak, Batang Ai, and Batang Rajang areas, and visiting them often involves a longboat trip. Generally erected next to rivers, most longhouses are stilt dwellings built of timber, with thatched roofs and bamboo or rattan woven walls tied together with fiber from creepers. Staying in a longhouse is the highlight of a visit to the province as the Iban make excellent hosts, often welcoming visitors with *tuak*, or rice wine, a meal, and providing a longhouse tour.

Traditional thatched roofs are now often replaced by the more durable corrugated iron.

Stilts support the structure, which is accessed by steps made of steeply angled tree trunks.

Private rooms, or *bilek*, line the *ruai*, a long, covered communal veranda.

A Traditional Longhouse

The main internal division of the longhouse is created by a wall through the center of the building. On one side is a wide communal veranda, while on the other is a row of bilek, or private rooms, each entered by a single door. The kitchen area is inside the bilek.

The area beneath the living quarters has chickens and pigs, rooting for scraps which fall through the bamboo slats.

A wide public veranda, or *ruai*, runs down the middle of the longhouse, with all *bilek* facing out onto it. The *ruai* is used for socializing and making handicraft items.

An outdoor veranda called *tanju* fronts the longhouse and runs along the length of the building. The veranda's split-bamboo floor is exposed to rain and sun. This area is used mainly for drying rice, coffee, cocoa beans, pepper, and even clothes.

❷⓿ Miri

516 miles (830 km) NE of Kuching. 🏙
300,000. **Tel** (082) 764-231. ✈ 🚌 ⛴
Sat & Sun. 🎭 Miri International Jazz
Festival (May), Hari Gawai (Jun).
🅦 **miricity.com.my**

Originally a quiet fishing village,
Sarawak's second-largest city
Miri emerged as a major
commercial center when
Malaysia's first oil well was
drilled here in 1910. In the
1970s, the onshore oilfields
closed down and Miri shifted its
focus to tourism.

Packed with markets and
cafés, the atmospheric old town
around Jalan China is the liveliest
part of the city. Among the most
interesting markets is Tamu
Muhibbah, or local market,
where upriver indigenous
people come to sell jungle
produce such as tropical fruits,
rattan mats, and Bario rice.

The **Al Taqwa Mosque**, with
its whitewashed arches and a
huge golden dome framed by
palm trees is also worth a visit.
Perhaps Miri's most significant
site, perched atop Canada Hill, is
Oil Well No. 1, which is known as
"the Grand Old Lady". The site of
Malaysia's first oil excavation, it is
now a National Monument.
Close to it, the **Petroleum
Museum** documents the
growth of this industry.

The superb reefs around Miri's
coast, teeming with electric-
blue angel fish and blue-
spotted stingrays, are ranked as
the best and healthiest reefs in

Vegetables laid out for sale in the Tamu
Muhibbah market, Miri

the country and have been a
boost to Miri's tourism industry.

🅲 Al Taqwa Mosque
Jalan Merpati. **Tel** (085) 412-291.
Open non-Muslims welcome outside
prayer times.

🏛 Petroleum Museum
Canada Hill. **Open** 9am–5pm Tue–
Sun. 📷

❷⓵ Niah Caves National Park

71 miles (115 km) S of Miri. 🛈 park
headquarters, Pengkalan Batu, Miri;
(085) 737-450. 🚌 from Bintulu or
from Miri to Batu Niah, then taxi.
Open 8am–5pm daily. 🎫 🍴 🚻 🏪
🐟 ⛰ may be booked in advance at
Miri's Visitor Information Center.
🅦 **sarawakforestry.com**

Considered by many to be the
most important archaeological
site in Southeast Asia, the Niah
caves are among Sarawak's

most spectacular attractions.
In 1958, Tom Harrison, curator
of the Sarawak Museum in
Kuching, discovered skulls
and tools at the mouth of the
Great Cave – evidence that the
caves had been inhabited by
humans 40,000 years ago.
With the enormous Great Cave
as its centerpiece, the national
park was established in 1975,
covering 12 sq miles (32 sq km)
of dense rain forest and
limestone outcrops.

From the Park Headquarters, a
short boat ride across Sungai
Niah takes visitors to the boardwalk that links the caves. The
first is Traders' Cave, named for
the guano and birds' nest
collectors who once sold their
harvest here. Farther along is
the Great Cave, one of the
world's largest caves. It measures a staggering 820 ft (250 m)
in width and has a 196-ft- (60-m-)
high cave mouth. It is home to
several species of swiftlets and
bats, and during the harvest
season, nest and bat guano
collectors camp inside the cave.
From within the Great Cave, the
trail continues to the Painted
Cave, where there are ancient
rock paintings made with red
hematite stone. Several small
boat-shaped coffins called
death-ships were also found
in the cave, indicating that it
may have been used once as a
burial chamber. The paintings
and the coffins are protected by
a fence. Visitors need to bring
their own torches.

Rock formations in the Painted Cave at Niah Caves National Park

Pantu waterfall at Lambir Hills National Park

㉒ Lambir Hills National Park

20 miles (32 km) S of Miri.
🛈 park headquarters, (085) 471-609.
🚌 from Miri. **Open** 8am–5pm daily.
🖼️ 🏕️ 🌳 ⛰️ may be booked in advance at the Visitor Information Center in Kuching or Miri.
🌐 **sarawakforestry.com**

With its range of rugged sandstone hills, mixed dipterocarp (hardwood) forest, low-lying *kerangas*, or scrubland, and teeming wildlife, Lambir Hills National Park is a popular weekend getaway from Miri. Among its main attractions are sparkling waterfalls that cascade into natural swimming pools. There are also some excellent jungle trails that lead to the falls, ranging from easy 15-minute strolls to all-day hikes. The longest is the 4-hour trek to the summit of Bukit Lambir for a scenic view of the park. Closest to the Park Headquarters is the Latak waterfall, with an enticing pool and sandy beach, while deeper into the jungle are the Pantu and Pancur waterfalls.

Although the animals here may be difficult to spot, the national park is home to flying squirrels, gibbons, pangolins, clouded leopard, and barking deer, as well as numerous species of birds. There are several Iban longhouses, including Rumah Nakat, which has an interesting traditional handicraft center.

㉓ Loagan Bunut National Park

75 miles (120 km) SE of Miri. **Tel** (085) 775-118. 🚌 from Miri to Lapok, then taxi. **Open** 8am–5pm daily. 🖼️ 🏕️ accommodation must be booked in advance at the Visitor Information Center in Kuching or Miri.
🌐 **sarawakforestry.com**

Consisting of Bunut Lake, Sarawak's biggest freshwater lake, and the surrounding dense peat swamp and dipterocarp forest, Loagan Bunut National Park is a bird-watcher's paradise. A profusion of bird species inhabit this park, including herons, darters, kingfishers, egrets, magpies, robins, and hornbills. The lake is dependent on the water levels of the Bunut and Tinjar rivers, and often dries up completely for a few weeks in February, May, and June. At this time, the local fishermen practice a unique type of fishing called *selambau* to catch fish that are stranded in the receding waters. The fish are scooped up in huge nets mounted on spoon-shaped wooden frames. Boat cruises on the lake's tranquil waters, especially rewarding in the early morning and dusk, can be arranged at the Park Headquarters. A few trails, lined with *tapang* and *belian* trees, lead through the forest. Limited access makes this a seldom-visited park, but new roads and visitor facilities are being planned to attract tourists to the park.

Kingfisher at Loagan Bunut

㉔ Kelabit Highlands

116 miles (190 km) SE of Miri. ✈️ from Miri to Bario. 🚗 from Miri.
🌐 **kelabit.net**

One of Borneo's most isolated and unspoilt regions, Kelabit Highlands is a 3,281-ft- (1,000-m-) high plateau that is home to the hospitable Kelabit people. A visit to one of their longhouses is a highlight of a trip to this spectacular region. Among the most populous of the highland settlements is **Bario**, which nestles in a lush valley. The village has a small airport and a few lodging houses, and these make it a good base for exploring the region. Day trips from Bario include a visit to the beautiful longhouse at Pa Umor. A longer and much more challenging outing is the 5-day trek along the Bario Loop. The trail offers delightful views, and trekkers have the option of making overnight stays at the Ramudu, Pa Dalih, or Long Dano longhouses. For serious mountain climbing head to **Gunung Murud**, located 12 miles (20 km) north of Bario. At 7,999 ft (2,438 m), Murud is Sarawak's highest peak and is seen as a holy mountain by the indigenous people of the highlands. Scaling its sheer walls should only be attempted by fit and experienced climbers. There are two main trails up the mountain and having a guide is advisable. All the treks can be arranged through the lodges at Bario.

Lush paddy fields near Bario in the Kelabit Highlands

㉕ Mulu National Park

Listed both as a UNESCO World Heritage Site and a Rainforest Conservation Area, Mulu National Park is one of Sarawak's premier tourist destinations. Named for the sandstone peak of Gunung Mulu, it is a region of great natural beauty. The park encompasses over 200 sq miles (500 sq km) of rain forest and has two mountain ranges and some of the largest caves in the world. Gorges, valleys, and underground passages in the park provide the ideal habitat for an abundance of flora and fauna, including several species of orchids and hornbills. Trekking up to the limestone pinnacles of Gunung Api, exploring Clearwater and Deer caves, and traversing the Canopy Skywalk are among the park's highlights.

★ **Clearwater Cave**
Thought to be the longest in Southeast Asia, the 62-mile- (100-km-) long Clearwater Cave features spectacular natural formations of helictites and photokarsts.

Key

⫘ Minor road

▪ ▪ Trail

▪ ▪ Park boundary

△ Peak

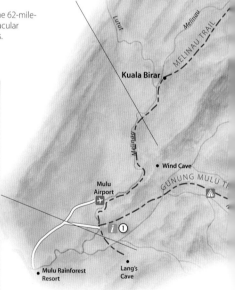

Kuala Birar

Wind Cave

Mulu Airport

Mulu Rainforest Resort

Lang's Cave

★ **Deer Cave and Bat Exodus**
The 571-ft- (175-m-) high cave mouth of Deer Cave is the largest in the world. At sunset, millions of freetail bats stream out of it in a writhing spiral as they fly off to look for food.

★ **The Pinnacles**
One of the park's most memorable sights, these 147-ft- (45-m-) high razor-sharp spikes of rock on Gunung Api were formed by erosion, and can only be reached by a steep climb.

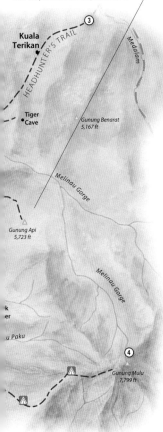

A visitor braving the Canopy Skywalk

Canopy Skywalk

Mulu National Park's popular attraction is the 1,575-ft- (480-m-) long Canopy Skywalk, which is among the longest in the world. A series of swaying walkways is held aloft by steel cables about 66 ft (20 m) above the ground, offering visitors the chance to explore the forest canopy, to get close up to the several species of birds that inhabit the park, and provides an aerial view of the swamp below. The 2-hour guided walk must be booked in advance.

0 km   3
0 miles   3

KEY

① **Park Headquarters**, located to the southwest of the park, is the starting point for all explorations of Gunung Mulu.

② **Gunung Mulu Trail**, a 4-day guided trek to the summit of Gunung Mulu, is exhilarating. It passes through some of the park's wildest terrain.

③ **Headhunter's Trail** is named for local indigenous people who used this route on raiding expeditions.

④ **Gunung Mulu**, at a height of 7,799 ft (2,377 m), is the second-highest peak in Sarawak.

Exploring the Park

Mulu National Park has exceptional facilities with well-maintained wooden walkways and a good network of paths. Most visitors arrive by plane and have accommodation options such as the five-star Marriott Royal Mulu Resort, chalets, and dormitories in the park. The Bat Exodus and the view from the Canopy Skywalk are fascinating. There are regular tours of the main caves.

㉖ Brunei

Located on the northwest coast of Borneo, East Malaysia and hemmed in by the borders of Sarawak, the Sultanate of Brunei Darussalam is among the world's smallest countries. It played a pivotal role in Borneo's history, with its sultans having once controlled vast tracts of the island's north and west. Today, Brunei occupies 2,226 sq miles (5,765 sq km). Most of the country is a low-lying coastal plain backed by rain forest and hills. Off the west coast lie vast oil fields, which are responsible for the country's affluence. It is divided into four districts: Brunei Muara which includes Bandar Seri Begawan, the capital; Tutong, an agricultural region; Belait, the center of the oil industry; and Temburong, an area of natural beauty.

A view of the capital city, Bandar Seri Begawan

Tasek Merimbun
Brunei's largest lake, this tranquil expanse of water is a popular spot for picnics and bird-watching. A wooden walkway leads to a tiny wooded island where eagles and falcons are commonly spotted.

Map labels: Pantai Seri Kenangan, Tutor, Kampung Abang, Sungai Liang, Lan, Kuala Belait, Seria, Sungai Liang Forest Reserve, Badas, Bela, BELAIT, TUT, Kuala Balai, Labi, Sukang, Penipir, Belait

Labi
This quiet agricultural town relies mainly on the harvest of fruits such as durian and rambutan. The 31-mile- (50-km-) long Labi Road is dotted with Iban longhouses.

Sultan of Brunei

Head of the world's oldest hereditary monarchy, Sultan Hassanal Bolkiah is Brunei's reigning sultan and prime minister, as well as its defense and finance minister. Best known for his legendary personal fortune and vast car collection, the sultan has attempted to share his nation's oil wealth by providing free education and health care for his people.

Sultan Hassanal Bolkiah, the reigning Sultan of Brunei

Key
▬ Major road
═ Minor road
—- International border
--- State border
△ Peak

★ **Sultan Omar Ali Saifuddien Mosque**
Built in 1958 and named for Brunei's 28th sultan, this mosque is a classic example of Islamic architecture. With its minarets and 171-ft- (52-m-) high golden dome reflected in the surrounding lagoon, it makes an impressive sight.

VISITORS' CHECKLIST

Practical Information
120 miles (193 km) NE of Miri.
🏙 390,000. 🛈 Jalan Menteri Besar, Bandar Seri Begawan; (673) 238-2822. 🎊 National Day (Feb), Sultan's Birthday (Jul).
w bruneitourism.travel

Transport
✈ 🚌 from Miri, Kuala Lumpur, Lawas.

★ **Kampung Ayer**
Built entirely on stilts along the Brunei River, Kampung Ayer is a cluster of 28 villages housing an estimated 30,000 people. The community is a reflection of the country's traditional way of life.

Berakas · Muara
Seresa
ndar Seri Begawan
RUNEI IUARA
Sipitang
Labu
Limbang · Limbang
Bantu Danau
Bangar
TEMBURONG
Batang Duri
Kampung Temada
Temburong
Ulu Temburong National Park
Bukit Pagon 6,070 ft

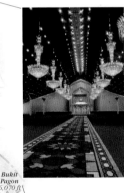

★ **Istana Nur-ul-Iman**
The world's largest residential palace, the Istana Nur-ul-Iman is the official home of the Sultan of Brunei. It contains nearly 2,000 rooms, a sumptuous throne room, and a banquet hall for 4,000 diners.

0 km ——— 20
0 miles ——— 20

KEY

① **Pantai Seri Kenangan** is a beautiful strip of beach separating the Tutong River from the South China Sea.

② **Bukit Pagon**, at a height of 6,070 ft (1,850 m), is the highest peak of Brunei and is located in Ulu Temburong National Park.

Ulu Temburong National Park
Covering about 10 percent of Brunei, this national park is the country's foremost nature preserve. Its canopy walkway gives visitors a chance to spot the flying lizards, hornbills, and gibbons that inhabit the park.

For keys to symbols *see back flap*

SABAH

Malaysia's second-largest state, with a population of three million, Sabah sits on the northeastern tip of Borneo. Located just south of the typhoon belt, this Land below the Wind is geographically stunning, with magnificent caves, coral reefs, forests, and mountains. It is also the ideal destination for adventure activities including mountain climbing, white-water rafting, and diving.

Archaeological excavations reveal evidence of prehistoric human habitation in eastern Sabah approximately 40,000 years ago. This remote province, with over 30 indigenous groups, as well as immigrants from China, Indonesia, and the Philippines, was nominally ruled by the sultans of Brunei for centuries until the British negotiated the rights to exploit the region's reserves of rubber, tobacco, and timber in the late 19th century. Although the British never had a stable leadership over Sabah, they clung on to power, with the region continuing to be known as North Borneo until it joined the Federation of Malaysia in 1963.

Today, Sabah's economy lags behind that of other states in Malaysia because of an inequitable distribution of wealth between the state and federal governments, and an influx of immigrants from neighboring countries. However, with ecotourism contributing to the state's finances, and abundant agricultural produce, such as palm oil, Sabah's economy is developing.

Sandakan, the administrative capital between 1883 and 1942, and Kota Kinabalu, the present state capital, were both almost completely destroyed during World War II, but today they have been rebuilt and are charming destinations. From Kota Kinabalu it is an easy journey north to the Tip of Borneo, south to the Padas River for white-water rafting, and northeast to Gunung Kinabalu for a challenging trek. Sandakan is a good base from which to visit the dive sites that lie off the east coast and the nature reserves at Sukau and Danum Valley. Sabah also offers visitors a cultural experience with its vibrant *tamus* (markets) held weekly, and fascinating longhouses.

Rafflesia, one of Sabah's most unusual and pungent attractions

◀ Sunrise striking St John's Peak in Kinabalu National Park

Exploring Sabah

The state is characterized by steep mountains, including Malaysia's three tallest peaks, and lush valleys teeming with magnificent wildlife and marine life. The highlights of a visit to Sabah are a trek up Gunung Kinabalu, diving trips from the islands of Sipadan and Lankayan, and white-water rafting on the Padas River. Danum Valley is excellent for wildlife spotting while the villages of Kota Belud, Gombizau, Bavanggazo, and Sumangkap offer an opportunity to interact with indigenous groups in memorable ways.

Key

— Major road
┅┅ Minor road
⌁ Railroad
▬▬ International border
▬▬ State border
△ Peak

Sights at a Glance

Towns and Village

1 Kota Kinabalu
7 Mari Mari Cultural Village
8 Kota Belud
9 Gombizau
10 Sumangkap
11 Bavanggazo
12 Kudat
15 Sandakan
23 Semporna
25 Tawau

Areas of Natural Beauty

4 Klias Wetlands
13 Tip of Borneo
20 Gomantong Caves
22 Danum Valley

Parks and Preserves

2 Tunku Abdul Rahman National Park
3 Tambunan Rafflesia Forest Reserve

14 *Kinabalu National Park pp190–91*
16 Sepilok Orangutan Rehabilitation Center
17 Turtle Island National Park
19 Kinabatangan Wildlife Sanctuary
21 Tabin Wildlife Reserve
26 Tawau Hills State Park

River

6 Padas River

Islands and Beaches

5 Pulau Labuan
18 Pulau Lankayan
24 *Pulau Sipadan pp200–201*

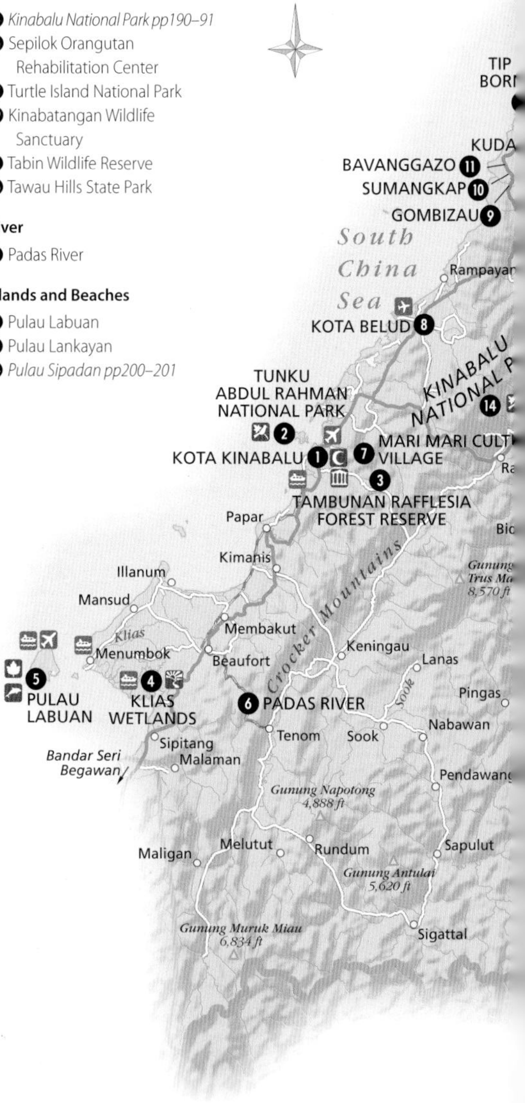

Lush tropical rain forest at Kinabalu National Park

For hotels and restaurants see p282 and pp298–9

Aerial view of Pulau Sipadan, one of Malaysia's top dive sites

Getting Around

Domestic flights are the best way of getting around Sabah. Daily flights connect Kota Kinabalu, Sandakan, Lahad Datu, Tawau, and Kudat. The state's main road connects Kota Kinabalu to Kudat in the north and Tawau and Sandakan in the east. The smaller roads often fall into disrepair, causing delays. The only rail line in Sabah is the short stretch connecting Kota Kinabalu to Tenom. Regular ferries connect Kota Kinabalu to most coastal towns, Menumbok to Pulau Labuan, and Sandakan to Turtle Island National Park. Visitors should be aware that there have been travel advisories issued by the UK and US governments advising against travel to some parts of Sabah (*see also p324*). At present these affect Tawau, Semporna, and east coast islands including Lankayan and Sipadan. Check your government's website for the latest situation.

Stilt village and State Mosque in Kota Kinabalu, the fastest-growing city and capital of Sabah

❶ Kota Kinabalu

190 miles (300 km) NE of Miri. ✈ 🚌
🚌 ℹ Sabah Tourism Board, 51 Jalan
Gaya; (088) 212- 121. 🛍 Sun.
W sabahtourism.com

The capital of Sabah, Kota
Kinabalu occupies a narrow
stretch of land between the
western seafront and a range of
forested hills. Formerly known
as Jesselton, it became the
provincial capital after World
War II, and was renamed Kota
Kinabalu in 1967. Most of its
historic buildings were
destroyed by bombing during
the war and the city had to be
completely rebuilt. Only three
structures remain of the old
town – the Land and Survey
building, the General Post
Office, and the Atkinson Clock, a
49-ft- (15-m-) tall timepiece
built in 1905 and named for the
city's first district officer. Despite
the lack of historical landmarks,
the city has charm, with friendly
people, bustling streets, and a
good range of accommodations,
restaurants, and bars. The city
center is small and easy to
explore on foot. The city's main
attractions include the lively
seafront *tamus*, or markets, such
as the Filipino Market, as well as
the Sabah Museum, and the
State Mosque. The larger City
Mosque, often referred to as the
Floating Mosque, was built in
2000 beside Likas Bay. Also
overlooking the bay is the
magnificent 31-story glass

building of the Sabah
Foundation. An observatory
on Signal Hill offers a sweeping
view of the city and offshore
islands. Kota Kinabalu is the
best base from which to explore
Sabah's northwest coast,
including the magnificent
Gunung Kinabalu *(see pp190–93)*
and Tunku Abdul Rahman
National Park.

🏛 Sabah Museum

Jalan Muzium. **Tel** (088) 253-199. 🚌
Open 9am–5pm daily. 🎫 📷 ♿ 📵
🖥 W museum.sabah.gov.my

The Sabah Museum is set amid
spacious grounds, and is
designed in the style of a
Rungus longhouse. The
museum has several floors,
with sections on ethnography,
natural history, ceramics,
history, and archaeology. The
ethnographic exhibits are
among the highlights of the
museum, and include examples

of musical instruments, swords,
spears, blowpipes, ethnic
costumes, and displays on the
various uses of bamboo. The
archaeology gallery displays
intricately carved coffins. A "time
tunnel" exhibit documents the
arrival of Filipino and Indonesian
immigrants, the colonial era, the
Japanese occupation, and the
incorporation of Sabah into the
Federation of Malaysia in 1963.
In front of the museum is a
small but interesting collection
of vintage cars.

The museum grounds also
contain a Heritage Village,
which has excellent examples
of houses of Sabah's main
indigenous groups. The Murut
house features an unusual
bouncing platform that is used
for communal dances. There is
also an attractive botanical
garden. Talks on a range of
topics can be arranged for
visitors by prior request.

The majestic façade of the Sabah State Mosque

C Sabah State Mosque

Jalan Sembutan. **Open** 8–11am & 2–4:30pm Mon–Thu, 8–10:30am & 2:30–4:30pm Fri, 8–11am & 2–4pm Sat & Sun.

Located close to the museum, southwest of the city center, this mosque is a striking example of contemporary Islamic architecture. Though set away from the bustle of the city center, its golden dome is visible from many parts of town. The mosque, built in the late 1970s, is one of the largest in Malaysia. It has a capacity of over 5,000 worshipers, and has a separate section for women to pray. While non-Muslims are permitted to go inside (except during prayer times), they should dress appropriately, remove their shoes before entering, and avoid visiting on Fridays.

Bright exterior of the popular Filipino Market

Filipino Market

Jalan Tun Fuad Stephens. **Open** 7am–7pm daily. **Central Market** Jalan Tun Fuad Stephens.

Several bustling markets line the city's waterfront, the most interesting of which is the Filipino Market, also known as the Handicrafts Market, named for the Filipino immigrants who run most of the stalls. A huge variety of souvenirs, shells, baskets, and bags are available, though these are not exclusively from the Philippines. The market is also a good place to buy cultured pearls and traditional medicines. Visitors should beware of pickpockets and fake pearls. Farther north is the **Central Market**, where snacks such as grilled chicken and the local favorite *murtabak*, a stuffed spicy pancake, are sold.

Visitors arriving on Pulau Sapi in the Tunku Abdul Rahman National Park

Tunku Abdul Rahman National Park

2 miles (3 km) W of Kota Kinabalu. Sabah Parks Office, Block K, Sinsuran Complex, Kota Kinabalu; (088) 523-500. on Pulau Manukan. on Manukan. camping allowed on all islands except Manukan and Sulug.

A short boat ride away from Kota Kinabalu, Tunku Abdul Rahman National Park is made up of five beautiful islands that cover an area of 19 sq miles (50 sq km). Named for the country's first prime minister, the park was established in 1974 to protect the fragile coral reefs around **Pulau Gaya**, **Pulau Sapi**, **Pulau Manukan**, **Pulau Mamutik**, and **Pulau Sulug**. Several varieties of marine life thrive in these reefs, including parrotfish, clownfish, batfish, and lionfish. Wildlife on the islands include long-tailed macaques, bearded pigs, pangolins, and pied hornbills.

Pulau Gaya is the biggest of the five islands. Covered in dense forest, it has about 12 miles (20 km) of trails and dazzling white-sand beaches such as Police Beach on the northeast coast. Although much of the coral around Pulau Gaya has been destroyed by dynamite fishing, the other islands have reefs teeming with marine life.

Just off the southwest tip of Pulau Gaya, and linked to it by a sandbar at low tide, Pulau Sapi is tiny in comparison but has some lovely waters that are ideal for swimming and snorkeling, as well as a short nature trail. The three other islands are clustered together a little farther south. Pulau Manukan, where the park headquarters is located, is the most popular of the five islands, especially for day trips. This crescent-shaped island's facilities include a resort and restaurant. Among the many activities on offer are snorkeling, glass-bottomed boat rides, sea kayaking, and parasailing. Scuba gear and underwater scooters can be hired on the island. Pulau Manukan has particularly good beaches on its eastern shore, but the large number of visitors and constant movement of boats sometimes cause the reefs to become murky.

The Coral Flyer, the world's longest zipline, connects Pulau Sapi and Pulau Gaya. It's an experience for the brave only – speeds reach up to 37 miles (60 km) per hour to cross between the two islands. Buy your ticket at Pulau Sapi Jetty.

Staff waiting to assist people arriving at speed on the Coral Flyer zipline

❸ Tambunan Rafflesia Forest Reserve

37 miles (60 km) E of Kota Kinabalu.
📞 ℹ (088) 899 589. **Open** 8am–
3pm daily. 🅿

Located near the top of the
5,410 ft- (1,649 m-) high
Sinsuron Pass in the Crocker
Mountain Range, the Tambunan
Rafflesia Forest Reserve was
set up to protect the unique
rafflesia flower. The botanical
name of the commonest
rafflesia, *Rafflesia arnoldi*, is
derived from Sir Stamford
Raffles, founder of Singapore,
and naturalist Dr. Joseph
Arnold, who discovered it in
Sumatra in 1818. A 15-lb (7-kg)
specimen was immediately sent
back to the Royal Society in
London. This parasitic plant is
pollinated by carrion flies and
emits a smell of rotting flesh to
attract them. Its natural habitat
is moist, shaded areas. The
flower takes about nine months
to bloom into the world's largest
flower, with brick-red petals and
white dots. The display is short-
lived as the petals begin to wilt
within a few days.

As the blooming season is
unpredictable and the rafflesia
flowers only for a few days in a
year, visitors are advised to
check in advance by calling the
information center. The reserve
has comprehensive information
on the rafflesia and its habitat.

Guides are available at the
information center, but are
mostly not necessary, since the
paths are well marked and staff
can give directions.

Proboscis monkeys, named for their long, drooping noses

❹ Klias Wetlands

62 miles (100 km) SW of Kota
Kinabalu. 🚌 to Kota Klias jetty.
🚤 tour boats from Kota Klias jetty.
🅿 from Kota Kinabalu.

Located on a peninsula about
75 miles (120 km) south of Kota
Kinabalu, the Klias Wetlands, a
mangrove forest interspersed
with countless channels of the
Sungai Klias, are a major ecotourism destination. Wildlife
here is rich and diverse: visitors
might spot several species of
monkey, such as the silver-leaf
and long-tailed macaque, an
amazing variety of birds, and
swarms of fireflies that illuminate
the riverside trees in the evenings. As dusk falls, crocodiles
gather at the water's edge to
hunt. The real highlight of the
wetlands, however, is the chance
to see the unique proboscis
monkey, a species native to
Borneo. They are timid but can
be seen feeding on tender
leaves near the edge
of the water. The
monkeys are named
for their long, droop-
ing noses that
particularly promi-
nent in males, often
twice as large as the
females. The males
also have a bulbous
belly. These distinc-
tive features have
earned the monkey
the nickname *orang
belanda*, meaning
Dutchman, in some

Rafflesia, the world's largest flower

parts of Borneo. Most tour firms
in Kota Kinabalu offer boat trips
to the wetlands. Independent
travel is possible, but joining a
tour group is a better option.

❺ Pulau Labuan

5 miles (8 km) W of the Klias Peninsula.
🏨 86,000. ✈ 🚤 ℹ (087) 423-445.

Located off the southwest coast
of Sabah, Pulau Labuan is a
small island with a significant
history. In 1846, the Sultan of
Brunei ceded the island to the
British who were particularly
keen to mine the island's large
coal deposits to provide fuel for
passing steamships. The island
remained a British territory for
almost 100 years, until it was
overrun by the Japanese at the
beginning of their occupation
of Borneo during World War II.
A few years later the Japanese
surrendered here at the end
of the war. In 1963, Pulau
Labuan joined the Federation
of Malaysia. Today, the island
is a pleasant place, with nice
beaches and popular as a
duty-free shopping haven.

Labuan Town is the main
settlement on the island.
Just north of Labuan is the
An-Nur Jamek Mosque, a
distinctive, futuristic structure.
The **Peace Park** at Layang
Layangan, 2 miles (4 km)
north of town, contains a war
memorial which marks the site
of the Japanese surrender.
An Allied war cemetery on

the east coast has nearly 4,000 graves of Allied soldiers who lost their lives in Borneo.

The island's waters are particularly popular among divers, especially for wreck diving. Several World War II and other shipwrecks lie in the waters off Labuan's coast. Dive operators organize visits to these interesting sites. The **Labuan Marine Park** is centered around Pulau Kuraman, a small island near the south coast, accessible by boats from the Labuan jetty. A number of activities such as diving, sailing, fishing, and organized short jungle walks are offered at the park. It also has some beautiful beaches, perfect for picnics and sunbathing.

6 Padas River

Pangi, near Tenom. 🚌 to Beaufort from Kota Kinabalu, then by train. 🚍 from Kota Kinabalu.

The Padas River weaves through the southwest region of Sabah, linking the small, quiet towns of Tenom and Beaufort. Known to be a turbulent river, it has flooded Beaufort several times. As a result, shophouses in the town are now built on stilts. Early photographs show Beaufort resembling the canal city of Venice. The Padas River is popular as a destination for great white-water rafting *(see p315)*. The boulder-strewn river cuts through lowland rainforest, and between April and July, the water level of the river creates

White-water rafting down the turbulent Padas River

15 miles (23 km) of Grade II and III rapids. The access point for rafting trips on the Padas River is at the town of Pangi, near Tenom, which can be reached by train from Beaufort. From Pangi, challenging rapids, with names such as Merry-Go-Round, Washing Machine, and Headhunter, tumble downstream. The river has several gentle stretches as well, where it is possible to hop out of the raft and float downstream with the current.

Rafting trips can be organized by tour companies in Kota Kinabalu who brief visitors well on safety procedures. As well as rafting trips, there is also the opportunity to take a tour of the southwest region of the state and ride on Borneo's only railway line from Beaufort to Tenom, tracing the Padas River and meandering through jungles.

Headstones of World War II soldiers at the Allied war cemetery in Labuan

The North Borneo Railway

When the British-run North Borneo Chartered Company began operating in the late 19th century, its managing director, William Cowie, developed a plan for a trans-Borneo railway stretching from Brunei Bay beside Pulau Labuan to Sandakan in the east of the province, cutting through steep ranges and uncharted jungles. Construction began in 1896 and by 1905 a line had been built from Weston, on Brunei Bay, to Beaufort in the southwest, and from there to both Jesselton, now known as Kota Kinabalu, and to Tenom, east of Beaufort. From Tenom it was extended a further 10 miles (16 km) to Melalap, where work came to a halt and was never continued. Cost of construction was high, and the rice tax levied on locals to pay for it resulted in rebellions against the British. The Chartered Company then ensured that the train paid for itself by refusing to build roads connecting Tenom, Beaufort, and Jesselton. Half-day trips are available on the old steam train, but they are quite expensive, although breakfast and lunch, served in tiffin boxes, are included in the ticket price. The train leaves Tanjung Aru at 10am every Wednesday and Saturday. A less expensive option is to take the standard train.

Tourists enjoying the view while on a train trip

Rope and timber bridge at the Mari Mari Cultural Village

❼ Mari Mari Cultural Village

Inanam, 9 miles (15 km) east of Kota Kinabalu. **Tel** (013) 881-4921. 🅟 arranged in Kota Kinabalu or booked online.
w marimariculturalvillage.com

A folk museum preserving Borneo ethnic culture, Mari Mari Cultural Village features the dwellings and cultural traditions of five Sabah tribes. On the tour you can see and experience the culture and lifestyle of the rice-farming Kadazan-Dusun, the longhouse-building Rungus, the hunter-fisherfolk the Lundayeh, the cowboy and sea gypsy Bajau, and the headhunting tribe, the Murut. The half-day tours include transport from hotels in and around Kota Kinabalu.

❽ Kota Belud

47 miles (75 km) N of Kota Kinabalu. 🅜 73,000. 🚌 🚆 Sun. 🎪 Tamu Besar (Oct/Nov).

Located on fertile alluvial plains, Kota Belud is a quiet town inhabited mainly by Bajau people, famed for their skill with horses. Gunung Kinabalu dominates the landscape to the east.

The town itself is small and unassuming, except on Sunday mornings when it springs to life during the weekly *tamu*, or market. Held at Jalan Hasbollah, a short distance from the town center, the *tamu* is the hub of local trade and is as much a social event as a commercial one. Local people from diverse ethnic groups such as Chinese, Indians, and Malay, come together to sell their goods while visitors soak up the atmosphere and enjoy a hearty breakfast at one of the many stalls. Just about anything one can imagine is on sale, from livestock, fruit, vegetables, and meat to hand-crafted knives, musical instruments, bark waistcoats, and local textiles. Tempting snacks, delicious local cakes, and drinks are also on offer. Vendors are very friendly, and expect potential buyers to haggle for their goods. The weekly *tamu* is busy from around 6am until early afternoon.

Tamu Besar, or the big market, is an annual festive event at Kota Belud which is celebrated amid cultural festivities and handicraft demonstrations. The highlight of the market are the stalls of horses for sale.

Traditionally dressed Bajau horsemen, commonly called Cowboys of the East, pose for the crowds. The Bajau with their resplendently dressed horses also display their unrivaled horse-riding skills at the Tamu Besar.

❾ Gombizau

56 miles (90 km) N of Kota Kinabalu. 🅜 140. 🚆 🅸 (013) 549-1885 (cell). **Open** 8:30am–5:30pm daily. 🅿 🅟 arranged in Kota Kinabalu. 🅰

Located up the coast from Kota Belud on the Kudat Peninsula in the north of the province, Kampung Gombizau is one of several smaller villages in the area that are taking part in the local government's scheme of One Village, One Product. The program encourages the communities to produce and market unique handmade products and handicrafts made from locally available material. The villagers, most of whom are part of the Rungus minority, dedicate their time to the industry of beekeeping and the sale of raw honey and beeswax. Royal jelly, a bee secretion which is a good dietary supplement and an ingredient in several beauty products, is also cultivated and sold here. Visitors are shown around the carefully tended beehives and can see how the bees are smoked out for the honeycombs to be removed.

❿ Sumangkap

57 miles (92 km) N of Kota Kinabalu. 🅜 431. 🚌 🅸 (019) 535-9943. **Open** 8am–6pm daily. 🅿 🅟 arranged in Kota Kinabalu. 🅰

A short drive from Gombizau is the village of Sumangkap, which resounds with the beating of metal being made into gongs and can thus boast Sabah's highest decibel count. One of the most important elements of Sabahan music, the gongs feature in all traditional celebrations. These gongs are skilfully crafted by local artisans. Set horizontally in frames or suspended vertically, gongs come in all sizes, from massive

Striking a massive gong in Kampung Sumangkap

ones that are 6 ft (2 m) in diameter and meant for use in temples, to tiny ones sold as souvenirs. Visitors can watch the gong-makers at work, as they beat out the raised center of an aluminum sheet to give the instrument its particular resonance and timbre.

⓫ Bavanggazo

61 miles (98 km) N of Kota Kinabalu.
🏔 250. 📧 ℹ️ (088) 614-088.
📷 🚗 🏠

The Rungus people, who live in the region around Kudat, have managed to maintain more of their traditions and culture than many other indigenous groups. A visit to a longhouse in the village of Bavanggazo, just off the road from Kota Belud to Kudat, is an excellent opportunity to appreciate Rungus heritage.

The longhouses are aligned in an auspicious east–west direction, with outward-sloping walls to allow for maximum ventilation. One such longhouse is **Matunggung**, which features traditional bamboo-slatted sides and a thatched roof, and contains the living quarters of approximately 100 families.

The Rungus are famed for their beadwork, and visitors to the longhouse can usually see women sitting on the communal veranda crafting shoulder bands, necklaces, and bracelets from multicolored beads, using motifs from Rungus folklore. The older Rungus women wear brass coils as jewelry. They are also skilled textile weavers, and use locally grown, hand-spun cotton on simple looms for their clothes.

Organized tours, which can be booked in Kota Kinabalu, include a visit to the villlages of Gombizau and Sumangkap as well as lunch at Bavanggazo. These tasty meals are made with fresh vegetables from the adjoining fields. Visitors have the option of staying overnight to attend a cultural performance of traditionally dressed dancers and gong players.

Symbolic globe at the Tip of Borneo marking the island's northernmost point

⓬ Kudat

118 miles (190 km) N of Kota Kinabalu.
🏔 75,000. ✈️ 🚌 Ekspress minibus service from Kota Kinabalu. 🚢 Sun.
🎏 Pesta Kelapa.

A small port sitting at the northern tip of Sabah, Kudat is inhabited by a large number of Chinese and Filipino traders. Sheltered by the Marudu Bay, the Kudat Peninsula was deemed suitable enough to be selected as the administrative capital of British North Borneo in 1882. However, the town's era of importance was short-lived, as frequent pirate attacks and a lack of fresh water forced the provincial capital to be shifted in 1883 to Sandakan (see p196).

There are not many sights in town, although a stroll around the harbor, watching fishing boats come and go, can be refreshing. A walk along the Sidek Esplanade around the bay is also rejuvenating. Kudat's main street, Jalan Lo Thien Chock, has some attractive

Rock pools at Bak Bak Beach, north of Kudat

shophouses and a bright Chinese temple. About 4 miles (7 km) north of town, the beach at **Bak Bak** is a popular picnic spot.

⓭ Tip of Borneo

124 miles (200 km) N of Kota Kinabalu.
🚌 Ekspress minibus service from Kota Kinabalu. 🚗 📷

The northernmost tip of Borneo, known locally as Tanjung Simpang Mangayau, which means battle junction, makes an excellent day trip from Kota Kinabalu. Located in the Kudat district, the tip can be reached after stopping off at the Gombizau bee farm, at the gong village of Sumangkap, and along the way at the Rungus longhouse at Bavanggazo.

A few miles before Kudat, a branch of the road forks to the left, passing under towering coconut palms and leading directly to a lovely windswept promontory that looks out over the South China Sea to the west and the Sulu Sea to the east.

Just before the headland, the road passes behind a sandy crescent shaded by casuarinas to Kalampunian Beach, where the Irranun people sell colorful shells. At the Tip of Borneo itself, a flagpole stands beside a giant globe of the world. An inscription on the globe recounts that Ferdinand Magellan spent 42 days here repairing his ship during his circumnavigation of the world between 1519 and 1522.

⑭ Kinabalu National Park

A UNESCO World Heritage site, the 754-sq km (291-sq mile) national park protects the environment around Gunung Kinabalu. Popular for its trails and wildlife, the park is home to 4,500 species of plants, including 1,500 varieties of orchids and nine types of pitcher plants. Also found here are large mammals such as orangutans, gibbons, and clouded leopards, unusual birds such as the Kinabalu friendly warbler and the Bornean mountain whistler, and a dazzling variety of butterflies and insects. At its southeast corner lies Poring Hot Springs, the ideal place to relax after the rigors of the park's trails.

Area of map Illustrated

Kiau   Lohan

Kundasang

Low's Peak 13,455 ft

Laban Rata Rest House

Layang Layang

Power Station

Kiau

Timpohon Gate

Park Headquarters

Bundu Tuhan

Kundasang

★ **Gunung Kinabalu**
At a towering 13,455 ft (4,101 m), the mountain offers unrivaled views from its summit. A reasonable degree of fitness is essential for attempting the climb *(see pp192–3)*.

Kinabalu Botanical Garden
The botanical garden behind the Park Headquarters features many varieties of plants from the mountain's middle ranges. All species are labeled, making a stroll around the grounds both informative and enjoyable.

★ **Silau Silau Trail**
This 50-minute walk along the length of the Silau Silau stream, from its source to its confluence with Sungai Liwagu, is excellent for bird-watching.

KEY

① **The Bukit Tupai Trail**, an easy 30-minute walk, leads up to a ridgetop with excellent views of Kinabalu's summit.

② **The alternative route to the summit of Gunung Kinabalu** begins 11 miles (17 km) east of Park Headquarters at Mesilau.

③ **The canopy walkway** is only 490 ft (150 m) long, but it gives a splendid bird's-eye view of the surrounding forest.

★ **Poring Hot Springs**
Fed by mineral waters, these springs have been developed into public and private baths. The site also features a short but exciting canopy walkway, an orchid farm, and a butterfly farm.

VISITORS' CHECKLIST

Practical Information
37 miles (60 km) NE of Kota Kinabalu.
ℹ️ Kota Kinabalu Resorts, 15 First Floor, Wisma Sabah (088) 243–629.
🚾 w sabahparks.gov.my
Kinabalu Botanical Garden:
Open daily. 📷 9am, noon, 3pm.

Transport
🚌

Exploring the Park

From the two main gates, at Mesilau and Timpohon, trails around the park along its ridgetops and streams pass through delightful terrain where quiet and observant walkers may see some of the region's mammals, such as bearded pigs and mouse deer. To make the climb up Gunung Kinabalu you need to book well in advance (passes are limited) and you must also be accompanied by a guide (see pp192–3).

Key

═══ Major road
─── Minor road
▬▬ Summit Trail
▬▬ Mesilau Trail
▬▬ Liwagu Trail
▬▬ Bukit Tupai Trail
⋯⋯ Mempening Trail
▬▬ Silau Silau Trail
▬▬ Via Ferrata Trail
▬ ▬ Park boundary
△ Peak

Poring Hot Springs ③

Mesilau Gate

↓ *Lohan*

| 0 km | 3 |
| 0 miles | 3 |

Flora and Fauna

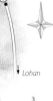

One of the richest areas in species diversity, the park's attractions include such mammals as tarsiers, squirrels, and tree shrews, birds such as hornbills, partridges, and mountain blackbirds, as well as a long list of colorful butterflies and beetles. The park is also home to several varieties of rare and exotic flora, including the extraordinary rafflesia (*see p186*).

Tarsiers are easily recognized by their long feet and large eyes. They are nocturnal primates that feed on insects, birds, and snakes.

Pitcher plants, which are one of the prime attractions of Kinabalu National Park, are carnivorous plants that attract and trap insects with their bright pigments and sweet nectar.

Slipper orchids are named for their bright slipper-shaped pouches that attract pollinating insects. These delicate plants are fast becoming an uncommon sight.

For keys to symbols *see back flap*

Climbing Gunung Kinabalu

The climb to the summit of Gunung Kinabalu begins at the Timpohon Gate, just above Park Headquarters. There is an alternative route, longer but less steep, which starts at Mesilau Nature Resort, 11 miles (17 km) to the east. The two trails meet at Layang Layang and continue to the Laban Rata Rest House, where most climbers break for the night. Some, however, travel another hour to the more basic rest house at Sayat Sayat, which has the benefit of a shorter clamber to the summit the next morning. The last, and toughest, part of the hike begins well before dawn to allow climbers to view the sunrise from Low's Peak. The descent takes five hours, so it is best to start back by noon to reach the base before dark.

The mighty Gunung Kinabalu rising above the clouds

The Summit Trail
From Timpohon Gate to the summit at Low's Peak, this trail takes at least two days to traverse. Handrails along the trickier stretches assist climbers.

Rhododendron Forests
Found between 5,900 ft (1,800 m) and 8,530 ft (2,600 m), these forests comprise 26 varieties of rhododendron, including the beautiful copper-leaved rhododendron.

Low's
13,4

St. John's Peak △
13,438 ft

Sou

Vil
She

Mempen
Shelter

Kamborangoh •
Telekoms Station

Ubah Shelter

Power Station •

① Kandis Shelter

Timpohon •
Gate

KEY

① **Tropical Montane Rainforests**, typically composed of oak, birch, and pine, as well as fern and moss, are found between 2,953 ft (900 m) and 5,900 ft (1,800 m), including the area around Park Headquarters.

② **Layang Layang**, at 8,599 ft (2,621 m), has a staff base and is the first rest stop for most climbers.

③ **South Peak**, as its name suggests, is the southernmost of Kinabalu's peaks. A near-perfect pinnacle, it provides lofty views of the surrounding area.

Park Headquarters
The jumping-off point for walks along trails, Park Headquarters has accommodations, restaurants, and a shop selling provisions for climbers.

For keys to symbols *see back flap*

Summit Peaks of Kinabalu
St. John's Peak, Donkey's Ears, and the Ugly
Sisters are just a few of the peaks that soar
near the summit of Gunung Kinabalu.

Low's Peak

Sir Hugh Low

The highest peak of
Gunung Kinabalu, Low's
Peak is named for Sir
Hugh Low, a naturalist
and British Colonial
Secretary on Pulau
Labuan. Ironically, he
never stood on its
summit despite three
attempts during the
1850s. On his second
attempt, in 1858, he was
accompanied by Spenser
St. John, the British Consul in Brunei, who made it to
the top of South Peak only to see other peaks around
it that stood still higher. It was not until 1888 that John
Whitehead, a zoologist, conquered the highest peak
while collecting new species of birds and mammals,
some of which are also named for Sir Hugh Low.

Sisters
228 ft

△ *Donkey's Ears*
13,300 ft

• **Sayat Sayat**
Rest House

Rata
ouse
emaing Hut
ndant Hut
Cave
r/Helipad

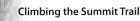

Gunting Lagadan Hut
Situated just above Laban
Rata, this simple rest
house can sleep up to
60 people in dormitories.
It also has sweeping views
of the mountain's upper
reaches, with Donkey's
Ears as a backdrop.

Climbing the Summit Trail

*You must book at least 6 months in advance. The park
allows only 192 climbers plus their guides to climb per
day, due to conservation issues and limited overnight
accommodations, which are always fully booked. The
climb is more fun when traveling light, but a few items
are essential, including a hat, sun block, sunglasses,
and a flashlight. Warm, waterproof clothing is a must.
Sleeping bags are provided free of charge at Laban
Rata and Sayat Sayat rest houses, and the shop at
Park Headquarters sells basic food.*

• **Chempaka**
Shelter

• **Mesilau Gate**

• **Nepenthes**
Shelter

• **Mesilau**

```
0 km          1
0 miles       1
```

Key

— — Summit Trail

— — Mesilau Trail

— — Via Ferrata Trail

△ Peak

Mesilau Trail
Located 11 miles (17 km) east of Park Headquarters, Mesilau provides a
quieter base for the climb. The trail from here is longer, quieter, and
offers a particularly good display of several species of pitcher plants.

Dive boats off the island of Pulau Sipadan in Sabah ▶

⑮ Sandakan

250 miles (400 km) E of Kota Kinabalu.
🚊 12,500. ✈ 🚌 *i* (089) 229-751.

Lying on the northern edge of Sandakan Bay, Sandakan is sandwiched between a steep escarpment and the Sulu Sea. During the late 18th century, exports of timber, pearls, birds' nests, and hornbill ivory made Sandakan a wealthy town. It became the administrative capital of North Borneo between 1884 and 1942, but was bombed out of existence by the end of World War II, like Kota Kinabalu. Much of the modern town is built on reclaimed land, but its indiscriminate architecture of concrete grids lacks the sense of space of Kota Kinabalu. These days, trade is focused on palm oil and cocoa crops.

There is little to interest visitors in the center of town, though the waterfront is lively with the constant movement of barges and ferries, and a daily fish market which is the biggest in Sabah. On the escarpment behind the town center is an Observation Pavilion that offers a spectacular view across the town and the harbor front.

Overlooking the pavilion is a well-preserved colonial building known as **Agnes Keith's House**. An American author who lived here in the 1930s, Agnes Keith wrote several books on Sabah and its culture. The house has ornate furnishings and wooden flooring, and the author's study still exudes an aura of tranquility. Next door, another

slice of colonial memorabilia, the **English Tea House** is a refreshing stop for tired visitors.

For many, the most moving sight in town is the **Sandakan Memorial Park**, about 7 miles (12 km) east of the town center. In 1944, over 2,000 Allied British and Australian prisoners of the Japanese POW camp were marched to Ranau near Gunung Kinabalu. Only six Australians survived. The small museum in the park, built by the Australian government, is a grim reminder of the tragedy.

🏛 **Agnes Keith's House**
Jalan Istana. **Open** 9am–5pm daily. 🖼

🏛 **Sandakan Memorial Park**
7 miles (12 km) E of Sandakan.
Tel (089) 275-400. **Open** daily. 📷

⑯ Sepilok Orangutan Rehabilitation Center

14 miles (23 km) E of Sandakan.
Tel (089) 531-180. 🚌 **Open** 9am–noon (11am Fri) & 2–4pm daily.
📷🖥🍴♿🖼 Sun Bear Conservation Center: **Open** 9am–3:30pm daily. 🖼

One of only four orangutan sanctuaries in the world, Sepilok was established in 1964 and is today one of Sabah's most popular attractions. Occupying 17 sq miles (43 sq km) of lowland rain forest, the center was set up to care for orphaned and injured animals, and teach them the skills needed to survive independently. The center aims to eventually reintroduce the orangutans into their natural

Orangutans at the Sepilok Orangutan Rehabilitation Center

habitat. At the entrance is the Nature Education Center which provides an insightful introduction to all that goes on behind the scenes, and also periodically screens a short, somewhat dated video on orangutans. A short walk from here are two feeding stations where the animals are fed at 10am and 3pm.

Next door to the center is the **Sun Bear Conservation Center**, dedicated to help protect the world's smallest bear. There are usually some 30–40 rescue bears that can be visited.

⑰ Turtle Island National Park

25 miles (40 km) N of Sandakan.
🚢 from Sandakan. *i* Crystal Quest, Sabah Park Jetty, Jalan Buli Sim-Sim, Sandakan, (089) 212-711. 🖼 📷 🍴 🖼 on Pulau Selingan. ♿
W sabahparks.org.my

The three small islands of Selingan, Bakungan Kecil, and Gulisan constitute this turtle sanctuary, commonly known as the Pulau Penyu National Park, where green and hawksbill turtles come ashore to nest.

The most rewarding time to visit the National Park is between July and October when visitors are most likely to see the turtles lay their eggs in the sand. As this often takes place in the evenings, one of the islands offers tourist accommodations. Vigilant rangers transfer the hatchlings

The impressive Agnes Keith's House, home of the American writer

to nurseries, from where they are regularly released into the sea. Sadly, the chance of survival for each hatchling is only about one in 100 eggs, as they often fall prey to poachers as well as natural predators.

Permissions to visit the islands must be obtained from Crystal Quest, who act as agents for Sabah Parks; local tour operators may be able to arrange this for you, or there is an office at the Sabah Parks Jetty, the departure point from Sandakan.

⓲ Pulau Lankayan

50 miles (80 km) N of Sandakan. 🚌 from Sandakan. 🛈 Pulau Sipadan Resorts, 484 Bandar Sabindo, Tawau; (089) 765-200. 🚗 📷 🚤 ⚠
🌐 lankayan-island.com

Just a 90-minute boat ride from Sandakan, Lankayan is a teardrop-shaped island, surrounded by dazzling white beaches and stunning coral reefs. It is visited mostly by divers for its colorful world of marine life, and, with only one resort, the place is rarely crowded. Some of the species that divers might spot around the Lankayan shipwreck, one of the many dive sites near the island, are glassfish, painted frogfish, and marble stingrays. Gazing into the waters from the jetty, visitors can often see black-tip sharks, especially in the months of April and May. Lankayan is a part of the Sugud Islands Marine Conservation Area, and its lush tropical vegetation is also worth a mention. The island is covered with screwpine (Pandanus amaryllifolins), which has a bloom resembling a pineapple.

⓳ Kinabatangan Wildlife Sanctuary

84 miles (135 km) S of Sandakan. 🚌 from Sandakan. 🚤 along Sungai Kinabatangan. 📷 🚤 🚤 in Sukau. ⚠

Sungai Kinabatangan is Sabah's longest river at 348 miles (560 km) and its lower reaches, bordered by dense forests, provide the largest corridor for wildlife in the country. A unique feature of the river are the oxbow lakes set back from the main course, creating abundant habitats for the diverse flora and fauna. Much of this area has been designated as the Kinabatangan Wildlife Sanctuary. It is easily visited on a day trip from Sandakan.

A river boat trip provides excellent opportunities for wildlife spotting. Sungai Menungal, a small tributary that joins the Kinabatangan just above Sukau, is a particularly successful spot for sightings. Proboscis monkeys, a species common in Borneo, and macaques that feed high up in the trees, are among the highlights. Visitors are almost certain to see a wide range of reptiles such as crocodiles, and birds such as the hornbill, oriental darter, and the blue-eared kingfisher.

⓴ Gomantong Caves

68 miles (110 km) S of Sandakan. 🚌 from Sandakan. 🛈 (089) 230-189. **Open** 8am–noon & 2–4:30pm daily. 📷 🚤 🚤 ⚠

The limestone caves of Gomantong are the largest caves in Sabah and home to a remarkable population of swiftlets and bats. Licensed locals clamber up bamboo poles to harvest swiftlet nests, which are the prime ingredient for bird's-nest soup, a delicacy in Chinese cuisine.

The two main caves are **Simud Hitam**, or black cave, and **Simud Putih**, or white cave, both of which are difficult to get to. However, visitors can venture into Simud Hitam aided by a boardwalk to avoid wading through ankle-deep bat guano which collects on the cave floor. Most tours of the caves include a trip down Sungai Kinabatangan.

The entrance into Simud Hitam at Gomantong Caves

㉑ Tabin Wildlife Reserve

137 miles (220 km) SE of Sandakan. 🚌 from Lahad Datu. 🛈 (088) 267-266. **Open** 8am–6pm daily. 🐾 🚻 organized by Tabin Wildlife Resort, **Tel** (088) 261-558. 🐾 🅦 tabinwildlife.com.my

Established as a protected area in 1984, the 473-sq mile (1,225-sq km) Tabin Wildlife Reserve is one of the last remaining habitats of the critically endangered Sumatran rhinoceros. Comprised mostly of secondary growth rain forest, this is a conservation zone for several other wildlife species as well, including endangered Borneo pygmy elephants, giant flying squirrels, orangutans, and several bird species including hornbills. Activities organized by the reserve in collaboration with Tabin Wildlife Resort are exciting ways to spot wildlife and include jungle walks, night safaris, and bird-watching trips.

The reserve offers visitors challenging walking trails, one of which leads to a waterfall that plunges into a river which is good for a swim. Another trail leads to a cluster of low, mud volcanoes.

㉒ Danum Valley

50 miles (80 km) W of Lahad Datu. 🚕 from Lahad Datu. 🛈 (088) 881-092. 📷 mandatory. 🐾

Covering an area of 168 sq miles (438 sq km), Danum Valley is a conservation area that consists of primary lowland rain forest,

Wild bearded pigs rooting for food in the Danum Valley

one of the most complex ecosystems, which is why it features high on most nature-lovers' itineraries on their visit to Sabah.

The surrounding logging concession, run by the Sabah Foundation, which has now been mostly reforested, acts as a buffer zone for the fantastic range of wildlife. Visitors are likely to spot elephants, barking deer, and slow loris on several guided walks along nature trails. Among the birds that are visible in this region are the great argus pheasant, the rhinoceros hornbill, and the crimson sunbird. Most visitors stay at the Borneo Rainforest Lodge by Sungai Danum, where a network of trails offers multiple options for exploring the area. The ideal time to observe wildlife is early morning and evening, when even the most cautious of animals, such as bearded pigs, emerge to root for food, while orangutans and

Bornean gibbons can be spotted often rustling about in treetops by the lodge. A steep 2-mile (3-km) climb leads to an ancient Kadazan Dusun burial site, high up in a cliff-top cave. The site contains old coffins and offers a spectacular view over the Segama River Valley.

㉓ Semporna

209 miles (336 km) SE of Sandakan. 🏔 150,000. 🚌 🎏 Regatta (Mar/Apr).

With most of its houses perched on wooden piles over the water, Semporna is a town juxtaposed between land and sea. This picturesque fishing town hovers over an ancient coral reef that supports a diverse variety of fish, soft corals, sponges, anemones, echinoderms, and mollusks.

The inhabitants are mainly the Bajau, a seafaring people who fish in the Celebes Sea to earn their living using delicately carved, traditional boats called *lipa lipa*, which they adorn with bright sails and colorful festoons.

Sempora is frequented by visitors who use it as a base for diving and snorkeling trips to the offshore islands of Mabul and Sipadan *(see pp200–201)*. Of the many island destinations that skirt the town of Semporna, the volcanic island of Pulau Bohey Dulang, also the site of a Japanese pearl culture station, is popular. The cliff-fringed Bohey Dulang is frequented by adventure lovers who trek up its highest peak for stunning views

Traditional stilt buildings in the harbor in Semporna

For hotels and restaurants see p282 and pp298–9

Ferry passengers disembarking at Tawau

of the surrounding islands. The area around Semporna has intrigued archaeologists since the discovery of stone tools at nearby Tingkayu, which pre-date similar implements found in the region by 10,000 years.

❷ Pulau Sipadan

See pp200–201.

❷ Tawau

223 miles (360 km) S of Sandakan. 🔼 178,000. ✈ 🚌
🚢 Tawau Central Market, daily. 🎭 Tawau Cultural Carnival (Mar).
🌐 sabahtourism.com

Cacao pod

Tawau sits on the coast in the extreme southeast of Sabah. It is a transport hub and a transit point for visitors heading toward Semporna and the offshore islands of Sipadan *(see pp200–201)*.

This bustling port began life as a modest Bajau settlement, but in 1878 the British North Borneo Company, attracted by the fine natural harbor and rich volcanic soil found in the region, settled in Tawau. They shipped in elephants from Burma to assist with logging in the forest.

Timber has always been the prime produce of this town, although the rich soil also sustains plantations of rubber, coconut, cocoa, and palm oil. In fact, Tawau is the cocoa capital of Borneo, and the cocoa estate at nearby Quoin Hill admits visitors to see the stages of processing cacao beans to chocolate. Palm oil is cultivated even more extensively in Tawau, and plantations of its fan-like fronds are scattered around the state of Sabah.

Tawau faces Kalimantan across the strait and has a high percentage of Indonesian and Filipino residents. While there are some squalid areas, the town center is a tidy blend of traditional wooden shophouses and modern concrete blocks. The cheerful street markets offer a wide mix of goods such as herbs, vegetables, clothes, and toys sold by mobile traders. Tawau's fish market is always busy, and exotic seafood is available at the open-air stalls seen all over town.

Tawau is the jumping-off point for trips to the Maliau Basin to the west, which is dubbed "Sabah's lost world" due to its inaccessibility and diversity of plant and animal life. This is a trip for enthusiasts as facilities offered to visitors are very basic.

❷ Tawau Hills State Park

15 miles (24 km) N of Tawau.
🚉 from Tawau. 🛈 (089) 925-719.
Open 7am–6pm daily. 🖼 🖼 🖼

A lush stretch of low hills and thick mossy rain forest, Tawau Hills State Park was established here in 1979 to protect the watershed of the Tawau, Merotai, Kinabutan, Mantri, and Balung rivers.

Occupying an area of about 104 sq miles (270 sq km), the park is a favorite among birders. The blue-banded kingfisher, wattled pheasant, blue-headed pitta, and the Bornean wren-babbler can be spotted here. Sightings of monkeys are also common.

The highest hill is the 4,268-ft- (1,300-m-) high Gunung Magdalena. A lower peak, Bombalai Hill, just 1,739 ft (530 m) high, is an extinct volcano that can be reached following a half-hour trail from the Park Headquarters. A 3-hour trek leads to some hot springs and Table Waterfall, where the crystal-clear river makes for a good swimming spot.

This park is much less busy than its more famous neighbors and is a good alternative for those looking for solitude.

Table Waterfall, Tawau Hills State Park

㉔ Pulau Sipadan

Rated among the world's top five dive sites, Pulau Sipadan is a limestone spire rising about 1,970 ft (600 m) from the sea-bed. Fringed with white and sandy beaches, the island is surrounded by a stunning coral reef teeming with over 3,000 species of marine life, including colorful butterflyfish, angelfish, and bright orange and electric-blue damselfish. Sightings of sharks, barracudas, turtles, and manta rays are also common in the waters around the reef.

★ Turtle Cavern
The eerie Turtle Cavern is an underwater cave stacked with the skeletal remains of green and hawksbill turtles that drifted into it and never found their way out.

Sempo
Mabul
Kapalc
islands

★ The Drop Off
Just east of the Sipadan jetty, the Drop Off is a seemingly endless wall of rock covered with several species of corals and sponges.

Diving Trips
Several tour operators arrange day and night dives, but only 120 divers are permitted to dive at the site each day. Qualified personnel accompany visitors on each diving trip.

KEY

① **Lobster Lairs** is a good place for spotting lionfish, lobsters, scorpionfish, and pipefish. This shallow dive site is an ideal spot for beginners.

② **Coral Garden**, where almost every species that inhabits these waters can be viewed, is a joy for the underwater photographer.

③ **Mid Reef**

④ **South Point**, a site for experienced divers, is popular for frequent sightings of hammerhead sharks and turtles.

Key

- - - Ferry route

Hanging Gardens
The reef descends gradually to a depth of 230 ft (70 m), where terraces covered with alcyonarian and gorgonian fan corals form the Hanging Gardens.

Barracuda Point
The site is named for the spectacular spirals of blacktail and chevron barracuda that come here to feed along a wall that harbors turtles and parrotfish.

0 meters 300
0 yards 300

②

★ White-Tip Avenue
A gap in the coral reef, White-Tip Avenue is frequented by white-tip sharks and gray reef sharks. Divers may encounter a school of bigeye trevallies and bumphead parrotfish.

③

Turtle Patch
This site offers frequent sightings of hammerhead and thresher sharks, triggerfish, bumphead parrotfish, and the green and hawksbill turtles that are commonly seen around Sipadan.

④

Staghorn Crest
This is a drop-off dive site with a fabulous garden of giant staghorn corals teeming with shoals of gobies, groupers, angelfish, and triggerfish. Currents can be strong here and divers need to be careful.

For keys to symbols see back flap

SINGAPORE
AREA BY AREA

INTRODUCING SINGAPORE

The small city-state of Singapore is bustling, cosmopolitan, trendy, modern, and plays a part on the world's financial and political stage that seems disproportionate to its size. Its varied traditions and intriguing mix of the old and new (in its people and way of life) make Singapore a great multicultural city in the truest sense.

Located at the tip of the Malay Peninsula on the Strait of Malacca, Singapore consists of one large island encircled by several smaller islets. Gleaming high-rise buildings and a fascinating diversity of foliage are crammed into a tiny area of just 269 sq m (697 sq km), some of it reclaimed land. Humidity and heavy downpours define its climate; showers are so sudden that the umbrella is a must-have accessory.

When Sir Stamford Raffles of the British East India Company landed on its shores in 1819, Singapore was little more than a nondescript fishing village. However, the town soon went on to become a British stronghold. After gaining independence from the British, Singapore was incorporated into the Federation of Malaysia in 1963, and went on to become a wholly independent nation in 1965.

Government and Politics

Singapore is a democratic republic that follows the British parliamentary system, with a government led by a prime minister. Political affairs have long been dominated by the People's Action Party, led by the late statesman Lee Kuan Yew from its inception in the 1960s right up to the 1990s. Even with the presence of an active opposition, a one-party system has prevailed on the whole. While critics deem it autocratic, the party is seen as having been instrumental in helping Singapore become the super-developed, modern nation that it is today. Singaporeans give particular credit to Lee Kuan Yew, who remains unrivaled in popularity as a nation builder.

The Economy

Singapore has a highly successful and transparent economy. Despite accusations of the government having too many stakes in the market, the economy is believed to be among the most powerful in the world, chiefly because of government efficiency, the exceptional infrastructure, minimal corruption, and a skilled workforce. Singapore's economy thrives on the electronics and chemical sectors, as well as business and financial services. Due to its strategic location

Towering skyscrapers dominate Singapore's skyline

 Neo-Classical civic buildings of Singapore with, south of the river, the financial district in the background

Ornately dressed performers of the Chinese opera

linking the mainland and the islands of Southeast Asia with the rest of the world, Singapore has the busiest port in the region. Canned food, biotechnology, rubber processing, and tourism have emerged as other key revenue-generating industries.

Peoples, Languages, and Religions

Singapore is a country of immigrants, with a multiracial ethnicity comprising 74.2 percent Chinese, 13.3 percent Malay, and 9.2 percent Indians, with a small number of Western expatriates. Ethnic neighborhoods, the norm in the 19th century, have given way to government-provided public housing. Old enclaves that have been left behind are now used only for shopping or entertainment that is unique to that particular community. The cultural heritage of the British colonialists is also deeply woven into the Singaporean lifestyle.

Malay, Mandarin Chinese, English, and Tamil are all official languages in Singapore. The unique "Singlish" – a patois that combines English with Malay and Chinese words and intonation – is understood by most resident Singaporeans but rarely by visitors.

Except for certain radical groups that are banned, religion is freely practiced. Mahayana Buddhism is the most common, followed by Islam, Christianity, and Hinduism. Since the racial riots of the 1960s, society has been considerably harmonized, with the government making every effort to keep it so.

Culture and the Arts

The arts flourish in this diverse city. Chinese opera and drama, Western classical music, Indian classical dance forms, and English theater are all part of local culture, and several theater and dance ensembles keep Malay culture alive. However, government censorship is rigid; each performance needs a seal of approval before being shown to the public. A plethora of museums, festivals, and religious places complement the visual arts.

Food is an integral part of Singaporean culture, and eating out is considered the best way of socializing. Although Chinese, Indian, and Malay flavors dominate, international cuisine ranging from African to Eastern European is also widely available. Being a food haven has added to the popularity of this gateway between the East and the West, and it remains as alluring today as it was centuries ago.

Worshipers at Sri Mariamman Temple

SINGAPORE THROUGH THE YEAR

Singapore's multicultural heritage has resulted in a calendar studded with holidays and vibrant festivals, both secular and religious. Many of the religious festivals are based on the lunar calendar *(see p321)*, so their dates vary annually. Check with the Singapore Tourism Board for exact timings. While some festivities, such as Chinese New Year and Hari Raya Puasa, are celebrated with pomp and pageantry all over the island, others are quieter local market and temple affairs. Visitors are welcome in temples and mosques as long as customs are respected. Other cultural events such as the Singapore Arts Festival further add to the year's festivities.

Paying respect to elders on Hari Raya Puasa

January to March

Ponggal *(Jan/Feb)*. A Tamil (south Indian) harvest festival celebrated at temples such as the Sri Srinivasa Perumal Temple *(see pp236–7)*. Rice is cooked in new pots and allowed to boil over to symbolize prosperity. It is then offered to the gods as thanksgiving.

Thaipusam *(Jan/Feb)*. A Hindu festival of penance in honor of Lord Murugan. Male devotees carry *kavadis*, or steel arches, anchored to their skin with hooks, in a long procession from the Sri Srinivasa Perumal Temple to the Chettiar Temple *(see p223)*.

Chinese New Year *(Jan/Feb)*. This vibrant Chinese festival is a two-week celebration culminating with Chap Goh Mei, marked by a final dinner and prayers. Chinatown is ablaze with lights and packed with shoppers.

Chingay Parade *(Jan/Feb)*. Part of the New Year festivities, a grand, lively parade of stiltwalkers, lion dancers, floats, and other multicultural performers travels down Orchard Road.

Qing Ming Festival *(Mar/Apr)*. Chinese families visit temples and ancestral graves to clean and restore them. Red candles and joss sticks are lit and offerings of rice, wine, and flowers are made.

Lion dance performance during the Chinese New Year

April to June

Vesak day *(May/Jun)*. Buddhists commemorate the birth, enlightenment, and death, of the Buddha on this day. Monks chant prayers at packed Buddhist temples and caged birds are set free to symbolize kindness. In the evening, candlelit processions set out from the temples. Thian Hock Keng Temple *(see pp228–9)* is a good place to see celebrations.

Singapore International Festival of Arts *(May/Jun)*. Organized by the National Arts Council, this premier arts festival has a captivating program of local, regional, and international art, drama, dance, and music.

Dragon Boat Festival and Boat Race *(Jun)*. This festival commemorates the death of the 4th-century Chinese poet Qu Yuan, who drowned himself in protest against political corruption. It is said that people searched for him in boats, beating drums and throwing rice dumplings into the water to distract the fish from attacking his body. Today, international teams compete in dragon-shaped boats to honor this event. The colorful spectacle takes place at Bedok Reservoir, which is a 20-minute taxi ride from the city center.

July to September

Great Singapore Sale *(May/Jul)*. Shops throughout the island hold sales during this period – the discounts can be extremely enticing *(see p253)*.

Singapore Food Festival *(Jul)*. Demonstrations from top chefs and special food markets draw large crowds.

National Day *(Aug 9)*. Singapore's Independence Day

is celebrated with a spectacular show at the Padang. The highlights include military parades, an airforce flypast, and cultural performances, with a laser and fireworks display as a final flourish.

Festival of the Hungry Ghosts *(Aug/Sep)*. The Chinese believe that during the seventh lunar month, souls of the dead return to earth to feast. Joss sticks, red candles, and paper money are burnt, and lavish feasts and dramatic Chinese street operas, *wayang (see p260)*, are held to appease the spirits.

Mid-Autumn Festival *(Aug/Sep)*. The full moon on the 15th day of the eighth month in the Chinese calendar is celebrated with mooncakes and lanterns. Traditionally a thanksgiving for a bountiful harvest, the festival also commemorates a 14th-century Chinese patriot who is said to have hidden notes to his companions in mooncakes while trying to overthrow the Yuan Dynasty.

Singapore Grand Prix *(Sep)*. Formula 1 cars race through the streets of Marina Bay in a spectacular night-time race on an illuminated track.

Lantern competition at the Chinese Garden during Mid-Autumn Festival

October to December

Hari Raya Puasa *(Sep–Oct)*. A day of celebration for the Muslim community to mark the end of Ramadan, the Muslim holy month. Areas such as

Offerings at the family altar during Deepavali

Sultan Mosque and Arab Street *(see p234)* come alive with festivities.

Deepavali *(Oct/Nov)*. The Hindu festival of lights marks Lord Krishna's victory over Narakasura – a triumph of good over evil. Homes and temples are decorated with oil lamps to attract Lakshmi, the goddess of prosperity, and Little India dazzles with lights and decorations. The precise date is established each year according to the Indian almanacs.

Thimithi Festival *(Oct/Nov)*. A festival procession begins at the Sri Srinivasa Perumal Temple and makes its way to the Sri Mariamman Temple *(see p224)* where devotees prove the strength of their faith by walking barefoot across a stretch of burning hot coals.

Festival of the Nine Emperor Gods *(Oct/Nov)*. A nine-day festival in honor of the Nine Emperor Gods, thought to bring good luck and longevity, is celebrated at Kiu Ong Yiah Temple on Upper Serangoon Road. Prayers, feasts, and Chinese opera performances are followed by a procession of the nine gods seated on elaborate chairs,

led by temple mediums with swords and whips. During this festival, many devotees also make a pilgrimage to the temple of Tua Pek Kong on Kusu Island (Turtle Island).

ZoukOut *(Dec)*. Around 40,000 people party at this annual outdoor dance music festival on Sentosa.

Christmas *(25 Dec)*. From mid-November onwards, Orchard Road is transformed into a stunning stretch of bright fairy lights and Christmas decorations.

Hari Raya Haji *(variable)*. A festival in honor of those Muslims who have made the pilgrimage to Mecca. It is marked by animal sacrifices and prayers at mosques.

Public Holidays

Local festivals follow the lunar calendar, and the dates are variable.

New Year's Day (Jan 1)
Hari Raya Puasa (variable)
Chinese New Year (Jan/Feb)
Hari Raya Haji (variable)
Good Friday (Mar/Apr)
Labor Day (May 1)
Vesak Day (May/Jun)
National Day (Aug 9)
Deepavali (Oct/Nov)
Christmas Day (Dec 25)

SINGAPORE AT A GLANCE

While most of Singapore's attractions lie at the heart of the city, south of the island, its compactness and efficient infrastructure make it easy to visit the outer reaches. The north, west, and east are studded with older suburbs, nature reserves, and historic sites. Despite being a model modern metropolis with skyscrapers, glitzy shopping malls, museums, and contemporary entertainment, a traditional Singapore survives beneath its glossy exterior. At its core is a multicultural heritage, revealed in the timeless elegance of colonial architecture, Chinatown's shophouses, and the uniquely juxtaposed temples, mosques, and churches.

Singapore's Top Ten Attractions

Raffles Hotel
See pp220–21

Orchard Road
See pp238–41

Chinatown
See pp224–9

Little India
See pp230–37

Singapore Botanic Gardens
See pp246–7

Singapore Flyer
See p218

Sentosa
See pp250–51

Chijmes
See p218

Boat Quay
See p227

Gardens by the Bay
See p217

◀ The Supertree Grove in the Gardens by the Bay

The Singapore River

The Singapore River winds through the heart of the main city and has long been the hub of its life and commerce. Flanked by the towering skyscrapers of the financial district on the southern bank and the stately colonial buildings on the northern bank, the river is lined with leafy walkways, shops, and eateries. River cruises depart from several piers along the bank.

UOB Plaza's entrance lobby is embellished with sculptures by Dali and Botero.

Cavenagh Bridge
Signs restricting horse-drawn carriages still stand at the city's only suspension bridge.

The Fullerton Hotel's colonial façade dominates the entrance to the river. The present building replaced Fort Fullerton in 1925.

Asian Civilizations Museum *(see p216)*

Merlion
This mythical half-fish, half-lion symbol of Singapore guards the river as it opens into Marina Bay.

Raffles' Landing Site
A plaque below a polymarble statue of Raffles marks the site of his original landing in 1819.

Anderson Bridge
This bridge was built in 1910 to relieve the increasing traffic on Cavenagh Bridge.

Parliament Complex
Opened in 1999, the new Parliament House complements the Victorian style of the original parliament building *(see p217)*, dating to 1827.

Boat Quay
Bars and restaurants bring new life to the restored row of old trading houses lining the southern bank of the river *(see p227)*.

Elgin Bridge
The present bridge was built in 1929 on the site of the first one across the river, and is named for Lord Elgin, then Governor General of India.

Clarke Quay
Refurbished warehouses form a colorful backdrop to this lively shopping and eating area *(see p223)*.

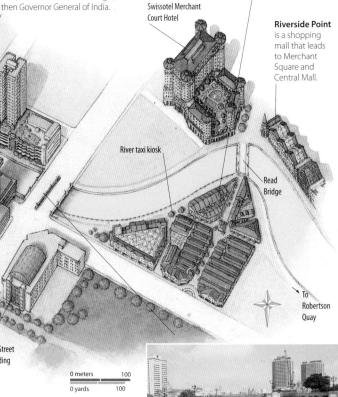

Swissotel Merchant Court Hotel

Riverside Point
is a shopping mall that leads to Merchant Square and Central Mall.

River taxi kiosk

Read Bridge

To Robertson Quay

Hill Street Building

| 0 meters | 100 |
| 0 yards | 100 |

Coleman Bridge
This bridge was named for George D Coleman, the architect who designed much of Singapore's urban landscape.

THE COLONIAL CORE AND CHINATOWN

Sir Stamford Raffles' city plan of 1822 designated the south of the river as the commercial district, and reserved the north for administrative offices. This northern area is known today as the Colonial Core. It is the heart of downtown Singapore and is dotted with historical landmarks. The Padang and Fort Canning Park are focal points of this area and have witnessed major events in Singapore's history. To the south of the river

lies the flourishing Central Business District, also known as the Golden Shoe due to its shoe-shaped district boundary. Adjoining the business district lies Chinatown. As trading houses grew along the south bank in the 19th century, coolies and Chinese merchants settled in the area and Raffles officially allocated it to the community. It is characterized by distinctive shophouses, temples, and markets.

Sights at a Glance

Attractions
9 Singapore Flyer

Historic Streets, Buildings, and Monuments
1 Raffles' Landing Site
4 Victoria Theater and Concert Hall
5 Old Parliament House
7 Marina Bay Sands
12 *Raffles Hotel pp220–21*
13 Chijmes
21 Clarke Quay
22 Chinatown Heritage Center
24 Temple Street
27 Tanjong Pagar Conservation Area
28 Ann Siang Hill
29 Telok Ayer Street
30 Lau Pa Sat
32 Raffles Place
33 Boat Quay

Museums and Galleries
2 Asian Civilisations Museum
6 National Gallery Singapore
14 Singapore Art Museum
16 National Museum of Singapore
17 Peranakan Museum

Parks and Gardens
3 Esplanade Park
8 Gardens by the Bay
19 Fort Canning Park

Shopping
11 Raffles City
25 Chinatown Complex

Churches and Temples
10 St. Andrew's Cathedral
15 Cathedral of the Good Shepherd
18 Armenian Church
20 Chettiar Temple
23 Sri Mariamman Temple
26 Buddha Tooth Relic Temple and Museum
31 *Thian Hock Keng Temple pp228–9*

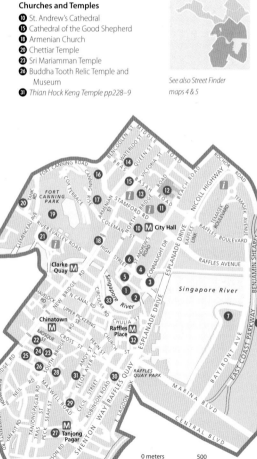

See also Street Finder maps 4 & 5

0 meters 500
0 yards 500

Street-by-Street: Around the Padang

The heart of Singapore's colonial district is the Padang, or square, which was once used by the 19th-century colonials as a site for big sporting events as well as National Day parades. Sporting activities from cricket and field hockey to soccer and rugby still take place here on a weekly basis. The square is flanked by grand Neo-Classical buildings such as the former Supreme Court and City Hall (now revamped as the National Gallery Singapore), the Parliament House, and the exclusive Singapore Cricket Club. Also of interest here is Esplanade Park, which lies on the eastern side of the Padang. One of the oldest parks in Singapore, it is home to many historical landmarks.

❻ ★ National Gallery Singapore
The gallery occupies imposing former civic buildings.

❹ ★ Victoria Theater and Concert Hall
Built in 1862, the Victoria Theater was originally the Town Hall. The Victoria Memorial Hall was added in 1905 to commemorate the death of Queen Victoria. Its name was later changed to the Victoria Concert Hall

Asian Civilisations Museum

Raffles' Landing Site

To the Boat Quay

PARLIAMENT PLACE

OLD PARLIAMENT LANE

❺ Old Parliament House
Constructed in 1827, this building was originally commissioned as a private residence for a Scottish merchant, John Argyle Maxwell.

The Time Capsule
Located in front of Empress Place, a small pyramid houses a time capsule prepared in 1990 to mark the 25th anniversary of Singapore's independence.

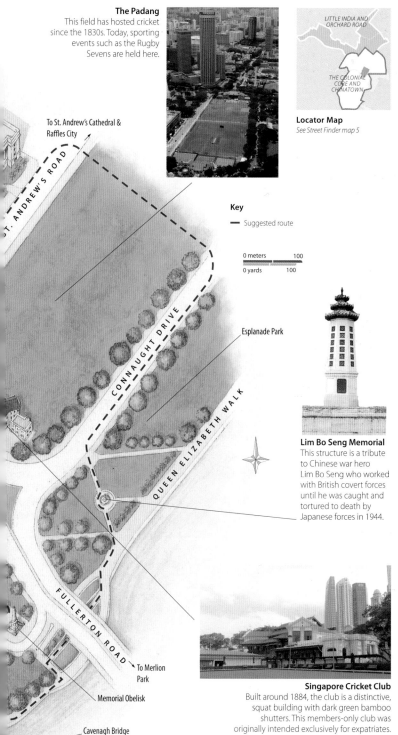

The Padang
This field has hosted cricket since the 1830s. Today, sporting events such as the Rugby Sevens are held here.

Locator Map
See Street Finder map 5

LITTLE INDIA AND ORCHARD ROAD

THE COLONIAL CORE AND CHINATOWN

To St. Andrew's Cathedral & Raffles City

ST. ANDREW'S ROAD

CONNAUGHT DRIVE

QUEEN ELIZABETH WALK

FULLERTON ROAD

To Merlion Park

Memorial Obelisk

Cavenagh Bridge

es Place

Esplanade Park

Key
— Suggested route

0 meters 100
0 yards 100

Lim Bo Seng Memorial
This structure is a tribute to Chinese war hero Lim Bo Seng who worked with British covert forces until he was caught and tortured to death by Japanese forces in 1944.

Singapore Cricket Club
Built around 1884, the club is a distinctive, squat building with dark green bamboo shutters. This members-only club was originally intended exclusively for expatriates.

Statue of Sir Stamford Raffles at the original landing site

❶ Raffles' Landing Site

North Boat Quay. **Map** 5 D3.
Ⓜ Raffles Place, City Hall. 🚌 7, 32, 51, 81, 124, 145, 197, 603, 851.

A statue of Sir Stamford Raffles gazing upon the flourishing Central Business District, complete with a plinth, marks the spot where he first set foot on Singapore soil, on the morning of January 29, 1819 (see p210). The modern poly-marble statue is a replica of the original bronze work cast by British sculptor-poet, Thomas Woolner, which was unveiled on the Padang on June 27, 1887. The original statue, which narrowly escaped being melted down during the Japanese invasion, now stands in front of the Victoria Concert Hall.

❷ Asian Civilisations Museum

1 Empress Place. **Map** 5 D3.
Tel 6332-2982. Ⓜ Raffles Place, City Hall. 🚌 75, 540, 608. **Open** 10am–7pm daily (to 9pm Fri). 🚻 ♿ 🏛
Ⓦ acm.org.sg

Home to over 1,600 artifacts that trace the history of the varied cultures and civilizations of Asia, the Asian Civilisations Museum is housed in the restored Empress Place Building. Named in honor of Queen Victoria and completed in 1867, the Palladian structure

was built by convicts and first functioned as a courthouse.
Today, this Neo-Classical structure showcases a wealth of exhibits in 11 themed galleries and four ACE (Asian Civilizations Education) Zones: South Asia, West Asia/Islam, Southeast Asia, and China. There is also a fascinating Singapore River Interpretive Gallery where the story of generations of immigrants who settled and worked on the banks of the Singapore River is told using old photographs.

❸ Esplanade Park

Connaught Drive. **Map** 5 E3. Ⓜ City Hall. 🚌 10, 70, 75, 82, 97, 100, 130, 131, 167, 196, 608.

Running along Connaught Drive from the underpass at Anderson Bridge to Stamford Road, Esplanade Park was one of the most popular outdoor spots for both the European and Asian communities during the colonial era.
The park contains Queen Elizabeth Walk and several landmarks, including the Cenotaph, which commemorates those who lost their lives during the two World Wars; the **Lim Bo Seng Memorial**, which eulogizes the World War II hero who died in Japanese captivity; and the Tan Kim Seng Fountain, which was built in honor of the philanthropist who set up Singapore's first freshwater supply. When **Esplanade – Theatres on the Bay** was built, there was debate over the radical architecture of the new building. Located on the

waterfront, the huge, spiked shells of the complex contain a plethora of performing arts venues, including a concert hall, theater, outdoor theater, and recital studio, as well as gallery space, a performing arts library, and a shopping mall.

❹ Victoria Theater and Concert Hall

9 Empress Place. **Map** 5 E2. **Tel** 6338-8283 (theater); 6338-6124, 6339-6120 (concert hall). Ⓜ Raffles Place, City Hall. 🚌 75, 540, 608. **Open** check website for opening times. 🚻 💻 🏛
Ⓦ nach.gov.sg

A splendid example of colonial architecture, Victoria Theater was built in 1862 by the British to showcase amateur dramatic productions and Gilbert and Sullivan operettas. The Victoria Memorial Hall was added in 1905 to celebrate Queen Victoria's jubilee. The Memorial Hall was renamed Victoria Concert Hall in 1980 when it became home to the Singapore Symphony Orchestra (see p260).
Over the years, the hall has been put to a variety of uses. During World War II, it was converted into a hospital. Its clock tower was set to Tokyo time when Japan occupied the island, and after the Japanese surrender, it was here that the war crimes tribunals were held.
The two buildings are the venue for a range of concerts, performances, and multi-cultural extravaganzas (see pp258–9). Tickets can be obtained at the box office or at outlets in Singapore's main shopping areas.

The massive riverside complex of Esplanade – Theaters on the Bay

The Neo-Palladian façade of the Old Parliament House

❺ Old Parliament House

1 Old Parliament Lane. **Map** 5 D3.
Tel 6332-6900. Ⓜ City Hall,
Raffles Place. 🚌 7, 32, 51, 81, 124,
145, 197, 603, 851. **Open** 10am–
9pm Mon–Fri, 11am–9pm Sat.
Box office opens 90 mins before
Sun events. 🏛 only for tours.
🎫 11am & 3pm daily. 🚻 📷 📱
🆆 theartshouse.com.sg

Singapore's oldest surviving
government building, the
Old Parliament House was
originally built as the residence
of Scottish merchant John
Argyle Maxwell in the late
1820s. It was designed in
Neo-Palladian style by G D
Coleman, an architect who was
to shape much of Singapore's
urban landscape. Maxwell
leased it to the government
for use as a courthouse. In the
1950s, it became the colonial
government's Assembly House,
and, in 1962, the Parliament
House of the independent
state. Outside the building
stands a handsome bronze
statue of an elephant, a gift
from the Thai monarch, Rama
V, after his 1871 visit to Singapore – the first visit to a foreign
nation by a Siamese king.

A new Parliament House was
built nearby in 1999. In 2004,
after careful restoration, the
old building was converted
into The Arts House, an elegant
arts and heritage space. The
center offers a range of contemporary visual and performance
arts, art house movies, and
improvisational theater.

❻ National Gallery Singapore

1 Saint Andrew's Road. **Map** 5 D2. **Tel**
6690-9400. Ⓜ City Hall. 🚌 7, 32, 51,
81, 124, 145, 197, 603, 851. **Open** see
website. 🏛 🆆 **nationalgallery.sg**

Right in the heart of the Civic
District, two striking buildings –
the City Hall and the former
Supreme Court – have been
refurbished and reborn as the
largest visual arts space in
Singapore, dedicated to the
display, promotion, research,
and study of Southeast Asian
and Singapore art, while also
hosting touring international
art exhibitions.

❼ Marina Bay Sands

10 Bayfront Avenue. **Map** 5 F3.
Tel 6688-8868. Ⓜ Bayfront. 🚌 97,
106, 133, 502, 518. 🚻 📱
🆆 **marinabaysands.com**

It is impossible to miss
the Marina Bay Sands, which
dominates Marina Bay.
Developed by the Las Vegas
Sands Corporation, the
integrated resort includes a
2,561-room hotel, a convention
center, the Shoppes at Marina
Bay Sands mall, and seven
celebrity-chef-run restaurants.
For entertainment, there are
two large theaters, an ice
skating rink, a casino, and two
Crystal Pavilions. Floating on
the water and four-stories high,
the pavilions house nightclubs
and shops full of designer
brands. Hotel guests can also
access the Skypark with its
infinity pool set on top of the
world's largest public
cantilevered platform. This tops
the complex and overhangs
the north tower.

❽ Gardens by the Bay

18 Marina Gardens Drive. **Map** 5 F3.
Tel 6420-6848. Ⓜ Bayfront. 🚌 400.
Open 5am–2am daily. Conservatories
9am–9pm; last ticket sold 8pm, last
entry 8:30pm. Skyway 9am–9pm.
🏛 for conservatories. 🎫 9am,
11am, 2pm & 4pm daily.
🆆 gardensbythebay.com.sg

Covering a vast area alongside
the waterfront, this award-
winning horticultural attraction
offers more than 250,000 rare
plants in landscaped gardens
and conservatories. The
outdoor gardens are divided
into three spaces – Bay South,
Bay East, and Bay Central.
Highlights include the Heritage
Gardens, where plants are
linked to the main ethnic
groups in Singapore, and the
Supertree Grove – 16-story-high
vertical gardens that collect
rainwater, generate solar power,
and act as venting ducts for the
conservatories. Suspended
between two Supertrees is the
OCBC Skyway. This walkway
offers visitors a bird's-eye view
of the gardens and the Marina
Bay area. A dazzling sound and
light show takes place nightly
amid the Supertrees.

The stunning Marina Bay Sands resort lit up
at night

The soaring silver blocks of the Raffles City complex

❾ Singapore Flyer

30 Raffles Avenue. **Map** 5 F2. **Tel** 6738-3338. Ⓜ Promenade. 🚌 106, 111, 133. **Open** 8:30am–10:30pm daily. 🖼
🖼 🖼 🆆 **singaporeflyer.com.sg**

One of Singapore's most eye-catching attractions is the world's second-tallest observation wheel, set on the edge of Marina Bay. As the wheel slowly turns, the city views from pods that reach 541 ft (165 m) above ground level are amazing. The trip takes about 30 minutes.

❿ St. Andrew's Cathedral

Coleman Street. **Map** 5 E2. **Tel** 6337-6104. Ⓜ City Hall. 🚌 7, 32, 51, 81, 124, 145, 197, 603, 851. 🕙 10:30am–2:30pm daily. 🖼 🖼 🖼 see website. 🖼 🆆 **livingstreams.org.sg**

Although an Anglican church, St. Andrew's was named for the patron saint of Scotland in recognition of the Scottish merchants who contributed funds to build it. The present cathedral dates from 1862 and was designed in an Early Gothic style reminiscent of England's Salis-bury Cathedral.

⓫ Raffles City

252 North Bridge Road. **Map** 3 D5, 5 E2. **Tel** 6433-2238. Ⓜ City Hall. 🚌 7, 36, 77, 97, 103, 124, 131, 147, 162, 166, 174, 190, 501, 511, 603. **Open** 10am–9:30pm daily. 🖼 🖼 🖼
🆆 **rafflescity.com.sg**

This huge complex comprises a shopping mall, high-rise offices, and two hotels – the Fairmont Singapore and Swissôtel the Stamford, the world's tallest hotel when it opened in 1985. Perched atop the Stamford are lavish bars and restaurants, including Jaan on Level 69, which has stunning panoramic views.

Popularly dubbed the Tin Can for its metallic appearance, Raffles City was designed by I M Pei, the architect famous for the glass pyramid in front of the Louvre in Paris and Bank of China skyscraper in Hong Kong.

⓬ Raffles Hotel

See pp220–21.

⓭ Chijmes

30 Victoria Street. **Map** 3 D5, 5 E1. **Tel** 6337-7810. Ⓜ City Hall. 🚌 2, 7, 12, 33, 81, 107, 130, 133, 147, 190, 520, 851, 960. **Open** 11am–3am daily. 🖼
🖼 🖼 🆆 **chijmes.com.sg**

Chijmes (pronounced "chimes"), an elegant walled complex of shops, bars, restaurants, and gallery spaces, was once the Convent of the Holy Infant Jesus. Founded by a French Jesuit priest in 1854 and run by nuns, the convent functioned as a school and a women's refuge, as well as a home for abandoned babies. In 1983, it was redeveloped into a shopping and restaurant complex. Quiet courtyards, cobbled paths,

Façade of the chapel of Chijmes, now an arts and dining venue

fountains, and covered Italianate walkways encircle shops that sell arts and crafts from China, the Philippines, Thailand, Malaysia, and India, as well as restaurants that serve everything from *sushi* to tapas. A flea market is held here most Sundays. The most striking building in the complex is the former chapel, designed in Neo-Gothic style by the Jesuit priest Father Nain.

Singapore Art Museum, a former Catholic boys' school

⓮ Singapore Art Museum

71 Bras Basah Road. **Map** 3 D5, 5 D1. **Tel** 6332-3222. Ⓜ Bras Basah, Dhoby Gaut. 🚌 7, 14, 16, 36, 77, 97, 131, 167, 171, 518, 602, 603, 605, 607, 700. **Open** 10am–7pm Mon–Sun, 10am–9pm Fri. 🖼 free for children under 6 years; also after 6pm Fri. 🖼 🖼 🖼 🖼
🆆 **singaporeartmuseum.sg**

A bronze statue of two schoolboys with 17th-century saint John Baptiste de la Salle stands above the porch of the Singapore Art Museum, a reminder that until 1987 this was St. Joseph's Institution, a Catholic boys' school.

Today, the building is a showcase for contemporary Asian art. Since the museum's opening, its permanent collection has grown from under 2,000 works of art to over 7,000 pieces, making it one of the world's largest public collections of modern and contemporary Southeast Asian art. The core of the museum's art, which includes sculptures, installations, and paintings, is richly supplemented by a regular roster of local and international traveling exhibitions, featuring 20th-century art from American and European compilations. Works from the museum's own collection are loaned out to international exhibitions.

Usually only a selection of works are on display at any given time. There are works by artists such as Georgette Chen, Liu Kang, Chen Chong Swee, Lim Tze Peng, and Huang Yao from Singapore, and those by regional artists such as Wong Hoy Cheong from Malaysia, Affandi from Indonesia, and Bui Xian Phai and Tran Trong Vu from Vietnam.

The old Classical-style building has been restored and skillfully converted for use as a museum. The former school chapel is used as an auditorium. While the chapel's original character has been retained, its central window has been replaced by a modern stained-glass work by Filipino artist Ramon Orlina. The building's two courtyards are used as exhibition spaces, arranged on either side of the Glass Hall, which is a glass-enclosed converted veranda decorated with blown-glass installations by American artist Dale Chihuly. The old classrooms are now galleries. The Learning Gallery showcases contemporary works by Singapore artists that have been especially selected to engage the imaginations of young people. The stylish gift shop has been voted one of the best museum shops in the world.

The Dome Café, ensconced in one of the naves of the museum, serves excellent sandwiches, cakes, and coffee drinks. There is also the Trattoria Lafiandra, which serves Italian cuisine. A trendy alfresco wine bar adds to the ambience.

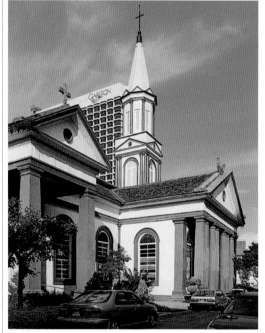
Renaissance-style exterior of the Cathedral of the Good Shepherd

Sculpture, Singapore Art Museum

❶ Cathedral of the Good Shepherd

Victoria Street. **Map** 3 D5, 5 D1. **Tel** 6337-2036. Ⓜ Bras Basah. 🚌 7, 14, 16, 36, 77, 97, 131, 167, 171, 501, 700, 957, 960. **Open** daily from mid-2016; phone ahead for hours and service times 🚻 🆆 veritas.org.sg

Singapore's oldest Catholic place of worship, this cathedral, built in the 1840s, reopens in 2016 following renovations. It was first administered by French missionary Father Jean-Marie Beurel, who also established the Convent of the Holy Infant Jesus and St. Joseph's Institution. Designed by noted colonial architect D L McSwiney in a Latin-cross pattern, the church combines a Renaissance-style exterior with Doric columns, Palladian porches, and a beautifully crafted timber ceiling. The octagonal steeple was a later addition by Charles Dyce.

The cathedral served as an emergency hospital during the invasion of Singapore in World War II, and was listed as a national monument in 1973.

Three interesting buildings stand within the church compound. The **Archbishop's House**, a 19th-century double-story bungalow with a projecting portico, casement windows, and enclosed verandas, is a simple structure in contrast to the cathedral. The **Resident's Quarters**, a U-shaped single-story building with Doric columns, and the **Priest's House** are more ornate and decorated with elaborate plasterwork.

Stained glass in the Cathedral of the Good Shepherd

⓬ Raffles Hotel

A legendary hotel and a national monument, Raffles, which opened in 1887, is a tranquil haven of white, veranda-enclosed, colonial-style buildings with terracotta-tiled pitched roofs. It was once the venue for grand colonial balls and dances, and its guest list boasted such names as Noel Coward, Somerset Maugham, Rudyard Kipling, Joseph Conrad, Charlie Chaplin, and Michael Jackson. The cool, calm refuges of its courtyards, gardens, and covered walkways can still be enjoyed by residents and visitors alike.

★ Long Bar
The Singapore Sling, the pink drink originally intended for women, was created in 1915 by Hainanese bartender Ngiam Tong Boon.

★ Ornamental Fountain
Made in Scotland in the early 1890s, the 20-ft- (6-m-) high cast-iron fountain was donated to the hotel in 1990 and now stands in the Palm Garden.

★ Lobby
The lobby, home to the Writers Bar, features photographs of some of the writers who have stayed at Raffles.

Palm Court
This area is a beautifully restored space lined with palm and frangipani trees. Collectively, the hotel's gardens house over 50,000 plants representing about 80 different species.

Raffles Courtyard
A menu of Italian dishes is served in this immaculate alfresco dining space with its tropical palms and native plants.

VISITORS' CHECKLIST

Practical Information
1 Beach Road. **Map** 5 E1.
Tel 6337-1886. 🖋 🖥 🏠
w raffles.com

Transport
M City Hall. 🚌 56, 82, 100, 518.

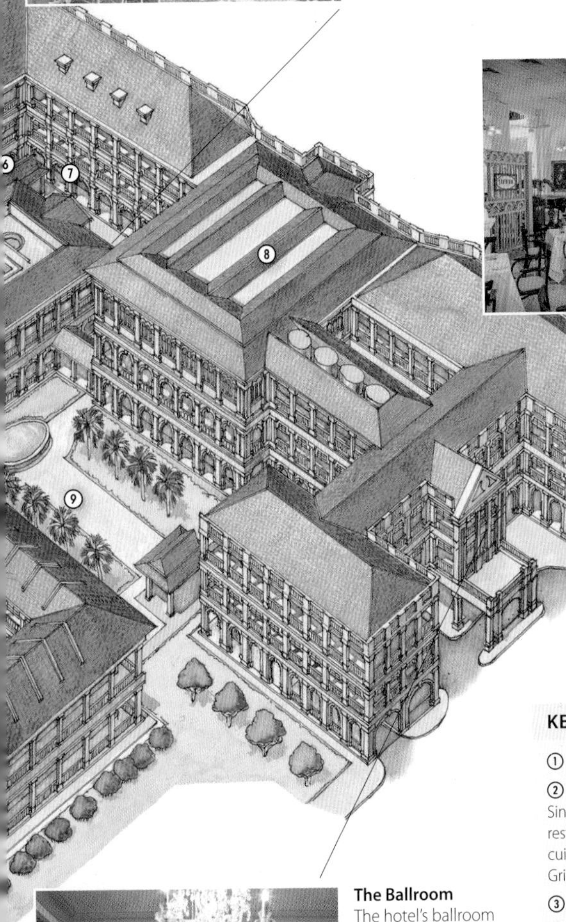

★ Tiffin Room
A north Indian curry buffet is offered for lunch and dinner here, punctuated by a strictly English afternoon tea.

The Ballroom
The hotel's ballroom is the epitome of formal elegance, with its high ceilings, sparkling chandeliers, and murals.

KEY

① **Writers Bar**

② **The Raffles Grill** is one of Singapore's most prestigious restaurants, serving fine French cuisine. The French doors of the Grill overlook the Palm Court.

③ **Tiffin Room**

④ **Bar and Billiard Room**

⑤ **Raffles Gift Shop**

⑥ **Ah Teng's Bakery**

⑦ **Long Bar Steakhouse** has a formal dress code and serves prime cuts of Australian and American beef and seafood.

⑧ **Jubilee Hall**

⑨ **The lawn's** tropical foliage combined with a gazebo provides the setting for garden receptions.

Neo-Classical façade of the Peranakan Museum

⑯ National Museum of Singapore

93 Stamford Road. **Map** 3 D5, 5 D1. **Tel** 6332-3659. Ⓜ Bras Basah, Dhoby Ghaut. 🚌 7, 14, 16, 36, 77, 97, 131, 166. **Open** 10am–6pm daily. 🅿️ 🅲 11am, 2pm daily, also 3:30pm Sat & Sun. 🗒️ 🏛️ 🌐 nationalmuseum.sg

Housed in a Neo-Palladian structure and crowned with a stunning stained-glass dome, the island's oldest museum opened in 1887. Known as the Raffles Museum and Library, it was famed for its remarkable collections of natural history, ethnology, and archaeology.

Following Singapore's independence in 1965, the museum was renamed the National Museum to reflect its new role and altered its focus to exhibitions that concentrated on the history and peoples of Singapore. The museum has a permanent collection, which features displays on food, fashion, and local history. There are also various exhibitions on a range of subjects from Chinese secret societies to botany, however, the highlights of the museum are the 11 artifacts that have collectively been christened the "Treasures of the National Museum."

The museum has been undergoing a S$10 million facelift, initiated as part of Singapore's landmark 50th anniversary celebrations in 2015, and parts of it may remain closed as a result until the second half of 2016. The revamp aims to give museum-goers a more comprehensive overview of Singapore's history, and to celebrate multiple voices in the nation's historical narrative.

⑰ Peranakan Museum

39 Armenian Street. **Map** 3 D5, 5 D2. **Tel** 6332-7591. Ⓜ City Hall, Bras Basah. 🚌 7, 14, 16, 36, 77, 97, 131, 166. **Open** 10am–7pm daily (to 9pm Fri). 🅿️ 🅲 11am, 2pm. 🏛️ 🌐 peranakanmuseum.sg

The building in which this museum is housed was originally the Tao Nan School, established in 1910 by three Chinese philanthropists for the education of boys from the Hokkien region of China. In 1997, this Neo-Classical building opened as the first wing of the Asian Civilisations Museum. Following an overhaul, it became a Peranakan-themed museum representing a pan-Southeast Asia perspective of Peranakan culture with a focus on its main centers, which include Singapore, Melaka, and Penang.

The museum explores the history and ethnology of the culture of these regions and also provides an interesting glimpse into their heritage, including language and religious customs. Exhibits include silver artifacts, porcelain, jewelry, and textiles.

⑱ Armenian Church

60 Hill Street. **Map** 3 D5, 5 D2. **Tel** 6334-0141. Ⓜ City Hall. 🚌 2, 12, 32, 33, 51, 103, 124, 147, 174, 190, 197, 851. **Open** 9am–5pm Mon–Fri, 9am–noon Sat. **Closed** Sun.

The Armenian Church of St. Gregory the Illuminator was the first permanent place of Christian worship in Singapore. The church was built in 1835 and the spire was added later, in 1850. It was able to seat a congregation of only 50 people, a reflection of the minority status of the local Armenian community then.

Designed by G D Coleman, the architect responsible for other landmarks of early Singapore such as St. Andrew's Cathedral (see p218), the church is an elegant example of tropical Neo-Classical architecture. The interior contains a photograph of the Armenian community from around 1917, as well as portraits of the patriarchs of the Armenian Church. In the

Interior of the Armenian Church

church's compound is the grave of Agnes Joaquim, who discovered an orchid hybrid in 1893. The flower was later named Vanda Miss Joaquim for her and adopted as Singapore's national flower.

⓳ Fort Canning Park

51 Canning Rise, Singapore, 179872. **Map** 2 C5, 4 C2. **Tel** 6332-1200. Ⓜ Dhoby Ghaut. 🚌 14, 32, 54, 77, 124, 139, 195. **Open** 6am–9pm daily.

Once the seat of Temasek, a 14th-century Malay kingdom, Fort Canning Park is now a verdant, tranquil oasis in the heart of the city. Because of the lovely view the site commands, Raffles built his bungalow here, and until the mid-19th century, it was home to Singapore's governors. The park was also the first site of Raffles' botanical garden.

In 1860, Fort Canning was built here; only the fort gate still stands. Nearby is the Fort Canning Center, formerly a barracks that now contains the Pinacotheque de Paris, an offshoot of a private fine art gallery that has made something of a name for itself in Paris. Another historic landmark is the Battle Box, a World War II bunker containing a museum that uses animatronics to recreate the 1942 surrender of the city to the Japanese. The Battle Box reopens in late 2016 following renovations.

Sculpture, Fort Canning Park

⓴ Chettiar Temple

Crossing of Tank Road and River Valley Road. **Map** 4 C2. **Tel** 6737- 9393. Ⓜ Dhoby Ghaut. 🚌 14, 32, 54, 65, 139, 195. **Open** 8am–noon, 5:30–8:30pm daily.

Built in 1984, this Shaivite Hindu temple replaced a much older one, founded in 1860 by wealthy Indian Chettiars (moneylenders). Dedicated to Lord Murugan (also known as Subramaniam), the colorful temple is believed to be one of the wealthiest and grandest in Singapore.

Craftsmen from southern India were specially brought in to create the temple's distinctive architectural features, which include a striking five-tiered *gopuram*, or entrance archway, massive patterned rosewood doors, and columns and prayer halls richly decorated with sculptures of Hindu deities.

The ceiling has 48 etched-glass panels of gods that are angled to catch the rising and setting sun. Another feature, a rarity for Hindu temples, is the presence of a *thoonganai maadam*, a representation of the rear of an elephant at rest. The dominance of the temple's main deity is apparent throughout the temple, with Lord Murugan represented in six of his holy abodes. Inside the temple are two connected rooms, the *mandapam* and the *antarala*, through which worshipers move to perform their devotions. The *antarala* leads to the innermost sanctum, the *garbhagraha*, which only priests

may enter. The Chettiar Temple plays an important role in the life of Hindu Shaivites as it is the culmination point of a spectacular procession that begins at Sri Srinivasa Perumal Temple *(see pp236–7)* during the annual Thaipusam festival, which occurs between January and February and honors Lord Murugan *(see p206)*.

The colorful *gopuram* of the Hindu Chettiar Temple

㉑ Clarke Quay

3 River Valley Road, Singapore 179019. **Map** 4 C2. Ⓜ Clarke Quay. 🚌 14, 32, 54, 65, 139, 195, or 3 min. walk from Hill Street. ⬚ 🖥 📷 🚩 flea market on Sat & Sun. 🅆 **clarkequay.com.sg**

Named for Sir Andrew Clarke, the second governor of Singapore, Clarke Quay is an upscale area along the banks of the Singapore River with waterfront shops and eateries. Lying near the mouth of the Singapore River, the site of Clarke Quay was a commercial hub during the late-19th century, containing ware-houses run by Chinese traders. It was redeveloped in the early 1990s into an entertainment precinct offering restaurants, wine bars, retail stores, craft stalls, street performers, and cruises in authentic bumboats (boats that bring provisions and commodities to ships at port). While it is relatively quiet during the day, Clarke Quay offers a lively atmosphere at night.

The wide frontage of the Fort Canning Center, now housing an art gallery

Figurines adorning the *gopuram*, or gateway, of Sri Mariamman Temple

temple has been repaired several times over the years. In its early days, the temple gave shelter to new immigrants and also served as a social center for the community.

Although many of the splendid friezes and statues depict the Hindu divine trinity of Brahma, Vishnu, and Shiva, as well as other Hindu deities, the temple is dedicated to the goddess Sri Mariamman (an incarnation of Shiva's wife Parvati), known for her power to cure disease. The temple is famous for the annual Thimithi festival *(see p207)* in autumn, during which devotees walk on hot coals as a sign of faith.

❷ Chinatown Heritage Centre

48 Pagoda Street. **Map** 4 C3. **Tel** 6221-9556. Ⓜ Chinatown. 🚌 61, 80, 197. **Open** 9am–8pm daily. 🅿️
Ⓦ chinatownheritagecentre.sg

A superb museum housed in three restored shophouses, the center provides one of the most vivid accounts of the history and culture of Chinese immigrants. Three levels of galleries recreate their living conditions and, together with first-hand accounts of former residents and a variety of artifacts, trace the lives of early settlers and evoke different periods of Chinatown's history.

❸ Sri Mariamman Temple

244 South Bridge Road. **Map** 4 C4. **Tel** 6223-4064. Ⓜ Chinatown. 🚌 51, 80, 124, 143, 174, 197. **Open** 7am–noon & 6–9pm daily.

The southern end of South Bridge Road is dominated by the *gopuram*, or entrance gateway, of the Sri Mariamman

Temple, vividly decorated with about 72 Hindu deities. The complex is encircled by a boundary wall topped with figures of sacred cows.

The oldest Hindu place of worship on the island, Sri Mariamman dates back to 1827 when the first temple, a simple wood and *attap*, or thatched-roof, was built on this site. The land belonged to an Indian merchant, Narain Pillai, who arrived in Singapore on the same ship as Sir Stamford Raffles. It was replaced by the present structure in 1843. The

❹ Temple Street

Map 4 C4. Ⓜ Chinatown. 🚌 51, 80, 124, 145, 174, 197, 608. 🅿️ 🖥️ 📷

The area bounded by Mosque, Pagoda, Temple, Terengganu, and Smith Streets is the place that Sir Stamford Raffles had first earmarked for the Chinese community. It grew into the hub of Chinese life and culture, with streets that were lined with temples, traditional craft stores, *kongsi*, or clan houses, restaurants, and shophouses, shuttered buildings where the ground floor was occupied by a shop while families lived on the upper floor. Some shophouses contained opium dens and brothels, giving the area a somewhat colorful reputation.

Sensitive restoration has meant that much of the original character of these shophouses

The entrance to a shop on Temple Street, Chinatown

has been retained. Many are painted in bright, contemporary colors. While escalating rents have driven out some of the traditional businesses, the area still features a variety of shops selling souvenirs, antiques, porcelain, and clothing. There are also several pleasant restaurants and cafés. The surrounding housing blocks also offer an authentic flavor of the old Chinatown. These streets come alive during Chinese New Year, with festivities, vibrant decorations, and food and gift stalls.

Restored double-story shophouses in the Tanjong Pagar Conservation Area

㉕ Chinatown Complex

New Bridge Road. **Map** 4 C4. Ⓜ Outram Park, Chinatown. 🚌 2, 12, 33, 54, 62, 63, 81, 124, 147, 961. **Open** 10am–10pm daily. 🚻 ▢ 🏛

On the corner of Terengganu Street and Sago Street, the Chinatown Complex houses one of the most boisterous wet markets in the city, offering a bewildering variety of fresh produce. The most startling meat and fish, including frogs, is on sale in the mornings.

㉖ Buddha Tooth Relic Temple and Museum

288 South Bridge Road. **Map** 4 C4. **Tel** 6220-0220. Ⓜ Outram Park, Chinatown, Tanjong Pagar. 🚌 1, 12, 33, 54, 63, 124, 143, 147, 961. **Open** 7am–7pm daily. 🌐 **btrts.org.sg**

Opened in 2007, this hugely popular temple gets its name from what Buddhists regard as the Sacred Buddha Tooth Relic. A Tang-styled Chinese Buddhist temple, it is based on the Buddhist *mandala*, a representation of the universe. Look out for bone and tongue relics in the Buddhist Culture Museum on the third floor. On the fourth floor is the Sacred Light Hall with the temple's centerpiece, the Buddha Tooth Relic, housed in a giant stupa made of gold. Only monks are allowed into the relic chamber.

㉗ Tanjong Pagar Conservation Area

Map 4 B5. Ⓜ Tanjong Pagar. 🚌 80, 145. 🚻 ▢ 🏛

Once a nutmeg plantation, this area at the southern tip of South Bridge Road boasts some of Singapore's most elegant stretches of renovated shophouses. One of the first of the old neighborhoods to be renovated, Tanjong Pagar is now home to many lively restaurants, bars, and hotels.

At the corner of Neil Road and Tanjong Pagar Road is the former Jinrickshaw Station, built in 1903. Jinrickshaws were first imported from Shanghai in the 1880s. By 1919 there were about 9,000 rickshaws and 20,000 rickshaw-pullers. The rickshaws were phased out by legislation after World War II and soon disappeared from the streets of Singapore.

Shophouse Styles

The shophouse is a memorable feature of Singapore's local architecture. Five styles, roughly chronological, have been identified – the Early, the First Transitional, the Late, the Second Transitional, and Art Deco styles.

The Early Style (1840–1900) shophouse is a squat, two-story building. The windows and façade are plain.

The First Transitional Style (early 1900s) shophouse is three stories high, such as this unit at Telok Ayer Street.

The Late Style (1900–1940) shophouse is flamboyantly ornamented with eclectic styles, as seen in this unit (No. 21) on Bukit Pasoh Road.

The Second Transitional Style (late 1930s) shophouse, such as this unit (No. 10) on Stanley Street, is much simpler and less ornate.

The Art Deco Style (1930–1960) shophouse is typified by classical geometric motifs, as illustrated by this unit (No. 30) located on Bukit Pasoh Road.

The distinctive architecture of Lau Pa Sat's food court

28 Ann Siang Hill

Map 4 C4. M Tanjong Pagar, Chinatown. 51, 61, 63, 80, 103, 124, 145, 174, 197, 603, 608, 851.

Once a clove and nutmeg plantation, Ann Siang Hill and its neighboring streets are today a hub of Chinese life and activity. The gently curving street, flanked by shophouses, makes for an interesting walking tour. Some of the shophouses feature *pintu pagar*, or half doors, reflecting Malay influence. Club Street nearby is noted for its dining and upmarket boutiques. It is also famous for its temple-carving shops and the clan associations and guilds that gave the street its name. Some, such as the **Victorian Chinese Weekly Entertainment Club**, still survive on the hill, their walls plastered with photographs of former members. Also striking are house numbers 33 and 35, designed by architect Frank Brewer, famed for his skilled plasterwork.

Row of restored shophouses on Ann Siang Hill

29 Telok Ayer Street

Map 5 D4. M Tanjong Pagar, Raffles Place. 10, 70, 75, 82, 97, 100, 107, 130, 167, 186.

Originally located on the seafront before modern land reclamation, Telok Ayer Street, which means water bay in Malay, retains much of the feel of 19th-century Singapore. On the street are a number of traditional businesses, as well as temples and mosques where early immigrants gave thanks for their safe passage. One of the most famous is the Hokkien **Thian Hock Keng Temple** *(see pp228–9)*, the city's oldest Chinese temple. The neighboring **Al Abrar Mosque** was built between 1850 and 1855 by Indian Muslims, who also built the nearby **Nagore Durgha** in the 1820s, a blend of Classical architecture and Indian-Islamic details such as arches and perforated grills. All three are national monuments. Farther down the street is the **Fuk Tak Chi Museum**, standing on the site of the former Hock Teckk Ch'i Temple. Among its display of Chinese artifacts is a diorama depicting Telok Ayer Street as it would have been in the 1850s. For a contrasting experience, the temple site also includes the tranquil, stylish Amoy boutique hotel.

30 Lau Pa Sat

18 Raffles Quay. **Map** 5 D4. M Raffles Place. 10, 70, 75, 82, 97, 100, 107, 130, 131, 167, 186. **Open** 24 hours.

Singapore's first municipal market, Telok Ayer Market, now renamed Lau Pa Sat, is an architecturally impressive food court offering an extensive variety of Asian cuisines and is a favorite lunch venue for locals. Originally commissioned by Raffles in 1822 on reclaimed land, the elegant octagonal cast-iron structure was designed by James MacRitchie and shipped over from a Glasgow foundry in 1894. It was declared a national monument in 1973.

The market was dismantled during MRT tunnel construction and was later painstakingly reassembled. The adjacent Boon Tat Street is closed off to traffic in the evenings for traditional hawker stalls to set up shop.

31 Thian Hock Keng Temple

See pp228–9.

㉜ Raffles Place

Map 5 D3. Ⓜ Raffles Place. 🚌 10, 70, 75, 82, 97, 100, 107, 130, 131, 167, 196.

Nowhere is Singapore's transition from a colonial backwater to a cutting edge, booming economy more apparent than in the gleaming skyscrapers of Raffles Place. This is the heart of the city's financial world, packed with well-known multinational corporations and financial institutions. Among the first banks to open here were the Hong Kong and Shanghai Bank and Standard Chartered Bank. The three tallest buildings in Singapore are located here – UOB Plaza and One Raffles Place Tower 1, both designed by renowned Japanese architect Kenzo Tange, and Republic Plaza. All the buildings are 920 ft (280 m) high. The Bank of China building is one of Southeast Asia's earliest skyscrapers.

Dotted around the area are installations of modern sculpture, including Salvador Dali's *Homage to Newton* (1985) and Fernando Botero's *Bird* (1990). The Merlion statue, symbol of the city, is also located nearby. **Clifford Pier**, which provided a location for Conrad's *Lord Jim*, is now a fine dining restaurant which has excellent views over the marina.

Dali's Homage to Newton, Raffles Place

Conrad's Lord Jim

Born to Polish parents in what is now Ukraine, Teodor Josef Konrad Korzeniowski sailed to many places, including the Malay states, between 1874 and 1894, becoming a mariner and a British subject in 1886. Joseph Conrad is perhaps the most celebrated English writer on late 19th-century Southeast Asia, and Singapore figures prominently in his works, especially in the novel

Joseph Conrad

Lord Jim. It was in this region that he heard of an English merchant navy officer, Austin Podmore Williams, who earned lasting disgrace by abandoning the steamer *Jeddah*, along with 953 Muslim pilgrims, in the Red Sea in 1880, dooming himself to a life of exile. He became the tragic model for Conrad's *Lord Jim*.

㉝ Boat Quay

Map 5 D3. Ⓜ Raffles Place. 🚌 2, 12, 33, 51, 54, 61, 81, 103, 145, 147, 166, 174, 190.

A thriving strip of restored shophouses converted into restaurants, shops, and bars, Boat Quay today is very different from the riverfront area of a century ago. The center of the city's commercial activities in the 1860s, most of its trading was handled from here. Shophouses crowded the curve of the south bank, the shape of which was thought to resemble the belly of a carp, an indicator of prosperity according to Chinese belief. The river teemed with bumboats, which were used to load and unload ships anchored on the river. By the 1960s, however, technological advances had changed the face of the shipping industry. New, high-tech container ports opened up farther up the river, claiming Boat Quay's role in the river's trade. Trading houses moved out and the area slowly declined. The government embarked upon a river-cleaning program which cleared out all the bumboats and the barges, leaving Boat Quay a desolate region.

The area has been restored as part of a government-led conservation project, reno-vating the old shophouses and godowns (warehouses) and revitalizing the riverfront area by pedestrianizing it. There are plenty of bars and restaurants with enchanting views of the river. A taxi service also plies for customers between Boat Quay and Clarke Quay.

Bars and restaurants lining the riverbank at Boat Quay, once a busy trading center

❸ Thian Hock Keng Temple

Built in 1839, Thian Hock Keng Temple is the oldest Chinese temple in Singapore. Constructed by Hokkien sailors on the site of a joss house, it was the most important center of worship for immigrants from their community. It was also where seafarers gave thanks for a safe passage to Singapore. Construction was paid for by individual donors, the main one being Hokkien leader Tan Tock Seng (1798–1850). The temple itself is laid out along a traditional north–south axis and has shrines dedicated to several deities. Today, people of all ages come to this temple to give their thanks to Ma Zhu Po, the goddess of the sea.

★ **Roof Decorations**
On the temple's roof ridge stand twin dragons that embody the principles of yin and yang. Between them is the "night-shining pearl," a glass globe that represents the sun.

Rear Hall
Dedicated to the moon goddess, Yue Gong Niang Niang, Rear Hall houses a shrine to the goddess. She is worshiped alongside Kuan Yin, the goddess of mercy. The sun god, Ri Gong Tai Zi, is also worshiped here.

★ **Secondary Shrines**
In the side hall to the left of the main courtyard stand shrines to Kai Zhang Shen Wang, an early immigrant, and Cheng Hang, a local deity.

KEY

① **Gift Shop**

② **The pagoda**, which used to house Chong Wen Ge, the first Chinese school in Singapore, was built in 1849.

③ **The roof ridge** is decorated with glazed tile chips.

④ **The furnace** is where paper money offerings and other gifts are burned to placate the spirits of the dead.

⑤ **The door** at the main entrance is decorated with temple guardians from Chinese mythology.

⑥ **The main hall** contains the image of Ma Zhu Po, the sea goddess. She is flanked by Guan Gong, the god of war, and Pao Sheng Da Di, the protector of life.

Ancestor Tablets
The spirits of ancestors are
believed to reside in these
venerated tablets.

Granite Pillars
The intricate columns
which support the roof,
made of granite from
China, are carved with
entwined dragons.

★ **Ceiling of Main Hall**
Gilded carvings on the temple's ceiling
depict stories from Chinese folklore. These
carvings have been restored by artisans from
China. The gray pillars supporting the ceiling
are made of granite from China.

LITTLE INDIA AND ORCHARD ROAD

Originally occupied by Europeans and Eurasians, Little India was settled by the Indians when they set up brick-kilns and cattle yards in the latter half of the 19th century. Packed with restaurants, shops, and ornate temples, the area is a mix of sights, scents, and sounds. With colonial architecture and a Middle Eastern ambience, Kampong Glam provides some of the best insights into Singapore's Malay community. Arab traders were the earliest settlers,

joining Buginese, Boyanese, and Javanese arrivals, to create a Muslim enclave. The ethnic area of Little India is the spiritual heart and commercial center of the local Indian community. Orchard Road lies to the northwest of the Colonial Core. In the 1840s it was a dirt road, lined with orchards and nutmeg plantations, but today it constitutes Singapore's most historic shopping district. Lavish hotels, cafés, pubs, and shopping malls are located here.

Sights at a Glance

Historic Streets and Buildings
❷ Malay Heritage Centre
❸ Arab Street
❼ Serangoon Road
❾ Dhoby Ghaut

Mosques and Temples
❶ Masjid Sultan
❹ Leong San See Temple
❺ Sakya Muni Buddha Gaya
❻ *Sri Srinivasa Perumal Temple pp236–7*
❽ Sri Veeramakaliamman Temple
❿ Peranakan Place and Emerald Hill
⓯ Goodwood Park Hotel

Shopping
⓫ The Centrepoint
⓬ ION Orchard
⓭ Ngee Ann City
⓮ Tangs
⓰ Tanglin Mall

See also Street Finder maps 1, 2 & 3

◀ Exuberant carving on the Sri Veeramakaliamman Temple, Little India

For keys to symbols *see back flap*

Street-by-Street: Kampong Glam

Kampong Glam is the focal point of Muslim life in Singapore. Its name is derived from the Malay words *kampung,* or village, and *gelam,* a tree that once grew abundantly in the area. In 1819, the area was given to Sultan Hussein Shah as part of a treaty by which Singapore was ceded to the British. The Sultan built his palace, the Istana Kampong Glam, and the stunning Masjid Sultan here and soon the area was filled with Muslims from diverse ethnic backgrounds. This early impact is reflected in the distinct Islamic flavor of its street names, shops, buildings, and restaurants. Arab Street is a major draw, with its intricate textiles, fine leather, and caneware. Good Malay food stalls can be found on Kandahar Street.

Alsagoff Arab School
Built in 1912, this was the first girls' school and the first Muslim school to be built in Singapore. It was named for a prominent Arab trader and philanthropist.

To Malabar Jama-Ath Mosque and old Malay cemetery

❷ ★ **Malay Heritage Centre**
Malay motifs combine with Palladian style in the former Istana Kampong Glam palace, now a Malay cultural center.

NORTH BRIDGE ROAD

❶ ★ **Masjid Sultan**
Designed by Irishman Denis Santry, this mosque dominates the skyline with its golden domes and four corner minarets.

KANDAHAR STREET

MUSCAT STREET

ARAB STREET

To Bugis MRT Station

Gedung Kuning
This yellow mansion, erected in the 1920s by Sultan Ali Iskandar Shah, is an example of Palladian-inspired architecture.

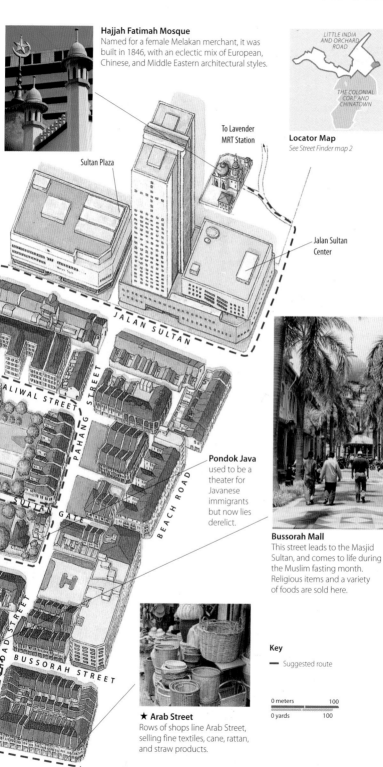

Hajjah Fatimah Mosque
Named for a female Melakan merchant, it was built in 1846, with an eclectic mix of European, Chinese, and Middle Eastern architectural styles.

Locator Map
See Street Finder map 2

LITTLE INDIA AND ORCHARD ROAD

THE COLONIAL CORE AND CHINATOWN

Sultan Plaza

To Lavender MRT Station

Jalan Sultan Center

JALAN SULTAN

ALIWAL STREET

PAHANG STREET

BEACH ROAD

SULTAN GATE

BAGHDAD STREET

BUSSORAH STREET

Pondok Java
used to be a theater for Javanese immigrants but now lies derelict.

Bussorah Mall
This street leads to the Masjid Sultan, and comes to life during the Muslim fasting month. Religious items and a variety of foods are sold here.

★ Arab Street
Rows of shops line Arab Street, selling fine textiles, cane, rattan, and straw products.

Key

— Suggested route

0 meters   100
0 yards   100

Main prayer hall inside the Masjid Sultan

❶ Masjid Sultan

3 Muscat Street. **Map** 3 E4. **Tel** 6293-4405. Ⓜ Bugis. 🚌 7, 32, 124, 145, 166, 174, 195, 197. **Open** 9:30am–noon & 2–4pm daily (2:30–4pm Fri). 🏛 voluntary. Note: visitors can only view the prayer hall from the foyer. 🌐 sultanmosque.org.sg

Named for Sultan Hussein Shah of Johor, the mosque was originally built in 1824 with the aid of a grant from the British East India Company, the result of a treaty between the Sultan and Stamford Raffles. It was replaced in 1928 by the present structure, designed by Irish architect Denis Santry. Arabesque in style with Moorish overtones, golden domes, balustrades, and arches, as well as a minaret at each corner, Singapore's largest mosque accommodates 5,000 worshipers in its main hall. Visitors are guided by multilingual docents.

❷ Malay Heritage Centre

Sultan Gate. **Map** 3 F4. **Tel** 6390-0450. Ⓜ Bugis. 🚌 107, 961, 980. **Open** Compound: 8am–8pm Tue–Sun (to 10pm Fri & Sat). Museum: 10am–6pm Tue–Sun. **Closed** Mon. 🏛

This cultural center and its museum, celebrating Malay history, culture, and arts, are housed in the Istana Kampong Glam, formerly the official royal residence of Sultan Hussein Shah, who ceded the sovereign rights of Singapore to the British. As part of this historic agreement, the Sultan built a wooden palace in 1820 and

named the area Kota Raja, or the King's Enclave. In 1840, his son, Sultan Ali Iskandar Shah, the last Sultan of Singapore, built the present palace. The Istana presides over extensive grounds. Several smaller Malay village-style houses were built within the walled compound. These housed the Sultan's large entourage which included his family of hundreds of relatives and servants. Also on the premises was the Kota Rajah Club, a sports club founded by a descendant of the Sultan, where young men of good breeding could enjoy recreational activities such as badminton.

According to the 1904 Sultan Hussein Ordinance, enacted by the British Government, the Sultan's descendants were entitled to live in the palace and receive an annual government stipend. Over the years, however, disputes and dwindling fortunes led the palace to gradually fall in ruins. It was then reclaimed by the government, which compensated the Sultan's descendants for their displacement.

❸ Arab Street

Map 3 E4. Ⓜ Bugis. 🚌 2, 7, 12, 32, 33, 51, 61, 62, 63, 125, 130, 145, 197, 520, 851, 960. 🚻 🛍 📷

Located within the smallest of Singapore's ethnic quarters, this street acquired its name from the Arab merchants who settled here when they came to trade in the 19th century. The vibrant colors of Arab Street are striking. It is a maze of shops that sell all manner of Middle Eastern and Islamic wares. Religious items such as prayer mats, holy beads, copies of the Koran, and skull caps jostle for space with excellent basketware, rattan, cane and straw work, leather products, jewelry, precious and semi-precious gems, and perfumes. Visitors should be prepared to bargain. The majestic Masjid Sultan looms over this pedestrianized tourist market strip.

Arab Street is most famous for its textile stores. Bales of colorful cotton, chiffon, organza, and silk cloth cram the shopfronts and spill onto the pavement. *Batik* from Indonesia and Malaysia, handmade or machine-printed with traditional designs, is typically sold in *sarong* lengths of 6 ft (2 m). Shops also sell readymade *batik* shorts, shirts, dresses, ties, and table linen. To complement the fabric sellers, specialist shops sell ostrich feathers, dazzling lamé in several shades, various types of sparkling sequins, and thread in a profusion of colors. Traditional Malay wedding outfits can also be found in shops on Arab Street.

Baskets and leather bags for sale on Arab Street

❹ Leong San See Temple

371 Race Course Road. **Map** 3 E1.
Tel 6298-9371. Ⓜ Farrer Park. 🚌 23,
64, 65, 111, 130, 131, 133, 139, 147.
Open 6am–6pm daily.

Situated across the road from the dazzling Sakya Muni Buddha Gaya Temple, the Leong San See Temple honors Kuan Yin, the goddess of mercy and compassion, and Shakyamuni Buddha. Leong San See, or dragon mountain temple, was built in 1917 by a Buddhist monk. Today, both Taoists and Buddhists worship here. The temple is beautifully decorated with timber beams and intricate carvings of phoenix, dragons, chimeras, and flowers. A courtyard in the temple contains many ancestral tablets.

Large gilded Buddha at Leong San See Temple

❺ Sakya Muni Buddha Gaya

366 Race Course Road. **Map** 3 E2. **Tel**
6294-0714. Ⓜ Farrer Park. 🚌 23, 64,
65, 106, 111, 125, 130, 131, 142, 147,
151, 857. **Open** 7:30am–5pm daily. ♿

Popularly known as the Temple of a Thousand Lights, Sakya Muni Buddha Gaya was built by Vuttisasara, a Thai monk. The temple has a Thai *wat* design, embellished with a mix of Chinese and Indian influences. To the left of the entrance is an ebony and mother-of-pearl replica of what is believed to be the footprint of the Buddha. Beyond, a 50-ft (15-m) seated statue of the Buddha is illuminated by the colored electric lights that give the temple its popular name.

Another relic that draws devotees here is a branch believed to be from the *bodhi*, or peepul, tree under which the Buddha gained his enlightenment. In a chamber behind the Seated Buddha is a statue of the Reclining Buddha. About 25 scenes from the Buddha's life are portrayed on the base of the statue. Visitors can have their futures foretold at a wheel of fortune near the prayer hall.

❻ Sri Srinivasa Perumal Temple

See pp236–7.

❼ Serangoon Road

Map 3 F1. Ⓜ Little India. 🚌 23, 64,
65, 106, 111, 125, 130, 131, 142, 147.
♿ 🚻 📷

The early Indian migrants to Singapore in the 19th century settled along the banks of the Rochor Canal. The area eventually became a trading and cattle-breeding center, evident from street names such as Kerbau Road, which means Buffalo Road in Malay. Over time, as more Indians arrived, Serangoon Road became the heart of "Little India," the religious, cultural, and economic center for the local Indian community.

One of the oldest roads in Singapore, Serangoon Road is a kaleidoscope of quintessential Indian life. Vying for attention are elaborate Hindu temples and ornate shophouses. The shopkeepers hang mirrors above their doors to ward off evil influences and sell jewelry, textiles, and Bollywood movie soundtracks. The area is full of Indian restaurants such as Komala Villas, famous for vegetarian food. The noise of fortune-telling parrots, street pedlars, and a heady aroma of spices and flowers fill the air.

❽ Sri Veeramakali-amman Temple

141 Serangoon Road. **Map** 3 D3.
Tel 6295-4538. Ⓜ Dhoby Ghaut,
Bugis. 🚌 23, 64, 65, 103, 106, 111, 125,
130, 131, 142, 147, 151, 857. **Open**
6am, 1pm, 4pm, 7:30pm daily. ♿ 📷

This temple, built in 1881 by Bengali laborers, is dedicated to the Hindu goddess Kali, who epitomizes the struggle of good over evil and is the consort of Shiva, the god of destruction. The name of the temple means Kali the Courageous.

The main altar of the temple has a black statue of Kali with each of her many arms and legs holding a weapon. She is flanked by her two sons Ganesh, the elephant god, and Murugan, the child god riding a peacock. The temple is especially crowded on Tuesdays and Fridays, which are Hindu holy days when devotees throng the temple to worship.

Sri Veeramakaliamman Temple, a temple in honor of the Hindu goddess Kali

❻ Sri Srinivasa Perumal Temple

One of the most important religious buildings in Singapore, this Hindu temple is devoted to the worship of Lord Vishnu (also known as Perumal). It is also one of the oldest temples in Singapore. Built in 1854, the temple was originally a simple structure with a *mandapam*, or a prayer hall, and the area around the temple had many ponds and vegetable gardens. In 1966, when the temple was consecrated, a six-tiered *gopuram*, or entrance tower, was built, funded by one of the earliest Indian migrants, P. Govindasamy Pillai. The temple is the starting point of the annual Thaipusam festival parade.

★ **Mandapam**
The main *mandapam* or prayer hall has a decorated ceiling that is supported by ornately carved columns.

★ **Subsidiary Shrines**
Several subsidiary shrines are dedicated to different deities. This shrine is in honor of Ganesh, the elephant-headed god who removes obstacles.

KEY

① **The inner sanctum** is where the main idol lies. Only priests can enter.

② **The office** provides information on temple activities.

Vimanams
Decorated *vimanams*, or domes, mark the position of the temple's subsidiary shrines.

Thaipusam Festival

This Hindu festival begins at dawn at the temple. Male devotees enter a trance-like state, carrying ornately decorated *kavadis*, or steel arches, attached by metal hooks to their torsos, with skewers pierced through their tongues and cheeks. Devotees take part in this act in penance for their sins and in honor of Lord Murugan, the god of bravery, power, beauty, and virtue. Women carry coconut milk pots, also fulfilling vows relating to penance. Accompanied by chanting and singing, they walk to Sri Thendayuthapani Temple on Tank Road, about 2 miles (3 km) away.

Devotee carrying an ornately decorated *kavadi*

Main Shrine
Here, devotees make offerings of ghee, flowers, and fruit, to the accompaniment of music and chanting. They also sprinkle their heads with holy water.

Vishnu
This sculpture of Vishnu shows him with four sacred instruments – the conch shell, club, lotus, and saber.

VISITORS' CHECKLIST

Practical Information
397 Serangoon Road. **Map** 3 E2. **Tel** 6298-5771. **Open** 6:30am–noon & 6–9pm daily. 👤 📷 on request.

Transport
Ⓜ Farrer Park. 🚌 23, 64, 65, 111, 130, 131, 139, 147, 857.

★ Gopuram
The 60-ft- (20-m-) high entrance tower has six tiers of sculptures.

②

Main Entrance
Statuary stands guard on either side of the massive wooden door. Devotees ring the bells before entering, asking the gods to grant their prayers.

Hanuman
This shrine is dedicated to Hanuman, the monkey god. In the Hindu epic, the *Ramayana*, he helps rescue Sita from the demon, Ravana.

Street-by-Street: Orchard Road

Stretching from Tanglin Mall to Plaza Singapura, the range and scale of retail outlets on Orchard Road make it an exemplary shopping experience. Shady trees dot the road between malls and department stores, including Singapore's oldest, Robinsons at The Heeren and the historic Tangs. These large, glitzy buildings are interspersed with smaller designer boutiques, antique stores, cafés, and food courts. Crowds throng the streets, especially on weekends.

⑬ Ngee Ann City
With seven floors, Ngee Ann City has plenty going on inside. It has more than 30 restaurants, a post office, banks, a Japanese department store, and more than 120 shops *(see pp240–41)*

Wheelock Place
Shaped like a steel and glass Christmas tree, Wheelock Place houses a department store and a few restaurants.

Paragon shopping center boasts a vast, shop-lined atrium. It houses five floors of gift, fashion, and lifestyle stores.

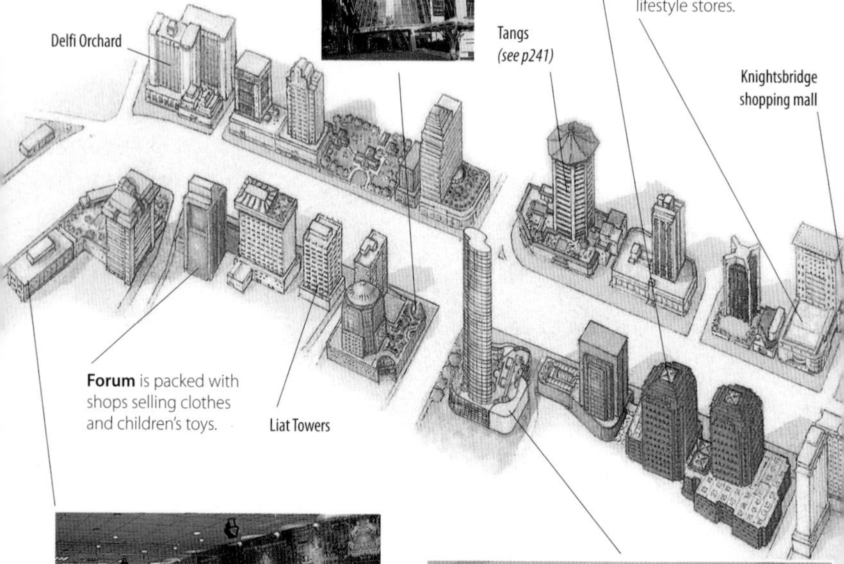

Delfi Orchard

Tangs *(see p241)*

Knightsbridge shopping mall

Forum is packed with shops selling clothes and children's toys.

Liat Towers

⑯ ★ Tanglin Mall
A paradise for antique lovers, Tanglin Mall is a treasure-house for old maps, bric-à-brac, books, furniture, carpets, and art

⑰ ★ ION Orchard
This vast, architecturally impressive center with shiny floors and snaking escalators offers a huge number of brands under one roof.

Locator Map
See Street Finder maps 1 & 2

⑩ ★ Peranakan Place
Beyond Peranakan Place's Baroque Chinese shophouse façade are modern, air-conditioned shops selling Eastern and Western goods, as well as restaurants, cafés, and pubs *(see p240)*.

⑪ The Centrepoint
The Centrepoint houses a diverse selection of stores over six floors and a basement. Its flagship store, Metro, has an excellent range of household goods. Cold Storage in the basement has one of the best supermarket selections *(see p240)*.

The Heeren is the place for trendy clothing, a huge music store, and the Robinsons department store.

Cuppage Plaza

0 meters	200
0 yards	200

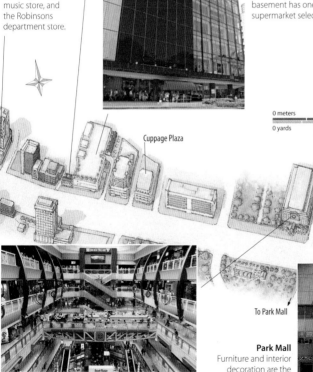

To Park Mall

Park Mall
Furniture and interior decoration are the themes of Park Mall. From the traditional to the avant garde, displays include items from Europe and Asia.

Plaza Singapura
One of the earliest malls on Orchard Road, Plaza Singapura was refurbished in the 1990s. As well as a department store, it houses a number of specialist outlets.

9 Dhoby Ghaut

Map 2 C4, 4 C1. M Dhoby Ghaut. 7, 14, 16, 36, 64, 65, 77, 85, 106, 111, 123, 124, 139, 143, 167, 171, 174, 190, 502, 518.

The area known as Dhoby Ghaut takes its name from the *dhobies*, or Indian laundrymen, who worked here many years ago, and *ghaut*, which means landing place in Hindi. *Dhobies* used to go door-to-door, collecting clothes from residents and recording the items in a book. They washed the clothes in the nearby stream, which ran down the side of Orchard Road, and dried them on land that is now occupied by the YMCA. This land was also once the site of detention and interrogation rooms used by the Japanese during World War II. Next to the YMCA is a white Presbyterian church established by Scottish settlers in 1877. It was once used as a supply base for Japanese civilians.

10 Peranakan Place and Emerald Hill

Emerald Hill Road. **Map** 2 B4. M Somerset. 7, 14, 16, 65, 77, 106, 111, 123, 124, 143, 167, 171, 174, 190. W peranakanplace.com

An upscale neighborhood of traditional residences, plush boutiques, and pricey eateries today, Peranakan Place and Emerald Hill were originally granted in 1845 to Englishman William Cuppage. Emerald Hill

was later acquired by the Peranakans *(see p26)*. From 1900 to 1930, 30 different owners built residential units along Emerald Hill Road resulting in a street lined with unique Peranakan architecture. Interesting features include the wooden *pintu pagar*, or half doors across unconventional doorways. Also visible are colorful ceramic tiles, mirrors above doors to ward off evil spirits, and animal reliefs to invite good luck. Toward Orchard Road, these terrace houses were converted into shophouses, with the first floors occupied by small stores and seamstresses.

The buildings on Peranakan Place have been carefully restored, making this area the only stretch of old shophouse architecture left on Orchard Road. It now houses restaurants, cafés, and boutiques.

11 The Centrepoint

176 Orchard Road. **Map** 2 B4. **Tel** 6737-9000. M Somerset. 7, 14, 16, 65, 77, 106, 111, 123, 124, 143, 167, 171, 174, 190. **Open** 10am–10pm daily. W fraserscentrepointmalls.com

This large shopping center first opened in 1858 and is one of Singapore's oldest malls. The store claims to have the best seasonal sales in Singapore, one of which coincides with the Great Singapore Sale held in June *(see p253)*. There is a host of other shops from branded Western retailers such as Marks & Spencer,

The Centrepoint shopping center, Orchard Road

Birkenstock, and Lacoste to Singaporean and Hong Kong fashion outlets, jewelry shops, interior decoration, and furniture shops.

12 ION Orchard

2 Orchard Turn. **Map** 1 F2. **Tel** 6238-8228. M Orchard. 14E, 124, 128, 143, 162. **Open** 10am–10pm daily. W ionorchard.com

The vast ION Orchard mall joined the shopping scene in 2009. With more than 300 stores, including designer names such as Louis Vuitton, Prada, and Cartier, the road's largest mall draws massive crowds, particularly at the weekend. An extensive food hall offers a myriad of choices, from the best hawker fare to international flavors. The art and exhibition gallery on the fourth floor is the largest of its kind in Singapore.

13 Ngee Ann City

391A Orchard Road. **Map** 2 A4. **Tel** 6506-0461. M Orchard. 7, 14, 16, 65, 77, 106, 111, 123, 124, 143, 167, 171, 174, 190. **Open** 10am–9:30pm daily. W ngeeanncity.com.sg

Popularly known as "Taka", Ngee Ann City has marble twin towers and a main entrance that has two silver columns and is guarded by two hand-carved *foo* dogs imported from China to bring prosperity. The building's atrium is five floors high, criss-crossed by escalators, and packed with over 100 local and

The multicolored shophouses near Peranakan Place

Modern sculpture and fountain in front of Ngee Ann City

international specialty stores. The dazzling array of some of the world's prestigious retailers includes Gucci, Chanel, Tiffany, Cartier, Tod's, Kenzo, Wedgwood, Burberry, Waterford, Bulgari, Louis Vuitton, Loewe, and Takashimaya, a Japanese department store.

Other facilities at the mall include a post office, a ticket-booking office, a great Kinokuniya bookstore, banks, a private health club, a night-club, and a café with a great view over the Civic Plaza.

⓮ Tangs

310 & 320 Orchard Road. **Map** 2 A3.
Tel 6737-5500. Ⓜ Orchard. 🚌 7, 14, 16, 36, 64, 65, 77, 106, 111, 123, 124, 132, 139, 143, 167, 171, 174, 190, 502, 518, 700. **Open** 10:30am–9:30pm Mon–Thu, 10:30am–11pm Fri & Sat, 11am–8:30pm Sun. 🚻
Ⓦ tangs.com.sg

The growth of Singapore's most famous department store reflects the vision of a young

Tangs department store, popular with both locals and visitors

Chinese immigrant of the 1920s. From selling his wares on a cart, the dynamic C K Tang nurtured his business into a store that rivals all others on Orchard Road. From under its distinctive pagoda-style roof, it now sells everything from cosmetics to rice cookers.

The distinctive tower of the elegant Goodwood Park Hotel

⓯ Goodwood Park Hotel

22 Scotts Road. **Map** 2 A3. **Tel** 6737-7411. Ⓜ Orchard. 🚌 54, 105, 124, 132, 143, 167, 171, 190, 518, 700. 🚻
🏊 Ⓦ goodwoodparkhotel.com

Originally the Teutonia Club for German expatriates in the early 1900s, the Goodwood Park Hotel was declared enemy property and seized by the government when World War I broke out in 1914. In 1929, the club was converted into a hotel. Designed by J Bidwell, the

architect who also designed its famous rival, Raffles Hotel, Goodwood competed furiously for famous guests – Charlie Chaplin stayed at Raffles while Goodwood boasted the Duke of Windsor as a patron.

When World War II broke out, Goodwood was again seized, this time by the occupying Japanese forces. After the war, it was chosen to be the venue of a court dealing with war crimes.

Today, this landmark, the only colonial hotel apart from Raffles, has returned to its former incarnation. Its elegant corridors are lined with art and antique furniture and in 1989, the Tower Wing of the hotel, distinguished by its gable ends with ornamental plaster work, was selected as a national monument. The hotel has also grown from its original 60 rooms into a 234-room luxury retreat with a fantastic range of restaurants.

⓰ Tanglin Mall

19 Tanglin Road. **Map** 1 E2. **Tel** 6737-0849. Ⓜ Orchard. 🚌 7, 36, 105, 111, 123, 132, 502. **Open** noon–6pm Mon–Sat. 🚻 🛗 📷 Ⓦ tanglinsc.com

Tucked away at the far end of Orchard Road and removed from the bustle is the quiet Tanglin Mall, unrivaled for its array of collectibles, vintage items, antiques, and art. Shop after shop offers a veritable treasure of Persian rugs, tapestries, curios made of jade and brass, and contemporary Southeast Asian art.

Tanglin, a favorite haunt of expatriates, is home to some of the "firsts" and "bests" of Singapore shopping. **Antiques of the Orient**, the best-stocked seller of antique maps and secondhand books in Singapore, has fascinating prints, postcards, and photographs. **Apsara** offers a good collection of Chinese and Burmese antiques. Also on offer are impeccably tailored men's suits, toy stores, sportswear, nail bars, and hairdressers, as well as some good restaurants.

FARTHER AFIELD

Some of Singapore's most interesting sights lie outside the city limits. Though much of its west is dominated by industrialized towns such as Jurong, it still contains some major tourist attractions including the theme park Haw Par Villa, the Science Centre Singapore, and the fascinating Jurong Bird Park. The central north area retains the island's spectacular primary rain forests and mangrove swamps and is dedicated to most of its nature reserves, such as Bukit Timah and Singapore Zoo. The Singapore Botanic

Gardens is a treasure-house of rare orchids and makes a peaceful retreat. Other sights of historic and religious significance include the museum at Changi village and Kusu Island. The island is famous for its turtle legend and is popular with Taoists and Muslims. To the south, Sentosa is the city's favorite getaway spot and now boasts the vast Resorts World complex with the Sealife Aquarium. East Coast Park offers a range of outdoor and indoor activities. The rustic island of Pulau Ubin is a peaceful retreat.

Sights at a Glance

Parks, Gardens, and Nature Preserves

1 Singapore Zoo
2 Bukit Timah Nature Reserve
4 Jurong Bird Park
6 *Singapore Botanic Gardens pp246–7*
10 East Coast Park

Museum

11 Changi Museum

Themed Attractions

3 Singapore Discovery Center
5 Science Centre Singapore
7 Haw Par Villa

Outlying Islands

8 Kusu Island
9 *Sentosa pp250–51*
12 Pulau Ubin

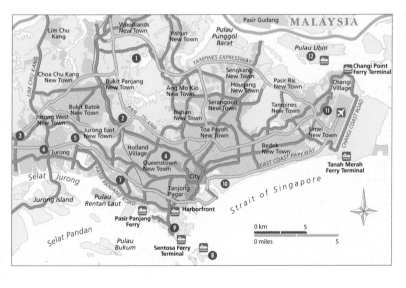

Key

Street Finder

Built-up area

Highway

Major road

Railroad

◀ Baby parrots at the Jurong Bird Park

For keys to symbols *see back flap*

The endangered Malayan tiger in Singapore Zoo

❶ Singapore Zoo

80 Mandai Lake Road. **Tel** 6269-3411.
Ⓜ Ang Mo Kio, Choa Chu Kang,
Woodlands. 🚌 138 from Ang Mo Kio,
927 from Choa Chu Kang, 926 from
Woodlands bus interchange (Sun &
public hols). **Open** 8:30am–6:30pm
daily. ♿ 🅿 🍴 optional. 📷 📹
Ⓦ zoo.com.sg Night Safari: **Open**
7:30pm–midnight daily (last adm
11pm). 📷 🚫

Set in refreshingly green
and peaceful surroundings,
the Singapore Zoo is one of
the world's few open zoos,
where animals roam freely in
landscaped enclosures that
simulate their habitats. Dry
and wet moats camouflaged
by waterfalls and vegetation
separate the animals from
visitors. While some animals,
such as leopards, jaguars, and
pumas still have to be kept in
glass enclosures, others such
as monkeys and peahens
roam freely.

The zoo houses about 3,000
animals, representing 290
species. Several of them are rare
such as the white (Bengal) tiger
and clouded leopard, while
others are endangered species
such as the Komodo dragon
and the Malayan tiger.

Major exhibits include Wild
Africa with its white rhinos and
magnificent lions, the Fragile
Forest, which is a walk-through
rain forest filled with butterflies,
bats, and birds, and the Primate
Kingdom featuring lion-tailed
macaques, brown capuchins,

and golden-lion tamarins. There
is also a children's petting zoo;
aquariums offering clear
underwater views of sea lions
and penguins; and a reptile
garden with several different
habitats. The zoo's breeding
program is well known and it
has the distinction of fostering
the world's first tropical birth of
a polar bear cub. There are daily
animal shows and feeding times
featuring sea lions, elephants,
primates, and reptiles. Visitors
also have the opportunity to
have breakfast or tea with the
orangutans, which makes it a
wonderful and memorable visit.

The **Night Safari**, sprawled
over 100 acres (40 ha) of lush
secondary forest next to the
zoo, is a night zoo and a wildlife
park combined. This unique
sight allows visitors to observe
the nocturnal activities of over
2,500 animals belonging to over
110 different species. A 45-
minute guided tram ride (with a
hop-on-hop-off option) takes
visitors through eight habitats
designed to resemble the
Himalayan, Indian, Nepalese,
African, Indo-Malayan, Southeast Asian, South American, and
Burmese geographical regions.
There is also a Wallaby Trail
where visitors can observe
some of Australia's native
nocturnal species, including
bush-tail possums, sugar gliders
and wallabies. The River Safari is
an extension to the Zoo and
Night Safari, focusing on river
fish, mammals, and reptiles.

❷ Bukit Timah Nature Reserve

177 Hindhede Drive. **Tel** 6468-5736.
Ⓜ Bukit Batok, then taxi. 🚌 67, 75,
171. **Closed** until mid-2016 for
renovations; check website for latest
details. 🅿 Ⓦ nparks.gov.sg

One of the only two rain forests
in the world that are within city
limits, Bukit Timah was
established as a reserve in
Singapore in 1883 to protect
the native biodiversity. Today,
about 410 acres (164 ha) of the
rain forest, which once covered
the entire island, still exist,
containing a cornucopia of flora
and fauna, and providing a
refuge for many mammals,
birds, and reptiles. Bukit Timah
has cycling and walking trails,
one of which leads to the
highest point, **Bukit Timah Hill**,
540 ft (164 m) above sea level.
The reserve should be open
again from mid-2016 following
closure for restoration work.

Cycling on the bike track at the Bukit Timah
Nature Reserve

❸ Singapore Discovery Center

510 Upper Jurong Road. **Tel** 6792-
6188. Ⓜ Boon Lay. 🚌 182, 193 from
Boon Lay. **Open** 9am–6pm Tue–Sun.
📷 ♿ 🍴 🅿 Ⓦ sdc.com.sg

Originally intended as a
museum to showcase the
history of Singapore Armed
Forces (SAF), the Singapore
Discovery Center today gives an
interesting glimpse into
Singaporean life. Visitors can
learn about Singapore's past,

Iguanas in the Reptile Garden, Singapore Zoo

❺ Science Centre Singapore

15 Science Centre Road, off Jurong Town Hall Road. **Tel** 6425-2500. Ⓜ Jurong East. 🚌 66, 178, 198, 335. **Open** 10am–6pm daily. ♿ 🚻 🖥 📷 Ⓦ **science.edu.sg**
Omnimax Theater: **Open** 9:30am–8:30pm Tue–Sun and public hols. 🎦
Ⓦ **omnitheatre.com.sg**

Acclaimed as one of the world's top ten science museums, the Science Centre Singapore has over 1,000 hands-on exhibits in eight galleries that are dedicated variously to aviation, space science, ecology, biotechnology, and IT among other disciplines. Visitors can explore innumerable scientific phenomena, and the Centre aims to make even the most complex of principles more accessible and easier to understand. The emphasis here is on fostering the learning of science and technology in a creative, entertaining, and interactive way.

Exhibits at the Science Centre include one that enables visitors to experience the world from within a fishbowl. There is also a mock television studio, where children are encouraged to become journalists for a day.

Next door, the **Omnimax Theater** features spectacular educational movies on science, technology, history, adventure sports, space, and the universe. The movies are projected on gigantic hemispherical screens in a 276-seat theater.

present, and future through various interactive exhibits. Located on the Singapore Armed Forces Training Institute's (SAFTI) grounds, the center is about 48,500 sq ft (4,500 sq m), with five main galleries and eight different themes.

Key milestone events that shaped present-day Singapore are presented through multimedia clips at The Gateway gallery, while the So Singapore Theatre is a fun way of finding out about how the different races live in harmony in Singapore. At the Singapore Works gallery interesting games teach visitors about the challenges Singapore faces being a small island with no resources of its own. Singapore Way deals with hopes, dreams, and aspirations, and the Visionarium gallery allows visitors an opportunity to contribute ideas to the Singapore of the future.

The center has a spectacular light and sound show with kaleidoscopic images of Singapore. For a truly sensory experience, a visit to Singapore's largest flat screen theater with 2D and 3D movies is a must. The center also has a popular shooting range.

❹ Jurong Bird Park

2 Jurong Hill, off Ayer Rajah Expressway. **Tel** 6265-0022. Ⓜ Boon Lay. 🚌 194, 251 from Boon Lay. **Open** 8:30am–6pm daily. 🎦 📷 🚻 🖥 Ⓦ **birdpark.com.sg**

More than 5,000 birds across 380 species from all over the world, including exotic and endangered birds, can be seen at Jurong Bird Park. The park has four aviaries, including the African Waterfall Aviary, the world's largest walk-in aviary. Here, visitors can walk among 1,500 free-flying birds against the backdrop of the world's tallest man-made waterfall. Other highlights include the Lory Loft, which is a towering aviary offering magnificent 360-degree views of the landscape. This enclosure showcases one of the largest collections of Southeast Asian birds in the world. The penguin enclosure has a recreated Antarctic environment. Daily birdshows include the World of Hawks, which features a demonstration of the hunting skills of birds of prey. The Birds 'n' Buddies show is an entertaining display by birds of different species who wear costumes and talk to each other. Children will love the Birdz of Play playground, which has both wet and dry bird-themed play zones.

Science Centre Singapore, a place to explore science and technology

❻ Singapore Botanic Gardens

The Singapore Botanic Gardens are located close to the bustling city and have served as a peaceful sanctuary since 1859. This idyllic garden sits on 130 acres (52 ha) of land and is dotted with lakes inhabited by swans, ducks, and turtles. The park is excellent for a stroll around its pretty waterfalls, landscaped fountains, and well-situated rest spots. Refrains of orchestral music can at times be heard from outdoor concerts. It has both primary jungle and manicured lawns. The gardens' orchid breeding program, begun in 1928, has produced more than 2,000 hybrids, with more being added each year. The garden has a reference library containing journals, rare books, and botanical illustrations dating back to 1875.

★National Orchid Garden
With over 1,000 species, this beautifully landscaped garden has the largest display of tropical orchids in the world.

VIP Orchid Garden
In 1928, the government started breeding hybrid orchids, and after 1957 started naming selected ones for distinguished guests.

Bandstand
This octagonal bandstand was popular in the 1860s, when promenading in the gardens while listening to music played by a band was a fashionable pastime.

KEY

① **Swan Lake** is home to a host of swans as well as a variety of pond flora.

② **Burkill Hall** was home to many of the Garden's past directors, including Isaac Henry Burkill and his son.

③ **The Tan Hoon Siang Mist House** contains rare orchid blooms. Cultural artifacts particular to the orchid's country of origin are displayed alongside.

Sculptures
Girl on a Swing (1984) is the first of a series of works created by Sydney Harpley.

★ **Yuen-Peng McNeice Bromeliad House**
The collection of 20,000 bromeliads, which come from the forests of Central and South America, was donated by Lady Yuen-Peng McNeice. More than 700 species and 500 hybrids can be seen.

Towards Eco Lake and Jacob Ballas Children's Garden

EJH Corner House
This colonial bungalow houses Au Jardin les Amis, which is one of Singapore's top fine-dining restaurants.

0 meters 100
0 yards 100

Visitors' Center
The center has an information counter, a café, a shop, and restrooms, as well as ample parking space. It has its own main entrance access from Evans Road. Volunteers lead free guided tours of selected areas of the gardens on Saturdays; times and details can usually be found on the website.

Symphony Lake
On an islet in the middle of Symphony Lake is the Shaw Foundation Symphony Stage. Concerts and performances are regularly held in the pavilion.

Exhibit from Chinese folklore at Haw Par Villa

❼ Haw Par Villa

262 Pasir Panjang Road. **Tel** 6872-2780. Ⓜ Harbourfront. 🚌 10, 30, 51,143, 200. **Open** 9am–7pm daily. 🔌 📷

This landscaped park and villa has picturesque surroundings, carp ponds, and statues and dioramas depicting aspects of Chinese folklore and traditional values. Established by the Aw brothers, Haw and Par, with the fortune they made from Tiger Balm, a camphor and menthol remedy still widely sold today, this theme park is based on Chinese legends and myths and aims to teach traditional values. Over 1,000 statues and tablets show mythical creatures and tell stories from Chinese folklore. The Ten Courts of Hell section is one of the most popular, graphically portraying the punishments for sins such as gambling and theft.

❽ Kusu Island

Tel 6534-9339 for ferry times. 🚌 402. ⛴ from Marina South Pier. 📷 includes ferry ticket. 🌐 **islandcruise.com.sg**

According to legend, Kusu Island, or Turtle Island, was actually a giant turtle which transformed itself into land to save two shipwrecked sailors, one Chinese and one Malay.

Located 3 miles (5 km) off Singapore, Kusu Island receives most of its visitors during the eleventh lunar month (October or November), when Taoist and Muslim devotees flock to the island on a pilgrimage. Taoists visit the island's Tua Pek Kong Temple, which is dedicated to the patron saint of merchants. Devotees pray for prosperity, good luck, and wealth, light joss sticks, and make offerings of flowers and food.

Muslim devotees climb 122 steps up a steep hill to visit a Malay shrine of Keramat Kusu. Childless couples mark their prayers by tying pieces of cloth around trees on their way up to the shrine.

The island is known for its two blue lagoons, its vast pristine beaches, and a wishing well. It has undergone much development and has a pleasant spot for picnics. However, overnight stays are not permitted on the island.

❾ Sentosa

See pp250–51.

❿ East Coast Park

Off East Coast Parkway (ECP). Ⓜ Bedok. 🚌 401. 🔌 📷 📷 🌐 **nparks.gov.sg**

The stretches of beach along East Coast Park are considered among the best in the country. The park stretches for more than 6 miles (10 km) along the coast from Changi Airport to Marina Bay. The seafront is lined with palm trees, shady rest areas, and park benches. For the fitness-conscious there are walking and jogging paths, well-marked cycling and in-line skating tracks, and a competition-standard skateboarding park. Bicycle hire shops in the area offer a choice of racers and mountain bikes or tandems for couples. There is also an in-line skate rental and repair store.

Fishing enthusiasts can set up their rods; picnickers can pitch tents on the beach; health buffs can work out at the outdoor fitness stations, and bird-watchers can take a walk through designated bird sanctuaries.

The pleasing sea breezes and scenic views of the East Coast Park make this a very fashionable place to live. The area is well provided with bars, chic restaurants, and a host of recreational facilities. The food on offer ranges from fast food and hawker fare to seafood and Western snacks. At the East Coast Recreation Center, indoor activities such as bowling, snooker, and children's games can be enjoyed. For watersports, kayaks and windsurf boards can

Taoist Tua Pek Kong Temple on Kusu Island

be hired from the Mana Mana Beach Restaurant and Bar. Holiday chalets can be rented for short-term stays. These chalets on the beachfront also provide facilities such as swimming pools, spas, and barbecue pits. The East Coast Park is a local favorite, especially for weekend family outings.

Families cycling along well-marked tracks at East Coast Park

❶ Changi Museum

1000 Upper Changi Road North. **Tel** 6214-2451. Ⓜ Tanah Merah, Tampines. 🚌 2, 29. **Open** 9:30am–5pm (4:30pm last admission). 🚩 5:30pm Sun. 📷 📖 🏛 Ⓦ changimuseum.sg

Changi Prison, which once served as a World War II prisoner-of-war (POW) camp for Allied troops, is still in use. Changi Museum is located just up the road from the prison, at the site of the Old Changi Prison Chapel. The museum is dedicated to all those who lived and died in Singapore, in particular the prisoners who suffered unspeakable torture at the hands of Japanese jailers during their internment here.

Over the years, the museum has amassed a valuable collection of photographs, paintings, and personal effects donated by former POWs and their families. A selection of photographs by George Aspinall, then a young Australian trooper, and more than 400 sketches by W R M Haxworth are among the works of art by various prison artists that are showcased here. Replicas of the Changi Murals, which were originally drawn by

prisoner Stanley Warren on the walls, are also on display.

In the museum's courtyard is a replica of the simple thatched-roof wooden chapel built by the POWs. The brass cross at the wreathed altar was crafted out of spent artillery casings.

Tour groups of ten or more people are required to inform the museum of their visit, at least three days in advance; call for further details.

❶ Pulau Ubin

Ⓜ Tanah Merah, Tampines. 🚌 2, 29. ⛴ from Changi Village. **Open** daily. 📷 📖 🏛 🚻 🚲

Singapore's second largest offshore island, Pulau Ubin, which sits in the Johor Strait between Changi and the mouth of the Johor River, is perhaps the last place left for a peek into the rustic atmosphere of Singapore as it was in the 1960s. A Malay and Chinese community once engaged in farming, granite quarrying, and fishing on the island. Today, only about 200 people live on Pulau Ubin. Measuring only 5 miles (8 km) across and 1 mile (1.5 km) wide, Pulau Ubin is the site of a traditional Malay fishing village. The remnants of rural kampung life can still be seen here: *attap,* or thatched-roof, and zinc-roofed wooden houses stand on stilts; *sampans,* or wooden fishing boats,

Jackfruit grown in Pulau Ubin

line the beach; and fishing nets spread out to dry in the sun.

The island has a variety of flora and fauna and includes species that once existed on the mainland but now can only be found here. These include various fruit trees such as coconut, durian, rambutan, and jackfruit, wild berries, wild orchids, the insect-trapping pitcher plant, several medicinal plants and herbs, and mangrove flora. The island's wildlife includes monkeys, monitor lizards, water hens, squirrels, fruit bats, and snakes such as pythons and cobras. The waters around the island teem with fish, crabs, and prawns. Pulau Ubin is also a good spot for bird-watchers as birds of prey such as eagles, kites, and hawks, and migratory birds nest here during the northern winter months. Bicycles can be rented from the jetty. The community center nearby has a good collection of photographs of life on the island during its heyday. There are also a few seafood restaurants, old-style coffee shops, and sundry shops that offer necessities for the visitor, such as insect repellent, sunblock, hats, canned drinks, and snacks. A couple of taxis ply the gravel tracks. Campsites, chalets, and lodges provide overnight accommodation on the island.

Rustic Malay kampung house on Pulau Ubin

9 Sentosa

Sentosa Island was once called Blakang Mati, which means "behind the dead" in Malay. One of the theories about the origins of this name speaks of a mysterious disease that claimed the lives of nearly all the original settlers. The British used the island as a military base until 1967. Today, Sentosa, which means "peace" in Malay, has been transformed into a recreational playground with museums, historical sights, theme parks, nature trails, and sporting activities. All the sights can be reached by the island's excellent transport network. Resorts World Sentosa, a major family attraction with a vast oceanarium, covers a large part of the island.

Sentosa's Wings of Time
This 25-minute extravaganza features majestic water effects, fireworks, and a light projection show at Sentosa's Siloso Beach.

★ Underwater World
In this tropical fish oceanarium, a moving walkway transports visitors through a 274-ft (83-m) tunnel to view 2,500 species of marine life.

★ Fort Siloso
The last bastion of the British during World War II, this fort was built in the 1880s and is an intriguing complex of bunkers, cannons, and underground passageways.

★ Adventure Cove Waterpark
The best waterpark in Singapore has rides both adults and children will enjoy, plus the opportunity to snorkel at an artificial reef teeming with fish.

For hotels and restaurants see p283 and p301

sentosa
sentosa

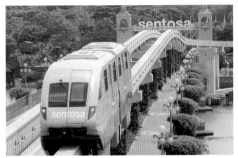

Sentosa Express
A monorail network, the Sentosa Express links Harbor Front, Vivocity, and St James Powerhouse MRT stations on the mainland to Beach and Imbiah stations. It also links sights within the island.

VISITORS' CHECKLIST

Practical Information
1.3 miles (2.1 km) S of Singapore.
Tel 6275-0388.
sentosa.com.sg

Transport
to Sentosa; or to Mount Faber or Harborfront Center, then cable car. Sentosa Express.

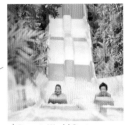

★Resorts World Sentosa
Offering something for everyone, this attraction has a marine-life park with the world's largest oceanarium, a Universal Studios theme park, casinos, shops, and restaurants.

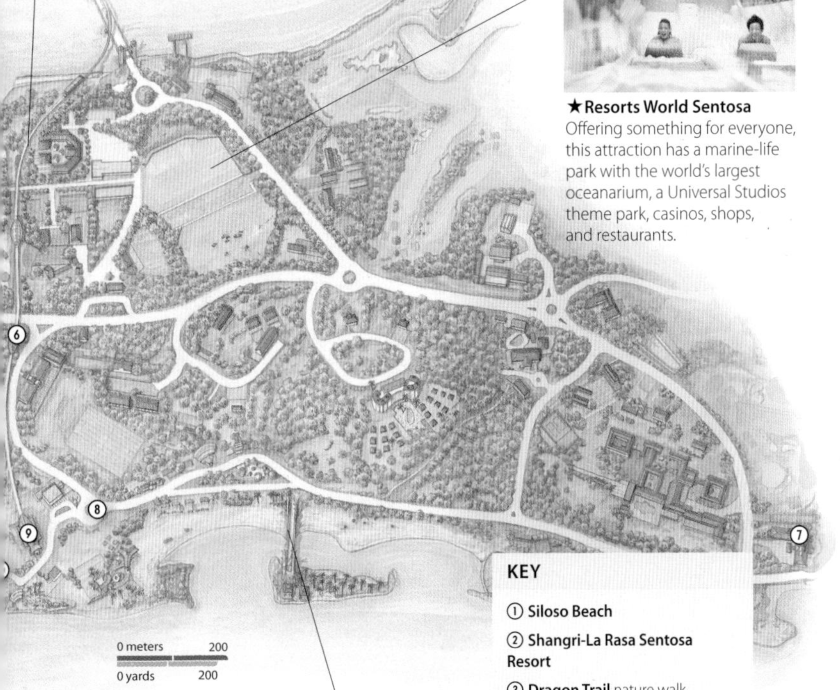

6
8
9
7
0 meters 200
0 yards 200

KEY

① **Siloso Beach**

② **Shangri-La Rasa Sentosa Resort**

③ **Dragon Trail** nature walk.

④ **Tiger Sky Tower** gives a bird's-eye view of Singapore's skyline.

⑤ **Cable car** from Mount Faber.

⑥ **Imbiah station**

⑦ **The Sentosa Golf Club** has two 18-hole championship golf courses and excellent facilities including chipping and putting greens, as well as a pro shop.

⑧ **Merlion Walk**

⑨ **Beach station**

⑩ **Sentosa's Wings of Time**

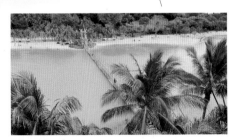

Palawan Beach
A suspension bridge links Palawan Beach to a small islet that is believed to be the southernmost tip of continental Asia.

SHOPPING IN SINGAPORE

Singapore is a shopper's paradise. Scores of shops at every turn offer almost unlimited choices. Whether you want to immerse yourself in the plush shopping arcades of Orchard Road or Raffles City, or scour the flea markets and back alleys of the ethnic quarters, Singapore caters to all tastes and budgets. Best known for its attractively priced electronic goods, such as computers, mobile phones, and cameras, Singapore also offers luxury brands, art, antiques, curios, jewelry, and more. Away from the

exclusive stores and boutiques, some of the most exciting shopping can be found in Little India, Chinatown, Arab Street, and Holland Village. A rich selection of traditional Southeast Asian handicrafts, such as fine caneware, *batik*, and textiles, is sold from stalls and specialist stores. Singapore is also famous for its bargains and sales, especially on electronic goods, but do spend some time browsing to find the best deals and only buy from reputable dealers.

VivoCity mall, with "wave" design features intended to echo its waterfront location

Department Stores and Malls

Orchard Road *(see pp238–9)*, with its vast stretch of glitzy department stores and malls, such as **Knightsbridge**, **Ngee Ann City**, **ION Orchard,** and **The Heeren**, is packed with just about everything one could want – shoes, clothes, books, music, jewelry, carpets, curios, and especially branded luxury items. **Tangs** *(see p241)* and **Robinsons** *(see p239)* at The Heeren are two of the oldest department stores on Orchard Road. **Park Mall** specializes in furniture and interior decoration. Major shopping malls can be found all over Singapore, including **VivoCity, Raffles Hotel Shopping Arcade, Holland Village, Marina Bay Sands** *(see p217)*, and **Raffles City Shopping Center.** For electronic goods, head to **Sim Lim Square** or **Funan Digitalife Mall**. Little India's **Mustafa Center**, a Singapore

favorite, sells every conceivable item, from electrical to household goods. Japanese chain stores **Isetan** and **Takashimaya** are very popular, as is the British retail outlet **Marks & Spencer**. Singapore's department stores and malls are well organized, with obliging staff, and usually an informative helpdesk.

Shopping Hours

Most shops and malls are open every day from 10am to 9pm, though a few stay open until 10pm or later. Mustafa Center in Little India is an exception – it is open 24 hours a day, making it great for a midnight shopping excursion. The mall at **Clarke Quay** opens at noon and stays open until midnight. Little India and Arab Street are best avoided on Fridays as several shops may be closed for the Muslim holy day. All 7-Eleven convenience stores are open 24 hours a day.

How to Pay

International credit cards are accepted at most shops – MasterCard, VISA, American Express, Diners Club, and Citibank. It used to be the case that a surcharge was added when a customer paid by credit card, but that practice has ended. However, some of Singapore's smaller shops and the hawker stalls still insist on being paid for purchases in cash.

Bargaining is an accepted practice in Singapore. Department stores generally have fixed prices, but most other shops, even in high-end malls, may be open to bargaining. It is best to be knowledgable about the correct value of a product. Start by asking the shopkeeper for his best price and then negotiate a suitable deal. Keep the exchange good-natured. Though several high-end shopping centers may accept traveler's checks in major

The Alessi Shop, a designer furnishing store in Park Mall

One of the many Southeast Asian handicrafts shops

currencies, it is always preferable to use the Singapore dollar. Traveler's checks can be cashed at a number of banks, which are open from 9:30am to 3:30pm on weekdays, and 10am to 1pm on Saturdays. Currency can be exchanged at all banks and hotels which display the "Licensed Money Changer" sign.

Sales

Daily newspapers such as *The Straits Times* have listings of all current sales. The free monthlies, *Where Singapore* and *Singapore Shopping Guide,* published by the Singapore Tourism Board, also give details on shopping options. But for the true thrill of Singapore's best bargains, time your trip during the Great Singapore Sale, held every year between May and July and promoted by the Singapore Tourism Board. This super-sale offers discounts of up to 80 percent on almost all goods and is the perfect chance to strike off all those things crowding your wish list. Visitors from neighboring countries are known to fly in just for this sale.

Goods Return Policies

Most large stores provide shoppers with a receipt, and accept returns of unused goods in original condition within seven days of purchase. Alternatively, an exchange may be offered. Keep all receipts until the end of your stay. Ensure that a warranty card that is recognized internationally is provided with any electronic product and is properly dated and stamped.

Consumer Claims

The country has an excellent redress policy for tourist complaints, such as being cheated by a retailer or finding that an international guarantee card has not been properly filled out. Visitors' complaints against retailers and travel companies can be registered via a consumer hotline at the **Consumers Association of Singapore (CASE)**. Consumers should first attempt to resolve the dispute with the business. Failing which, consumers can seek CASE's assistance to settle the dispute. Tourists can file complaints with the Singapore Tourism Board. If the dispute cannot be settled by CASE, the

consumer may file a claim in court for civil remedies. Most claims should be filed under the Small Claims Tribunal.

Permits and Laws

Singapore has a reputation for stringent laws prohibiting the purchase and transportation of weapons, endangered species, and narcotics. Even the smallest offence is not overlooked and can result in a fine, caning, or brief imprisonment. Visitors should be very careful about what they buy, and where they make their purchases. Also, don't carry anyone else's luggage.

Visitors trying their hand at haggling at a busy Sunday flea market in Singapore

Taxes and Refunds

In Singapore, a 7 percent Goods and Services Tax (GST) is levied on most goods and services. A tax refund can be claimed on purchases worth S$100 or more made at shops that display a "Tax Free Shopping" logo. Claims for refunds can be made at GST counters at **Changi International Airport** or you can use the **Electronic Tourist Refund Scheme (eTRS)**. Kiosks that allow you to process a claim via the eTRS system are located in the departures areas at the airport and at the city's two cruise terminals. Receipts and purchased items should be retained as they will be needed for verification before a refund is given. Refunds are limited to S$500 per person, and a credit card will be required as proof of identity. For further details visit the eTRS website.

Interior of Ngee Ann City, one of Singapore's premier shopping malls

Where to Shop

Malls and shopping centers are considered convenient places to shop, as an extensive range of products is available under one roof. Some malls have become popular for a particular product, such as Sim Lim Square and Funan Digitalife Mall, which are known for electronic goods. There are several smaller boutiques and specialist outlets to choose from. Many warehouses and traditional shophouses throughout the city, such as those that line the river, have been renovated into shopping venues. Little India, Chinatown, and Arab Street brim with shops and galleries that sell handicrafts from their respective regions as well as from other Asian countries.

Clothes and Fabrics

In Singapore, you will find international designer brands, such as **Gucci**, **Calvin Klein**, **Burberry**, **Emporio Armani**, **Hugo Boss**, **Vera Wang**, **Giordano**, and **Chanel**, located along Orchard Road and at the other major shopping areas. Rising local designer **Max Tan** can be found at the hip lifestyle store Eggccessorize. The latest collections from top Indian fashion designers are displayed at the upscale **Mumbai Se**.

For a great selection of textiles, the best areas are **Arab Street** (see p234) and **Serangoon Road** (see p235) in Little India. Indonesian and Malaysian *batik* silks are available on Arab Street, sold mostly by the meter. *Batiks* are also sold in *sarong* lengths (about 6 ft/2 m) and as ready-made garments. Indian *saris* (a 6-yard/5.5-m length of cloth) can be found in Little India. **Chinatown** (see pp224–7) specializes in Chinese silk and traditional garments such as *cheongsam* and *samfoo*, which can be bought readymade.

Chinese silk garments are available at Tangs. Sizes of ready-made garments are in keeping with the petite Asian body frame.

Jewelry

For exclusive platinum and 18-carat gold jewelry, luxury brands such as **Bulgari** and **Tiffany** have outlets at Raffles Hotel Shopping Arcade, Orchard Road, and Raffles City Shopping Center. Local jewelers **Choo Yilin** and **Lee Hwa** are reputed for their excellent craftsmanship. For antiques or gold fashioned in ethnic designs, such as Chinese ornaments and Indian jewelry, Chinatown and Little India offer the best selection. Cheaper imitations of the gold jewelry are available as well. Chinatown is also a good place to buy Chinese jade jewelry. The hawker stalls at **Clarke Quay** (see p223) offer a good range of trendy silver pieces.

Handmade mask

Shoes and Bags

All the international designer labels offer a superb selection of shoes and bags at their stores on Orchard Road and other upmarket shopping arcades. **Louis Vuitton**, **Fendi**, and **Ferragamo** are popular with shoppers. **Charles & Keith** and **Substance** are among the sought-after brands for shoes. Singapore is also known for its wide range of footwear at affordable prices especially at Tangs and **On Pedder**. Arab Street is the place to head to for fine leather products.

Antiques and Crafts

Antiques and handicrafts available in Singapore are predominantly Southeast Asian. **Tanglin Mall** (see p241) is the popular place for antiques and art. Old maps and curios from the Southeast are stocked at **Antiques of the Orient**. The many shops at Clarke Quay, the renovated warehouses along Dempsey Road, and **Lim's Arts & Living** are also good places. For good handmade Kashmiri, Persian, and Turkish carpets, **Amir & Sons** in Kampong Glam, the oldest carpet shop in Singapore, is worth a visit. Arab Street is known for Southeast Asian crafts such as fine cane products. Chinatown offers religious and architectural artifacts. Brass statues and lamps can be found both in Little India as well as in Chinatown.

Stacks of traditional Oriental textiles in vivid colors and patterns

DIRECTORY

Department Stores and Malls

Funan Digitalife Mall
109 North Bridge Road.
Map 3 E4. **Tel** 6336-8327.
W funan.com.sg

The Heeren
260 Orchard Road.
Map 2 B4. **Tel** 6738-4388.
W heeren.com.sg

Holland Village
211 Holland Avenue.
Tel 6465-0213.
W holland-village-singapore.com

ION Orchard
2 Orchard Turn.
Map 1 F2. **Tel** 6838-6520.
W ionorchard.com

Isetan
350 Orchard Road.
Map 1 F2. **Tel** 6733-1111.
W isetan.com.sg

Knightsbridge
270 Orchard Road.
Map 2 A4.
Tel 6593-6999.
W knightsbridge.com.sg

Marks & Spencer
501 Orchard Road. **Map** 1
F2. **Tel** 6733-8122.
W marksandspencer.com

Mustafa Center
145 Syed Alwi Road.
Map 3 E2. **Tel** 6295-5855.
W mustafa.com.sg

Ngee Ann City
391 Orchard Road.
Map 2 A4. **Tel** 6506-0461.
W ngeeanncity.com.sg

Parco Marina Bay
The Shoppes @ Marina
Bay Sands, 2 Bayfront
Avenue. **Map** 5 F3.
Tel 6595-9100.
W parco.com.sg

Park Mall
9 Penang Road. **Map** 2 C5.
Tel 6339-4031.

Raffles City Shopping Center
252 North Bridge Road.
Map 5 E2. **Tel** 6338-7766.
W rafflescity.com

Raffles Hotel Shopping Arcade
328 North Bridge Road.
Map 5 E1.
Tel 6337-1886.
W raf600hotel.com/arcade

The Shoppes @ Marina Bay Sands
2 Bayfront Avenue.
Map 5 F3. **Tel** 6688- 8868.
W marinabaysands.com

Sim Lim Square
1 Rochor Canal Road.
Map 3 E4.
Tel 6338-3859.

Takashimaya
391 Orchard Road.
Map 2 A4. **Tel** 6738-1111.
W takashimaya-sin.com

Tanglin Mall
163 Tanglin Road.
Map 1 E2. **Tel** 6736-4922.
W tanglinsc.com.sg

Tangs
310/320 Orchard Road.
Map 2 A3. **Tel** 6737-5500.
W tangs.com.sg

VivoCity
1 Harbourfront Walk.
Tel 6377-6870.
W vivocity.com.sg

Consumer Claims

Consumers Association of Singapore (CASE)
170 Ghim Moh Road.
Tel 6100-0315.
W case.org.sg

Small Claims Tribunal
1 Havelock Square.
Map 4 C3.
Tel 6435-5937.
W smallclaims.gov.sg

Taxes and Refunds

Changi International Airport
50 Airport Boulevard.
Tel 6542-1122.
W changiairport.com.
Open 24 hours.

Electronic Tourist Refund Scheme
W customs.gov.sg

Harbourfront Centre (International Passenger Terminal)
1 Maritime Square.
Tel 6711-6311.
W harbourfrontcentre.com.sg

Marina Bay Cruise Centre
61 Marina Coastal Drive.
W mbccs.com.sg

Clothes and Fabrics

Chanel
01-25 Ngee Ann City.
Map 2 A4.
Tel 6733-5120.
W chanel.com

Emporio Armani
B1-29/30 The Shoppes @
Marina Bay Sands, 2
Bayfront Avenue.
Map 5 F3. **Tel** 6304-1458.

Giordano
B2-28 Ngee Ann City.
Map 2 A4.
Tel 6736-4302.

Gucci
01-40 Paragon, 290
Orchard Road.
Map 2 A4. **Tel** 6734-2528.

Hugo Boss
01-03 Ngee Ann City, 391
Orchard Road. **Map** 2 A4.
Tel 6735-0233.

Max Tan
Egg-ccessorize, Orchard
Central, 181 Orchard road.
Map 2 B4.

Mumbai Se
02-03 Palais Renaissance,
390 Orchard Road.
Map 1 F2. **Tel** 6733-7188.

Vera Wang
L1-29A, The Shoppes @
Marina Bay Sands, 2
Bayfront Avenue.
Map 5 F3. **Tel** 9759-8815.

Jewelry

Bulgari
02-1/3 Ngee Ann City.
Map 2 A4. **Tel** 6735-6689.
W bulgari.com

Choo Yilin
331 Joo Chiat Road.
Tel 6348-1010.
W chooyilin.com

Lee Hwa
01-23, 200 Victoria Street.
Map 3 D5. **Tel** 6334-2838.
W leehwajewellery.com

Tiffany
01-05 Raffles Hotel
Shopping Arcade, 328
North Bridge Road.
Map 5 E1.
Tel 6334-0168.
W tiffany.com/locations

Shoes and Bags

Charles & Keith
01-05 Wisma Atria, 435
Orchard Road.
Map 2 A4. **Tel** 6238-3312.
W charleskeith.com

Fendi
01-32 Ngee Ann City.
Map 2 A4. **Tel** 6733-0337.
W fendi.com

Ferragamo
290 Orchard Road.
Map 1 F2. **Tel** 6738-3206.

Louis Vuitton
01-20/24 Ngee Ann City,
391 Orchard Road.
Map 2 A4.
Tel 6734-7760.
W louisvitton.com
One of several branches

On Pedder
Takashimaya, 391
Orchard Road. **Map** 2 A4.
6 Scotts Road. **Map** 2 A3.
W onpedder.com.

Substance
02-12 Wheelock Place,
501 Orchard Road.
Map 1 F2. **Tel** 6836-0111.

Antiques and Crafts

Amir & Sons
Lucky Plaza,
304 Orchard Road.
Map 1 F2. **Tel** 6734-9112.

Antiques of the Orient
02-40 Tanglin Mall.
Map 1 D3.
Tel 6734 9351.
W aoto.com.sg

Lim's Arts & Living
Vivocity,
1 Harbourfront Walk.
Tel 7652-1345.

Sim Lim Square, one of Singapore's specialist electronics and computer malls

Electronic Goods

The absence of import duties makes Singapore one of the most popular places to buy electronic gadgets. Several stores stock the latest high-tech audio-visual products. Latest models are available at specialist centers such as **The Sony Center**. **Sim Lim Square** and **Mustafa Center** are the best for music systems, televisions, and DVD players. The **Funan Digitalife Mall** is good for audio products. Make sure a world-wide guarantee is provided and that your purchase is compatible with the voltage system in your country.

Cameras and Watches

Most electronics shops and dedicated camera shops stock brands such as Nikon, Canon, and Olympus. **Cathay Photo Store** and Mustafa Center have a good range of all the popular camera brand names. The shops also offer equipment for professional photographers. A huge range of watches is available at most shopping centers. Many companies such as **Rolex** and **Swatch** have their own outlets, while **The Hour Glass** stocks an expensive range, including the exquisite Gerald Genta, De Bethune, and steely Daniel Roth pieces. The bustling **Lucky Plaza** is known for cameras and watches. Branded secondhand watches can also be bought at **Peng Kwee**. The **Camera Workshop** at Peninsula Shopping Center sells secondhand cameras and collector's models.

Computers

Funan Digitalife Mall, the main computer shopping center in Singapore, also claims to be the largest computer store in Asia. Located between the Excelsior and Peninsula Hotels in the Colonial Core, it has six floors packed with shops selling computers, software, and other electronic equipment. Prices here can be lower than elsewhere and special deals and offers are often available. Two popular computer shops are **Proton-Wisma Computers** and **The Mac Shop** at the Funan Center. Other good places to buy computers include **Suntec City Mall** and **Sim Lim Square** (see p255). As with many stores, bargaining is an accepted practice.

Books and Music

HMV has the most extensive selection of music with over 200,000 CD titles. Separate floors are dedicated to different genres, including classical music, jazz, rock, and pop. **MPH** also has a good selection. It is also popular for its excellent children's books section. Japanese bookstore **Kinokuniya** stocks a number of titles in several languages. They sell Chinese books and also have a bargain section. **Times the Bookstore** is another favorite.

Singapore Memorabilia

The ubiquitous Merlion, the half-fish, half-lion symbol of Singapore, is the most popular souvenir. A wide range of items sporting the symbol is available, including coffee mugs, T-shirts, pendants, stuffed toys, musical trinket boxes, china plates, key rings, and much more. There are gift shops at most Singapore national gardens and museums, which also offer an interesting collection of mementos. Museum shops such as those at the **National Museum of Singapore** offer an array of products inspired by the collections on display. The **Gardens Shop** at the Singapore Botanic Gardens (see pp246–7) stocks an eclectic range of books on natural history. Raffles Hotel has the excellent **Raffles Hotel Gift Shop**.

For a very different experience, **Sungei Road Thieves' Market** is Singapore's oldest flea market, stretching between Kelantan Road and Weld Road. In Kampung Glam, **The Heritage Shop** specializes in objects from yesteryear. It has thousands of collectibles for sale, mostly from 1930s to 1960s Singapore.

Orchids

Orchids are the country's national flower and more than 3,000 varieties of this exotic flower are grown at the **National Orchid Garden**, part of Singapore Botanic Gardens. Every year new hybrids are added to the collection. At the gift shop, orchids can be packed and shipped home upon request. **Toh Garden** is an orchid grower specializing in locally cultivated orchid hybrids and imported orchid genera.

Orchids can be shipped overseas for visitors by the National Orchid Garden

Unique gold-plated orchids can be purchased at the **RISIS Store** on Orchard Road.

Gourmet Food

Singapore is a renowned gourmet destination and a number of specialty foods are available as gifts and souvenirs. Aromatic ground spices from Little India can be used to flavor curries and marinades. Singaporean delicacies such as *kaya*, a toast spread, and the Hainan chicken-rice paste mix, along with other ready-to-serve foods are available at all **Bee Cheng Hiang** outlets, Kee's Gourmet Boutique and the **Chinatown Heritage Centre** *(see p224)*. **The Tea Chapter** in Chinatown has a delightful selection of teapots, cups, accessories, and fine teas for sale. **Brown Rice Paradise** and **Tierney's Gourmet** are also worth a visit. Handmade chocolates and premium quality caviar are some of the gourmet foods from around the world stocked at **Thos. S.B. Raffles**.

DIRECTORY

Electronic Goods

Funan Digitalife Mall
109 North Bridge Road.
Map 3 E4. **Tel** 6336-8327.
W funan.com.sg

Mustafa Center
145 Syed Alwi Road.
Map 3 E3. **Tel** 6295-5855.
W mustafa.com.sg

The Sony Center
02-28 to 37, 313 Somerset Road. **Map** 2 A4.
Tel 6634 9497.
W sony.com.sg

Cameras and Watches

Camera Workshop
Peninsula Shopping Center, 3 Coleman Street.
Map 5 D2. **Tel** 6336-1956.

Cathay Photo Store
6 Raffles Boulevard, Marina Square. **Map** 5 F2
Tel 6339-6188.
W cathayphoto.com.sg

The Hour Glass
290 Orchard Road. **Map** 2 A4. **Tel** 6735-6466.
W thehourglass.com

Lucky Plaza
304 Orchard Road.
Map 1 F2. **Tel** 6235-3294.
W luckyplaza.com.sg

Peng Kwee
01-45A Peninsula Plaza, 111 North Bridge Street.
Map 3 E4. **Tel** 6334-0155.
W 2ndhandwatch.com

Rolex
1-01 Tong Building, 302 Orchard Road. **Map** 1 F2.
Tel 6737-9033.
W rolex.com

Swatch
81-27 Plaza Singapura, 68 Orchard Road.
Map 1 F2.
Tel 6334-8042.
W swatch.com

Computers

The Mac Shop
4–11 Funan Digitalife Center. **Map** 5 D2.
Tel 6334-1633.
W apple.com.sg

Proton-Wisma Computers
109 North Bridge Road.
Map 3 E4. **Tel** 6338-3066.

Books and Music

HMV
6 Raffles Boulevard, Marina Square. **Map** 5 F2.
Tel 6733-1822.
W hmv.com.sg

Kinokuniya
03-10 Ngee Ann City, 391 Orchard Road. **Map** 2 A4.
Tel 6737-5021.
W kinokuniya.com.sg
One of several branches.

MPH
Raffles City Shopping Centre, 252 North Bridge Road. **Map** 5 E2. **Tel** 6336-4232. W mph.com.sg

Times the Bookstore
04-08 The Centrepoint, 176 Orchard Road.
Map 1 F2. **Tel** 6734-9022.
One of several branches.

Singapore Memorabilia

The Heritage Shop
93 Jalan Sultan.
Map 3 F3.
Tel 6223-7982.

The Gardens Shop
Singapore Botanic Gardens, 1 Cluny Road.
Map 1 D1. **Tel** 6475-2319.
W sbg.org.sg

National Museum of Singapore
93 Stamford Road.
Map 3 D5. **Tel** 6336-3670.
W nationalmuseum.sg

Raffles Hotel Gift Shop
01-01 Raffles Hotel, 1 Beach Road. **Map** 3 E5.
Tel 6412-1143.
W raffleshotelgifts.com

Sungei Road Thieves' Market
Sungei Road. **Map** 3 D4.

Orchids

National Orchid Garden
1 Cluny Road. **Map** 1 D1.
Tel 6471-7361.
W sbg.org.sg

RISIS Store
320 Orchard Rd.
Map 2 A3. **Tel** 6835-2492.
W risis.com

Toh Garden
11 Lorong Pasu.
Tel 6763-9186.
W tohgarden.com

Gourmet Food

Bee Cheng Hiang
1359 Serangoon Road.
Map 3 E1. **Tel** 6291-5753.
W bch.com.sg

Brown Rice Paradise
02-35 Tanglin Mall, 163 Tanglin Road. **Map** 1 D3.
Tel 6738-1121.
W mybrp.com.sg

Chinatown Heritage Centre
48 Pagoda Street.
Map 4 C3. **Tel** 6338-6877.
W chinatownheritagecentre.sg

The Tea Chapter
9–11 Neil Road/Tanjong Pagar. **Map** 4 C4.
Tel 6226-3026.
W tea-chapter.com.sg

Thos. S.B. Raffles
01-30 Raffles Hotel Arcade,1 Beach Road.
Map 3 E5.
Tel 6412-1148.
W raffleshotelgifts.com

Tierney's Gourmet
02-01/04 Serene Center, 10 Jalan Serene.
Tel 6466-7451.

ENTERTAINMENT IN SINGAPORE

In its endeavor to become a regional center for the arts, Singapore delights visitors with a diverse array of entertainment, ranging from classical to contemporary. Professional and amateur theater groups, dance troupes, and orchestras offer Asian performances and Western productions. The lively scene is enhanced by the presence of international artists, who come to participate in the many arts festivals held throughout the year.

Performance venues are scattered throughout the island, but among those that hold pride of place are the Riverside Arts District, the striking Esplanade – Theaters on the Bay, and the open-air Fort Canning Park. Singaporeans love their nightlife and its increasingly eclectic mix of venues – jazz clubs, blues bars, nightclubs, karaoke lounges, and traditional pubs – will be sufficient to satisfy all tastes.

Information

Daily newspapers, such as *The Straits Times* carry comprehensive listings of current and upcoming events. Brochures at hotels and free publications including *Where Singapore*, *Juice*, and *I-S (Inside Singapore)* also carry detailed listings and reviews.

Internet websites such as www. singaporetheatre.com are also an excellent resource for all the latest information, especially if you want to book tickets for an event in advance of your trip.

Tickets

It is best to purchase tickets at least two days in advance at the venue itself, though some shows may be totally booked out months ahead. Internet booking is now a convenient option. **Gatecrash** and **SISTIC** are two outlets that handle tickets for most events. Check the schedules on their websites, by telephone, or by visiting one of their many locations across the island. Tickets, once purchased, are not usually refundable or exchangeable. For Indian cultural shows, the **Annalakshmi Restaurant** hands out free tickets.

Disabled Access

Although most entertainment venues are located in heritage buildings or renovated warehouses, several of them have added disabled access. In newer venues, such as the Esplanade, such facilities have been provided. It is always best to call ahead and confirm.

Venues

Ever since its opening, **Esplanade – Theaters on the Bay** has been the focal point for the performing arts, though the elegant **Chijmes Hall**, **Jubilee Hall**, and **Victoria Theater & Concert Hall** are still traditional favorites for theater and musical performances. The **Shaw Foundation Symphony Stage**, perched on a lake at the Singapore Botanic Gardens, is a popular outdoor venue.

Singapore Indoor Stadium, the **National Stadium**, and the **University Cultural Center** are preferred for large concerts, especially for international artists, while the **DBS Arts Center** and **The Substation** are for smaller, more intimate events and specialize in more offbeat acts.

Festivals

Singapore hosts several performing arts festivals throughout the year. The riveting **Singapore Arts Festival**, held every August to September, is one of the highlights, drawing both up-and-coming and well-established acts from Singapore and all over the world. The **Buskers' Festival** for street performers is held on Sentosa every September. The **Singapore International Film Festival** in December, which screens about 300 movies, has been held every year for over 15 years. It showcases mainstream cinema, documentaries, and animation from around the world.

More recently, **The Substation** has been organizing an alternative Singapore Short Film Festival in March. The most popular, and allegedly Asia's largest, outdoor cinema festival is **Films at the Fort** every June at the Fort Canning Park. The **Singapore Piano Festival** also draws crowds.

Chijmes Hall, the restored chapel of a former convent, now a concert venue

Free Performances and Open-Air Shows

Free events are held regularly at Esplanade – Theaters on the Bay. A list of the frequently changing performances, including world music and drama, is available on their website *(see Directory)*. Indian classical music and dance shows, such as Bharatnatyam and Odissi, are organized at different venues by the **Temple of Fine Arts**, a non-profit making arts organization. Tickets for shows hosted by Temple of Fine Arts are also available at Annalakshmi Restaurant. "Ballet under the Stars", organised by **Singapore Dance Theater**, is a delightful event at Fort Canning Park. Classical music concerts, including performances by the **Singapore Symphony Orchestra**, are held at the Singapore Botanic Gardens, while street musicians often play by the Singapore River. Every Sunday, **Chijmes** has live music.

The Singapore Symphony Orchestra in concert, Botanic Gardens

DIRECTORY

Information

Juice
Tel 6733-1111.
🔲 juiceonline.com

The Straits Times
Tel 6319-5397.
🔲 straitstimes.com

Tickets

Annalakshmi Restaurant
133 New Bridge Road,
B1-02 Chinatown Point.
Tel 6339-9993.
🔲 annalakshmi.com.sg

Gatecrash
🔲 gatecrash.com.sg

SISTIC
Tel 6348-5555.
🔲 sistic.com.sg
Several locations from Raffles City; Victoria Concert Hall Box Office.

Venues

Chijmes Hall
30 Victoria Street.
Map 3 D5.
Tel 6334-3801.
🔲 chijmes.com.sg

DBS Arts Center
20 Merbau Road.
Map 4 C2.
Tel 6733-8166.
🔲 srt.com.sg

Esplanade – Theaters on the Bay
1 Esplanade Drive,
Marina Bay.
Map 5 E2.
Tel 6828-8222.
🔲 esplanade.com

Jubilee Hall
Raffles Hotel.
Map 3 E5.
Tel 6412-1319.
🔲 raffles.com

National Stadium
2 Stadium Walk.
Tel 6653-8900.
🔲 sportshub.com.sg

The Room Upstairs
42 Waterloo Street.
Map 3 D4.
Tel 6837- 0842.

Shaw Foundation Symphony Stage
Botanic Gardens,
1 Cluny Road.
Map 1 D2.
Tel 6471-7361.
🔲 sbg.org.sg

Singapore Indoor Stadium
2 Stadium Walk.
Tel 6344-2660.

The Substation
45 Armenian Street.
Map 3 D5.
Tel 6337-7535.
🔲 substation.org

University Cultural Center
50 Kent Ridge Crescent. **Tel** 6516-2492.
🔲 nus.edu.sg

Victoria Theater & Concert Hall
9 Empress Place.
Map 5 D3.
Tel 6338-8283.
🔲 nac.gov.sg

Festivals

Buskers' Festival
🔲 singapore-buskers.com

Films at the Fort
🔲 filmsatthefort.com.sg

Singapore Arts Festival
Tel 6345-8488.
🔲 nac.gov.sg

Singapore International Film Festival
🔲 filmfest.org.sg

Singapore Piano Festival
🔲 pianofestival.com.sg

Free Performances and Open-Air Shows

Chijmes
30 Victoria Street.
Map 3 D5. Tel 6336-1818.
🔲 chijmes.com.sg

Singapore Dance Theater
2nd Story, Fort Canning Center, Cox Terrace.
Map 5 D1.
Tel 6338-0611.
🔲 singaporedancetheatre.com

Singapore Symphony Orchestra
Victoria Concert Hall,
11 Empress Place.
Map 5 D3.
Tel 6338-1230
🔲 sso.org.sg

Temple of Fine Arts
20 Havelock Road,
Central Square.
Tel 6535-0509.
🔲 templeoffinearts.org

Wayang (Chinese Opera) performance on an elaborate stage on Teochew street

Western Classical Music and Dance

The **Singapore Symphony Orchestra** *(see p259)* was founded in 1979 and performs regularly at its home base, the Esplanade, and the Victoria Concert Hall. The concerts often feature special guest conductors, composers, and soloists. The **Singapore Dance Theater** *(see p259)*, the state's foremost dance company, presents classic and contemporary Western ballet, while the **Odyssey Dance Theater** and **Ecnad** stage contemporary and fusion dance performances.

Chinese Opera, Malay and Indian Music

Traditional Chinese opera, or *wayang*, is a cultural street event best seen during the Festival of the Hungry Ghosts *(see pp206–7)*. The **Chinese Opera Institute** and the **Chinese Theater Circle** also stage a 2-hour opera every Friday and Saturday, complete with explanations. The **Singapore Chinese Orchestra**, the island's only professional Chinese orchestra, plays Indian and Malay music as well as Chinese pieces.

For traditional Malay culture, the Malay Heritage Centre *(see p234)* in Kampong Glam often holds music and dance performances – call the venue for details. A rich repertoire of Indian classical dance and music is presented by the **Temple of Fine Arts** *(see p259)*, as well as the **Nrityalaya Aesthetics Society**.

Theater and Musicals

Singapore's vibrant theater scene ranges from runaway Broadway and West End hits on international tour to local groups performing contemporary productions by local playwrights. Well-known companies are the **Action Theater**, **Singapore Repertory Theater**, **TheaterWorks**, **Toy Factory**, and **The Necessary Stage**. While most productions are in English, albeit with an all-Asian cast, vernacular Chinese dialects, as well as Malay and Tamil theater, are represented too. Troupes such as **The Singapore Stage Club**, set up in 1945, with members from around the world, perform pantomimes, especially at Christmas.

Cinema

Most of the films shown in Singapore are in English, with Chinese subtitles. Other language films have both English and Chinese subtitles. Hollywood blockbusters and Indian films are extremely popular and there are many multiplex cinemas to choose from, such as the **Golden Village** and **Shaw Beach Road Cineplex**. For a luxurious experience, choose the "gold class" option: for around S$25 a ticket, you get a reclining armchair, blankets, lots of room and waitstaff serving you food and drink. Art-house films in European languages are screened by the **Singapore Film Society** at the **Alliance Française**, or **Goethe Institute**. The **British Council** organizes regular shows of critically acclaimed movies. Films by young local directors such as Royston Tan and Kelvin Tong draw large audiences.

Nightlife

The island has plenty to offer visitors looking for bars and clubs. The three main destinations for nightlife are Clarke Quay, Boat Quay, and Dempsey Hill. Swing to the blues and rock and roll at Clarke Quay's **Crazy Elephant** and at **Harry's Bar** on Boat Quay. Singapore's first Irish pub that plays Irish music, **Molly Malone's**, is located by the riverside. **Brix** on Orchard Road, **Sa Vanh** in Chinatown, and **Tanjong Beach Club** on Sentosa Island are a few of the favorite venues. The wine bars offer friendly service and intimate ambience. Most of them are

Local rock band playing at the Crazy Elephant

located in renovated shop-houses. Though all are fairly popular, the ones that attract the most crowds are **No. 5**, the city's first wine bar, which has a rustic feel to it with unpolished wooden floors and Persian carpets; **1-Altitude**, one of the highest open-air bars in the world, and the busy **KU DE TA**. Karaoke rooms (also known as KTV stations) are hugely popular, and even the smallest pub will feature a karaoke station.

Dance clubs are always packed and tend to play alternative music – trance, progressive trance, and garage. **Kilo Lounge** is one of the more "underground" clubs in Singapore's mainly mainstream scene. For a mind-thumping dance night, **Attica** is also one of the venues that top the list of favorites. The trendy **Zouk** complex houses **Velvet Underground** and **Phuture**. The Velvet Underground has a main dance floor and a separate bar

for chilling out. Enter a futuristic world with trendy murals on Phuture's walls and enjoy all sorts of hip music, hip-hop, and drum 'n' bass at the club. **Pangaea** specializes in a range of music from electro, trance, and house to progressive. This super-club hosts talented local and international DJs. Check the website for more details.

The majority of these clubs charge a cover price between S$20 and S$30.

DIRECTORY

Music and Dance

Chinese Opera Institute
111 Middle Road.
Map 3 D4. **Tel** 6339-1292.
🌐 www.coi.org.sg

Ecnad
04–05 182 Cecil Street.
Map 5 D4.
Tel 6226-6772.
🌐 ecnad.org

Malay Village
39 Geylang Road.
Tel 6748-4700.

Nrityalaya Aesthetics Society
Stamford Arts Center,
155 Waterloo Street.
Map 3 D4. **Tel** 6336-6537.
🌐 nas.org.sg

Odyssey Dance Theater
04–04, 182 Cecil Street.
Map 5 D4.
Tel 6221-5516.
🌐 odysseydance-theatre.com

Singapore Chinese Orchestra
Singapore Conference
Hall, 7 Shenton Way,.
Map 5 D5. **Tel** 6440-3839.
🌐 sco.org.sg

Theater and Musicals

Action Theater
42 Waterloo Street.
Map 3 D4. **Tel** 6837-0842.
🌐 centre42.sg

The Necessary Stage
278 Marine Parade Road.
Tel 6440-8115.
🌐 necessary.org

Singapore Repertory Theater
DBS Arts Center, 20
Merbau Road. **Map** 4 C2.
Tel 6733-8166. 🌐 srt.com.sg

The Singapore Stage Club
203 Henderson Road.
Tel 6454-5200.
🌐 stageclub.com

TheaterWorks
72–13 Mohamed Sultan
Road. **Map** 2 B5.
Tel 6737-7213.
🌐 theatreworks.org.sg

Toy Factory
15 A Smith Street.
Map 4 C4. **Tel** 6222-1526.
🌐 toyfactory.org.sg

Cinema

Alliance Française
1 Sarkies Road.
Map 2 A2.
Tel 6737-8422.
🌐 alliancefrancaise.org.sg

British Council
30 Napier Road.
Map 1 D2.
Tel 6473-1111.
🌐 britishcouncil.org/sg

Goethe Institute
136 Neil Road.
Tel 6735-4555.
🌐 goethe.de/ins/sg

Golden Village
Marina Leisureplex, Raffles
Avenue. **Map** 5 F2.
Tel 1900 912-1234.
🌐 gv.com.sg
One of several branches.

Shaw Beach Road Cineplex
Shaw Tower, 100 Beach
Road. **Map** 3 F4.
Tel 6738-0555.
🌐 shaw.com.sg
One of several branches.

Singapore Film Society
03–01 Marina Leisureplex,
5A Raffles Avenue.
Map 5 F2. **Tel** 90-170-160.
🌐 sfs.org.sg

Nightlife

1-Altitude
1 Raffles Place. **Map** 5 D3
Tel 6438-0410

Attica
01-03 Clarke Quay, 3A
River Valley Road.
Map 1 E4.
Tel 6333-9973.
🌐 attica.com.sg

Brix
Grand Hyatt Singapore,
10 Scotts Road.
Map 2 A3. **Tel** 6738-1234.

Crazy Elephant
Clarke Quay, 3E River
Valley Road. **Map** 1 E4.
Tel 6337-7859.
🌐 crazyelephant.com

Harry's Bar
28 Boat Quay. **Map** 5 D3.
Tel 6538-3029.
🌐 harrys.com.sg

Kilo Lounge
66 Kampong Bugis.
Tel 6467-3987

KU DE TA
Marina Bay Sands,
1 Bayfront Ave. **Map** 5 F3.
Tel 6688-7688.

Molly Malone's
56 Circular Road.
Map 5 D3.
Tel 6536-2029.
🌐 molly-malone.com

No. 5
5 Emerald Hill.
Tel 6732-0818.
🌐 no5.emerald-hill.com

Pangaea
Marina Bay Sands,
1 Bayfront Avenue.
Map 5 F3. **Tel** 8611-7013
🌐 pangaea.sg

Sa Vanh
49 Club Street.
Map 4 C4.
Tel 6323-0145.

Tanjong Beach Club
120 Tanjong Beach Walk,
Sentosa Island.
Tel 6270-1355.
🌐 tanjongbeachclub.com

Zouk, Velvet Underground, and Phuture
17 Jiak Kim Street.
Tel 6738-2988.
🌐 zoukclub.com

OUTDOOR ACTIVITIES IN SINGAPORE

Singapore is not only a place for shopping and dining, but also for a range of exciting outdoor activities. Being a tropical island, all the favorite watersports such as diving, sailing, water-skiing, and wakeboarding are available throughout the year. The most popular spots for these are the Kallang River located to the east of the city, East Coast Park, and Sentosa. Ample cycling trails are provided around the outer reaches of the island and within its beautiful nature reserves. Golf and fitness activities are widely enjoyed here. Tennis is also a popular sport but can be strenuous and it's best to play early in the day. The tropical sun can be strong, so adequate protection is required.

Golf driving range at East Coast Park

Golf

Singapore has a number of beautifully kept golf courses. Visitors are permitted to play at most clubs, but only on weekdays. However, the **Seletar Country Club** is open to non-members on the weekends. The other popular golf clubs include **Marina Bay Golf Course** in the center of town, **Sentosa Golf Club**, and the **Raffles Country Club** where there is a spectacular view of the South China Sea.

Diving

Singapore is one of the most economical places in the world for diving lessons. PADI (Professional Association of Diving Instructors) courses for beginners as well as advanced divers are available. There are a number of reputable dive schools to choose from, including the **Big Bubble Center**, **Waikiki Dive Center**, **Scuba Corner**, **Gill Divers**, and **Friendly Waters Seasports Services**. Besides offering dive lessons, most schools also rent out equipment and organize dive trips. These excursions range from a day's outing to explore local Singapore waters to longer dive tours and live-aboard trips that cover popular dive spots off Malaysia's east coast, Thailand, or Indonesia's Riau Archipelago. For an exciting up-close encounter, you can also dive with the sharks at Underwater World on Sentosa *(see p250)*.

Water-Skiing and Wakeboarding

Several individual operators rent out equipment and offer professional instruction. The facilities of the **Cowabunga Ski Center** are among the best in Singapore. **Seabreeze** on Sentosa offers wakeboarding and wakesurfing lessons.

Sailing and Windsurfing

Most sailing and windsurfing facilities are located on the east coast of the island. Among these are the **Mana Mana Beach Restaurant and Bar**, **National Sailing Center**, **Marina at Keppel Bay**, **Raffles Marina**, **Republic of Singapore Yacht Club**, **SAFRA Seasports Center**, and **Changi Sailing Club**, which offer various marine activities, including sail boat charters (permits may be required), windsurf boards for hire, and boat berthing docks. Some hold large regattas and many conduct training courses. Call or check websites for details.

Adventure Sports Clubs

Singapore Adventurers' Club organizes a range of exciting activities such as trekking, cycling tours, canoeing, and sailing. Most of its activities are open to all, with the exception of a few members-only events. Intensive courses in kayaking, rock climbing, and abseiling are offered all year round by **Outward Bound Singapore** located at Pulau Ubin and East Coast Park.

Diving, a popular activity in SIngapore

Nature watch

Nature Society (Singapore) organizes bird-watching trips twice each month to various locations. Call or check its website for more details. In addition, spotting the diverse species of animals, birds, and plants protected within Singapore's stunning nature reserves can be a truly rewarding experience.

Cycling

Cycling is an excellent way to explore the attractions that lie outside Singapore's city limits. Hiring a bike on Sentosa is a good alternative to the island's monorail system. For a leisurely ride along the seashore of the East Coast Park, bikes can be rented at the **Sunsport Center**. The varied landscape of the tracks at the Bukit Timah Nature Reserve *(see p244)* offers a more challenging experience, but you will need to bring your own bike. Pulau Ubin *(see p249)* off the northeastern coast is a favorite cycling destination. With its maze of trails, it is particularly good for mountain biking. You can also combine cycling with seeing the sights on a **Let's Go Bike Singapore** tour.

Tennis

Tennis courts can be booked every day between 7am and 10pm at various centers, such as the **Kallang Squash and Tennis**

A game in progress at Singapore Tennis Center

Center, and **Farrer Park Tennis Court**. The **Singapore Tennis Center** offers one-on-one coaching, and you can put your name on a partner list and hire a court. An Instant Tennis course for beginners is available at a very reasonable fee.

DIRECTORY

Golf

Marina Bay Golf Course
80 Rhu Cross. **Tel** 6342-5730. **W** mbgc.com.sg

Raffles Country Club
450 Jalan Ahmad Ibrahim.
Tel 6861-6888.
W rcc.org.sg

Seletar Country Club
101 Seletar Club Road,
Seletar Airbase.
Tel 6481-4812.
W seletarclub.com.sg

Sentosa Golf Club
27 Bukit Manis Road.
Tel 6275-0022.
W sentosagolf.com

Diving

Big Bubble Center
57 Cantonment Road.
Map 4 B4. **Tel** 6222-6862.
W bigbubble.com

Friendly Waters Seasports Services
01-36 The Riverwalk,
20 Upper Circular Road.
Map 5 D3. **Tel** 6557-0016.
W friendlywaters.
com.sg

Gill Divers
37B Hong Kong Street.
Map 5 D3. **Tel** 6734-9373.
W gilldivers.com

Scuba Corner
Block 809 French Road.
Map 3 F3. **Tel** 6338-6563.
W scubacorner.com.sg

Waikiki Dive Center
Block 462, Crawford Lane.
Tel 6291-1290.
W waikikidive.com

Water-Skiing and Wakeboarding

Cowabunga Ski Center
10 Stadium Lane.
Tel 6344-8813.
W extreme.com.sg

SeaBreeze
36 Siloso Beach, Sentosa.
Tel 6376-4336.
W seabreeze.com.sg

Sailing and Windsurfing

Changi Sailing Club
32 Netheravon Road.
Tel 6545-2876.
W csc.org.sg

Mana Mana Beach Restaurant and Bar
1212 East Coast Parkway.
Tel 6339-8878.
W manamana.com

Marina at Keppel Bay
Lot 1016 and 2003,
Bukit Chermin Road.
Tel 6270-6665. **W** marina
keppelbay.com

National Sailing Center
1500 East Coast Parkway.
Map 5 F4. **Tel** 6444-4555.
W sailing.org.sg

Raffles Marina
10 Tuas West Drive.
Tel 6861-8000. **W**
rafflesmarina.com.sg

Republic of Singapore Yacht Club
52 West Coast Ferry Road.
Tel 6768-9288.
W rsyc.org.sg

SAFRA Seasports Center
10 Changi Coast Walk.
Tel 6546-5880.
W nsrcc.com.sg

Adventure Sports Clubs

Outward Bound Singapore
9 Stadium Link,
Pulau Ubin.
Tel 6545-9008.
W obs.nyc.gov.sg

Singapore Adventurers' Club
74B Lorong 27, Geylang.
Tel 6749-0557.
W sac.org

Nature Watch

Nature Society (Singapore)
02–05 The Sunflower,
510 Geylang Road.
Tel 6741-2036.
W nss.org.sg

Cycling

Lets Go Bike Singapore
High Street Centre B1-58
(Basement 1 Shop 58).
Tel 9004-4332.
W letsgobike
singapore.com

Sunsport Center
East Coast Parkway.
Map 5 F4. **Tel** 6440-9827.

Tennis

Farrer Park Tennis Court
Rutland Road.
Tel 6299-4166.

Kallang Squash and Tennis Center
Stadium Road.
Tel 6348-1291.

Singapore Tennis Center
1020 East Coast Parkway.
Map 5 F4.
Tel 6442-5966.
W singtennis.org.sg

SINGAPORE STREET FINDER

The key map below shows the area of Singapore covered in this Street Finder. Map references given for sights, shops, and entertainment venues described in the Singapore section of this guide refer to the maps on the following pages. Map references are also given for Singapore hotels *(see pp282–3)* and restaurants *(see pp299–301)* recommended in the *Where to Stay* and *Where to Eat and Drink* sections.

Major sights are also marked. A complete index of street names and places of interest shown on the maps follows on pages 270–73. The first figure in the map reference indicates which Street Finder map to turn to, and the letter and the number which follow refer to the grid on the map. The key, below, indicates the scale of the maps and other features marked on them, including post offices and tourist information centers.

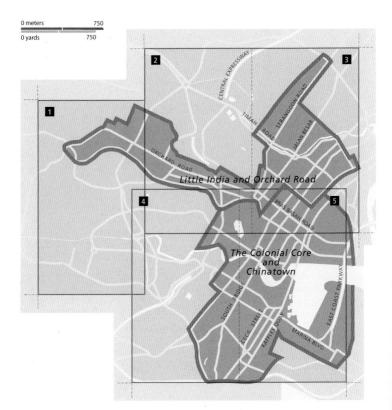

| 0 meters | 750 |
| 0 yards | 750 |

2 **3**

1

CENTRAL EXPRESSWAY

SERANGOON ROAD

TIMAH ROAD

JALAN BESAR

ORCHARD ROAD

Little India and Orchard Road

BRAS BASAH ROAD

4 **5**

The Colonial Core and Chinatown

SOUTH BRIDGE

EAST COAST PARKWAY

CECIL STREET

RAFFLES QUAY

MARINA BLVD

Key

Major sight	Church
Place of interest	Buddhist temple
Other building	Mosque
M MRT station	Synagogue
Bus station	Railroad
Hospital	Expressway
Police station	Pedestrian bridge
i Tourist information	
Indian temple	

Scale of Map Pages

| 0 meters | 250 |
| 0 yards | 250 |

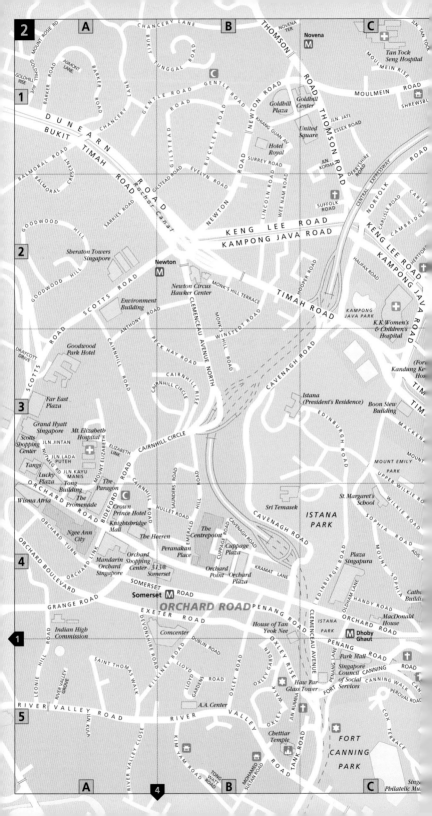

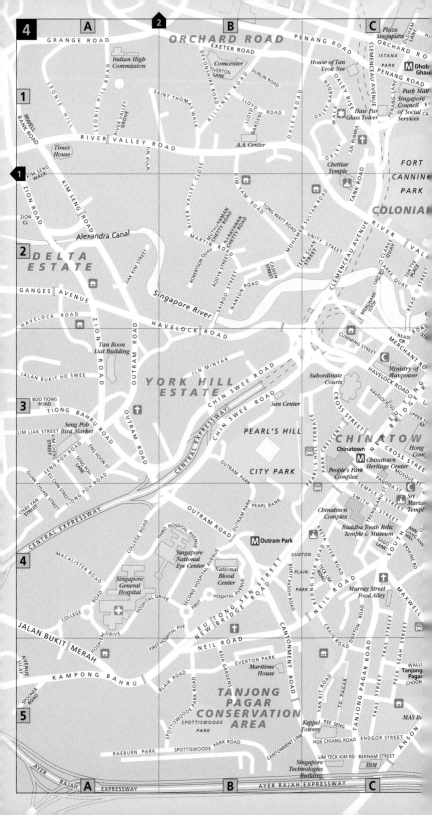

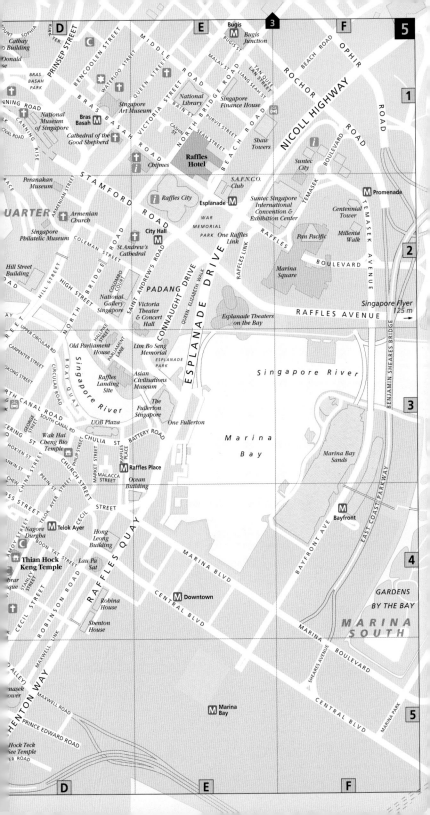

Street Finder Index

TRAVELERS' NEEDS

WHERE TO STAY

Both Malaysia and Singapore offer a variety of accommodations, from luxury hotels to simple guesthouses. Prices are fairly reasonable, although Malaysian Borneo and Singapore tend to be more expensive than Peninsular Malaysia. Top international hotel chains are well-represented, and there are some beautiful resorts in idyllic settings. Mid-range options include some lovely boutique hotels and locally run chains.

Budget travelers will find excellent guesthouses and hostels offering dormitory beds, and, in some parts of the country, homestays can be arranged. An overnight stay in a longhouse is a wonderful way to experience Dayak culture. Malaysia's national parks provide cabins and campsites, making it possible to stay in the heart of the rain forest. For more information, refer to the detailed listings on pages 278–83.

Immaculate old-world simplicity at the upscale Raffles in Singapore (p283)

Ratings

Top- and mid-range hotels are accredited with star ratings according to the level of luxury, facilities, and services they offer but guesthouses have no such ratings. While these ratings help in selecting accommodations, it is wise to visit the official websites of individual hotels to check what they offer.

International and Resort Hotels

Several of the world's best-known international hotel chains are represented in Malaysia and Singapore, offering luxurious rooms and impeccable service. Many incorporate features of local architecture in an effort to make their rooms more personal. The resorts, set in beautiful surroundings, have spas, watersports and fitness facilities, golf courses, and a range of shops, restaurants, and bars, giving guests no reason to step out of the resort during their stay. Staying at hotels

where colonial history marries luxury, such as the Majestic in Melaka (see p280) and Raffles in Singapore (see p283), makes for a memorable experience.

Mid-Range Hotels

As international chains have moved into the region, some mid-range hotels with excelllent facilities have had to reduce their prices in order to compete, and now provide very good value for money. This category includes boutique hotels, which focus on generating an exotic and relaxing ambience. They are usually more intimate than the chain hotels, and can offer personalized services. Budget accommodation has long been available in shophouses (see p32), but there is a growing trend for converting these into boutique hotels, creating attractive options for a heritage stay.

Budget Hotels and Guesthouses

All Malaysian cities and towns have budget hotels and guesthouses in tourist areas

that are both economical and often, a good source of local information. While facilities are basic, some include free breakfast and Internet access. Homestays are becoming popular, offering an opportunity to get to know Malaysians outside the tourist industry. The local tourist offices always have a list of homestay programs. Singapore has a number of award-winning hostels with excellent facilities.

Longhouses

Travelers to Malaysian Borneo, particularly Sarawak, can experience a night in a longhouse, the traditional dwelling of many indigenous groups, such as the Bidayuh (see p167) and the Iban (see p173). Most visitors to longhouses organize their trips through tour agents, such as Borneo Adventure (see p317) and Sabah Tourism Board (see p323), who arrange stays at working longhouses. Facilities are generally very basic, consisting of little more than a floor mattress and mosquito net, although some longhouses have now

Live music to accompany sundowners at The Majestic in Melaka (p280)

◀ Traditional kite-making at Khota Baru

Lavish suite accommodations at the Mulu Marriott Resort & Spa *(p282)*

installed Western-style toilets to make the stay a little more comfortable for their guests.

National Parks and Camping

National Parks and preserves throughout Malaysia offer reasonably comfortable lodges or cabin-style huts, usually located around the park's headquarters. They also have campsites where visitors may rent a tent or pitch their own, including on beaches, but the facilities are basic. For information, bookings, and permits, contact the **Department of Wildlife and National Parks**, **Sarawak Forestry Corporation**, and **Sabah National Parks**.

Rates and Reservations

Room rates tend to remain steady through the year, increasing only during festivals such as Hari Raya Puasa, Chinese New Year *(see pp34–5)*, and Christmas, when all types of accommodations fill up and advance booking becomes necessary. At quieter times, especially during the monsoon season between November and February, rates drop significantly and discounts can be obtained on the east coast. Prior reservations are essential at top-end hotels for the best prices. Note that hotel and guesthouse prices are substantially higher in Kuala Lumpur than in the rest of Malaysia. Hotels in Singapore are more expensive still, with prices similar to what you'd expect to pay in the West.

Hidden Costs

Most budget and mid-range hotels quote net prices that include all taxes. However, top-end hotels in Malaysia display a price amount with the symbol "++" after the rate, which means that 10 percent service charge and 6 percent government tax will be added to it. In Singapore, this symbol becomes "+++", which refers to 10 percent service charge, 17 percent Goods and Services Tax, and 1 percent government tax. Food and beverage items in luxury hotels and restaurants also have taxes and service charges added on.

Traveling with Kids

Hotel staff in both Malaysia and Singapore tend to indulge younger guests. Even at basic hotels, under-12s can often stay for free in their parents' room. Not all hotels have playgrounds and other special facilities for kids, but most are very flexible about providing extra beds in rooms and special meals. Cots and high chairs are available with some notice. Some resort hotels organize activities for kids and offer babysitting services.

Cabin-style huts at the Sepilok Nature Resort, Sabah *(p282)*

Special Needs

Apart from top-end hotels, few places offer special facilities for the disabled in Malaysia or Singapore *(see p322)*. For the mobility impaired, facilities are limited to ramps and elevators. Some five-star hotels have wheelchair-user-friendly rooms.

Recommended Hotels

The hotels listed on pages 278–83 reflect the main types of accommodations in Malaysia, Borneo, and Singapore. Prices are given in Malaysian ringgit, Singapore dollar, or Brunei dollar, which is equal in value to the Singapore dollar, as appropriate.

Modern hotels range from five-star to budget. Resorts, which are frequently in the mid- or top price range, are usually in coastal areas or nestled in the rain forest. Boutique hotels are small and intimate, often in beautifully restored colonial buildings. Beach hotels are usually in the lower price category. Guesthouses tend to be inexpensive, and are often family-run, while hostels cater to Asia's plethora of backpackers. Self-catering accommodation is in serviced apartments, always available in the capital cities, while at historic hotels colonial history meets luxury.

The establishments highlighted as DK Choices offer something particularly special, such as a beautiful setting, eco-friendly credentials, excellent service and facilities, or a combination of these.

DIRECTORY

National Parks and Camping

Department of Wildlife and National Parks
Kuala Lumpur. **Tel** (03) 9086-6800. 🔳 wildlife.gov.my

Sabah National Parks
Kota Kinabalu. **Tel** (088) 523-500. 🔳 sabahparks.org.my

Sarawak Forestry Corporation
Kuching. **Tel** (082) 610-088. 🔳 sarawakforestry.com

Places to Stay

Kuala Lumpur

KLCC

Mandarin Oriental
Modern   **Map** 2 F5
Kuala Lumpur City Center
Tel *(03) 2380-8888*
W mandarinoriental.com
Right by the Petronas Towers, this hotel has a luxury spa, pools, tennis courts, and top restaurants.

Traders Hotel
Modern   **Map** 2 F5
Kuala Lumpur City Center
Tel *(03) 2332-9888*
W shangri-la.com/kualalumpur/traders
The elegant rooms have great views of the city's skyline, as does the trendy 33rd floor Sky Bar.

Bukit Bintang and the Golden Triangle

Classic Inn
Modern   **Map** 5 C3
36 Jalan 1/77a, Changkat Thambi Dollah
Tel *(03) 2148-8648*
W classicinn.com.my
In a colonial-style building, rooms are welcoming and there's a café.

Orange Pekoe Guesthouse
Modern
1-1 Jalan Angsoka
Tel *(03) 2110-2000*
W orangepekoe.com.my
Comfortable rooms, friendly staff, a veranda, and communal lounge with cable TV feature here.

Rainforest Bed & Breakfast
Guesthouse
27 Jalan Mesui
Tel *(03) 2145-3525*
W rainforestbnbhotel.com
This welcoming place bursts with greenery in jungle lodge style. The cosy rooms feature solid furniture.

Dorsett Regency
Modern   **Map** 5 C3
172 Jalan Imbi
Tel *(03) 2716-1000*
W dorsettregency.com
Some of the rooms in this tower block have great city views; there's a pool, too.

The Mesui Hotel
Modern
9 Jalan Mesui
Tel *(03) 2144-8188*
W themesuihotel.com
Retro furnishings add '70s style. Rooms have quirky wall designs.

Anggun Boutique Hotel
Boutique   **Map** 5 B2
7 & 9 Tengkat Tong Shin
Tel *(03) 2145-8003*
W anggunkl.com
Pretty rooms with antique furnishings overlook an interior courtyard with a fishpond.

Fraser Place
Modern
Lot 163, 10 Jalan Perak
Tel *(03) 2118-6288*
W kualalumpur.fraserhospitality.com
Stylish highrise rooms have floor-to-ceiling windows. There's a gym and rooftop infinity pool.

Hotel Maya
Modern   **Map** 1 C5
138 Jalan Ampang
Tel *(03) 2711-8866*
W hotelmaya.com.my
Rooms feature floor-to-ceiling glass panels and great city views. There's a hydrotherapy pool and gym, as well as yoga classes.

DK Choice

Villa Samadhi
Boutique
8 Jalan Madge
Tel *(03) 2143-2300*
W villasamadhi.com.my
This luxurious hotel has designer Asian furnishings in individually styled rooms. The Sarang rooms have private plunge pools, while the spacious ground-level rooms have private balconies with direct access to the lagoon pool. Great Western breakfasts.

Traditional thatch roofing and hanging lanterns at Villa Samadhi, Kuala Lumpur

Price Guide

Prices are based on one night's stay in high season for a standard double room, inclusive of service charges and taxes.

/$	up to RM/$120
/$$	RM/$120 to RM/$300
/$$$	over RM/$300

Chow Kit and Little India

Crossroads Hotel
Modern   **Map** 1 B2
1 Jalan Raja Muda Abdul Aziz
Tel *(03) 2698-7000*
W crossroads-hotel.com
Just a short walk from Chow Kit Market, this hotel has spotless rooms with dark furnishings.

Chinatown

Back Home
Hostel   **Map** 4 F2
30 Jalan Tun H.S. Lee
Tel *(03) 2022-0788*
W backhome.com.my
Modern rooms featuring open brick walls and hardwood floors give onto an interior courtyard with coffee tables.

The Explorers Guesthouse
Hostel   **Map** 4 F3
128 & 130 Jalan Tun H.S. Lee
Tel *(03) 2022-2928*
W theexplorersguesthouse.com
The lobby area features a peaceful water feature and dream-catchers, while the small cosy rooms are spic-and-span.

Swiss Inn
Modern   **Map** 4 F3
62 Jalan Sultan
Tel *(03) 2072-3333*
W swissgarden.com
This hotel has rooms with hip, bright designs over seven floors.

DK Choice

Hotel Majestic
Historic   **Map** 4 E4
5 Jalan Sultan Hishamuddin
Tel *(03) 2785-8000*
W majestickl.com
In a stunning 1930s restored building, Hotel Majestic bursts with colonial charm. The sumptuously decorated suites in the Majestic Wing have butler service. The Art Deco-style, 15-story Tower Wing has deluxe rooms and suites. Facilities include two swimming pools, a spa, a barbershop, and a movie screening room.

Northwest Peninsula

ALOR STAR: Holiday Villa
Modern
Lot 162, 163 Jalan Tunku Ibrahim
Tel *(04) 734-9999*
w holidayvillaalorsetar.com
Suited to both business and leisure travelers, this hotel has restaurants, a pool, and a spa.

CAMERON HIGHLANDS: Father's Guest House
Hostel
4 Jalan Mentigi
Tel *(016) 566-1111*
w fathers.cameronhighlands.com
Rooms are modern with good facilities. The staff organize guided treks and tours.

CAMERON HIGHLANDS: Smokehouse Hotel
Historic
Next to the golf course in Tanah Rata
Tel *(05) 491-1215*
w smokehousehotel.com
Evoking the colonial era amid lush greenery, this is the classiest place to stay in the Cameron Highlands.

FRASER'S HILL: Puncak Inn
Modern
Jalan Genting
Tel *(09) 362-2007*
This homey hotel has plainly furnished but comfortable rooms.

IPOH: D'Eastern Hotel
Modern
118 Jalan Sultan Idris Shah
Tel *(05) 254-3936*
The simply decorated en-suite rooms are very spacious.

IPOH: French Hotel
Modern
60 & 62 Jalan Dato Onn Jaafar
Tel *(05) 241-3030*
w frenchhotel.com.my
This compact, centrally located hotel boasts chic touches and great breakfasts; exceptional value.

PANGKOR: Anjungan
Beach Hotel
6610 Nipah Bay
Tel *(05) 685-1500*
w anjunganresortpangkor.com
Rooms are set around a boat-shaped swimming pool with the beach just across the road.

PENANG: Old Penang Guest House
Hostel
53 Love Lane, Georgetown
Tel *(04) 263-8805*
w oldpenang.com
A slickly renovated shophouse with rooms and dorms, as well as an airy downstairs lounge.

Relaxed home-from-home atmosphere at 23 Love Lane, Penang

DK Choice

PENANG: 23 Love Lane
Boutique
23 Love Lane, Georgetown
Tel *(04) 262 1323*
w 23lovelane.com
In a lovingly restored colonial-era villa, 23 Love Lane has eclectic, elegant decor and lush, restful gardens; the feel is of an expansive family home rather than a hotel. Breakfast is served in their adjacent restaurant.

PENANG: E & O
Historic
10 Lebuh Farquhar
Tel *(04) 222-2000*
w eohotels.com
Enjoy colonial splendor and butler service at Penang's *grande dame* of hotels (see p111).

PULAU LANGKAWI: Sunset Beach Resort
Beach Hotel
Jalan Pantai Tengah
Tel *(04) 955-1751*
w sungroup-langkawi.com
Cosy rooms in warm hues are set in lush grounds planted with ferns and scented plumeria trees.

DK Choice

PULAU LANGKAWI: Bon Ton/ Temple Tree
Resorts
Pantai Cenang, 1 mile (2 km) north of main beach area
Tel *(04) 955-1688*
w bontonresort.com.my; templetree.com.my
These two idyllic resorts feature vintage timber houses that have been fully restored; some sleep two, others a family. Both resorts sit in landscaped grounds with palm trees, a swimming pool, and restaurant.

PULAU LANGKAWI: The Danna
Beach Hotel
Telaga Harbour Park, Pantai Kok
Tel *(04) 959-3288*
w thedanna.com
A grand marbled lobby and beachside infinity pool complement the lavish, spacious rooms.

TAIPING: Sentosa Villa
Resort
Jalan 8, Taman Sentosa
Tel *(05) 805-1000*
w sentosa-villa.com
This compound with a rustic hideaway feel has rooms and mini-villas. There is a cool stream for swimming in.

Southern Peninsula

JOHOR BAHRU: Renaissance
Modern
2 Jalan Permas 11
Tel *(07) 381-3333*
w marriott.com/hotels
State-of-the-art facilities, including a spa, fitness center, and pool, feature at this five-star hotel.

MELAKA: Wayfarer Guesthouse
Guesthouse
104 Lorong Hang Jebat
Tel *(06) 281-9469*
w wayfarermelaka.com
Rooms in this former rubber-trading house are spacious; some have beautiful views of the river.

MELAKA: 45 Lekiu
Serviced Apartment
45 Jalan Hang Lekiu
Tel *(012) 698-4917*
w 45lekiu.com
This stylish two-floor apartment has sleek furnishings, its own pool, and a rooftop terrace with lovely views over the city.

DK Choice

MELAKA: The Majestic

Historic
188 Jalan Bunga Raya
Tel *(06) 289-8000*
🅦 majesticmalacca.com
Set in a stunning 1920s mansion, this hotel offers sumptuous rooms with teakwood fittings and rolltop baths. Indulgent spa therapies are based on the healing heritage of the Peranakans. The restaurant offers traditional local cuisine.

MELAKA:
The Opposite Place
Boutique
18 Jalan Hang Lekiu
Tel *(016) 274-9686*
🅦 opposite-place.com
This hotel has just two stylish individually designed suites. The café serves superb Western dishes.

PULAU TIOMAN:
Japamala Resort & Spa
Resort
Kampung Lanting, north of Nipah
Tel *(07) 419-7777*
🅦 japamalaresorts.com
Nestled amid tropical rain forest, this exclusive eco-luxe resort offers Malay village-style villas.

PULAU TIOMAN:
Tunamaya Resort
Resort
Lots 20 & 21, Kampung Mukut
Tel *(07) 798-8108*
🅦 tunamayaresort.com
Contemporary villas have modern amenities and garden or sea views; there's a spa, pool, and dive center.

DK Choice

SEREMBAN:
The Dusun
Resort
Kampung Kolan Air, Mukim Pantai
🅦 thedusun.com.my
At this beautiful orchard retreat the Malay village-style units have rainforest views, kitchenettes, and barbecue stoves (catered meals are available only upon request). The lush grounds have two infinity pools.

SERIBUAT ARCHIPELAGO:
Batu Batu
Resort
Pulau Tengah
Tel *(017) 755-2813*
🅦 batubatu.com.my
This upmarket private island resort has villas in lush grounds; popular with both couples and families.

The Majestic in Melaka, incorporating influences from Peranakan culture

SERIBUAT ARCHIPELAGO:
Rimba Beach Resort
Resort
Pulau Sibu
Tel *(012) 710-6855*
🅦 resortmalaysia.com
Rustic beach chalets are shaded by palm trees at this laid-back resort with a young clientele.

SRI MENANTI: Sri Menanti
Resort
Modern
Pekan Sri Menanti
Tel *(06) 497-0049*
Right by the Istana Lama, this whitewashed hotel offers rooms and chalets around a pool.

Eastern and Central Peninsula

CHERATING: Tanjung Inn
Beach Hotel
11 Jln Kuantan Kememan
Tel *(09) 581-9081*
🅦 tanjunginn.com
Simple fan-cooled chalets and stylish Malay village-style houses are set around a tranquil garden.

KOTA BHARU: Tune
Modern
KBCC, Jalan Hamzah
Tel *(09) 744-3822*
🅦 tunehotels.com
Book well in advance for the best rates at this excellent-value hotel that is part of the AirAsia group.

KOTA BHARU: Pasir
Belanda
Guesthouse
Jalan PCB, Banggol District
Tel *(09) 747-7046*
🅦 pasirbelanda.com
Traditional Malay chalets are set around a garden with a pool; *batik* and cookery lessons are offered.

KOTA BHARU:
Renaissance
Modern
Kota Sri Mutiara, Jalan Sultan Yahya Petra
Tel *(09) 746-2233*
🅦 marriott.com
This luxurious hotel has an attractive pool, spa, and gym, as well as two restaurants.

KUALA TERENGGANU: Duyong
Marina & Resort
Modern
Pulau Duyong
Tel *(09) 627-7888*
🅦 duyongmarinaresort.com
Comfortable wooden chalets, a swimming pool, and a restaurant overlook the river at this resort.

KUANTAN:
Hyatt Regency
Modern
Jalan Telok Chempedak
Tel *(09) 518-1234*
🅦 kuantan.regency.hyatt.com
An upmarket beach retreat with a gym, tennis and squash courts, two pools, restaurants, and a bar.

PERHENTIAN ISLANDS: Mama's
Chalet
Beach Hotel
Lot 137, Kg. Seberang Genting, Perhentian Besar
Tel *(09) 690-4600*
🅦 mamaschalet.com.my
The chalets, some sea-facing, have private facilities; there's also a restaurant.

PERHENTIAN ISLANDS: Bubbles
Dive Resort
Resort
Tanjung Tukas, Perhentian Besar
Tel *(012) 983-8038*
🅦 bubblesdc.com
A friendly resort, Bubbles has its own stretch of beach, plus a dive shop and turtle hatchery.

PERHENTIAN ISLANDS:
Tunabay Island Resort
Beach Hotel
Perhentian Besar
Tel *(09) 690-2902*
🅦 tunabay.com.my
Wooden chalets have modern furnishings and there's a popular bar and restaurant.

PERHENTIAN ISLANDS: Bubu
Long Beach Resort
Beach Hotel
Pasir Panjang (Long Beach), Perhentian Kecil
Tel *(09) 697-8888*
🅦 buburesort.com.my
This is the most comfortable option on Long Beach. The deluxe villas nestle in greenery on a stretch of powdery white sand.

PULAU KAPAS: Kapas Beach Chalet (KBC)
Beach Hotel
Lot 85, Pulau Kapas
Tel *(012) 288-2008*
A-frame huts with private facilities are offered at this Malay-Dutch-run retreat with a very laid-back atmosphere.

PULAU KAPAS: Kapas Turtle Valley
Beach Hotel
Southeast coast, Pulau Kapas
Tel *(013) 354-3650*
[W] kapasturtlevalley.com
In a secluded cove, this welcoming Dutch-run resort offers eight comfortable chalets on a beautiful stretch of beach. The restaurant serves excellent international dishes. Book ahead.

PULAU REDANG: Redang Kalong
Resort
Teluk Kalong Beach
Tel *(03) 7960-7163*
[W] redangkalong.com
The simply furnished rooms have sea views, and there's a good on-site dive center.

PULAU REDANG: The Taaras Beach & Spa Resort
Resort
Teluk Dalam Beach
Tel *(09) 221-3997*
[W] thetaaras.com
A spa, dive shop, restaurants, pools, and tennis courts feature at this luxury resort.

DK Choice

PULAU TENGGOL: Tanjong Jara Resort
Resort
Batu 8, off Jalan Dungun, Dungun
Tel *(03) 2783-1000*
[W] tanjongjararesort.com
Set in peaceful tropical gardens, this exclusive retreat is sumptuously designed to reflect the 17th-century grand wooden palaces of Malay sultans. The well-appointed rooms with timber furnishings are dotted around the extensive grounds. There is a relaxing spa.

TAMAN NEGARA: Mutiara Taman Negara
Modern
Across the river from Kuala Tahan
Tel *(09) 266-3500*
[W] mutiarahotels.com
The upmarket, comfortable chalets are set in secluded, lush grounds shaded by towering trees in this national park.

Sarawak

BINTULU: Park City Everly
Modern
Jalan Tun Razak, I mile (2 km) NW of center
Tel *(086) 318-888*
[W] bintulu.theeverlyhotel.com
The best hotel in Bintulu has plush rooms, some with sea views, and is near restaurants, bars, and a mall.

BRUNEI: The Brunei $$
Modern
95 Jalan Pemancha, Bandar Seri Begawan
Tel *(073) 224-4828*
[W] thebruneihotel.com
Very near the waterfront and offering the best value in the capital, The Brunei has stylish rooms and a good restaurant.

BRUNEI: Empire Hotel $$
Resort
Jerudong BG3122, Negara Brunei Darussalam, 9 miles (15 km) from the capital
Tel *(073) 241-8888*
[W] theempirehotel.com
This elaborate combination of hotel and country club has its own golf course, pools, and a cinema.

DAMAI BEACH: Damai Beach Resort
Beach Hotel
Teluk Bandung beach
Tel *(082) 846-999*
[W] damaibeachresort.com
Rooms are spread over the beach and hilltop at this resort. The most striking are those in the style of a Bidayuh house with a conical roof.

DAMAI BEACH: The Village House
Resort
Pantai Puteri Santubong
Tel *(082) 846-166*
[W] villagehouse.com.my
Nestling in the shadow of Mount Santubong and located near Damai Beach, the rooms in this timber building are set around a central pool and feature traditional textiles as well as modern fittings.

KELABIT HIGHLANDS: Junglebluesdream
Guesthouse
Bario
Tel *(019) 884-9892*
[W] junglebluesdream.weebly.com
The longhouse-style residence of a Kelabit artist and his Danish partner, this homestay is also an art gallery. The owners can offer advice on jungle treks in the area.

KUCHING: Batik Boutique Hotel
Modern
38 Jalan Padungan
Tel *(082) 422-845*
[W] batikboutiquehotel.com
The most stylish downtown hotel has a good restaurant and bar, plus a courtyard garden.

KUCHING: Pullman Hotel
Modern
1A Jalan Mathies
Tel *(082) 222-888*
[W] pullmankuching.com
Suitable for both business and leisure travelers, this hilltop tower offers a full range of amenities and good city and river views.

MIRI: Dillenia
Hostel
Lot 846, Jalan Sida
Tel *(085) 434-204*
This perenially popular hostel has a knowledgeable owner who can offer travel advice and arrange transport to various destinations.

MIRI: Dynasty Hotel
Modern
Lot 683, Block 9, Jalan Pujut-Lutong
Tel *(085) 421-111*
[W] dynastyhotelmiri.com.my
A short walk from Miri's popular markets, this pleasant hotel with a marbled lobby has 130 rooms.

Tented four-poster beds at the island retreat Kapas Turtle Valley

For more information on types of hotels *see pp276–7*

MULU: Mulu Marriott Resort & Spa (RM)(RM)(RM)
Resort
About a mile (2 km) from Mulu airport and the Mulu park entrance
Tel *(085) 792-388*
W marriott.com
The plushest of Mulu's hotels, this sprawling, venerable complex has a pool, spa, and tennis courts.

SIBU: Tanahmas (RM)(RM)
Modern
Lot 277, Block 5, Jalan Kampung Nyabor, off Jalan Chambers
Tel *(084) 333-188*
W tanahmas.com.my
This centrally located tower block has spacious rooms, a pool, gym, a couple of restaurants, and business facilities.

Sabah

KINABALU NATIONAL PARK: Mesilau Nature Resort (RM)(RM)(RM)
Resort
Jalan Cinta Mata Mesilau, Jalan Kundasang Kauluan, A4 road
Tel *(088) 871-519*
W suterasanctuarylodges.com.my
On a river with plenty of birdlife, this peaceful resort has dorms, chalets, and lodges.

KOTA KINABALU: Jesselton (RM)(RM)
Modern
69 Jalan Gaya
Tel *(088) 223-333*
W jesseltonhotel.com
Designed to look like a colonial house, this welcoming hotel offers well-appointed rooms.

KOTA KINABALU: Langkah Syabas (RM)(RM)
Beach Hotel
Jalan Papar Baru, Kampung Laut Kinarut, Kinarut
Tel *(088) 752-000*
W langkahsyabas.com.my
Twelve miles (20 km) south of Kota Kinabalu, this resort offers chalets grouped around a pool.

DK Choice

KOTA KINABALU: Hyatt Regency (RM)(RM)(RM)
Modern
Jalan Dutuk Salleh Sulong
Tel *(088) 221-234*
W kinabalu.regency.hyatt.com
This sumptuous hotel has an inviting pool and comfortable rooms with wonderful sea views. There's a well-equipped gym and spa. The restaurant features an open kitchen and serves local and international dishes.

PULAU LANKAYAN: Lankayan Island Dive Resort (RM)(RM)(RM)
Resort
Pulau Lankayan
Tel *(089) 673-999*
W lankayan-island.com
The wooden seafront chalets are roomy and comfortable. There's a reputable dive shop on-site.

SEPILOK: Sepilok Nature Resort (RM)(RM)
Resort
Jalan Sepilok Mile 14k
Tel *(089) 673-999*
W sepilok.com
Spacious eco-friendly chalets are set around a lake in the jungle. There is an acclaimed restaurant.

TIP OF BORNEO: Tampat Do Aman (RM)
Beach Hotel
Peti Surat 115
Tel *(013) 880-8395*
W tampatdoaman.com
Choose from simple, comfortable rooms in a longhouse, private huts and fan-cooled chalets.

TUNKU ABDUL RAHMAN NATIONAL PARK: Bunga Raya Resort (RM)(RM)(RM)
Resort
Polish Bay, Pulau Gaya
Tel *(088) 380-390*
W bungarayaresort.com
Nestled in the forest, this luxurious hideaway has access to a beautiful white-sand beach.

TUNKU ABDUL RAHMAN NATIONAL PARK: Gayana Eco Resort (RM)(RM)(RM)
Resort
Malohom Bay, Pulau Gaya
Tel *(088) 380-390*
W gayana-eco-resort.com
Set on a peaceful lagoon, these luxurious villas are on stilts. There's an infinity pool.

Singapore

Colonial Core and Chinatown

Wink $
Hostel **Map** 4 C3
8A Mosque Street
Tel *6222-2940*
W winkhostel.com
This slick establishment has dorms with capsule-style beds, some sleeping two. Each has its own power outlet and locker.

The Inn at Temple Street $$
Modern **Map** 4 C4
36 Temple Street
Tel *6221-5333*
W theinn.com.sg
In a centrally located shophouse, this is a simple, good-value option.

DK Choice

New Majestic $$
Boutique **Map** 4 B4
31–37 Bukit Pasoh Road
Tel *6511-4700*
W newmajestichotel.com
Masquerading as a gallery of contemporary art, every room at this hotel has been styled by a different designer, some with flamboyant murals, others minimalist and understated. The swimming pool has glass portholes into the restaurant below. Book early to benefit from good rates.

Carlton $$$
Modern **Map** 5 E1
76 Bras Basah Road
Tel *6338-8333*
W carltonhotel.sg
Plush rooms feature designer touches at this luxurious hotel.

Mulu Marriott Resort, a landmark easily spotted from incoming flights

Fort Canning $$$
Historic   Map 4 C1
11 Canning Walk
Tel *6559-6770*
w hfcsingapore.com
In a former British military building within Fort Canning Park, this luxurious hotel has rooms with quirky touches – some have the bathtub almost next to the bed.

Fullerton $$$
Historic   Map 5 E3
1 Fullerton Square
Tel *6733-8388*
w fullertonhotel.com
With Neo-Classical façades and an Art Deco atrium with massive Egyptian temple-style pillars, the opulent Fullerton is one of Singapore's most stunning hotels.

Marina Bay Sands $$$
Modern   Map 5 F3
10 Bayfront Avenue
Tel *6688-8868*
w marinabaysands.com
There's a definite thrill in staying at this iconic building just by Gardens by the Bay. The infinity pool affords unrivalled views of the Colonial Core.

Parkroyal on Kitchener $$$
Modern   Map 3 E2
3 Upper Pickering Street
Tel *6809-8888*
w parkroyalhotels.com
This luxury hotel prides itself on connecting with nature by using wood furnishing and glass for natural light. The curvy-edged green terraces are intended to echo rice paddies.

DK Choice

Raffles $$$
Historic   Map 5 E1
1 Beach Road
Tel *6337-1886*
w raffleshotel.com
Raffles is a byword for colonial charm and opulence. Beyond its whitewashed Neo-Classical façade are serene courtyard gardens and luxurious suites, all with butler service, plus excellent restaurants and the Long Bar, where the Singapore Sling was first concocted.

Sofitel So $$$
Boutique   Map 5 D4
35 Robinson Road
Tel *6701-6800*
w sofitel.com
Partly designed by Karl Lagerfeld, this supremely chic hotel has a mixture of ornate, Baroque-inspired decor and modern, quirky touches.

Designer decor in an individually styled room at the New Majestic, Singapore

Little India and Orchard Road

The Inn Crowd $
Hostel   Map 3 D3
73 Dunlop Street
Tel *6296-9169*
w theinncrowd.com
Probably the best-value hostel in Singapore has well-kept dorms and private rooms that, unusually, have TVs. Staff organize offbeat excursions.

The Big Hotel $$
Modern   Map 3 D4
200 Middle Road
Tel *6809-7998*
w bighotel.com
This arty, chic hotel's rooms have minimalist styling and high-tec comforts such as in-room tablets.

Lloyd's Inn $$
Modern   Map 2 B5
2 Lloyd Road
Tel *6737-7309*
w lloydsinn.com
Smart designer fittings, a roof terrace, and a landscaped garden feature at this minimalist hotel.

The Quincy $$
Modern   Map 2 A3
22 Mount Elizabeth
Tel *6738-5888*
w quincy.com.sg
Oozing contemporary style, this smart hotel has a lovely infinity pool on the 12th floor.

The Sultan $$
Modern   Map 3 F4
101 Jalan Sultan
Tel *6723-7101*
w thesultan.com.sg
Occupying a series of refurbished shophouses, this relaxed hotel's rooms are individually decorated with understated flair. For a quiet stay, ask for an attic room.

Wanderlust $$
Boutique   Map 3 D3
2 Dickson Road
Tel *6396-3322*
w wanderlusthotel.com
Rooms are color-coded or decked out in eccentric artwork at this very quirky hotel.

Goodwood Park $$$
Historic   Map 2 A3
22 Scotts Road
Tel *6737-7411*
w goodwoodparkhotel.com
Only a 5-minute walk from Orchard Road, this hotel in a colonial-era landmark building has every luxury and excellent restaurants and coffee lounges.

Mandarin Orchard $$$
Modern   Map 2 A4
333 Orchard Road
Tel *6737-4411*
w meritushotels.com
The perenially popular Mandarin Orchard has elegant rooms and its own swanky shopping mall. Staff wear traditional Chinese-inspired uniforms.

Shangri-La $$$
Modern   Map 1 E1
22 Orange Grove Road
Tel *6737-3644*
w shangri-la.com
Amid the tropical gardens of this opulent green haven are three wings of plush rooms and restaurants. Facilities include tennis courts and a spa.

Farther Afield

Santa Grand East Coast $$
Boutique
171 East Coast Road, Katong
Tel *6344-6866*
w santagrandhotels.com
This hotel has an attractive shophouse façade, bright Peranakan-themed rooms, and a rooftop pool.

Siloso Beach Resort $$
Resort
51 Imbiah Walk
Tel *6722-3333*
w silosobeachresort.com
The main draw here is the excellent swimming pool with a waterfall and slides.

Capella $$$
Resort
1 The Knolls, Sentosa
Tel *6377-8888*
w capellahotels.com/singapore
Sentosa's most lavish hotel is set around splendid former British officers' quarters. Rooms are chic and contemporary, there's a top-notch spa, and three pools.

For more information on types of hotels *see pp276–7*

WHERE TO EAT AND DRINK

With their clever combinations of textures and flavors, the cuisines of Malaysia and Singapore offer exciting dining discoveries for the visitor. Dishes of Malay, Chinese, and Indian origin are widely available, reflecting the three major communities that make up the population of the two countries. Whether you eat at a sumptuous restaurant in a top hotel or a simple street stall in a local market, you're usually assured of a decent meal, if not an excellent one. The major cities of Kuala Lumpur and Singapore boast a dazzling array of international cuisines, and many provincial cities, including Kota Bharu, Georgetown, Melaka, and Kuching, usually offer a good variety, including Italian, French, Mexican, Vietnamese, and Japanese, plus a range of Western-style venues.

Types of Restaurants

Though the cuisines available in Malaysia and Singapore are amazingly varied, eateries are essentially of three types: hawker stalls, *kedai kopi* or coffee shops, and restaurants that range from the simple to the lavish.

Hawker stalls are not only the cheapest, with food often as good as the best restaurant, but also a real cultural experience. Despite the name, many stalls are no longer found on the street but are instead collected into indoor hawker centers or food courts. *Kedai kopi* are no-frills neighborhood cafés that usually offer a limited range of dishes at cheap prices, and are, along with hawker centers, the favored place to eat for most locals. The *kedai kopi* either has a handful of "stalls", resembling a mini-food court, or a central kitchen serving up a limited range of dishes.

Restaurants vary from simple shopfronts to establishments that serve gourmet food in elegant surroundings. The most expensive are those in Kuala Lumpur and Singapore. Prices in the restaurant listings on pages 290–301 are given in Malaysian ringgit or Singapore dollars as appropriate (and in Brunei using the Brunei dollar, which is equal in value to the Singapore dollar).

Reading the Menu

Virtually all restaurants and many coffee shops and hawker stalls display the names of the dishes they offer in English. If they don't have English menus, it is acceptable to just point at your choice of dish. The problem is not so much finding out what is on offer but what to select, such is the wide variety.

Menus are often organized according to the main ingredient, such as chicken, beef, pork, seafood, and vegetables (note that pork is unavailable not just at halal eateries, but also at most Malaysian hotel restaurants and at Chinese restaurants in some Muslim-majority areas). There are usually a few individual meals, but most people tend to eat in groups and choose a variety of dishes in order to sample more. Portions are relatively generous and for a couple, three dishes will usually suffice.

Table Etiquette

Most Malay, Chinese, and Indian food is chopped up for quick cooking, so a knife is not required. Generally a fork and spoon are the preferred eating utensils (local people mainly use the spoon). Chopsticks are useful for noodle dishes but are not used for rice unless it is in a rice bowl, in which case the chopsticks are used, shovel-like, to bring the rice to the mouth. Diners are presented with an individual plate or bowl, and help themselves from the platters of stir-fried dishes, curries, soups, and salads in the center of the table.

Reservations

Reservations are not generally necessary except at the most popular or upscale restaurants, although in Singapore it's advisable to book at weekends, when most families go out for a meal. People with special dietary needs should mention it to the restaurant manager before making a reservation. *Kedai kopi* don't take bookings, but meals there are over so quickly that you'll seldom have to wait more than a few minutes for a table.

Drinks

Alcoholic drinks, especially beer, are generally available but prices can be high; hawker centers and *kedai kopi* tend to be cheapest. Muslim restaurants, however, along with many Chinese eateries in the conservative northeast of the Peninsula, serve no alcohol at all. Freshly squeezed fruit juices are widely available at hawker stalls, and the variety of exotic tropical fruits

Outside seating at Nerovivo, among European options in Kuala Lumpur *(p291)*

has an irresistible appeal, though note that sugar is almost always added unless you specify otherwise. *Tuak*, or rice wine, is brewed in the longhouses of Sabah and Sarawak, but visitors should note that it can vary from weak and cloying to extremely potent.

Payment and Tipping

Top-end and many mid-range restaurants accept credit cards, but in general it is best to carry sufficient cash to pay the bill. Tipping is not common: bills may include a service charge and tax, and a tip is not expected at *kedai kopi* and hawker stalls; only at cheaper restaurants without a service charge might you want to offer a tip.

Street Food

Sampling street food is one of the highlights of a visit to Malaysia and Singapore, not just because many dishes served at hawker stalls are unfamiliar to foreign visitors, but also because the food is generally prepared with great expertise. Another advantage of hawker stalls is that it is often possible to sample Malay, Chinese, and Indian cuisine, all in one spot. Some stalls specialize in just one or a handful of rice or noodle dishes, others serve up a range of curries, egg dishes, pancakes, or satay, and all are inexpensive.

Chic interior of Ristorante Beccari, Kuching *(p297)*

Vegetarians

It can be difficult for vegetarians to find dishes that don't contain any meat or seafood. However, most Indian restaurants have a selection of vegetarian dishes and Chinese restaurants can prepare vegetable stir-fries, though note that cooks often use oyster sauce as seasoning unless you ask for it to be omitted. Many cities also have Chinese vegetarian eateries that use soya or gluten-based meat substitutes to emulate traditional dishes as well as street food.

Eating with Children

There are no restrictions on children entering restaurants in Malaysia and Singapore; in fact, in most places they are welcome. Some restaurants offer special children's meals. Mild Chinese soups and rice dishes are best for those unaccustomed to spicy food. High standards of food preparation and quality control are maintained, yet care should be taken as children traveling here could be prone to food- and water-related ailments.

Smoking

Smoking is prohibited in enclosed, air-conditioned environments, which comprise two-thirds of the restaurants in Malaysia and Singapore. However, about one-third of the eateries have a terrace or outdoor smoking area.

Recommended Restaurants

The restaurants recommended on pages 290–301 have been selected on the basis of their popularity, quality, and value for money. A range of establishments catering to different tastes has been included, so that there are places to sample local specialties in every area, plus a range of restaurants offering international cuisine, especially in the major cities. Many excellent hawker centers and *kedai kopi* are featured, to give an authentic idea of the Malaysian and Singaporean dining experience.

Restaurants highlighted as DK Choices stand out for one or more exceptional features: perhaps a unique setting, or the breadth as well as the quality of the food. These special places have stood the test of time and boast a loyal following, and are worth seeking out.

Traditional and improvised decor at the relaxed Calanthe Art Café, Melaka *(p294)*

The Flavors of Malay Cuisine

Malaysians and Singaporeans live to eat, so it is not surprising that markets offer an abundance of fresh tropical fruit and vegetables, meat, and seafood. Mounds of cabbages, eggplants, mangoes, and pineapples are stacked up beside bowls of dried shrimp and fresh crabs, slabs of beef, and marinated ducks. Some stalls specialize in types of rice, the staple of Malay cuisine; others in flavorings and pastes, such as *rempah* and *belacan*, essential to Malay cooking. Though many dishes are unknown outside the region, *satay* has become a worldwide favorite.

Galangal, lemongrass, and bird's-eye chilies

Stall at the Chow Kit fish market, Kuala Lumpur

Nasi and Mee

Rice (*nasi*) and noodles (*mee*) form the basis of any Malay meal, though the preparation of both is almost as varied as the sauces, broths, and curries that accompany them.

Rice may be served fried, steamed, glutinous, or boiled into *bubur*, a savoury soup or porridge. It is commonly steamed, and eaten with a selection of toppings (*nasi campur*). It is also sometimes enhanced with coconut milk (*santan*), in *nasi lemak*.

Noodles may be made from wheat, wheat and egg, rice, or mung beans and are served fried or as a soup with vegetables and meat or seafood. Typical Malay noodle dishes are *laksa* and *mee rebus*, both of which are usually served with scrumptious spicy sauce.

Rempah and Sambal

The carefully blended seasoning pastes are the secret to the mouthwatering flavors

Jambu air (water apple)
Durian
Mangga (mango)
Belimbing (star fruit)
Betik (papaya)
Nenas (pineapple)
Limau (pomelo)
Kaktus madu (dragon fruit)

Tropical fruits of the region

Malay Dishes and Specialties

Chicken *satay*

Breakfast can be almost anything in Malaysia and Singapore, but a couple of favorites are *laksa* (spicy noodle soup) and *nasi lemak* (a rice dish). Lunch is usually a one-dish meal, which might easily be *nasi campur* or *mee goreng*. Dinner generally brings family groups or friends together to share a variety of classic Malay dishes, such as *satay* (spicy meat skewers with a peanut sauce), *rendang*, and *ayam panggang* (chicken marinated with garlic and lime, grilled and served with a hot *sambal*). This is likely to be followed by an *ais kacang* or a plate of fresh fruit. Constantly passionate about food, locals don't miss out on a late-night supper, indulging in anything from a steaming hot bowl of rice soup to a plate of barbecued chicken wings.

Mee goreng are yellow noodles, stir-fried with vegetables and meat, fish, or tofu, and garnished with lime.

A woman selling fruit and other produce at a market in Kota Belud

of Malay food. The most widely used paste is *rempah*, for which garlic, lemongrass, shallots, galangal, and ginger are pounded in a mortar. Cinnamon, coriander seeds, cloves, and peppercorns are added to thicken curries, or are fried in oil until fragrant before being added to meat or vegetables.

Sambal is a chili paste that is served as a side dish. *Sambal ulek* is a blend of chili, salt, and vinegar, while the hugely popular *sambal belacan* is made of chili, salt, and sugar pounded with fermented shrimp paste, and served with a wedge of lime.

Peranakan and Bornean Cuisine

Malay cuisine is influenced by Chinese, Indian, Thai, Indonesian, and other cultures, but there are several regional variations, of which Bornean and Peranakan, or Straits Chinese, food are the most distinctive. In Malaysia, Peranakan cuisine came into existence when Chinese traders settled in the region and married local Nyonya women. They combined spicy Malay pastes with ingredients that are usual in Malay food, such as pork and duck, using Chinese cooking techniques

Grilling *satay* at the Gurney Drive hawker center in Penang

but adding elements of Portuguese, Indian, and Thai cuisine. A typical Peranakan dish is *mee siam*, or fine rice noodles in a spicy, sweet-sour gravy.

Visitors to Malaysian Borneo can sample local specialties such as *linut* (in Sarawak) and *ambuyat* (in Sabah), both translucent pastes made of sago starch, *paku* (jungle ferns), and *jaruk* (wild boar mixed with salt and rice and cooked in a bamboo tube).

REGIONAL LAKSAS

Every state has its own version of this noodle soup, a national favorite, including:

Assam laksa
From the Penang region, this uses tamarind to give a sour edge, as well as flaked fish, wild ginger buds, and *belacan*. Pineapple is shredded for a sweet garnish.

Laksa Johor
A very rich fish *laksa* flavored with coconut milk, cumin, coriander seeds, and turmeric. It is garnished with cucumber, bean sprouts, and Vietnamese mint.

Sarawak laksa
This features chicken, and prawns in tangy *kalamansi* lime. Toasted rice and coconut give the soup a brownish color.

Singapore laksa
Deep-fried anchovies, *belacan*, and coconut milk are used to make a rich, sour soup that is topped with fish cakes.

Rendang, influenced by Indonesian cuisine, is a fiery, dry curry made with chicken, mutton, or beef.

Laksa lemak, found around Kuala Lumpur and known as curry *laksa*, features prawns, tofu, and egg.

Ais kacang is a vivid dessert concoction of shaved ice with syrup, jelly, corn, red beans, and evaporated milk.

The Flavors of Malay-Chinese Cuisine

The Chinese had been trading in the region for centuries, but it was not until the 19th century that immigrants began settling in large numbers, attracted by tin- and gold-mining, and plantation agriculture. The greatest concentration of settlers was in Singapore, where Chinese cuisine still predominates, though its influence is apparent throughout Malaysia. In Malay cuisine, rice and noodles are a staple in most meals, of which the latter is a major Chinese import. Key elements in all regional variations of Chinese food are the use of fresh produce and the balance of tastes and textures.

Dried shiitake mushrooms

Frying street snacks in Chinatown, Kuala Lumpur

Regional Influences

The Chinese food in Malaysia and Singapore is usually Cantonese, noted for its mild flavorings and specialties such as *dim sum* (steamed or fried filled dumplings and buns).

Hakka cuisine, from the provinces of Guangdong and Fujian, mixes fresh and preserved ingredients.

Deep-fried bean-curd is a Hakka specialty, and pork (especially belly) is the preferred meat.

Hainanese food features fresh ingredients and the sparing use of spices. It has given Malaysia and Singapore one of their most common dishes – Hainanese chicken rice, garnished with cucumber, and chili and ginger dips. Hokkien, sometimes called

peasant food, is still the source of delicate spring rolls. Noodles are found in many dishes, such as *Hokkien mee*, thick wheat noodles stir-fried with seafood or pork.

Teochew cuisine, from Chiuchow, is famed for *muay* porridge – a pale rice broth served with crayfish, salted eggs, and vegetables.

Xiao long bao — Coriander dumplings — Chive dumplings — Pork buns — Shao mai — Prawn dumplings — Seafood dumplings

Selection of steamed dumplings that make up a typical *dim sum* meal

ON THE CHINESE MENU

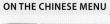

Aromatic soup of pork ribs, shiitake mushrooms, and cilantro

Bak kut teh (Hokkien) Pork rib soup.

Cao fan (Cantonese) Fried rice.

Char kway teow (Hokkien) Spicy flat rice noodles with cockles, sausage, and egg in soy sauce.

Cha siew mee (Cantonese) Egg noodles in soup with minced pork dumplings.

Chee cheong fun (Hokkien) Rice flour rolls stuffed with shrimp or pork.

Hay mee (Hokkien) Prawn and pork rib noodle soup.

Lou ark (Teochew) Braised duck.

Lui char fan (Hakka) Rice porridge with ground peanuts, sweet potato leaves, peppercorns, and mint.

Pai quat (Cantonese) Steamed pork ribs with black beans.

Sek bak (Hokkien) Pork belly in spicy black bean sauce.

Sha bou fan (Cantonese) Rice in a claypot with chicken, sausage, salted fish, and soy sauce.

Shao mai (Cantonese) Minced pork wrapped in dumplings.

The Flavors of Malay-Indian Cuisine

The main period of Indian immigration was the 19th century, when laborers were shipped across to work on rubber plantations operated by the British. Most were Hindus from southern India and, like the Chinese, they brought a major influence to Malay cuisine. Although rice is a staple, Indian food is also characterized by its use of pulses and various types of flatbread, such as *roti*, *naan*, and *chapati*. The most commonly used flavorings are chili, cumin, garam masala, coriander, mustard seed, turmeric, yogurt, coconut, and ghee.

Naan bread

Baskets of chilies in the market at Langkawi, Malaysia

North and South

Northern Indian cuisine is characterized by the use of dairy products to make rich, thick sauces. Many dishes are baked in a cylindrical clay oven called a *tandoor*; these include *naan* breads and the famous *tandoori* chicken now enjoyed worldwide. Breads are eaten in preference to rice. In contrast to the emphasis on bread and meat in the northern Indian diet, southern Indian food is always accompanied by rice and many vegetarian dishes. Despite the hotter climate, dishes from south India tend to be spicy and are distinguished by the liberal use of coconut milk, lentils, and curry leaves. The *thali* is a popular southern Indian meal, comprising small portions of a variety of dishes and condiments.

Mamak Cuisine

A third type of Indian food frequently found in Malaysia is that produced by Indian Muslims. These dishes are mostly sold at hawker stalls, and include *mee goreng* (spicy fried noodles), *rojak* (deep-fried vegetables and seafood in a sweet and spicy sauce), and *mee rebus* (a mix of yellow noodles and beansprouts in a sweet potato gravy, topped with a boiled egg).

Fish in coconut tamarind sauce · Mung bean *dal* · Pilau · *Roti canai* · Chickpea masala · Coconut chutney · Banana chutney · *Raita* · Lemon pickle · Prawn curry

Example of a *thali*, laid out on a banana leaf

Indian Favorites in Malaysia

Red lentils

From early morning, cooks at *roti* stalls throughout Malaysia can be seen spinning dough into a flat disk, folding it in on itself, then frying it on a griddle to make *roti canai*, which can either be dipped in a bowl of curry sauce or sprinkled with sugar for a less spicy breakfast. At lunchtime, one of the most popular dishes sold at Indian Muslim hawker stalls is the vegetarian *mee rebus*. For dinner, among the many delicious and filling options are *biryani* and a *thali*. The former has a base of seasoned rice cooked with saffron, nuts, and vegetables, and is served with meat or seafood, and vegetables. The latter consists of a tray or banana leaf, laden with vegetable, fish, or meat curries, pulses (*dal*), pickles, and yogurt (*raita*), as well as rice, breads, or poppadoms.

Lamb *biryani*, fragrant with saffron and other spices

Where to Eat and Drink

Kuala Lumpur

KLCC

Acme Bar & Coffee (ABC)
Western
Ground Floor, The Troika,
19 Persiaran KLCC
Tel *(03) 2162-2288*
The all-day weekend brunches
are a highlight at this bright
and airy café with floor-to-
ceiling windows and low-
hanging light bulbs.

Cantaloupe
French
Level 23A, Tower B, The Troika,
19 Persiaran KLCC
Tel *(03) 2162-0886*   **Closed** *lunch*
Mon–Sat
The real draw here is the
bird's-eye views of the city;
there's also a popular Sunday
lunch that attracts visitors
and expats alike.

Fuego
South American
Level 23A, Tower B, The Troika,
19 Persiaran KLCC
Tel *(03) 2162-0886*   **Closed** *lunch*
This swanky tapas bar with open-
air seating offers incredible views
of the Petronas Towers.

Marini's on 57
Italian   **Map** 2 E4
Level 57, Menara 3 Petronas
Tel *(03) 2386-6030*   **Closed** *lunch*
Kuala Lumpur's highest rooftop
bar is one of the best places to
enjoy a pre-prandial cocktail,
while the award-winning
restaurant serves creatively
presented dishes.

Bukit Bintang and the Golden Triangle

Din Tain Fung
Chinese   **Map** 6 D2
Level 6, Pavilion KL Mall
Tel *(03) 2148-8292*
Part of a bustling chain, Din Tain
Fung has an open-plan kitchen
and specializes in pork dumplings,
which are traditionally eaten
dipped in ginger vinegar.

Muar
Malay   **Map** 5 B2
6G Tengkat Tong Shin
Tel *(03) 2144-2072*   **Closed** *Mon*
Cuisine from Muar, a small coastal
town known for its variations of
Chinese and Malay dishes is
served in a simple interior. It's the
perfect spot to grab a quick bite.

Feeka
Western   **Map** 5 C2
19 Jalan Mesui
Tel *(03) 2110-4599*
Delicious home-made pastries
and a range of light meals are
served at this laid-back café.

Hakka
Chinese   **Map** 6 D1
90 Jalan Raja Chulan
Tel *(03) 2143-1908*
This superb Hakka restaurant
with open-air seating offers
particularly good seafood dishes.

Lot 10 Hutong
Asian   **Map** 6 D2
Basement, Lot 10 Mall, Jalan Bukit
Bintang
You can sample everything from
noodles to dumplings at this
gourmet heritage village with
dozens of excellent hawker
stalls specializing in Malay and
Asian cuisine.

Luk Yu Tea House
Chinese   **Map** 6 D2
Basement, Starhill Gallery, 181 Jalan
Bukit Bintang
Tel *(03) 2782-3850*
Hong Kong-style pork-free *dim*
sum are served at this welcoming
restaurant shaped like a teapot.
There are plenty of teas on offer.

The Magnificent Fish &
Chip Bar
British   **Map** 5 C2
28 Changkat Bukit Bintang
Tel *(03) 2142-7021*
Authentic fish and chips are
served in newspaper wrapping.
There's an all-day English breakfast
and Guinness-and-steak pie.

European wine-bar interior at the
Italian Neroteca

Pinchos
Spanish   **Map** 5 C2
18 Changkat Bukit Bintang
Tel *(03) 2145-8482*   **Closed** *lunch,*
Mon
Enjoy the dishes at the bar or at
wooden tables as you people-
watch at this buzzing tapas joint,
which swarms with customers
most evenings.

Pisco Bar
Peruvian & Spanish   **Map** 5 C2
29 Jalan Mesui
Tel *(03) 2142-2900*   **Closed** *lunch,*
Mon
This popular bar rustles up
potent pisco sours, the Peruvian
drink of choice. There are tasty
Peruvian and Spanish tapas, too.

Sao Nam
Vietnamese   **Map** 5 B2
25 Tengkat Tong Shin
Tel *(03) 2144-1225*
An award-winning restaurant,
Sao Nam is popular with
international travelers. The menu
includes spring rolls and
mangosteen and prawn salad.

Albion
British   **Map** 5 C2
31 Jalan Berangan
Tel *(03) 2141-9282*   **Closed** *Mon*
Authentic modern British
cuisine including top-notch
Sunday roasts with Yorkshire
pudding, as well as excellent
slow-roasted pork belly.

Frangipani
Modern European   **Map** 5 C2
25 Changkat Bukit Bintang
Tel *(03) 2144-3001*   **Closed** *lunch;*
Mon
First-rate nouvelle cuisine is
served at this sleek restaurant. It
also has a very trendy bar that
buzzes on weekends, attracting
both a straight and gay clientele.

Havana
Western   **Map** 5 C2
Changkat Bukit Bintang
Tel *(03) 2142-7170*   **Closed** *lunch*
Specializing in steaks, burgers,
and beef ribs cooked over a
charcoal grill, this busy restaurant
gets packed on the weekends.
There's a popular bar and club by
the same name upstairs.

Marble 8 Steakhouse
Western
163 Jalan Binjai
Tel *(03) 2386-6030* **Closed** *Sat lunch*
Fine cuts of Wagyu and Angus beef are on the menu at this fine-dining steakhouse. There are excellent views of the Petronas Towers. The swish M8 bar is the ideal place to enjoy cocktails.

Neroteca
Italian **Map** 5 C2
Unit G1, Seri Bukit Ceylon, 8 Lorong Ceylon
Tel *(03) 2070-0530* **Closed** *Sat lunch*
The stylish Neroteca is a great spot to enjoy a glass of wine and nibble on some cold cuts, or enjoy a hearty Italian meal. It's also popular for Sunday brunch.

Nerovivo
Italian **Map** 5 B2
3a Jalan Ceylon
Tel *(03) 2070-3120* **Closed** *Sat lunch, Sun*
A range of well-executed classic Italian dishes, including excellent meat and seafood mains, is served ar this upscale restaurant with modern decor. Book ahead.

DK Choice

Shook!
Asian/Western **Map** 6 D2
Basement, Starhill Gallery, 181 Jalan Bukit Bintang
Tel *(03) 2719-8535*
Attracting a well-heeled crowd of locals and expats, this excellent restaurant with four show kitchens serves Italian, Chinese, Japanese, and Western grill dishes. The walk-in cellar holds over 3,000 bottles, which means there's an extensive wine list. There's daily live jazz, too.

Sushi Hinata
Japanese **Map** 5 C1
A-0-1, Ground Floor, St Mary Residence, 1 Jalan Tengah
Tel *(03) 2022-1349* **Closed** *Sun*
Sushi and sashimi is lovingly prepared at the open counter of this small restaurant, which is considered to be among the capital's very best.

twenty.one
European **Map** 5 C2
20–21 Changkat Bukit Bintang
Tel *(03) 2142-0021*
One of Changkat's most popular venues, this restaurant, bar, and club has it all – from excellent modern European fare to a trendy first-floor bar and dance area with balcony.

The modern interior of popular Nerovivo

Zenzero
Italian **Map** 5 C1
Ground Floor, St Mary Place, 1 Jalan Tengah
Tel *(03) 2022-3883* **Closed** *Sat lunch*
Undoubtedly one of the city's best Italian restaurants, the menu at Zenzero changes seasonally, and there's an extensive wine list.

Chinatown

Central Market Food Court
Asian **Map** 4 F3
Jalan Hang Kasturi
Tel *1300-22-8688*
An array of different dishes are on offer from Malaysia and beyond, including traditional Nyonya cuisine and Japanese pancakes.

Nam Heong
Chinese **Map** 4 F3
56 Jalan Sultan
Tel *(03) 2078-5879* **Closed** *eve*
This is a popular spot for original Haiwanese chicken rice prepared in the open kitchen.

Old China Café
Chinese & Malay **Map** 4 F4
11 Jalan Balai Polis
Tel *(03) 207-25915*
Brimming with old-world charm, this atmospheric café serves hearty, classic dishes.

DK Choice

Contango
Asian/Western **Map** 4 E4
Majestic Hotel, Jalan Sultan Hishamuddin
Tel *(03) 2785-8000*
At this buffet restaurant there's a mouthwatering array of freshly prepared dishes ranging from Indian, Chinese, and Malay to Italian, rustled up before your very eyes in an open kitchen. There's a good selection of desserts and wines.

Farther Afield

DK Choice

Annalakshmi
Indian
Temple of Fine Arts, 116 Jalan Berhala, Brickfields
Tel *(03) 2274-3799* **Closed** *Mon*
An excellent lunchtime buffet and evening à-la-carte menu of authentic South Indian dishes is served at this restaurant set in the Temple of Fine Arts. The profits of the evening menu support various projects in the Indian community.

Sri Nirwana Maju
Indian
43 Jalan Telawi 3, Bangsar
Tel *(03) 2287-8445*
Excellent meat and fish curries are served in an informml setting at this bustling banana-leaf curry house. Long queues are to be expected.

Alexis Bistro
Asian/Western
29 Jalan Telawi 3, Bangsar
Tel *(03) 2284-2880* **Closed** *eve*
Especially popular among Kuala Lumpur's expats, this stylish café, bistro, and wine bar offers modern takes on traditional Asian and Western dishes, including pizza and pasta, as well as a mouthwatering selection of home-made cakes. There are frequent live jazz performances.

La Bodega
Spanish
16 Jalan Telawi 2, Bangsar
Tel *(03) 2287-8318*
This branch of a tapas chain has an adjacent deli and serves Spanish food products imported from Spain. It has a particularly loyal expat clientele who flock here for its paella and tapas.

For more information on types of restaurants *see pp284–5*

Mercat
Spanish
51G Jalan Telawi 3, Bangsar
Tel *(03) 2201-5288*   **Closed** *Mon*
Superb Catalan tapas, as well as heartier mains, are served at this bustling gastro-bar. The pork and beef meatballs with cuttlefish and peas is one of their most popular dishes.

WTF
International
98 Lorong Maarof, Bangsar
Tel *(019) 261-7070*
The Indian vegetarian dishes are exquisite, but there are plenty of other cuisines to choose from including Chinese and Mexican. The acronym stands for What Tasty Food.

Yeast
French
24G Jalan Telawi 2, Bangsar
Tel *(03) 2282-0118*   **Closed** *Mon*
This boulangerie, café, and bistro is the ideal spot for a morning snack and a coffee. The menu includes French favorites such as *boeuf bourguignon*.

Rendez-Vous
French
100 Lorong Maarof, Bangsar
Tel *(03) 2202-0206*   **Closed** *Mon*
A wide selection of typical French meat and seafood dishes as well as delicious desserts are served in a welcoming interior. There is an extensive wine list of bottles from the most renowned vineyards in France.

Northwest Peninsula

ALOR STAR: Lot 7 Food Court
Chinese
Jalan Sekerat
The best of the food courts close to Alor Star's Chinatown has a vast range of rice and noodle dishes, as well as more eclectic options such as oyster omelette, and even Chinese renditions of lamb chops with chips.

CAMERON HIGHLANDS: Kumar
Indian
26 Jalan Besar (Main Road), Tanah Rata
Tel *(05) 491-2624*
At this informal diner with friendly wait stafff the chefs rustle up traditional dishes such as Tandoori chicken, roti, curries on banana leaves, freshly prepared *naan* bread and even versions of

China House, which segues from restaurant to night spot as the evening draws on

Chinese stir-fries. This venue is especially popular with young travelers.

CAMERON HIGHLANDS: Cameron AA Curry House
International
44B Jalan Besar (Main Road), corner of Lorong Perdah, Tanah Rata
Tel *(016) 526-9097*
Despite the name, this convivial restaurant actually majors on Italian food. The pizzas are especially popular – a medium-sized pizza is big enough for two to share. They also serve pasta dishes and omelettes, currries, and kebabs.

CAMERON HIGHLANDS: Cameron Organic
Chinese
Jalan Angsana, Brinchang
Tel *(05) 491-4807*
Steamboats – Chinese fondues, where diners cook platters of sliced meat, seafood, and vegetables in pots of boiling stock at the table – are a mainstay of dining in the chilly Cameron Highlands. This restaurant stands out from the rest by using organic vegetables and offering a choice of chicken or vegetable stock.

CAMERON HIGHLANDS: Smokehouse
British
The Smokehouse Hotel, by the golf course, Tanah Rata
Tel *(05) 491-1215*
The very British Smokehouse hotel maintains the theme at its restaurant, which distinguishes itself with roasts such as beef Wellington and excellent cream teas with scones and jam. Almost uniquely among

hotels in Malaysia, the cooked breakfasts feature pork bacon rather than a halal substitute.

IPOH: Haji Yahaya
Malay
Jalan Dato Onn Jaafar
At this delightful corner *kedai kopi* there is an excellent selection of curries, spicy fried chicken, and fish dishes, as well as unusual offerings such as *nasi kerabu* – a bluish rice, traditionally colored using a flower, that is a specialty of Kota Bharu.

IPOH: Foh San
Chinese
51 Jalan Leong Sin Nam
Tel *(05) 254-0308*   **Closed** *eve, Tue*
Order by pointing at your selected dishes at this airy dim sum restaurant where most of the bamboo steamers of dumplings, glutinous rice, and other morsels sit in glass cabinets. There are a few more substantial dishes too, such as *chee cheong fun* (rice noodle rolls in a savory sauce).

IPOH: Plan B
Western–Asian Fusion
75 Jalan Panglima
Tel *(05) 249-8286*
With glass paneling and modern brickwork the sleekest restaurant in Ipoh's old town has an eclectic menu of excellent pasta dishes, burgers, and sophisticated versions of Asian favorites such as Vietnamese beef noodles. There is also a wonderful dessert menu – try the apple sugee cake, made with semolina.

LANGKAWI: Warung Janggus
Malay
Jalan Pantai Cenang, center of Cenang beach   **Closed** *Tue*
This humble eatery looks like little more than a garage, but its lunchtime spread is one of the best in Langkawi: bank on two dozen or more stir-fries, curries, and stews, ranging from braised crab to mango salad. In the evening the accent is on barbecued fish.

LANGKAWI: Orkid Ria
Chinese
Lot 1225, Jalan Pantai Cenang, northern end of Cenang beach
Tel *(04) 955-4128*
Specializing in seafood, Orkid Ria offers excellent fish and shellfish that's grilled, steamed, or fried to order. It's all priced by weight, so be careful not to over-order. There is also a good range of vegetable and meat dishes.

LANGKAWI: Unkaizan
Japanese
Lot 395, Jalan Telok Baru, southern end of Tengah beach
Tel *(04) 955-4118* **Closed** *lunch; every other Wed*
It's worth seeking out this secluded restaurant, up a leafy hillside, for the excellent-value set meals and a wide range of sushi and sashimi, plus daily specials and Japanese ice-cream.

LANGKAWI: The Cliff
Malay–Western Fusion
Lot 63 & 40, Jalan Pantai Cenang, southern end of Cenang beach
Tel *(04) 953-3228*
The artfully presented Malay fare has eclectic influences; try the *sup ekor lembu* (oxtail soup) or king prawns with an oaty coating. Sunset views from the bar are unrivalled – arrive early and sit by the parapet.

PANGKOR: Sea View
Chinese
Sea View Hotel, Pasir Bogak
Tel *(04) 685-1605*
This long-established favorite with, as the name suggests, a view of the Strait of Malacca, has an extensive menu focused on seafood, plus some Western main courses and snacks. Try the tamarind prawns, steamed red snapper, or chicken with cashews.

PENANG: Red Garden Food Paradise
Chinese/East Asian
20 Lebuh Leith, Georgetown
Tel *(012) 421-6767* **Closed** *lunch*
Phenomenally popular, this food court is packed with stalls offering seafood, curries, satay, and numerous rice and noodle dishes, including some Japanese fare. Wandering staff take orders for beer and soft drinks, and there are even Chinese song-and-dance acts on some nights.

PENANG: Mugshot
Western
302 Lebuh Chulia, Georgetown
Tel *(012) 405-6276*
A superb bakery and café, Mugshot specializes in bagels and artisan breads. A beef and rocket bagel with their excellent coffee or drinking yoghurt (with unusual flavors such as jackfruit) will set you up nicely for the day.

PENANG: Perut Rumah
Peranakan (Nyonya)
17 Jalan Kelawei, Georgetown
Tel *(04) 227-9917*
Inside a suburban house is this gorgeous dining hall with geometrically patterned floor tiles and marble tables. It serves fine Peranakan cuisine, including *kuih pai tee* (crisp pastry cups with a spring-roll-like filling) and *inche kabin* (a Penang dish of fried chicken).

PENANG: Tai Tong
Chinese
45 Lebuh Cintra, Georgetown
Tel *(04) 263-6625*
At one of the most endearingly old-fashioned dim sum restaurants in the country, staff push trolleys laden with morsels. There is also a wide range of other Cantoneses dishes that are cooked to order, from fried chicken to vegetable stir-fries.

PENANG: Woodlands
Indian Vegetarian
60 Lebuh Penang, Georgetown
Tel *(04) 263-9764*
This low-key restaurant has some South Indian dishes, although it's the North Indian fare that stands out: try the *palak paneer* (spinach with cheese) and *malai kofta* (dumplings in a creamy sauce), both excellent with the freshly made *naan* bread.

DK Choice
PENANG: China House
Asian
153 & 155 Lebuh Pantai, Georgetown
Tel *(04) 263-7299*
Three beautifully restored heritage buildings have been merged into a huge restaurant, nightspot, and gallery, a favorite meeting place for Penang's movers and shakers. The superb food ranges from Middle Eastern wraps to delicious pies and pan-Asian bento boxes; the cakes are stunning, with at least two dozen varieties on offer at any time. There are jazz and acoustic live sets after 9pm.

PENANG: Sarkies
International
E & O Hotel, 10 Lebuh Farquhar, Georgetown
Tel *(04) 222-2000*
Unless you're staying here, there's no better way to glimpse the colonial splendor of the E & O Hotel than to enjoy a buffet lunch or dinner at the Sarkies restaurant. The spread includes roasts, grilled seafood, sushi, curries, Malaysian hawker standards, and a wide range of cakes and desserts.

PENANG: Via Pre
Italian
5 Pengkalan Weld, Georgetown
Tel *(04) 262-0560*
Among Malaysia's best Italian restaurants, Via Pre serves excellent pizza and pasta dishes. Their wild boar ragout and mushroom spaghetti are particular hits with locals. There is a good range of cured hams, antipasti, and desserts, too.

TAIPING: Taman Tasik Food Court
Chinese
Facing the southwestern side of Lake Gardens
In a city dotted with food courts, this is one of the best, featuring the usual hawker staples such as seafood noodles and less common dishes such as "century eggs" porridge (rice gruel with gelatinous pickled eggs). It is best visited in the evening when more of the stalls are open.

TAIPING: Soon Lee
Chinese
11-15 Jalan Lim Swee Aun
Tel *(05) 807-6624*
Taiping's largest Chinese restaurant has a chandeliered main section specializing in seafood, and a smaller vegetarian area. Specialties include pig's trotters and butter prawns. Ask the staff about the daily specials.

Sarkies restaurant in Penang's prestigious E & O hotel

For more information on types of restaurants *see pp284–5*

Southern Peninsula

JOHOR BAHRU: Hiap Joo Bakery & Biscuit Factory
Chinese
13 Jalan Tan Hiok Nee
Tel *(07) 223-1703* **Closed** *eve; Sun*
This historic bakery uses a wood-fired oven to prepare a range of baked goods, including coconut buns and banana cake.

JOHOR BAHRU: Roost Juice & Bar
International
9 Jalan Dhoby **Closed** *Sun lunch*
With recycled furniture and bric-a-brac (including a toy corner), this unique café and restaurant serves great juices and a range of dishes such as beef noodles and Nyonya fish fillets.

JOHOR BAHRU: Carabao
Thai
16 Jalan Dato Abdullah Tahir
Tel *(07) 335-9333*
The lengthy menu includes plenty of Thai favorites at this open-fronted restaurant built with natural materials.

JOHOR BAHRU: Chez Papa
French
38 & 40 Jalan Jaya, Taman Maju Jaya
Tel *(07) 333-4988* **Closed** *Sun*
Seating is at wooden tables or at the bar in this atmospheric bistro and wine bar. The menu includes plenty of traditional rustic fare such as stews, and there's an extensive wine list.

KUKUP: New Kukup Restaurant
Chinese
1 Kukup Laut
Tel *(07) 696-0216*
A large open-fronted restaurant on the waterfront, New Kukup specializes in seafood dishes with stir-fried vegetables.

MELAKA: Calanthe Art Café
Malay
11 Jalan Hang Kasturi
Tel *(06) 292-2960* **Closed** *Tue*
Vinyl discs and recycled cans decorate the interior of this trendy café and restaurant serving great coffee and classic dishes.

MELAKA: Capitol Satay
Malay
41 Lorong Bukit China
Tel *(06) 283-5508* **Closed** *lunch; Mon*
This is a great place to sample satay – grilled skewered fish, meat, or vegetables dipped in peanut sauce.

MELAKA: The Daily Fix Café
Western
55 Jalan Hang Jebat
Tel *(06) 283-4858* **Closed** *eve; Tue*
Home-baked cakes and refreshing drinks are served at this relaxed café located at the back of a souvenir shop.

MELAKA: Jonker 88
Malay
88 Jalan Hang Jebat
Tel *(019) 397-5665*
Try a bowl of tasty *laksa* (noodles) followed by *baba cendol*, a traditional Malay dessert, at this popular eatery.

MELAKA: Low Yong Moh
Chinese
32 Jalan Tukang Emas
Tel *(06) 282-1235* **Closed** *eve; Tue*
Prawn, pork, and fish dim sum as well as buns stuffed with pork are the specialties here. Closes at 1pm.

MELAKA: Baboon House
American
89 Jalan Tun Tan Cheng Lock
Tel *(06) 283-1635* **Closed** *eve; Tue*
This quirky art café with rustic furniture and artworks decorating the walls specializes in beefburgers.

MELAKA: Eat at 18 Café
Western
18 Jalan Hang Lekiu
Tel *(06) 281-4679* **Closed** *eve; Tue*
Excellent salads, light meals, and home-made desserts are served at this welcoming café filled with artworks and books.

MELAKA: Eleven Bistro & Restaurant
Portuguese–Malay
9, 11, & 13 Jalan Hang Lekir
Tel *(06) 282-0011*
The food here combines the best of Portuguese and Malay cuisines. The lively bar has a DJ after 10pm.

MELAKA: Limau Limau
European
9 Jalan Hang Lekiu
Tel *(012) 698-4917* **Closed** *eve; Wed*
Salads, sandwiches and juices are served at this tiny café with mismatched furniture.

MELAKA: Nancy's Kitchen
Peranakan
7 Jalan Hang Lekir
Tel *(06) 283-6099* **Closed** *eve; Tue*
This is the place to try traditional Nyonya dishes, and there's a little store at the back where customers can buy Nyonya ingredients.

DK Choice

MELAKA: Pak Putra
Indian
56 & 58 Jalan Kota Laksamana
Tel *(012) 601-5876* **Closed** *lunch; every other Mon*
This laid-back restaurant with tables spilling onto the street serves exceptionally tasty dishes including mutton *rogan josh* and chicken curries. The fluffy, super-fresh *naan* bread is a highlight. It gets particularly busy on weekend evenings so it's wise to arrive early.

MELAKA: Teo Soon Loong Chan
Chinese
55 Jalan Hang Kasturi
Tel *(06) 282-2353*
Traditional Teochew dishes are served in an informal setting. The oyster noodles are a favorite.

MELAKA: Veggie Planet
Vegetarian
41 Jalan Melaka Raya 8, Taman Melaka Raya
Tel *(06) 292-2819*
Organic dishes including Nyonya curry and all manner of delicious soups and salads are served at this welcoming café.

Rustic interior and fun decor at the French Chez Papa, Johor Bahru

MERSING: Syed Ali
Indian/Malay
72–73 Jalan Sulaiman
Tel *(016) 716-3124*
The Indian and Malay dishes at this self-service canteen-style restaurant are among the best in town.

MERSING: Loke Tien Yuen
Chinese
55 Jalan Abu Bakar
Tel *(07) 799-1639*
This friendly restaurant has been attracting custom for years. The menu includes a good range of seafood dishes.

SEREMBAN: Pasar Besar Market
Mixed Asian
Jalan Pasar **Closed** *from 1:30pm (noon on Tue)*
The local market is renowned for its excellent beef noodle stands – stalls 648 and 742 are particularly recommended.

TIOMAN ISLAND: Sunset Bar
Western
Air Batang (ABC) **Closed** *lunch*
Popular for a sundowner, this bustling beach bar serves snacks and good pizzas too.

TIOMAN ISLAND: Tioman Cabana
International
South Tekek
Tel *(013) 717-6677*
Great homemade burgers and a selection of freshly prepared local dishes are served at this relaxed beach bar with a rustic feel.

Eastern and Central Peninsula

CHERATING: Don't Tell Mama
Western
BT28 Kampung, Cherating Lama
Tel *(019) 996-1723* **Closed** *lunch*
With a quirky interior and chilled background music, this surfer hangout serves tasty cheese and chicken burgers, steak, fish and chips, salads, pasta dishes, and sandwiches.

KOTA BHARU: Cikgu
Malay
Jalan Hilir Kota, Kampung Kraftangan
Tel *(019) 946-6665* **Closed** *eve; Fri*
Vegetable curry and catfish in spicy sauce are among the Malay dishes at this laid-back self-service eatery.

Tioman Cabana, a beach bar on Tioman Island

KOTA BHARU: Medan Selera Night Market
Asian
Off Jalan Pintu Pong, Jalan Zainal Abidin, Besut **Closed** *lunch*
This night food market offers a range of dishes including fish curry, *murtabak* (stuffed savory pancakes), and hearty oxtail soup.

KOTA BHARU: Shan Sri Devi
South Indian
4213F Jalan Kebun Sultan
Tel *(09) 746-2592*
Popular with locals, this bustling restaurant specializes in tasty banana-leaf curries.

KOTA BHARU: Muhibah
Vegetarian
Jalan Pintu Pong
Tel *(09) 744-3668*
A café-bakery serves pastries while the restaurant offers traditional Malay meat-free dishes.

KUALA TERENGGANU: Asia Signature
Malay
134 Jalan Sultan Zainal Abidin
Tel *(09) 620-5421*
A handful of vegetarian versions of Malay classics and tasty dim sum are on the menu here.

KUALA TERENGGANU: Madam Bee's Kitchen
Peranakan
177 Jalan Kampung Cina
Tel *(012) 988-7495* **Closed** *Wed*
Local dishes such as *loh mee* (egg noodles with chicken and crab) feature at this intimate restaurant.

KUALA TERENGGANU: Star Anise
Chinese/Western
82 Jalan Kampung Cina
Tel *(017) 664-2368*
With outdoor seating in the heart of Chinatown, this café serves locally grown tea and great coffee.

KUALA TERENGGANU: Vinum Exchange
Western
221 Jalan Kampung Cina
Tel *(09) 638-1353*
One of the very few places in the city to serve alcohol, this little drinking hole also serves food such as pork chops as well as coffee and pastries.

KUANTAN: Akob Patin House
Malay
Tapak PCCL Jalan Besar
Tel *(019) 987-4463* **Closed** *eve; Sun*
This river-front eatery specializes in the local delicacy, *patin* (silver catfish) served with chili, tamarind, and durian. Its sister location is on Lorong Tun Ismail.

KUANTAN: Tjantek Art Bistro
Western
46 Jalan Besar
Tel *(09) 516-4144* **Closed** *lunch; Sun*
One of Kuantan's more atmospheric establishments, Tjantek Art Bistro has low lighting, vintage artwork, and a simple menu of pasta dishes and sandwiches. No alcohol is served but there are great freshly squeezed fruit juices.

PERHENTIAN ISLANDS: Ewan's Café
Malay
Coral Bay, Perhentian Kecil
This bustling breezy restaurant gets packed at lunchtime for its tasty Malay dishes with chicken, vegetables, or prawns.

PERHENTIAN ISLANDS: Mandalika
Malay/Western
Teluk Dalam, Perhentian Besar
At this laid-back beach shack there are nightly barbecues and a wide-ranging menu which includes fish and chips.

For more information on types of restaurants *see pp284–5*

PERHENTIAN ISLANDS: Panorama Café
Western
Perhentian Kecil
A popular spot for evening movie screenings, this place serves good pizzas.

PERHENTIAN ISLANDS: Tuna Café
Western
Perhentian Besar
One of the best restaurants on either of the islands, this open-fronted eatery serves a variety of Western dishes and there are evening barbecues, too.

PERHENTIAN ISLANDS: World Café
Western
Long Beach, Pulau Perhentian Kecil
Tel *(03) 2142-6688*
Grilled lobster and tasty sandwiches are among the dishes on the menu at this bustling beachside café-restaurant. As it's one of the best places to eat on the island, it gets very busy at mealtimes and in the late afternoon, when people congregate here over a sundowner.

DK Choice

PULAU KAPAS: Koko's
Malay
T111, Western shore
Tel *(010) 926-5088*
This excellent English–Malay-run beachside restaurant features rustic wooden tables and chairs on a powdery stretch of sand. The Malay chef rustles up superb fresh fish, prawns, and squid cooked in a mouth-watering coconut sauce. His friendly English partner waits on the tables.

PULAU KAPAS: Kapas Turtle Valley
International
Southwestern shore
Tel *(013) 354-3650*
The excellent restaurant at this small, secluded resort serves delicious wide-ranging dishes.

TAMAN NEGARA: Floating Restaurants
Asian/Western
Riverfront, Kuala Tahan
On the to-do list for many visitors here is dining on one of the "floating restaurants" – ramshackle timber structures on rafts. The food may not be of the highest quality but it's worth trying instead for the experience and the ridiculously low prices.

DK Choice

TAMAN NEGARA: Seri Mutiara
International
Mutiara Taman Negara Resort, across the river from Kuala Tahan
Tel *(09) 266-3500*
This open-fronted restaurant attracts visitors with its extensive menu of Western, Chinese, Indian, and Malay favorites, including *nasi lemak* (rice dish cooked in coconut milk and pandan leaf), pizza, and T-bone steak. It's a particularly welcome treat after a few days of jungle trekking.

Sarawak

BINTULU: Famous Mama Café
Indian
10 Jalan Somerville
Tel *(086) 336-541*
Popular with young locals who come here to socialize over a meal or a drink or two, this simple eatery serves very good-value curries, biryani rice dishes, and rotis.

BINTULU: King Hua
Chinese
Jalan Keppel (lane close to Jalan Masjid)
Tel *(086) 337-255*
Humble, comfort food is served at this popular restaurant. They'll happily cook up whatever you feel like eating if they have the ingredients to hand. Otherwise, stick to the extensive menu of seafood, meat, and vegetable dishes.

An informal meal of oven-grilled meats and tasty curries at Lyn's Thandoori

BINTULU: Riverfront Inn Café
Western/Malay
256 Taman Sri Dagang
Tel *(086) 333-111*
Part of a hotel, this is a reliable option for Western standards like spaghetti, burgers, and fish and chips, as well as hearty cooked breakfasts of sausage, beans, and eggs. They also do a range of Malaysian dishes and are open for very late meals.

BRUNEI: Tarindak d'Seni $$
Malay
Arts and Handicrafts Complex, Jalan Residency, Bandar Seri Begawan
Tel *(073) 224-0422*
This modern restaurant is the best place to sample local food, with splendid lunch and dinner buffets of curries, stir-fries, and local *kuih* (puddings) as well as some Western desserts. One offering that's hard to find elsewhere is *ambuyat*, a Bruneian delicacy of sago starch which is dipped into various sauces .

BRUNEI: Thiam Hock $$
Chinese
5 Yong Siong Hai Building, Gadong, Bandar Seri Begawan
Tel *(073) 244-1679*
In the busy commercial suburb of Gadong, this long-standing restaurant is popular for its signature dish of fish head in a spicy tamarind sauce, its crispy chicken, and a wide range of noodle dishes.

KUCHING: Aroma Café
Bornean
Ground Floor Sublot 126, Jalan Tabuan
Tel *(082) 417-163*   **Closed** *Sun*
Try very reasonably priced local dishes such as *ayam pansoh* (chicken steamed in bamboo tubes) and *umai* (raw fish salad) at this humble eatery. Portions are generous and the lunchtime spread is particularly good value.

KUCHING: James Brooke Bistro & Café
Western/Malay
Jalan Tunku Abdul Rahman, close to the Hilton hotel
Tel *(014) 520-4007*
In a prime position facing the river, this popular open-sided restaurant serves authentic local dishes such as Sarawak *laksa* (spicy noodle soup) and Western standards such as beef stroganoff. The veranda surrounding the restaurant provides outside seating.

KUCHING:
Lyn's Thandoori
Indian

No. 7, Lot 267, Jalan Song Thian Cheok
Tel *(082) 234-934*
The homey Lyn's Thandoori specializes, unsurprisingly, in Tandoori chicken, although there's also a wide range of mainly North Indian-style curries and biryanis – including chicken tikka masala and *gobi Manchurian* (sweet-and-sour spiced cauliflower).

KUCHING: My Village
Barok
Bornean
Jalan Brooke, Kampung Boyan, north bank of the Sarawak River
Tel *(082) 448-970*   **Closed** *lunch*
Styled like a longhouse, this informal restaurant's signature dish is *ayam penyet* – chicken tenderized and then fried. It also offers grilled seafood dishes and fried rice with the olive-like *dabai* fruit, which is a Bornean delicacy.

KUCHING: Top Spot Food
Court
Chinese/Malay
Jalan Padungan   **Closed** *lunch*
The top floor of a multistory car park might seem an uninviting place to eat, but this is one of the most delightful dining spots in Kuching – packed with stalls specializing in seafood cooked to order, as well as other dishes such as the crepe-like oyster omelette.

KUCHING: Bla Bla Bla
Asian–Western fusion
27 Jalan Tabuan
Tel *(082) 233-944*   **Closed** *lunch; Tue*
The courtyard water feature with its carp sets the tone at this chic restaurant. The house specialty is the superb Malaysian *midin* (fern) salad. The mozarella-stuffed ostrich is another menu highlight. Other dishes include non-Asian ingredients such as salmon. Desserts can be just as eclectic and include pavlova and cheesecake.

KUCHING:
The Carvery
Brazilian
Abell Hotel, 22 Jalan Tunku Abdul Rahman
Tel *(082) 239-449*
Dedicated carnivores will delight in the all-you-can-eat *churrasco* barbecue buffet, featuring at least nine types of lamb, chicken, beef, and fish served on skewers. Vegetarians can help themselves to the salad buffet.

DK Choice

KUCHING: Jambu
International
32 Jalan Crookshank
Tel *(082) 235-292*   **Closed** *lunch; Mon*
Housed in a grand yet convivial colonial-era residence a little way south of the center, Jambu offers an eclectic menu that includes Mexican, Italian, and French cuisine as well as their own take on *laksa* – which is very similar to the way it's served in the south of Peninsular Malaysia. There are sweet treats too, including their trademark Moroccan date tart.

KUCHING: The Junk
Western
80 Jalan Wayang
Tel *(082) 259-450*   **Closed** *lunch; Tue*
The junkstore-like decor echoes the name of this popular eatery. Come here for standards such as fish and chips or pizza, or, more ambitiously, lamb shank or salmon gnocchi. There are rice-wine-based cocktails too.

KUCHING: Ristorante
Beccari
Italian
Merdeka Palace Hotel, Jalan Tun Abang Haji Openg
Tel *(082) 258-000*
Best known for its thin-crust pizzas cooked in a wood-fired oven, Beccari also serves pasta dishes and larger mains such as rack of lamb with gnocchi. On Sunday evenings there's a massive buffet spread, with roasts and pasta, and cheesecake for dessert.

MIRI: Krishna's
Indian
Jalan Kubu
Tel *(085) 430-095*
This delightful, friendly restaurant serves up enormous tasty portions of curries with rice and poppadoms, mostly eaten off banana-leaf platters. Their specialty is the prized Malaysian delicacy, fish head curry.

MIRI: Puma Sera
Malay/Indonesian
Jalan Maju
Tel *(013) 840-1868*
Puma Sera serves good-value curries, stir-fries, and stews. Dishes include catfish curry, *ulam* (traditional Malay salad), and *ayam lapanan* – chicken served with eight different accompaniments including condiments and rice.

Ristorante Beccari, located in Kuching's Merdeka Palace Hotel

MIRI: Barcelona
Western/Malay
Lot 1190, Jalan North Yu Seng
Tel *(085) 413-388*
This bar and bistro passes for a major nightspot in central Miri, and also serves a vast range of pizzas and tapas dishes. For conservative local palates, they also do upmarket versions of hawker favorites like *nasi lemak* and fried noodles.

MIRI: The Summit Café
Bornean
Centre Point Phase 1, 1246 Jalan Melayu   **Closed** *eve; Sun*
At this restaurant serving food from the Kelabit Highlands dishes include smoked, shredded wild boar and *nuba laya*, a sort of steamed rice cake, plus the Malaysian favorite, *nasi lemak*. The café shuts once the day's food has sold out.

MULU: Mulu National Park
Café
Malay/Western
Mulu National Park headquarters
Tel *(085) 792-300*
Run privately like the rest of the park facilities, Mulu's café turns out to be one of the soundest places to eat in the remote settlement. There's excellent and fiery Sarawak *laksa*, some Indian dishes, plus Western breakfasts, sandwiches, and snacks.

SIBU: Café Café
Asian
10 Jalan Chew Geok Lin
Tel *(084) 328-101*   **Closed** *Mon*
An unexpectedly smart two-story eatery right by the Rajang river, Café Café serves up local and more generally East Asian fare, including Malay beef *rendang* (curry) and Thai chicken salad, plus Western cakes for dessert.

For more information on types of restaurants *see pp284–5*

SIBU: Hock Chu Leu
Chinese
28 Jalan Tukang Besi
Tel *(084) 316-524*   **Closed** *Tue*
Much of Sibu's Chinese population emigrated from Fuzhou city in southeast China, and their ancestral cuisine is showcased at this very simple upstairs restaurant. The house specialty is *ang jow kai*, a red chicken stew that gets its color from the sediment in a particular Chinese rice wine.

SIBU: Payung Café
Asian
20F Jalan Lanang
Tel *(016) 890-6061*
This down-to-earth, eclectically decorated restaurant offers interesting twists on Southeast Asian fare. Try the mushroom rolls (based on Malaysian *popiah*, steamed spring rolls) and the durian milkshake, made with the notoriously odorous fruit.

Sabah

KINABALU NATIONAL PARK: Paanataran Kinabalu
Asian
At the turning for the park HQ
Tel *(088) 889-117*
Conveniently located for fueling up before a hike, this is a decent restaurant serving Chinese and Malay dishes, with a handful of Western snacks and breakfasts on offer too.

KINABALU NATIONAL PARK: Balsam
International
Within the park HQ
The varied buffet consisting of Indian, Malay, Chinese, and Western dishes is popular among hiking groups; perhaps because of this, it is on the pricey side.

KOTA KINABALU: Jesselton Point Hawker Centre
Asian
Jesselton Point, Jalan Haji Saman
Locals pour into this hawker center in the evenings to enjoy the tasty street food on offer, including satay and fried fish.

KOTA KINABALU: Night Market
Mixed Asian
Jalan Tun Fuad Stephens   **Closed** lunch
When the sun sets the sellers here set up their stalls, packing them with exotic fruits, fresh fish, and barbecued meats.

DK Choice
KOTA KINABALU: El Centro
International
32 Jalan Haji Saman
Tel *(019) 893-5499*
Popular with visitors and locals alike, this British-run restaurant serves hearty portions of international dishes infused with local flavors. Artworks decorate the cosy interior. Great for evening cocktails.

KOTA KINABALU: Grazie
Italian
Third Floor, Suria Sabah Mall
Tel *(019) 821-6936*
The Italian dishes have an Asian twist. Particularly good are the wood-fired pizzas.

KOTA KIBANALU: Jarrod & Rawlins
Western
KK Times Square
Tel *(088) 231-890*
This pub includes a deli selling imported foodstuffs such as sausages, cheeses, and steaks.

KOTA KINABALU: Jothy's Banana Leaf
Indian
1/G9, Api-Api Centre
Tel *(088) 261-595*
The South Indian curries here are particularly good and use the freshest meat, fish, and seafood.

KOTA KINABALU: Suang Tain Seafood Restaurant
Malay
Sedco Complex, Jalan Kampung Air 4
Tel *(088) 223-080*
A local favorite that has been going strong since the 1980s,

Fish head curry, a popular Malay delicacy with Indian and Chinese origins

---

Suang Tain (meaning Twin Sky) is renowned for its crab dishes.

KOTA KINABALU: Tam Nak Thai
Thai
Third Floor, Suria Sabah Mall
Tel *(016) 832-9928* **Closed** *Sun lunch*
Favorites such as green curry are served at this bustling eatery that gets very busy in the evenings.

KOTA KINABALU: Waterfront
International
Jalan Tun Fuad Stephens
Tel *(088) 249-333*
The lively boardwalk lined with cafés, restaurants, and bars includes The Aussie, which specializies in barbecued Australian meat dishes with Asian influences and Kohinoor, serving Indian cuisine.

SANDAKAN: Nam Choon
Malay
Block A, Lot 2a, Old Slipway
Tel *(089) 216-922*   **Closed** *eve*
This local favorite only serves four dishes including chicken rice and fish balls, served with complimentary tea.

DK Choice
SANDAKAN: Ba Lin
Western
Level 8, Nak Hotel, Jalan Pelahuban Lama
Tel *(089) 272-988*
The rooftop bar and restaurant on the 8th floor of this modern, rather unassuming hotel is a pleasant surprise. The stylish setting offers good views of Sandakan. The menu, which looks like a newspaper, includes great brunches, along with superb pizzas and pasta, and meat dishes.

SANDAKAN: English Tea House
British
2002 Jalan Istana
Tel *(089) 222-544*
A colonial-style restaurant with a croquet lawn, English Tea House serves staples such as shepherd's pie and afternoon tea with scones and jam.

SANDAKAN: Sim Sim Seafood Restaurant
Malay
Bridge 8, Sim Sim Water Village
Tel *(012) 842-7131*   **Closed** *Wed*
Renowned for its top-quality fresh seafood, this restaurant on stilts is a popular choice among locals.

SANDAKAN: Taste (RM)(RM)
Western
Lot 2-3, Block 9, Bandar Indah, Mile 4
Tel *(012) 818-1819* **Closed** *lunch*
This bar and steakhouse serves
various Western-style dishes,
although it's mainly known for its
range of local and imported
alcoholic drinks.

SEMPORNA: Anjung Lepa (RM)
Malay
Seafest Hotel, Jalan Kastam
Tel *(089) 782-333* **Closed** *lunch*
On the waterfront terrace, this
restaurant with outdoor seating
offers fried rice and noodle
options, as well as a handful of
seafood dishes.

**SEMPORNA: Mabul Café and
Seafood Restaurant** (RM)
Malay
Semporna Seafront
Tel *(089) 781-785*
Dishes in generous portions
including stir-fried chicken,
prawns, and squid with rice are
served here. The service can be
a little erratic.

**SEMPORNA:
Scuba Junkie** (RM)(RM)
Western
36 Semporna Seafront
Tel (089) 785-372
Aimed at the dive crowd, this
New Zealand-run establishment
has a lively bar, great pizzas,
sandwiches, burgers, and salads.

Singapore

Colonial Core and Chinatown

Bee Heong Palace $
Chinese **Map** 5 D4
134 Telok Ayer Street
Tel *6222-9074* **Closed** *Mon*
Specializing in Hokkien cuisine
from southeast China, this
restaurant serves dishes such
as *kong bak*, buns stuffed with
braised pork belly, and delightful
rolls made with minced prawns
and pork.

Lau Pa Sat $
Asian **Map** 5 D4
18 Raffles Quay
Beneath the Victorian wrought-
iron arches of the old Teluk Ayer
market, this is the most visually
appealing of Singapore's hawker
centers. Stalls serve up the usual
mix of Chinese, Malay, and Indian
food, with some Japanese,
Korean, and Indochinese fare too.
In the evenings, a row of satay
stalls sets up outside.

Low-rise seating emphasizing the magnificent Art Deco setting of Clifford Pier

Lee Tong Kee $
Chinese **Map** 4 C4
278 South Bridge Road
Tel *6226-0417* **Closed** *Mon eve, Tue*
The speciality here is Ipoh-style
hor fun (tagliatelle-style wide
rice noodles). They come with
chicken and prawns, or beef. The
signature sweet-salty lime juice
makes a good accompaniment.

Maxwell Food Centre $
Asian **Map** 4 C4
*Corner of Maxwell Road and South
Bridge Road* **Closed** *eve*
It can be hot and stuffy, but this
is one of the most popular
hawker centers in Singapore. One
or two stalls are locally famous
(Tian Tian has people lining up
for its chicken rice); others serve
excellent Indonesian curries and
Chinese noodle dishes.

Annalakshmi Janatha $$
Indian Vegetarian **Map** 5 D4
104 Amoy Street
Tel *6223-0809* **Closed** *eve; Sun*
At this restaurant run by
volunteers there is a superb
buffet spread of curries, plain
and biryani rice, samosas, south
Indian specialties such as *vadai*
(savory donuts), plus sweets and
fruit for dessert. There are no set
prices – you pay what you feel
your meal was worth, and
proceeds go to an Indian
cultural organization.

Clifford Pier $$
Asian/Western **Map** 5 E3
80 Collyer Quay
Tel *6597-5266*
In a superb setting beneath the
lofty arched ceiling of the old Art
Deco boat terminal, Clifford Pier's
menu is dominated by a refined,
modern take on traditional
dishes. Menu highlights include
laksa, steamed spring rolls, and
bak kut teh (pork rib soup). Pasta
and fish and chips figure too.

Sky on 57 $$
Asian–French Fusion **Map** 5 F3
*Marina Bay Sands, 10 Bayfront
Avenue*
Tel *6688-8857*
Offering a panoramic view of
Singapore and the bay, this fine-
dining restaurant in the Marina
Bay Sands hotel serves innovative
Franco-Asian dishes such as king
prawn *laksa*, halibut in a Thai-
style green curry with wild rice,
and lamb in an Asian pesto
with artichokes.

Spizza $$
Italian **Map** 5 D4
29 Club Street
Tel *6224-2525*
This modern restaurant has a
different thin-crust pizza for
every letter of the alphabet, from
the very traditional to one
slathered in chocolate spread
and banana. Pasta, gnocchi, and
lasagne are on the menu too.

Tak Po $$
Chinese **Map** 4 C4
42 Smith St
Tel *6225-0302*
Order steamed pork ribs,
dumplings, rice porridge, and
more substantial dishes by
ticking boxes on the slips of
paper handed out at this
reasonably priced dim sum
restaurant. The custard tarts
make an excellent dessert.

Urban Bites $$
Middle Eastern **Map** 5 D4
161 Telok Ayer Street
Tel *6327-9460* **Closed** *Mon & Wed
eve*
Although plainer than its rivals,
this is the best Lebanese
restaurant in town. The meze
and kebabs are terrific, and they
also serve *manakeesh*, delicious
chewy flatbreads topped with
herbs or cheese. Crepes and
baklava are among the desserts.

For more information on types of restaurants see pp284–5

Elegant, minimalist interior at the lofty 1-Altitude

DK Choice

1-Altitude $$$
European **Map** 5 D3
Levels 61–63, One Raffles Place
Tel 6438-0410 **Closed** *lunch*
There's no more amazing setting for a meal than this swanky 62nd-floor restaurant with stunning views. Menus change regularly, but expect the likes of lamb with eggplant and hazelnut purée, or truffle gnocchi. There is also a rooftop alfresco bar on the 63rd floor.

Bacchanalia $$$
Fusion **Map** 5 D2
Freemasons' Hall, 23A Coleman St
Tel 6509-1453 **Closed** *Sun*
Portions are designed for sampling, so order, for example, three main courses for two people. The belly pork with cabbage, apple, and capers is a trademark dish.

Flutes $$$
European **Map** 5 D1
Ground floor, National Museum, 93 Stamford Road
Tel 6338-8770
This elegant eatery offers beaufully crafted dishes such as lobster bolognaise and, for Sunday lunch, English roast beef with all the trimmings. From Friday to Sunday they are also open for afternoon teas of sandwiches, scones, and quiche.

Sabio $$$
Spanish **Map** 4 C4
5 Duxton Hill
Tel 6690-7562
At this compact, Spanish-owned venue there is a huge range of authentic high-quality tapas, plus

hams and chorizos. The wine list is just as vast, encompassing sangria, sherries, and a profusion of cocktails. No reservations.

Shiraz $$$
Middle Eastern **Map** 4 C2
3A River Valley Road, 01–06 Clarke Quay
Tel 6334-2282
A contemporary Persian restaurant, Shiraz serves large flavorsome kebabs, including some based on seafood rather than the usual chicken or lamb, on fragrant saffron rice. There is belly-dancing on some nights.

Supertree by Indochine $$$
Indonesian **Map** 5 F4
#03-01, Gardens By The Bay, 18 Marina Gardens Drive
Tel 6694-8489
Perched atop the tallest Supertree (the metal towers in Gardens by the Bay whose sides are planted with climbers), this restaurant offers great views of Marina Bay. The lychee pork beignets and Vietnamese rolls stuffed with prawns and herbs show why it has been going strong for years.

Little India and Orchard Road

Ah Chew Desserts $
Chinese **Map** 3 E5
#01-11,1 Liang Seah Street
Tel 6339-8198
The desserts make extensive use of snowy crushed ice, syrups, and ingredients surprising to Western palates such as pulses. Here you can try a vast selection, including *pulot hitam* (black glutinous rice in coconut milk) and peanut paste (like peanut butter, only a broth).

Haji Maimunah $
Malay **Map** 3 E4
11 & 15 Jalan Pisang
Tel 6297-4294 **Closed** *Sun*
Truely authentic Malay food (as opposed to superficially similar Indonesian fare) can be hard to find. This plain *kedai kopi* does the genuine article, including delicacies such as spicy snails in coconut milk, plus a good range of *kuih*, Malay sweetmeats based on glutinous rice, tapioca, and other tropical ingredients. May close during Ramadan.

Kampong Glam Café $
Malay **Map** 3 F4
17 Bussorah Street
Tel 6294-1697
Few places to socialize and people-watch are more endearing than this *kedai kopi*, a

stone's throw from the Masjid Sultan. Order rice or noodles cooked to order, or choose from an excellent spread of curries and stir-fries, and wash it down with *teh tarik* (frothy, sweet milky tea).

Newton Food Center $
Asian **Map** 2 B2
500 Clemenceau Avenue North
This is popular with tourists for its numerous open-air stalls and closeness to Orchard Road, although prices are a little above average as a result. The food is generally excellent and wide-ranging: satay, oyster omelette, and *sup kambing* (Malay mutton stew), plus seafood are sold by weight. More stalls open in the evening than for lunch.

Warung M Nasir $
Indonesian **Map** 2 B5
69 Killiney Road
Tel 6734-6228
A tiny, modern café, Warung M Nasir has long been highly rated for traditional dishes such as beef *rendang*, *ayam balado* (tangy spiced chicken), and *tempeh* (fermented soya cakes, prepared in a variety of ways). Desserts are both traditional and Western.

Banana Leaf Apolo $$
Indian **Map** 5 D3
54 Race Course Road
Tel 6293-8682
As the name suggests, this friendly eatery majors on banana-leaf meals, with staff ladling out South Indian mutton, fish, or chicken curries onto leaf "plates", along with rice and accompaniments. They're famed for their fish head curry, and there's plenty for vegetarians too.

Comfy seating at Bacchanalia, which serves plates for sharing

Bistro Du Vin $$
French **Map** 1 F2
#01-14 Shaw Centre, 1 Scotts Road
Tel *6733-7763*
The contemporary, informal Bistro du Vin serves up good-value dishes such as onion soup, duck leg confit, and coq au vin. There are tasty desserts too, including an impressive Grand Marnier soufflé.

Chao Shan Cuisine $$
Chinese **Map** 3 E5
85 Beach Road
Tel *6336-2390*
Specializing in Teochew cuisine from southeast China, this unpretentious family-run eatery serves classics such as roast goose, but the chef will cook anything to order as long as they have the ingredients.

Crystal Jade La Mian Xiao Long Bao $$
Chinese **Map** 2 A4
#04-27 Ngee Ann City, 391 Orchard Road
Tel *6238-1661*
Shanghai and northern Chinese cuisine: the *xiao long bao* of the name are delectable Shanghai-style steamed pork buns. They're also known for *la mian*, traditional hand-stretched noodles.

Herbivore $$
Japanese Vegetarian **Map** 3 D4
1-13 Fortune Centre, 190 Middle Road
Tel *6333-1612*
This exemplary modern restaurant manages to offer a full range of Japanese food using soy and other meat substitutes. The set meal platters are particularly recommended. It gets busy at weekends, when they may not take reservations.

Kiseki $$
Japanese **Map** 2 B4
#08-01 Orchard Central, 181 Orchard Road
Tel *6736-1216*
The sumo wrestler statue at the entrance hints at what can happen to waistlines here: buffet tables groan with everything from sashimi to yakitori, and there's an equally impressive dessert section. Note that pricing on weekends is nearly double the weekday lunch cost.

Marché $$
Swiss **Map** 2 B4
Basement, 313@Somerset, 313 Orchard Road
Tel *6834-4041*
Each counter specializes in a different item at this delicatessen-style restaurant:

Massaman chicken curry with Thai-style pancake, a signature dish at Thai Express

salads, pasta, crepes, and the obligatory rösti. Each customer is given a plastic card which stores all their orders.

Saravanaa Bhavan $$
Indian Vegetarian **Map** 3 E2
84 Syed Alwi Road
Tel *6297-7755*
This is a branch of a chain that started in Chennai and extends beyond Tamil food to offer dishes like *bisibelabath* (a rice, lentil, and vegetable concoction from Karnataka). The menu includes biryanis, *uthappam* (something between a crepe and a pizza), and north Indian curries too.

Thai Express $$
Thai **Map** 2 C4
#03-24 Plaza Singapura, 68 Orchard Road
Tel *6339-5442*
The menu at this modern restaurant is dominated by one-bowl dishes of noodles (notably Thai *laksas*) or rice with red or green curry. There are plenty of veggie options and side dishes such as battered crab.

PS Café $$$
Internationl **Map** 1 F2
Level 2, Palais Renaissance, 390 Orchard Road
Tel *9834-8232*
In what resembles a glasshouse, PS Café has long been known for well-presented, creative cooking. Brunches are hearty – try the superfood salad of blueberries, almonds, and quinoa, or spicy crab tart – but it's hard to go wrong here at any time of day.

Straits Kitchen $$$
Chinese/Peranakan **Map** 2 A3
Grand Hyatt Hotel, 10 Scotts Road
Tel *6738-1234*
The very best in Singapore cooking is offered under one roof with the extravagant lunch and

evening buffets. They cover street food perennials (such as carrot cake – a savory dish of rice flour and white radish fried in egg), Malay and Indian standards (satay, roti), and some Peranakan fare.

Farther Afield

Food Republic $
Asian
Level 3, VivoCity mall, 1 Harbourfront Walk
Tel *6276-0521*
Food Republic is a food-court chain that prides itself on selecting hawkers based on culinary skill. Their outlet at the gateway to Sentosa has scissor-cut curry rice (a food spread where you order by pointing and someone cuts up the rice portion with scissors for ease of eating), good Indonesian *nasi padang* (steamed rice dishes), and much more.

Guan Hoe Soon $$
Peranakan
38/40 Joo Chiat Place, Katong
Tel *6344-2761*
Katong is the Singapore suburb where Peranakan culture still has a toehold, and this is one of the best restaurants for the cuisine. Sample classics like *bak wan kepiting* (crab and pork balls), *chap chye* (a vegetable and fungus stir-fry), and *otak otak* (slivered, spicy dumplings).

Samy's $$
Indian
Block 25, Dempsey Road, close to the Botanic Gardens
Tel *6472-2080* **Closed** *Tue*
There are few more atmospheric places to have a traditional Indian meal on banana-leaf platters than here, under whirring ceiling fans at a former British military base. Both north and south Indian food is available, but it is best known for fish head curry.

For more information on types of restaurants see pp284–5

SHOPPING IN MALAYSIA

Malaysia is an affluent country with a rapidly developing economy and Malaysians love to shop. There is an astonishing variety of shopping options, from the latest electronic gadgets to a wealth of traditional art and handicraft items. Differences exist between the range, quality, and prices available in the various regions, with the large cities on the western coast of Peninsular Malaysia, notably Kuala Lumpur, Penang, and Johor Bahru, offering sophisticated malls, and the smaller east coast cities, such as Kota Bharu and Kuala Terengganu, acting as the repository of Malay artistry, especially *batik*, colorful kites, and shadow puppets. Sarawak and Sabah in Malaysian Borneo are unrivaled for their array of ethnic products, skilfully crafted by the indigenous people.

Department Stores and Shopping Malls

Shopping malls, ranging from modest establishments to plush, air-conditioned, multistory buildings, are ubiquitous in Malaysian towns and cities. They contain a mix of large department stores that sell branded goods, supermarkets offering both local and imported food, and dozens of smaller shops that stock everything from mobile phones, computers, electronic goods, and English and Malay books, to a wealth of souvenirs, clothes, shoes, and accessories, such as bags and watches. Nearly all shopping malls have fast-food outlets, while the upmarket ones also feature expensive restaurants. Many have multiplex movie theaters, food courts, Internet cafés, and branches of banks with facilities such as money changing and ATMs. Malls in west coast cities, especially those in Kuala Lumpur, compare with the glitziest outlets in the Western countries and are an excellent source of a wide range of international luxury brands. Besides those in the malls, there are several independent department stores, such as Kuala Lumpur's Isetan, which is part of a Japanese chain.

Local Markets (Tamus) and Stalls

Malaysia is brimming with local markets, or *tamus*. Almost every town and village has at least one bustling central market, usually containing a multitude of stalls offering a bewildering selection of goods, from local crafts to clothes and household items. Very often there is also a wet market selling fresh meat, fruits, and vegetables. Numerous hawker stalls offer an array of local delicacies. Prices are reasonable, the quality is generally good, and standards of hygiene are very high, even in fish markets, which are regularly hosed.

Another enduringly popular feature and a highlight for many of a trip to Malaysia are its *pasar malams*, or night markets. The most fascinating of these are in Kuala Lumpur *(see pp62–83)*, Johor Bahru *(see p134)*, Penang *(see pp106–15)*, Kuching *(see pp160–63)*, and Kota Kinabalu *(see p184)*.

Most state capitals and the larger towns of Malaysia and Singapore often have ethnic enclaves, such as Chinatown and Little India, which are excellent places to buy Chinese and Indian products.

Shopping Hours

Business hours for shops can vary substantially throughout Malaysia, but most establishments are open from 9am to 6:30pm, Monday to Saturday. Malls and major emporia open later, usually between 10am and 10:30am and stay open longer, until 9:30pm or 10pm. Most major malls are open seven

The Sungei Wang Plaza in Kuala Lumpur's Golden Triangle *(see p306)*

days a week. Shops in the conservative Islamic east coast states of Kelantan and Terengganu are closed on Friday, the Muslim Sabbath.

Methods of Payment

Cash is universally accepted and a few places in major cities also take US dollars and euros. However, money changers are found everywhere. Credit cards are widely accepted except in the smallest of stores. The preferred cards include VISA, MasterCard, and JCB, while larger establishments also accept American Express and Diners Club cards. A very small number of shops levy a service charge, but this is becoming less common.

Sales Tax

Malaysia charges a 6 percent Goods and Services Tax (GST). For food and accommodation, however, customers can expect to pay a service tax of 10 percent at luxury hotels and restaurants, in addition to the government tax of 6 percent. Malaysia has some designated duty-free areas, including Pulau Langkawi in the west and Pulau Labuan in the east, designed to attract shoppers. There are also duty-free areas in Kelantan at Rantau Panjang and Pengkalan Kubur, as well as in Kedah at Padang Besar and Bukit Kayu Hitam.

Fresh fish sold at a market in Tawau, Sabah

Bargaining

In Malaysia, bargaining is an accepted practice. However, whether to bargain or not depends on the kind of market shoppers are in. Top-end department stores, shopping malls, and government emporia have fixed prices, though the latter offer good fixed-price deals.

In most local markets and stalls, bargaining is not just accepted but is also expected. Buyers can often obtain a substantial reduction in the original price. Remember to keep the exchange polite and good-natured, and if a keen price is important to you, it is always a good idea to browse in several shops and know the fair price of the product you wish to buy before you begin negotiating. A good rule of thumb is to offer half the initial price and go from there.

Guarantees

Buyers should always be careful with their selection at the time of purchase to avoid problems later. Most government shops and large department stores will accept the return of faulty goods, but it might not be as easily done for products bought at street stalls, especially antique shops that are not recommended or guaranteed by the government.

Photography

Malaysia, like Singapore, tends to be at the cutting edge of photographic technology. Deals are just as great as in Singapore, and sometimes better, due to good exchange rates. The range of products is excellent, though digital technology has swept aside slide film. Print film remains available, and film-developing facilities are ubiquitous, fast, and cheap.

Imitations

Although the sale of imitation goods and knock-offs is illegal in Malaysia, and there is a growing clampdown on the sale of illicit goods, such products continue to be sold at small stores and stalls. Since most of these products are very cheap and of poor quality and because such trade breaches property rights, the purchase of fakes, such as faux designer bags, clothing, and illegal copies of VCDs and DVDs, although tempting, is best avoided.

A shopping street in Kuala Lumpur at night

What to Buy in Malaysia

Glitzy shopping malls, bustling local markets, vibrant *pasar malams* (night markets), and small craft shops across Malaysia offer a good range of souvenirs for visitors to take home. Traditionally styled Malay, Chinese, and Indian artifacts are widely available; however, some craft items are restricted to specific regions. The country can boast an astonishing range of products, including antique furniture, *ikat* cloth, *batik* prints, woodcarvings, and shadow puppets, besides handicraft items produced by indigenous people.

Visitors at a chic shopping mall in Kuala Lumpur

Malay Products

With the rising demand for ethnic Malay goods, aided by Malaysia's thriving tourism and patronage offered by the country's leading banks and oil companies, art in Malaysia is flourishing as never before. Malay goods are available almost everywhere, but are especially visible in Kuala Lumpur, Johor Bahru, Kelantan, and Terengganu.

Wayang Kulit
Shadow puppet theater, or *wayang kulit*, is a Malay folk art whose traditions are passed on orally. These colorful leather puppets are available in Kelantan and Kuala Lumpur.

Silverware
The best Malay silverware, with its trademark filigree embellishments, is produced in Terengganu and Kelantan. These areas specialize in belt buckles and tobacco boxes.

Batik Fabric
Malay *batik* uses wax and dyes to print on fabrics. Shirts, skirts, and sarongs in *batik*-print are best bought from Malaysia's east coast.

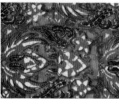

Songket Silk Fabrics
Belonging to the brocade family of textiles, *songket* is hand-woven on looms and features elaborate patterns created with a gold and silver weft.

Kites
While the principal designs of traditional Malay kites are derived from nature, decorations are unique to each craftsman. Kite-making shops can be found in villages along the east coast of Peninsular Malaysia.

Ceramic Items
Shaped by hand, pottery is produced in Selangor and Perak. Ayer Itam, a small town in Peninsular Malaysia, is known for its pottery and porcelain crafts. The Cameron Highlands are also a good place to buy ceramics.

Masks
Traditionally, Malaysian and Southeast Asian masks represent people, demons, and deities. They are cultural icons that help preserve tradition, religion, and history. Malay ceremonial masks are commonly available in Melaka.

Products from Malaysian Borneo

Sabah and Sarawak are unrivaled for items crafted by indigenous people and by Malay Christians, including fine *ikat* cloth, shamanistic religious paraphernalia, and woodcarvings.

Ikat Design
Often a symbol of status and power, *ikat*, meaning to tie in Malay, is a style of weaving created by dyeing the warp. The best *ikat* is produced in Sarawak.

Bamboo Products
Items made of bamboo, palm leaf, and rattan, including finely woven baskets and hats, are available in bazaars throughout Sarawak and Sabah.

Woodcarvings
Woodcarvings depicting people, spirits, and animals in the shamanistic tradition are widely available in Kuching, Kota Kinabalu, and at Selangor's small Orang Asli Museum.

Chinese Products

Malaysia is especially popular for locally produced Peranakan or Straits Chinese goods, including antique furniture and ceramics. Standard Chinese wares are imported from Hong Kong and the Chinese mainland.

Good Luck Charms
Chinese good luck charms in bright, attractive colors make cheap and fun purchases. They are available almost everywhere.

Chinese Antique Furniture
Antique furniture of the Baba-Nyonya tradition, made from hardwood with exquisite carvings, is available in Melaka, where Jalan Hang Jebat *(see p130)* is a treasure-house for antique lovers.

Chinese Ceramics
Baba-Nyonya vases, which are unique to Malaysia, and imported china-ware are available in big retail outlets in Melaka, on the west cost of Peninsular Malaysia.

Indian Products

Indian enclaves in Penang, Kuala Lumpur, and Johor Bahru exude a heady aroma of spices and have several authentic silk stores recreating an ambience similar to that in southern Indian states.

Brassware
Fine brass goods, a Tamil tradition transplanted to Malaysia, comprise household objects, decorative ware, and religious items.

Indian Silk Sarees
Traditional southern Indian *kanchipuram* silk sarees are available in the fabric stores of Little India in Georgetown as well as in shopping malls across Malaysia.

Indian Spices
Spices, such as pepper, cardamom, saffron, cloves, mace, nutmeg, and cinnamon, are widely available in Malaysia.

Where to Shop

There are good shops just about everywhere in Malaysia, from big cities on the peninsula to smaller towns and villages in Malaysian Borneo. The larger metropolises, especially Kuala Lumpur, Penang, Johor Bahru, and Kuching, have fantastic malls selling a fine range of products. The smaller east coast cities, such as Kota Bharu and Kuala Terengganu, are the center of traditional Malay arts and crafts, while Sarawak and Sabah are unrivaled for their ethnic goods.

Kuala Lumpur

The main shopping areas in Kuala Lumpur are around Bukit Bintang and Jalan Sultan Ismail in the heart of the Golden Triangle. Major malls here include **Bukit Bintang Plaza**, **Lot 10**, **Starhill Gallery**, and the huge **Pavilion KL**. **Sungei Wang Plaza** and **Low Yat Plaza**, also in the Golden Triangle, specialize in electronic goods. Among the upmarket malls, Suria KLCC in the Petronas Towers (see p78) is popular, and the **Mid Valley Megamall** is worth visiting. **Publika** is also a good addition to KL's shopping scene. Perhaps the best market in Malaysia for tourists is **Central Market**, which sells local souvenirs. There is a great variety of batik and handicraft goods for sale at Kompleks Budaya Kraf (see p81). The market at Jalan Tuanku Abdul Rahman (see p76) offers great bargains, with the **Globe Silk Store** popular for tailor-made clothes. The street springs to life at night with a pasar malam. Jalan Petaling (see p70) is great for bargain hunting.

Penang

After Kuala Lumpur, the best place to shop is Penang, with outlets selling local crafts, antiques, and electronic items at competitive prices. Jalan Penang is the best shopping street in Georgetown, with **Komtar**, a shopping mall located in a massive 56-story building, and **Chowrasta Bazaar** for spices. The five-story **Queensbay Mall** in Penang is the largest mall in northern Malaysia. Little India (see p108) offers an array of southern Indian products, while Batu Ferringhi (see p114) has a vibrant night market.

An antiques store displaying Peranakan artifacts, Melaka

Pulau Langkawi

One of the major attractions of Pulau Langkawi is its status as a duty-free shopping zone. The island's capital, Kuah, is where most duty-free shops are located. Popular outlets include the **Langkawi Fair Shopping Mall** and the **Jetty Point Duty-Free Complex**, both in Kuah. The **Zon Duty Free Shopping Paradise** at Pantai Cenang and **Sunmall** at Pantai Tengah are worth visiting, although they mainly stock cosmetics, cigarettes, and alcohol.

Melaka

The restored Chinese district in Melaka is the place to look for antiques, both genuine and imitation, as well as all kinds of Chinese and Peranakan goods. Jalan Hang Jebat (see p130) sells beautiful porcelain, coins, old lamps, songket fabric, and antique furniture. There is a range of handicraft and souvenir shops in Taman Merdeka and a pasar malam on Jalan Paramesawara. The **Mahkota Parade** shopping complex on Jalan Merdeka is Melaka's largest shopping venue.

Johor Bahru

Regarded as one of Malaysia's most prosperous towns, Johor Bahru is located across the causeway from Singapore, whose citizens often come to shop, notably at **Justco Terbau Shopping Mall**, **Pelangi Leisure Mall**, **Perling Mall**, and **Plaza Pelangi** in Johor Bahru. All these

Jalan Petaling, the commercial heart of Chinatown, Kuala Lumpur

malls specialize in designer goods, clothing, luxury goods, and accessories. **Johor Premium Outlets** is a popular factory outlet in the Iskandar Malaysia zone.

Kota Bharu and Kuala Terengganu

The east coast of Peninsular Malaysia abounds with shops selling traditional Malay crafts such as *batik* and *songket* fabric, silverware, woodcarvings, and colorful kites. The handicraft workshops along the road to Pantai Cahaya Bulan and **Kompleks Bazaar Buluh Kubu** in Kota Bharu are good stops for their displays of *batik* items.

In Kuala Terengganu, Jalan Bandar near the Central Market has several small shops selling local handicrafts and *batik* cloth, which are open on all days except on Fridays. The **Noor Arfa Craft Complex** is also a favorite for traditional crafts, especially *batik* and *songket*.

Kuching, Sarawak

Kuching is one of Malaysia's best shopping destinations, rivaled only by Penang and Melaka. The city is filled with stores selling souvenirs, *ikat* cloth, and Asian antiques. It also specializes in artifacts made by indigenous peoples. Jalan Satok's Sunday market sells a variety of crafts and fresh produce. Demonstrations of these crafts are held daily at **Sarawak Handicraft Center**.

Kota Kinabalu, Sabah

The capital of Sabah, Kota Kinabalu, has several local handicraft shops selling goods of reasonable quality. The Filipino Market *(see p185)* at the waterfront is the best market and sells basketware and colorful woven ponchos. The products on display serve as a reminder of how much closer Sabah is to the Philippines than to Peninsular Malaysia.

Woman selling *batik* silk in the new Central Market in Kota Bharu

DIRECTORY

Kuala Lumpur

Bukit Bintang Plaza
Jalan Bukit Bintang. **Map** 5 C3. **Tel** (03) 4252-1781.
🔲 allmalaysia.info

Central Market
Jalan Hang Kasturi.
Map 4 E2. **Tel** (03) 2274-6542. 🔲 centralmarket.com.my

Globe Silk Store
185 Jalan Tuanku Abdul Rahman. **Map** 1 B5.
Tel (03) 2692-2888.
🔲 allmalaysia.info

Lot 10
Map 6 D2.
🔲 ytlcommunity.com

Low Yat Plaza
Lot 7, Jalan 1/77.
Tel (03) 2148-3651.
🔲 plazalowyat.com

Mid Valley Megamall
🔲 midvalley.com.my

Pavilion KL
168 Jalan Bukit Bintang.
🔲 pavilion-kl.com

Publika
Jalan Dutamas 1,
Hartamas Heights.
Tel (03) 6205-2768.
🔲 publika.com.my

Starhill Gallery
🔲 starhillgallery.com

Sungei Wang Plaza
99 Bukit Bintang. **Map** 6 D3. **Tel** (03) 2144-9988.
🔲 sungeiwang.com

Penang

Chowrasta Bazaar
Jalan Penang, Penang.

Komtar
Jalan Penang.
🔲 allmalaysia.info

Queensbay Mall
🔲 queensbaymall malaysia.com

Pulau Langkawi

Jetty Point Duty-Free Complex
🔲 jettypointlangkawi.com/dutyfree_shops.htm

Langkawi Fair Shopping Mall
Persian Putra, Kuah.
Tel (04) 969-8100.

Sunmall
Jalan Teluk Baru.
Tel (07) 955-8300.
🔲 sungrouplangkawi.com

Zon Duty Free Shopping Paradise
Pantai Cenang.
Tel (04) 955-6100.

Melaka

Mahkota Parade
1 Jalan Merdeka.
Tel (06) 282-6151.
🔲 allmalaysia.info

Johor Bahru

Johor Premium Outlets
🔲 premiumoutlets.com.my

Justco Terbau Shopping Mall
Tel (07) 354-2131.
🔲 justco.com.my

Pelangi Leisure Mall
Jalan Serampang Teman Pelangi.
🔲 allmalaysia.info

Perling Mall
Jalan Persisiran Perling.
🔲 perlingmall.com.my

Plaza Pelangi
Jalan Kuning.
Tel (07) 276-2216.

Kota Bharu and Kuala Terengganu

Kompleks Bazaar Buluh Kubu
Central Market, Kota Bharu.
🔲 allmalaysia.info

Noor Arfa Craft Complex
Chendering Terengganu.
🔲 virtualmalaysia.com

Kuching, Sarawak

Sarawak Handicraft Center
🔲 sarawakhandicraft.com.my

ENTERTAINMENT IN MALAYSIA

Entertainment in Malaysia can range from a traditional dance performance by the indigenous Iban people to the hip nightclubs in Kuala Lumpur. As the capital, Kuala Lumpur boasts a wide choice of entertainment, including theater, concerts, and art exhibitions. However, state capitals such as Johor Bahru, Kuching, and Kota Kinabalu also cater for

night-time revelry with a variety of nightclubs and karaoke bars. Malaysia's festivals through the year *(see pp56–9)* are often accompanied by traditional performing arts. Theme parks, such as LEGOLAND® Malaysia near Johor Bahru, are a great way to enjoy an all-day outing with children, while cinema enthusiasts can watch the latest Hollywood films at multiplexes.

Contemporary artwork at the National Art Gallery *(see p77)*, Kuala Lumpur

Event Listings

For comprehensive listings of current and upcoming events including art exhibitions, theatrical performances, and concerts in Kuala Lumpur, check English-language dailies such as **The Star** and **New Straits Times**. Another useful publication is **Juice**, a monthly magazine that lists the trendiest clubs. Up-to-date listings from all these publications are also available on their official websites. The **Kakiseni** website is an excellent arts portal and **TimeOut KL** online provides not only listings but a wealth of information regarding places to stay, restaurants, outdoor activities, and street maps.

There is no central ticket booking organization in Kuala Lumpur, so it is necessary to contact each venue directly or ask hotel staff for help with booking tickets. Unfortunately, not many older entertainment venues are equipped with facilities for the disabled, although most modern establishments provide such amenities. Call individual venues in advance to check for details before booking.

Art Exhibitions

There are several art halls in Kuala Lumpur, which host frequently changing exhibitions. The **National Art Gallery** *(see p77)* showcases works of over 2,500 artists and painters, especially works by contemporary Malaysian artists. The gallery also hosts rotating exhibitions throughout the year. Another impressive art gallery is **Galeri Petronas** at Suria KLCC *(see p79)*, which has three separate halls of international standard. It houses Malaysia's largest private art collection. For detailed

information on Kuala Lumpur's other art galleries it is best to visit the Kakiseni website.

Theme Parks

Peninsular Malaysia has several theme parks that offer exciting all-day amusement for the entire family. Children especially enjoy the action-packed environment. The newest, opening in 2016, is Twentieth Century Fox World, the film brand's first theme park and part of Malaysia's Resorts World Genting, an hour outside of Kuala Lumpur. The large park will feature more than 25 rides and attractions based on Fox films such as *Ice Age*, *Rio*, *Planet of the Apes*, and *Night at the Museum*. **LEGOLAND® Malaysia**, is a massively popular theme park, with over 40 rides, huge models of the Petronas Towers and other Asian landmarks rendered in the plastic bricks, a 4-D film screening studio, and a fun water park. Wet World Water Park in Shah Alam *(see p82)* and **Sunway Lagoon** are other water theme parks with water chutes and wave pools.

LEGOLAND® Malaysia, popular with kids of all ages

The long-running Coliseum Cinema

Theater

Kuala Lumpur hosts a great variety of theatrical performances throughout the year. Apart from touring Broadway hits, traditional and experimental musicals, comedies, and tragedies written by international as well as local playwrights, are also staged. There is a particularly active fringe theater scene in Kuala Lumpur, with groups such as Instant Café producing thought-provoking plays. The venues are as varied as the productions, ranging from the state-of-the-art **Kuala Lumpur Performing Arts Center** to the simple **Old China Café**.

Traditional Malaysian theater is the shadow puppet play, or *wayang kulit*, accompanied by a *gamelan*, music played by a traditional Indonesian percussion orchestra. Once the main form of entertainment in Malay villages, it is now mostly performed in some rural parts of the east coast states of Terengganu and Kelantan. One good place to catch a show is at Gelanggang Seni in Kota Bharu *(see pp152–3)* and a typical performance often lasts about 8 hours. Chinese opera, or *wayang*, a mix of dialog, dance, and music is also traditionally performed in the country. Street shows are held mostly during festivals such as the Chinese New Year *(see p34)*.

Cinema

Kuala Lumpur and big towns around the country have numerous movie halls and multiplex cinemas, which screen the latest Hollywood releases, usually with the original soundtrack and subtitles in Malay and Chinese. Movies from China, India, and other Asian countries are also screened. Most cinemas have air conditioning. Some of the biggest cinema chains are **Golden Screen Cinemas**, **Tanjong Golden Village**, and **Cathay Cineplexes**. The oldest cinema in Kuala Lumpur, still functioning today, is the Coliseum Cinema *(see p76)*. Cinema listings, show times, and tickets are available on the **Cinema Online** website.

Traditional and Classical Music

Reflecting a blend of cultures, predominantly Indian, Chinese, Muslim, and Indonesian, traditional Malaysian music is based largely around several types of drums – an influence of the *gamelan* – and other percussion instruments. Modern composers are constantly

Musicians playing a traditional Malay instrument

experimenting with a fusion of new and traditional instruments such as synthesizers in an attempt to keep classical music popular among the younger generation. Traditional music performances are frequently held at the Malaysian Tourism Information Complex *(see p80)* and the National Theater *(see p77)* both in Kuala Lumpur. Occasionally the National Theater hosts classical music concerts featuring the National Symphony Orchestra. The main classical venue in Kuala Lumpur is **Dewan Filharmonik Petronas**, Malaysia's first classical concert hall and home to the Malaysian Philharmonic Orchestra. It stages classical concerts and hosts local and international cultural performances. There is a strict dress code here.

The grand auditorium at the Dewan Filharmonik

Hard Rock Café, one of the best venues in Kuala Lumpur for live bands

Contemporary Music

Extremely popular among Malaysian youth, contemporary Western music often provides inspiration for local groups who create songs in Malay that are set to pop, rock, hip-hop, or underground beats. Touring pop stars of international repute occasionally perform in Kuala Lumpur. The Arena of the Stars stadium in Genting Highlands *(see p96)* is a popular venue for such concerts. Some of the most popular contemporary live music venues in Kuala Lumpur are the **Hard Rock Café**, **No Black Tie**, and **KL Live**. Many famous DJs from Europe also visit Kuala Lumpur's hippest clubs.

Dancer performing *datun julud*

Traditional Dance

Like its music, Malaysia's traditional dances are strongly influenced by Islamic, Indian, and Chinese cultures, though they have evolved into their own unique styles. Many of these dance forms continue to enjoy widespread popularity in the country and are performed during special occasions and festivals. Perhaps the most popular traditional dance is *joget*, which has its origins in Portuguese folk dance and is performed by couples who blend fast and graceful movements with playful humor. *Mak yong* combines romantic drama, dance, and operatic singing.

Originally presented only in Kelantan's royal courts, it is now enjoyed by all. *Silat* is an elegant dance that developed from martial arts and is accompanied by percussion music. It is often performed at weddings and festivals. One of the most popular dances from Sarawak is the *datun julud*, or hornbill dance. Created by the Kenyah people, it is based on the story of a prince blessed with a grandson and involves a single female dancer who waves fans of hornbill feathers to the sound of a *sape*, or a traditional guitar. A good place to enjoy traditional music and dance in Sarawak is the Sarawak Cultural Village *(see p165)*. In Kuala Lumpur, dance performances are held at the Malaysia Tourism Information Complex, as well as at the National Theater.

Pubs, Bars, and Karaoke

Kuala Lumpur has a dizzying range of nightlife haunts that cater to every taste. The greatest concentration of pubs and bars is in the Golden Triangle *(see p80)*. Located here is **Pisco Bar**, a well-stocked bar, live music venue, boutique, and art gallery in one, as well as the **Beach Club Café**, which mostly plays old favorites and is often packed to the rafters. The capital's other pulsating nightspot is around Bangsar. Bars such as **Finnegan's** serving Kilkenny beer and **La Bodega** with its Spanish ambience infuse it with a cosmopolitan feel. Another bar worth a visit for lovers of rhythm and blues music is **Modesto's**.

Karaoke is hugely popular in most Asian countries, and Malaysia is no exception. Among Kuala Lumpur's chic, luxurious, and commonly visited karaoke bars are **Cherry Blossom**, **Deluxe Nite Club**, and **Club De Vegas**.

Other main towns in the country with a fair choice of pubs and bars are Kuching, Johor Bahru, Kota Kinabalu, and several in Penang. Since drinks can be expensive in Malaysia, it is worth looking out for places that offer happy hour prices, typically two drinks for the price of one. Generally, happy hour is between 5 and 8pm. Many bars feature live music, especially at weekends, for which there is usually a cover charge of around RM20.

Men performing *silat*, or a traditional martial art dance, in Kelantan

Nightclubs and Discos

Although nightclubs and discos can be found in all large Malaysian towns, Kuala Lumpur has the widest choice of venues. Most places don't pick up pace until around 10pm, but are throbbing with life until the early hours of dawn. Several locations feature Ladies' Nights when women can get free entry. The popularity of individual clubs tends to fluctuate, but the hottest spots in town can usually be found around the junction of Jalan P. Ramlee and Jalan Sultan Ismail. Most places play European and British house music, and frequently feature well-known international DJs. Among the trendiest places are

Zouk Club, **Desire**, **Maison**, **Luna Bar**, and **Sky Bar** in the Traders Hotel. Both Luna Bar and Sky Bar have the advantage of offering fantastic views of the

Petronas Towers. Discos tend to be located in upscale shopping malls or in hotels, and among the most popular clubs are **Liquid Bar** and **Sultan Lounge**.

A crowded dance floor in a Malaysian club

DIRECTORY

Event Listings

Juice
w juiceonline.com

Kakiseni
w kakiseni.com

New Straits Times
w nst.com.my

The Star
w thestar.com.my

Timeout KL
w timeout.com/kl

Theme Parks

Legoland® Malaysia
7 Jalan Legoland, Bandar Medini, Nusajaya, Johor.
Tel (07) 597 8888.
w legoland.com.my

Sunway Lagoon
11/11 Bandar Sunway, Petaling Jaya, Selangor.
Tel (03) 5635-8000.
w sunwaylagoon.com

Theater

Kuala Lumpur Performing Arts Center
Jalan Strachan, Kuala Lumpur. Tel (03) 4047-7000. w klpac.com

Old China Café
11, Jalan Balai Polis, Kuala Lumpur.
Tel (03) 2072-5915.

Cinema

Cathay Cineplexes
2 Selangor Darul Ehsan.
Tel (03) 7727-8051.

Cinema Online
w cinemaonline.com. my

Golden Screen Cinemas
Mid Valley Megamall, Bangsar.
Tel (03) 2938-3366.

Tanjong Golden Village
Level 3 Suria KLCC. Map 2 F5. Tel (03) 7492-2929.

Traditional and Classical Music

Dewan Filharmonik Petronas
Petronas Towers.
Map 2 E4. Tel (03) 2051-7007. w malaysian filharmonik.com

Contemporary Music

Hard Rock Café
Jalan Sultan Ismail, Kuala Lumpur. Map 2 D5.
Tel (03) 2715-5555.

No Black Tie
17 Lorong Mesui, Kuala Lumpur.
Tel (03) 2142-3737.

Pubs, Bars, and Karaoke

Beach Club Café
97 Jalan P. Ramlee, Kuala Lumpur. Map 2 D5.
Tel (03) 2166-9919.

La Bodega
31 Tengkat Tong Shin, Kuala Lumpur.
Tel (03) 2142-6368.

Cherry Blossom
Sun Kompleks, Off Jalan Bukit Bintang, Kuala Lumpur. Map 5 C3.
Tel (03) 2144-4895.

Club De Vegas
3 Jalan Imbi, Kuala Lumpur. Map 5 C3.
Tel (03) 2141-3888.

Deluxe Nite Club
Ampang Park Shopping Center, Jalan Ampang, Kuala Lumpur.
Tel (03) 2162-1399.

Finnegan's
51 Jalan Sultan Ismail, Kuala Lumpur.
Tel (03) 2145-1930.

KL Live
1st Floor, Life Centre, 20 Jalan Sultan Ismail, Kuala Lumpur. Tel (03) 2162-2570.

Modesto's
Sri Hartamas, Kuala Lumpur. Map 2 E5.
Tel (03) 6201-7898.

Pisco Bar
329 Jalan Mesui (off Jalan Nagasari), Bukit Bintang.
Map 5 C2.
Tel (03) 2142-2900.

Nightclubs and Discos

Desire
Jalan Doraisamy, Kuala Lumpur. Map 1 B4.
Tel (02) 200-1926.

Liquid Bar
Jalan Hang Kasturi.

Luna Bar
Menara Panglobal, Jalan Puncak. Map 5 B1.
Tel (03) 2332-7777.

Maison
8 Jalan Yap Ah Shak, Kuala Lumpur. Map 1 B5.
Tel (03) 2694-3341.

Sky Bar
Traders Hotel, KLCC. Map 2 F5. Tel (03) 2332-9888.

Sultan Lounge
Mandarin Oriental, Jalan Pinang.
Tel (03) 2380-8888.

Zouk Club
Jalan Ampang, Kuala Lumpur. Map 2 E4.
Tel (03) 2171-1997.

OUTDOOR ACTIVITIES IN MALAYSIA

From the summit of Gunung Kinabalu to the depths of the South China Sea, Malaysia offers an array of opportunities to enjoy the country's natural wonders. Pristine offshore islands such as the Perhentians, Tioman, and Sipadan attract divers with their stunning coral reefs and rich marine life. Most beach resorts offer adventure sports such as windsurfing, water-skiing, and snorkeling. The oldest rain forests in the world with their towering trees, tangled vines, and gaping limestone caves are wonderful to explore. Tour agents cater to the needs of special interest groups, from climbers to bird-watchers, while river cruises are a comfortable way of visiting the mangrove swamps on the coast of Malaysian Borneo. The agreeable climate is perfect for golf enthusiasts.

Speedboat tour at Bako National Park *(see pp168–9)*, Sarawak

Guided Tours

Tourism in Malaysia is well developed and tour operators, such as **CPH Travel Agency** and **Asian Overland Services**, offer a wide range of choices. Depending on a visitor's time and budget, everything from a half-day city tour to a 10-day tour of the country is available.

Independent travelers can join tour groups, such as **S.I. Tours** and **Exotic Adventure**, to visit sights and participate in activities that would otherwise be prohibitively expensive. For example, a tour is the best way to access Sarawak's Mulu National Park *(see pp176–7)*, hike up Gunung Kinabalu *(see pp190–93)* in Sabah, or join a white-water rafting expedition down Sungai Padas *(see p187)*. The advantage of joining a guided tour is that the local guide's knowledge can enrich the experience of visiting a place you may never return to.

Bookings and Permits for National Parks

At most national parks and reserves in Malaysia, visitors can pay the entry fees at Park Headquarters within the reserve's boundaries or at the entrance. However, booking in advance is advisable for a few of the parks, such as Tanjung Datu National Park *(see p166)* and Semenggoh Wildlife Centre *(see p167)*. Permits and entrance tickets can be obtained at the **National Parks Booking Office** in Kuching *(see p161)* or at its branch in Miri. Visitors entering Endau-Rompin National Park *(see p143)* from Johor also have the option of buying a permit from the Forestry Commission online. Some parks require official permits for professional filming and photography, as well as for activities such as trekking and fishing. These can be obtained either at the park itself or, if in Sarawak, from the National Parks Booking Offices. Many parks offer accommodations and, while it is not mandatory to book in advance for all, it is advisable to do so as preserves and parks tend to get busy, especially during weekends and holidays. Some parks may require permits for camping. The National Parks Booking Offices also handle accommodation bookings.

Trekking

Malaysia's national parks are ideal for those wishing to trek through scenic landscape and observe the country's wildlife. At 13,455 ft (4,101 m), Sabah's Gunung Kinabalu is one of the highest peaks in the world that can be climbed without special climbing equipment, so it is not surprising that hundreds set out every day with the intention of

Braving the Pinnacles at Mulu National Park

Following the jungle trail near Asah waterfall *(see p136)*, Southern Peninsula

standing on its summit. Park authorities advise against climbing Kinabalu independently and hiring a guide is recommended. A climbing permit can be purchased on arrival at Park Headquarters. Most climbers take two days to reach this summit with an overnight stay in one of the mountain huts, such as the one at Laban Rata, 10,738 ft (3,273 m) above sea level. It is essential to pre-book, particularly in the peak season (April). Wear good walking boots and warm, waterproof clothing, and bring a sleeping bag, water, and high-energy food. A flashlight is invaluable since climbs can start early in the morning to catch the sunrise at the summit.

For less strenuous climbs, there are alternatives, ranging from a trek up Taman Negara's Gunung Tahan *(see pp144–5)* to the climb up Sarawak's Gunung Mulu *(see p177)* or the Pinnacles on Gunung Api *(see p177)*. Malaysia's terrain is challenging, and it is wise to trek with local tour companies, such as **Jungle School**.

In parks that lie within the protected area of **Sarawak Forestry Corporation**, such as Mulu National Park, guides are mandatory while trekking. Taman Negara is best for beginners as it has trails for every level of ability. Bako National Park *(see pp168–9)* in Sarawak has several easy trails, while Gunung Mulu and

Gunung Kinabalu test the fittest of walkers. Peradayan Forest Reserve in Brunei also offers many good trails.

Most of Malaysia's forests are ecologically fragile and protected by the **Department of Wildlife and National Parks**. While many visitors opt to trek on their own following color-coded trails, treks can be organized by the department or private companies, such as **Borneo Adventure** or Jungle School.

Hikers should shield themselves from the sun and drink lots of water to avoid dehydration. Leech socks can also be very useful, especially during the wet season.

Caving

Malaysia's landscape, riddled with some of the world's largest limestone caves, lures spelunkers from around the world. Many *guas*, or caves, such as Lang's Cave in Gulung Mulu, are covered with beautiful stalactites and stalagmites, while others, such as the nearby Deer Cave, offer opportunities for adventure caving, following rarely visited routes.

The caves at Niah *(see p174)* and Mulu National Park in Sarawak attract millions of bats and birds, which roost in their dank interiors. Sabah's Gomantong Caves *(see p197)* are famed for their swiftlet nests. Locals clamber up bamboo poles to retrieve the nests, considered a gastronomic delicacy by some. The best time to see the cave's wildlife is at dusk, during the changeover when bats come hurtling out for their night feeding and swiftlets return to their nests.

Though smaller than the caves in Borneo, the illuminated caverns at Tempurong in Selangor and the Hindu shrines at Batu Caves *(see p96)* are remarkable. For those intrigued by their hidden recesses, the **Malaysian Nature Society Caving Group** offers quick courses and arranges cave explorations.

Gua Kelam, or cave of darkness, in Kuala Perlis

Diving in Malaysia

The idyllic islands scattered around the coast of Malaysia provide easy access to the country's spectacular dive sites. While Malaysia is a strong draw for experienced divers, it is also a good training ground for amateurs, with numerous diving outfits offering lessons (*see p317*) in the waters around islands such as Pulau Tioman, Pulau Redang, and the Perhentian Islands. Some of the more common marine creatures that divers can hope to spot are whale sharks, manta rays, starfish, and a variety of sea turtles. The monsoon season reduces visibility and makes diving less rewarding. The best time to visit the west coast of Peninsular Malaysia is from November to May, while March to October are the ideal months for a trip to the east coast of the peninsula and around Sabah and Sarawak. The islands off the southwest coast of Sabah are suitable for diving all year round.

Types of Diving

Malaysia's coastline offers wreck diving, snorkeling, and coral reef diving. While wreck dives enable experienced divers to glimpse Malaysia's underwater treasures, coral reefs can be explored by snorkelers and scuba divers.

Malaysia's Best Dive Sites

- Miri *see p174*
- Perhentian Islands *see p148*
- Pulau Kapas *see p146*
- Pulau Labuan *see p186*
- Pulau Lankayan *see p197*
- Pulau Redang *see p148*
- Pulau Sipadan *see pp200–201*
- Pulau Sulug *see p185*
- Pulau Tenggol *see p146*
- Pulau Tioman *see pp136–7*

Wreck dives allow divers to explore old shipwrecks. The easiest wreck to navigate is the Cement Wreck, which sank in 1980 off the coast of Labuan.

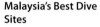

Scuba diving in Malaysia offers the opportunity to experience its coral reef system, which supports aquatic organisms numbering up to at least 200 species.

Snorkeling needs only a mask and a snorkel. It is a great way to watch underwater life at close quarters.

Marine Life

The waters off Malaysia are a treasure trove of marine species. East coast islands such as Tioman are home to black marlin and yellowfin, schools of barracuda, and reef sharks.

Starfish, also known as sea stars, are bright and vibrantly colored. These boneless species glide across the ocean floor.

Whale Sharks are gentle and slow plankton-feeding sharks. The largest living fish species, they grow to 39 ft (12 m) in length.

Green Sea Turtles are an endangered species. The adult turtle's algae diet is responsible for its green color.

White-water rafting along one of Malaysia's rivers

Diving and Snorkeling

Diving is a popular activity for both locals and visitors in Malaysia. Numerous scuba-diving and marine clubs as well as beach resorts offer equipment for hire. Most dive operators have five-day PADI courses leading to certification as a diver and also organize trips to dive sites. **Borneo Dream and Sea Sports**, **Pulau Sipadan Resort and Tours**, and **Borneo Dive** are some of Malaysia's best tour operators.

In several places, coral reefs are in shallow water, making it easy for snorkelers to get among them and explore the pristine vistas and vibrant corals. However, care should be taken not to touch the corals as they can sting and are easily damaged. The number of divers permitted at any one time in Pulau Sipadan (see pp200–201) is limited, and booking in advance is a must.

Water Sports

Paragliding, windsurfing, water-skiing, wakeboarding, and jet-skiing are just some of the water sports on offer at Malaysia's beach resorts. **Sea Quest Tours and Travel** organizes glass-bottom boat cruises along the coast. They also arrange sunset cruises and island-hopping tours.

Some travel insurance companies do not cover injuries sustained while taking part in water sports, so policies should be checked before signing up.

White-Water Rafting

The frothing rivers that tumble out of Malaysia's rugged mountains become rapids en route to the sea. They once formed an impassable barrier for many explorers. Today, however, they form the perfect setting for a white-water rafting adventure. Rapids are graded from Class I to V, but anything above Class III will need an expert guide. One of the top sites is Sabah's spectacular Padas Gorge (see p187) with Class III–IV rapids that leave paddlers exhilarated. Sungai Sungkei and Sungai Kampar in Perak, north of Kuala Lumpur, feature gentler rapids.

No previous experience is necessary for white-water rafting, as tour operators such as **Nomad Adventure** and **Exotic Adventure** run through safety procedures before setting off. Rafters wear helmets and protective jackets and have to be good swimmers. The experience varies, as rivers offer a sedate drift in the drier months and a soaking roller-coaster ride after severe rain. Children above 12 are allowed on such trips provided they are good swimmers and are accompanied by parents or legal guardians.

River Cruises

A comparatively recent phenomenon on Malaysia's ecotourism scene is a cruise through lush rain forests and mangrove swamps. These cruises usually set out in the early mornings or late afternoons, and as the boat glides over the water, knowledgeable guides help spot long-tail macaques, silver langurs, and proboscis monkeys, as well as birds such as hornbills feeding in the trees close to the water's edge.

Such cruises are available in Pulau Langkawi (see pp118–21) and Taman Negara (see pp144–5) on the peninsula, or at the Klias Wetlands (see p186) and Kinabatangan Wildlife Sanctuary in Sabah (see p197). Irrawaddy dolphins are occasionally seen splashing in the shallows around the mouth of the Sungai Santubong in Sarawak. On disembarking from the cruise, tour groups such as **S.I. Tours** and **Borneo Eco Tours** often treat their guests to a buffet dinner before driving them back to their hotels.

Kayaking tour in mangrove swamps

A golfer enjoying a round in a spectacular setting

Golf

With affordable caddies, low green fees, and equipment hire at reasonable rates, the country's well-planned courses attract golfers from all over the world. Day visitors can usually enjoy a game for a fee.

Almost 200 golf courses are currently available, with locations ranging from the cool Fraser's Hill (see p97) to the coastline of Borneo. A few of the most popular courses in Peninsular Malaysia include the **Cameron Highlands Golf Club**. Kuala Lumpur has the **Kuala Lumpur Golf and Country Club**, and on the city's outskirts are the designer **Mines Resort Golf and Country Club** course and the **Templer Park Golf Club**. Further afield on Langkawi is the award-winning **Els Club** and **Gunung Raya Golf Resort**.

Wildlife Viewing

People visit Malaysia in great numbers to view its tropical biodiversity comprising over 200 kinds of mammals, many thousands of flowering plants, and a spectrum of butterflies. Malaysia's wildlife includes orangutans, Borneo gibbons, proboscis monkeys, and hornbills. It may be necessary to trek through jungles or climb up mountains to spot

rarer species. Fraser's Hill and Taman Negara (see pp144–5) are both easily accessible wild-life-spotting areas.

Another popular activity is an organized tour to spot orang-utans in their natural habitat at Semonggoh Wildlife Centre in Sarawak (see p167), or at Sepilok Orangutan Rehabilitation Center (see p196) in Sabah. Wildlife enthusiasts can also see green and hawksbill turtles nesting and observe hatchlings being released by rangers on islands such as Gulisan, Bakungan Kecil, and Pulau Selingam, and on a trip to Turtle Island National Park (see p196). **WWF**, the global conservation organization, plans events to support the terrain threatened by poaching and deforestation.

Bird-Watching

With more than 600 identified species, Malaysia is a paradise for bird-watchers. Part of the reason for this great diversity is that Malaysia has many different habitats, including montane forests, lowland forests, mangrove swamps, and wetlands, which provide good nesting conditions for all kinds of birds. Apart from the eight varieties of hornbill that can be seen gliding over the rain forest canopy, crested serpent eagles, mangrove pittas, kingfishers, and trogons delight bird-watchers.

In Malaysian Borneo, Sarawak is the perfect place for a wildlife holiday and is often referred to as the Land of the Hornbill. Kinabalu National Park (see pp190–91) in Sabah has a fantastic variety of flycatchers and magpies. Among the best locations on Peninsular Malaysia for bird-watching are Kuala Selangor Nature Park and Fraser's Hill, where swiftlets and cuckoos predominate. Enthusiastic twitchers might like to join in one of many birding events, such as the Fraser's Hill International Bird Race (see p97) that takes place annually in June.

Borneo Mainland Travel and Tours, **Birdtour Asia**, **Malaysian Nature Society Birding Group**, **Rockjumper**, and **Birding Pal** are among the tour operators and groups that organize bird-watching itineraries. Binoculars, a good field-guide, and a hat will prove to be very useful.

Enthusiastic bird-watchers on a jungle tour

DIRECTORY

Guided Tours

Asian Overland Services
Ampang Point, Kuala Lumpur. **Tel** (03) 4252-9100. w **asianoverland.com.my**

CPH Travel Agency
Kuching, Sarawak.
Tel (082) 414-921.
w **cphtravel.com.my**

Exotic Adventure
Lot 1, 1st Floor, Block D, Segama Complex, Kota Kinabalu, Sabah.
Tel (088) 486-886.
w **exotic-adventure.com**

S.I. Tours
Lot 1002–1003, Wisma Khoo, Siak Chiew, Sandakan, Sabah.
Tel (089) 673-502.
w **sitoursborneo.com**

Bookings and Permits for National Parks

Sarawak National Parks Booking Office
w **sarawakforestry.com**

Trekking

Borneo Adventure
Gaya Center, Jalan Tun Fuad Stephens, Kota Kinabalu, Sabah.
Tel (088) 486-800.
w **borneoadventure.com**

Department of Wildlife and National Parks
Jalan Charas, Kuala Lumpur.
Tel (03) 9075-2872.
w **wildlife.gov.my**

Jungle School
The Heritage Unit, Kuala Lumpur. **Tel** (019) 342-2049. w **jungleschool.com.my**

Sarawak Forestry Corporation
Hock Lee Center, Jalan Datuk Abang Abdul Rahim, Kuching, Sarawak.
Tel (082) 348-001.
w **sarawakforestry.com**

Caving

Malaysian Nature Society Caving Group
641 JKR Jalan Kelantan, Bukit Persekutuan, Kuala Lumpur. **Map** 3 A4.
Tel (03) 2287-9422.
w **mns.org.my**

Diving and Snorkeling

Borneo Divers and Sea Sports
Tel (088) 222-226.
w **borneodivers.info**

Borneo Dream
Tel (088) 244-064.
w **borneodream.com**

Pulau Sipadan Resort and Tours
1st floor, No. 484, Block P, Bandar Sabindo, Tawau, Sabah.
Tel (089) 765-200.
w **sipadan-resort.com**

Water Sports

Sea Quest Tours and Travel
1 Sutera Harbour Boulevard, Kota Kinabalu, Sabah. **Tel** (088) 248-006.
w **seaquesttours.net**

White-Water Rafting

Exotic Adventure
Lot 1, 1st Floor, Block D, Segama Complex, Kota Kinabalu, Sabah.
Tel (088) 486-886.
w **exotic-adventure.com**

Nomad Adventure
4.06B, 4th Floor, The Summit Subang USJ, Persiaran Kewajipan, USJ 1, Subang Jaya, Selangor.
Tel (603) 8024-5152.
w **nomadadventure.com**

River Cruises

Borneo Eco Tours
Pusat Perindustrian Kolonbong Jaya, Kota Kinabalu.
Tel (088) 438-300.
w **borneoecotours.com**

Golf

Cameron Highlands Golf Club
PO Box 66, 39007 Tanah Rata, Cameron Highlands, Pahang.
Tel (05) 491-1126.

Els Club
Pulau Langkawi.
Tel (04) 959-2700.
w **elsclubmalaysia.com**

Gunung Raya Golf Resort
Jalan Air Hangat, Kisap, Langkawi.
Tel (04) 966-8148.
w **golfgr.com.my**

Kuala Lumpur Golf and Country Club
10 Jalan 1/70D, off Jalan Bukit Kiara, Kuala Lumpur.
Tel (03) 2011-9188.
w **klgcc.com**

Mines Resort Golf and Country Club
The Mines Resort City, Selangor Darul Ehsan.
Tel (03) 943-2288.
w **minesgolfclub.com**

Templer Park Golf Club
Rawang, Selangor.
Tel (03) 6091-9111.
w **tpcc.com.my**

Wildlife Viewing

WWF (Worldwide Fund for Nature)
49 Jalan SS23/15 Taman Sea, Petaling Jaya, Selangor.
Tel (03) 7803-3772.

Suite 1–6 W11 6th Floor, CPS Tower, Center Point Complex No. 1, Jalan Center Point, Kota Kinabalu, Sabah.
Tel (088) 262-420.
w **wwf.org.my**

Bird-Watching

Birding Pal
w **www.birdingpal.org**

Birdtour Asia
w **birdtourasia.com**

Borneo Mainland Travel and Tours
1081, 1st Floor, Jalan Merpati, Miri, Sarawak.
Tel (085) 433-511.
w **borneomainland.com**

Malaysian Nature Society Birding Group
641 JKR Jalan Kelantan, Bukit Persekutuan, Kuala Lumpur.
Map 3 A4.
Tel (03) 2287-9422.
w **mns.org.my**

Rockjumper
w **rockjumperbirding.com**

SURVIVAL GUIDE

PRACTICAL INFORMATION

Malaysia is one of Asia's top tourist destinations, appealing to package tourists and independent travelers alike. The government of Malaysia, long aware of the country's potential as a tropical paradise, has been promoting tourism for decades. Visitors will find that tour operators are efficient, hotels are well maintained, traveling around is usually smooth, and local people are generally friendly in Singapore,

Malaysia, and Brunei. Visitors should be aware of petty crime, especially bag-snatching, in Kuala Lumpur, and of a risk of criminality on Pulau Tioman and eastern Sabah, so some common-sense caution is needed *(see p324)*. However, most visits are trouble free. Singapore, on the other hand, is an exceptionally safe country, largely free of violent crime, dirt, and most tropical diseases.

A percussionist at the Rainforest World Music Festival *(see p165)*

When to Go

Malaysia, Singapore, and Brunei fall entirely within the tropics, so all three countries have a hot and humid climate all year round, with temperatures hovering around 30° C (86° F) and rarely dipping below 20° C (68° F). Visitors keen to lounge on a beach or participate in adventure sports should avoid the monsoons. The rainy season affects the west coast of the peninsula between May and September. On the east coast and in Malaysian Borneo, the monsoon falls between November and February. It is worth timing a visit to coincide with one of the country's major festivals, such as the Merdeka Eve celebration *(see p58)* or the Rainforest World Music Festival *(see p165)*. Chinese and Hindu festivals in Singapore take place in January and February.

Visas and Passports

Visitors need a passport that is valid for at least six months from the date of arrival. A visa can be obtained overseas at Malaysian embassies, though many nationalities are granted one on arrival. Citizens of some European, African, South American, and ASEAN countries can stay in Malaysia for a month without a visa. Citizens of the UK, USA, New Zealand, Australia, Canada, and Ireland are automatically allowed to stay for three months, which can be extended for another two months by applying to the Immigration Department. The Malaysian **Foreign Office** website has further details.

Brunei does not require visas from citizens of the UK, USA, and most European nations. Depending on your nationality, you will be allowed to stay for either 30 or 90 days. Australians are issued with a visa on arrival for 30 days while Canadians can stay for only two weeks. However, an initial stamp, valid

for between two weeks and three months, may be extended by applying to the Immigration Department in Bandar Seri Begawan, the capital of Brunei. Citizens of most other nationalities are given 72-hour transit visas.

Singapore stamps in citizens from the UK, USA, Australia, New Zealand, and Canada for an initial 30 days, or travelers can cross into Malaysia or any other country and then return for three months.

Customs Information

Duty-free limits are 50 cigars, 200 cigarettes, or 225g of tobacco, as well as a liter of either wine or spirits in Malaysia. Duty is payable on all tobacco in Singapore, and you can bring in one liter of wine, one of spirits and one of beer. Visitors who are carrying over US$2,500 need to fill a Declaration Form on arrival.

These three countries take a very hard line on illegal drugs. Possession can result in a

Visitor's Center at Suntec City Mall, Singapore

◀ Cycle rickshaws waiting for tourists in front of the Stadthuys in Melaka

Visitors watching orangutans at the Sepilok Orangutan Rehabilitation Center *(see p196)*

lengthy prison term or the death penalty in Malaysia, Singapore, and Brunei.

Visitor Information

Anyone considering a visit to Malaysia, Singapore, and Brunei will find useful information on the official websites of **Tourism Malaysia**, the **Singapore Tourism Board**, and **Tourism Brunei**. The websites provide details of festivals, hotels, and resorts. The tourist boards, aided by their efficient network of domestic and overseas offices, offer a wide range of pamphlets on the most attractive tourist destinations. For information on Malaysian Borneo, both the **Sabah Tourism Board** and the **Sarawak Tourism Board** have detailed websites. Most hotels operate a tour service or can make arrangements for guests while backpackers' lodges are generally excellent sources of local information.

Guide of Singapore Tourism Board

Opening Hours

Government offices in Malaysia are open 8:30am–5:30pm, Monday to Friday. Museums keep similar hours, though it is worth checking specific locations as some museums are closed Mondays. In Malaysia's more devout Muslim states, such as Kedah, Terrangganu, and Kelantan, offices are also closed on Friday. Post offices are generally open betwen 8am and 6pm, Monday to Saturday. In Singapore, government offices remain open between 8:30am and 5pm, Monday to Friday. In Brunei, government offices are open between 7:45am and 4:30pm and remain closed on Friday and Sunday. For details on the opening hours of banks see pp326–7, and for shops see pp302–3.

Admission Charges

Most museums charge a nominal entry fee both in Malaysia and in Singapore. Most national parks charge RM10, except Kinabalu National Park, where the fee is RM15. Some of the more developed attractions charge a higher entry fee, including the Sepilok Orangutan Rehabilitation Center (RM30) and Sarawak Cultural Village (RM60). Night safaris tend to be expensive. Both countries have lower rates for children.

Local Time

Malaysia, Singapore, and Brunei are 8 hours ahead of Greenwich Mean Time (GMT), 16 hours ahead of US Pacific Standard Time (PST) and 13 hours ahead of Eastern Standard Time (EST) in the USA. However, Malaysia does not have daylight saving time; visitors should note that time differences will change when countries observing daylight saving move their clocks forward.

Lunar Calendar

Malaysia and Singapore use the Gregorian (Western) calendar for administrative purposes, but many of their festivals, particularly Islamic or Chinese, are celebrated according to the lunar calendar. This means they fall on a different day each year. The main difference between the Chinese and Islamic lunar calendars is that the former uses an intercalary month, so that festivals occur mostly at the same time each year, while Islamic festivals occur about 10 days earlier each year. Most festivals are planned to coincide with the night of the full moon. To find exact dates of any festival, it is best to check the tourist board website of the country concerned.

Electricity

The electrical current in the region is 220–240 volts at 50 hertz. Equipment using 110 volts requires a converter. Adaptors are cheap and available in most big towns. Most wall sockets accommodate three-pronged square pin plugs as used in the UK.

Family boat ride on Sungai Santubong

Traveling with Children

Parents traveling with children will often be surprised and delighted to find that their children are usually treated with affection and care almost everywhere in Malaysia, Singapore, and Brunei. An example of this is in restaurants, where the staff are often helpful, and willing to occupy children while parents have their meal. Malaysia is particularly child-friendly, with a wide range of places to visit that interest people of all ages. Childcare products are available throughout the region except in rural areas and remote destinations. Children's health, however, requires protection, especially against exposure to heat, and food- and water-related ailments.

Women Travelers

Malaysia, Singapore, and Brunei are reasonably safe for women traveling alone. It is important to bear in mind, though, that due to the conservative nature of Malaysian culture, unaccompanied Western women may attract attention, particularly in rural districts and Muslim areas. Women travelers are unlikely to be harassed if they are considerate of local customs, wear modest clothing, and avoid taking risks such as hitchhiking and walking alone at night.

Disabled Travelers

Singapore provides the best facilities for the disabled, while Malaysia unfortunately offers little in the way of assistance. Many hotels, banks, cinemas, and shopping centers in Singapore provide ramps and other amenities for those with special needs, but these are less common in Malaysia. Facilities are slowly improving, however. Public transport lacks wheelchair accessibility, and towns have high kerbs and uneven sidewalks. Travel websites for the disabled, such as **Global Access News**, offer some guidance.

Gay and Lesbian Travelers

Officially, neither Malaysia nor Singapore welcomes gay and lesbian travelers, and delivers strict punishment for homosexual acts. Nevertheless, a number of bars and clubs in Singapore and Kuala Lumpur bolster a thriving gay scene. For more information on gay and lesbian issues and events across Asia consult the website **Utopia**.

What to Wear

Light, casual clothes in cotton and other natural fibers are ideal for the tropical climate of Malaysia, Singapore, and Brunei, which are hot and humid year-round. Hats and sunglasses are also advisable. A sweater and windproof jacket are recommended for those visiting hill stations. As there is some rainfall throughout the year in Malaysia, a raincoat is handy. It is also important to carry a few long-sleeved shirts and pairs of trousers or full-length dresses, not just as protection from the sun, but also for visits to conservative rural areas and religious venues as well as visits to smart restaurants and hotels. Singapore is generally smarter than Malaysia when it comes to dining out.

Since laundry services are available in most hotels and guesthouses and cheap clothing, such as T-shirts and *batik* shirts, can be bought everywhere, it is easy to travel light.

Photography

Natural beauty, teeming wildlife, and stunning architecture ensure that most places in Malaysia, Singapore, and Brunei are extremely photogenic. People are generally quite happy to have their picture taken, but to avoid causing offence, always request their permission first, especially while visiting the indigenous people. Similarly, it is advisable to ask a priest or *imam* at all temples and mosques before taking pictures there.

Photo shops in Malaysia's big cities and in Singapore are well stocked with equipment, memory cards, and print film; prices are cheaper than in the West. Professional slide film is only available in big cities, and even then it might be better to

Stalls selling clothes and other wares at Jalan Petaling market

Arm wrestling between a tourist and a local

carry your own, as it tends to be improperly stored. It is worth using photographic services, such as film processing, before heading home. It is also easy and cheap to get images on a memory card transferred onto a DVD and to get prints from digital images.

Social Customs

The majority of the Malaysian population is conservative, but visitors will find most social customs flexible and generally easy to comply with. Loud behavior is considered rude. As a rule, do not point at people or objects using the index finger; instead indicate with the thumb or the whole hand. Although men shake hands, wait for a hand to be offered. Also note that in Muslim company it is impolite to touch people with the left hand or on the head. Public displays of affection such as hugging and kissing are also frowned upon. Topless sunbathing and nudity on beaches are taboo.

Before entering a Malaysian home, visitors should take their shoes off. Never help yourself to food without it being offered first and avoid eating with the left hand.

While most big cities have a modern outlook in terms of fashion, Muslim women still dress conservatively. Care must be taken to dress modestly, with arms and legs covered, when visiting rural areas, temples,

mosques, and other religious places, as well as in Muslim areas or homes. Non-Muslim women may be forbidden to enter mosques in some places.

Language

Bahasa Malayu, which means Malay language, is the official language of Malaysia and Brunei. In Singapore, English and Mandarin are also widely spoken, though visitors may also hear Tamil, Cantonese, Hindi, or any number of indigenous languages that are still used by the multi-ethnic population. Visitors who learn even a few Malay phrases will endear themselves to their hosts.

Conversion Chart

Malaysia, Singapore, and Brunei use the metric system for weights and measures.
Imperial to Metric
1 inch = 2.5 centimeters
1 foot = 30 centimeters
1 mile = 1.6 kilometers
1 ounce = 28 grams
1 pound = 454 grams
1 US pint = 0.473 liter
1 US quart = 0.947 liter
1 US gallon = 3.6 liters
Metric to Imperial
1 centimeter = 0.4 inch
1 meter = 3 feet 3 inches
1 kilometer = 0.6 mile
1 gram = 0.04 ounce
1 liter = 2.1 US pints

Personal Security and Health

Malaysia, Singapore, and Brunei are all relatively safe to travel in as crime rates are low, though petty crime is on the rise in Kuala Lumpur. The same common-sense safety rules apply here as anywhere else: be vigilant, especially in tourist hotspots where pickpockets and bag-snatchers may operate. However, Sabah's eastern coast and islands have been subject to travel warnings issued by both the US State Department and British Foreign Office, after kidnappings. Check current advisories on your government's website before travel to this area.

Singapore policeman and a patrol car

Police

Most visitors never have cause for dealings with the police, unless reporting a theft or loss. In Malaysia, areas with large numbers of tourists are also patrolled by special tourist police who offer extra protection.

Singapore has strict laws that prohibit smoking in public places, littering, and even chewing gum, for which steep fines ranging from S$50–1,000 are imposed. The police here are particularly vigilant. Although sometimes tourists may be let off with a warning for these offences, it is best to respect local laws.

General Precautions

While traveling in the region is relatively safe, some basic precautions should be followed. Avoid carrying large sums of money or wearing expensive jewelry; leave them in your hotel safe. Keep money and passports in a money

Tourist police in Malaysia

belt beneath clothing to prevent the risk of pick-pocketing. Valuables such as cameras and mobile phones should be hidden from view. In Kuala Lumpur, it is becoming quite common for thieves on motorcycles to grab bags and phones so be aware of your surrounds. Avoid walking along dimly lit streets after dark or leaving purses unattended.

It is a good idea to have photocopies of your travel insurance papers, passport, and documents, in case of theft or loss (see below).

Lost and Stolen Property

If you are robbed, report the theft immediately to the local police station. A police report will be necessary to make an insurance claim later. Lost or stolen credit cards and traveler's checks must be reported to the issuing bank to prevent with-drawals and cards must be canceled thereafter for replacements. If a passport is lost or stolen,

contact your embassy or consulate in order to obtain a replacement (see p323).

Narcotics

Malaysia and Singapore are very strict when it comes to penalties for possessing or smuggling narcotics, and anyone caught carrying them can expect either a long time in prison or possibly the death sentence. Brunei, too, carries the death penalty for drug trafficking.

Health Precautions

Standards of health and hygiene are high in Malaysia and Singapore. No inoculations are necessary, unless you have recently visited countries where yellow fever is prevalent. If so, you will need to show proof of vaccination on arrival.

Most areas of Malaysia have no risk of malaria. There is a risk of malaria in deep hinterland areas of Sabah and Sarawak and in Temara Negara National Park in Peninsular Malaysia. There is low to no risk of malaria in Kuala Lumpur and other urban/suburban areas and coastal regions.

Dengue fever, which is also transmitted by mosquitoes, is an increasing problem. It causes high fever, joint pain, and headaches, usually running its course in one week to 10 days. There is no vaccine for it, but a checkup is recommended to avoid any complications.

The most common problem for travelers is diarrhea and stomach upsets caused by a change in diet, water, and climate. To reduce the risk of diarrhea, drink only bottled or boiled water, avoid ice in drinks and raw food, and eat only in clean places.

The greatest danger of traveling to the tropics is the heat, which can easily cause dehydration and sunburn. Drink plenty of water, stay in the shade, and protect yourself from direct sunlight with a hat, sunscreen, and sunglasses. The tropical climate can play havoc

A private hospital in Singapore, a country with superb health care

with open cuts and burns, so treat these immediately. Bring a well-stocked medical kit to help tackle minor problems. If a problem persists, seek medical advice immediately.

Hospitals and Medical Treatment

All large towns in Malaysia have a district hospital as well as private clinics. Most are clean and all doctors speak some English. Private clinics catering specifically for expatriates and tourists are usually more expensive than local facilities. Private hospitals in both Malaysia and Singapore are popular destinations for medical tourism thanks to their keen pricing compared with other countries.

While amenities in the major cities are well developed, with hospitals in Kuala Lumpur such as **Gleneagles Medical Center**

and **Prince Court Medical Centre** among the best, reliable medical care can be difficult to find in rural areas. Brunei has adequate health care facilities but serious health problems are better treated in Singapore, which has world-class medical facilities. Major hospitals here include **Raffles Hospital** and **Singapore General**.

Pharmacies

Even the smallest towns in Malaysia have well-stocked pharmacies. The **Guardian Pharmacy** has a large number of outlets in Malaysia and Singapore. Another well-known pharmacy in Singapore is the **Changi General Hospital Pharmacy**. Medication may be bought over the counter in Malaysia without a doctor's prescription, but that is not possible in Singapore. When traveling, be sure to carry a good supply of your prescription medicines.

Travel and Health Insurance

It is essential to take out travel insurance before traveling to the region. Ensure that it covers you for injury, sickness, accident, emergency hospital treatment, and repatriation as well as medical assistance. You will need extra coverage if you participate in high-risk activities such as diving or mountain climbing.

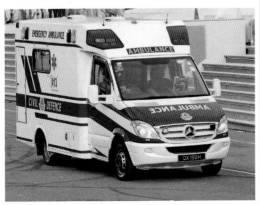

Ambulance in Singapore

Banking and Currency

Banks are generally easy to find in Malaysia, Singapore, and Brunei. Commercial and merchant banks freely allow non-residents to open foreign currency accounts without too many restrictions on the movement of funds through these accounts. Visitors can bring any amount of foreign currency into or out of Malaysia or Singapore, although it must be declared at customs. However, there is a limit of the equivalent of US$10,000 in ringgit allowed into or out of Malaysia.

Citibank, one of the many international banks in Singapore

Banks

Maybank is Malaysia's largest bank. International banks, such as **Citibank** and **HSBC**, are also established in all three countries. Malaysian banking hours are from 9:30am to 4pm from Monday to Friday and 9:30 to 11:30am on Saturday. In the Muslim states of Kedah, Terengganu, and Kelantan, however, the banks are open from 9:30am to 4pm from Saturday to Wednesday, and from 9:30 to 11am on Thursday; they remain closed on Friday. Banks in Singapore are open from 9:30am to 3pm from Monday to Friday, and from 9:30 to 11:30am on Saturday.

Changing Money

Cash and traveler's checks can be exchanged at large branches of all banks for a small service fee. Most major currencies such as dollars and euros are easily exchangeable, though outside the big cities, it can be difficult to exchange other currencies such as the Thai baht or the Indonesian rupiah. Top-end hotels will also exchange dollars and some common currencies, but rates are usually less favorable than at banks. Licensed money changers generally stay open until 6pm and often offer the best rates. Exchange facilities can be difficult to find in remote areas, especially in Sarawak and Sabah, so carry adequate cash at all times.

ATMs

Automatic teller machines (ATMs) are now ubiquitous in Malaysia, except in the more isolated areas, and have long been so in Singapore. ATMs only issue the currency of the respective country, and there is a daily withdrawal limit of around US$800. A fee is levied for each transaction, usually about US$3 on foreign cards.

Credit Cards and Traveler's Checks

Major credit cards can be used in most urban and tourist areas, with **VISA** and **MasterCard** being the most widely accepted. They can also be used at ATMs for withdrawals and at major banks for cash advances. Traveler's checks, commonly issued by **American Express** and VISA, can be exchanged at major banks. Lost or stolen traveler's checks and credit cards must be reported to the issuer.

Currency

The Malaysian unit of currency is the ringgit, denoted by RM before the price of an item. Locals often refer to it, rather confusingly, as dollars. It is further divided into 100 sen although tourists are unlikely to need these small denomination coins unless shopping in a local market. In Singapore, the unit of currency is the Singapore dollar, written S$, which is made up of 100 cents. The Brunei dollar is at par with the Singapore dollar and is legal tender in Singapore.

DIRECTORY

Banks

Citibank
Menara Citibank,165 Jalan Ampang, Kuala Lumpur.
Tel (03) 2383-8585.
W citibank.com.my
40A Orchard Road 01-00, Singapore. **Map** 1 F2.
Tel 6225-5225.
W citibank.com.sg.

HSBC
W hsbc.com.my
W hsbc.com.sg

Maybank
3rd Floor (West Wing),
100 Jalan Tun Perak, Kuala Lumpur. **Map** 4 E1. **Tel** (03) 2074-7266. W maybank.com.my
3 Battery Road, Singapore.
Map 5 E3. **Tel** 6550-7158.
W maybank.com.sg

Credit Cards and Traveler's Checks

American Express
Malaysia **Tel** (0377) 124-314.
Singapore **Tel** 1-800 823-2090.

MasterCard
Malaysia **Tel** 6209-9288.
Singapore **Tel** +1-636-722-7111.

VISA
Malaysia **Tel** 1-800 802997 (stolen cards).
Singapore **Tel** 1-800 448-1250 (stolen cards).

Malay Ringgit

Bank notes are issued in denominations of RM1, RM2, RM5, RM10, RM20, RM50, and RM100. All notes bear the image of Malaysia's first prime minister, Tunku Abdul Rahman. The ringgit is divided into 100 sen, available in coins of 1, 5, 10, 20, and 50 sen.

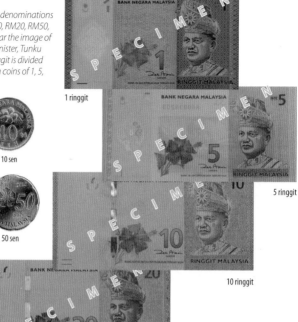

1 ringgit

5 ringgit

10 ringgit

20 ringgit

5 sen

10 sen

20 sen

50 sen

Singapore Dollar

The Singapore dollar is made up of 100 cents, and coins are minted in denominations of 1 (slowly being phased out), 5, 10, 20, and 50 cents. S$1 coins are also circulated. Singapore dollars are issued in notes of S$1, S$2, S$5, S$10, S$20, S$50, S$100, S$500, and S$1,000. There is a S$10,000 note, but it is rare.

1 cent

5 cents

10 cents

20 cents

50 cents

1 Singapore dollar

2 dollars

5 dollars

10 dollars

50 dollars

100 dollars

Communications and Media

The communications network in Malaysia, Singapore, and Brunei is fast and efficient, offering a variety of local, national, and worldwide services. Local and international calls can be made from public telephones in all but the smallest of islands. Cell phone facilities and Internet access are particularly impressive, with networks that compete with the best in the West. The postal system is reliable and well organized. International publications and several locally published English newspapers and magazines are available in big cities.

Card- and coin-operated SingTel public telephone booths in Singapore

International and Local Phone Calls

Public telephones can be found all over Singapore, Malaysia, and Brunei. They are both phonecard- and coin-operated, and most also accept credit cards. **Telekom Malaysia** is a national operator while **SingTel** is Singapore's main telephone company. Local calls in Malaysia cost 10 sen for unlimited time, and 10 cents for three minutes in Singapore. Public telephones in all three countries offer international direct dialing (IDD), and it is best to use a phonecard for these calls. Phonecards of several companies are available at petrol stations and convenience stores, such as 7-Eleven, in denominations of between RM5 and RM50 in Malaysia, S$2 and S$50 in Singapore, and B$10 and B$100 in Brunei. Most big hotels in the region have IDD facilities, but this service is extremely expensive. It will almost always work out

cheapest to phone home using a VoIP (voice over IP) service such as Skype.

Malaysian phone numbers generally consist of six or seven digits, except in Kuala Lumpur which has eight-digit phone numbers. All numbers are preceded by a two- or three-digit area code. Phone numbers all across Singapore consist of eight digits and there is no area code within the country.

Cell Phones

Generally, cell phone network coverage is good in Malaysia, except in the remote regions of Sarawak and Sabah where some networks work better than others. There is complete coverage across Singapore. Cell phones with international roaming service will automatically tune into one of the local networks, but this service is very expensive. It is best to buy a local prepaid SIM card, such as **Maxis**, **Digi**, and **Celcom** in Malaysia, or **SingTel** and **M1** in Singapore; these are all widely available and are inexpensive to buy and top up. Text messaging is cheap, and

many local network companies offer a certain number of free messages as promotions.

Internet Facilities

The entire region has fully embraced the use of the Internet and cheap Internet access is available even in remote locations. Internet cafés in Malaysia charge by the hour and they can be found in the major cities. Rates in Singapore are comparable. Bigger hotels often have Internet access in rooms or in a business center, but this is usually more expensive than the Internet cafés. Many backpacker lodges offer free Internet access to their guests. For those traveling with laptops and smartphones, Wi-Fi facilities are highly advanced in both Singapore and Malaysia. Note that wall sockets accommodate three-pronged, square-pin plugs, and adaptors are easily available in most big towns.

Postal Services

Post offices, run by the **Malaysian Postal Service** and **Singapore Post** respectively, are found all over Malaysia and Singapore and are generally very efficient. Each Malaysian town has a General Post Office (GPO) with poste restante, as do the GPOs in Singapore and Brunei. In Malaysia, post offices are open from 8am to 5pm Monday to Friday, and some Saturdays, though in the states of Kedah, Terengganu, and Kelantan they close on Friday instead of Sunday. The opening hours in

A well-equipped Internet café in Malaysia

Singapore are from 8am to 6pm Monday to Friday, and from 8am to 2pm on Saturday. Brunei post offices open from 7:45am to 4:30pm Monday to Thursday and Saturday, and from 8 to 11am and 2 to 4pm on Friday.

Letters and parcels posted from Malaysian towns usually take a week to reach overseas destinations. Anything posted from remote places in Sabah and Sarawak may take a few weeks to reach its destination. Postcards and aerograms cost 50 sen from Malaysia, and 50 cents from Singapore for the same service. Postcards from Brunei to any destination cost 30 cents. Most major post offices in the region have fax facilities too. Several well-known international courier services such as **DHL**, **Federal Express**, and **United Parcel Service (UPS)** operate in both Malaysia and Singapore as do local courier companies such as **Nationwide Express**.

Television and Radio

Both Malaysia and Singapore have a huge selection of international satellite television channels. Terrestrial TV stations are closely monitored for signs of criticism of the respective governments. RTM1 and RTM2 are Malaysia's government-run TV stations, which broadcast uncontroversial programs in Bahasa Malayu. Commercial stations such as NTV7 feature English news, and international soaps and films.

Six government-run radio stations air programs in various languages including English. Singapore's television and radio channels offer a mixture of English, Tamil, Chinese, and Malay programs. Brunei has five TV channels with many imported programs and two radio channels.

Newspapers and Magazines

A wide range of international publications is available in most major hotels, bookstores, and newsstands in Singapore,

Virtual Malaysia magazine, packed with useful information

and big cities in Malaysia, such as Kuala Lumpur. These include magazines such as *Newsweek* and *Time* and newspapers such as the *International New York Times*. Both countries have local newspapers in English, though government censorship is strict, and dissenting views are rarely published. The leading English daily in Malaysia is *The Star*, besides *New Straits Times*, *The Sun*, and *The Malay Mail*. These are all good sources of information for upcoming events. In Sabah and Sarawak, the leading newspapers are *New Sabah Times* and the *Sarawak Tribune*. Malaysia also publishes some English magazines, including *Virtual Malaysia*. Singapore's main English papers are *The Straits Times* and *New Paper*, while Borneo's main newspaper is *Borneo Bulletin*.

DIRECTORY

Telephone Calls and Cell Phones

Celcom
w celcom.com.my

Digi
w digi.com.my

M1
w m1.com.sg

Maxis
w maxis.com.my

SingTel
w singtel.com

Telekom Malaysia
w tm.com.my

Postal Services

DHL
Malaysia **Tel** (03) 7964-2800.
Singapore **Tel** 6880-6060.
w dhl.com

Federal Express
Malaysia **Tel** (03) 2179-0370.
Singapore **Tel** 1 800 743 2626.
w fedex.com

Malaysian Postal Service
w pos.com.my

Nationwide Express
Malaysia **Tel** (03) 5512-7000.
Singapore **Tel** 6285-4223.

Singapore Post
w singpost.com.sg

United Parcel Service
Malaysia **Tel** (03) 7784-1233.
Singapore **Tel** 6883-7000.
w ups.com/asia

Useful Dialling Codes

- The country code for Malaysia is 60; Singapore 65; Brunei 673.
- To call these countries from abroad, dial your international access code, the country code, the area code minus the first 0 (except Singapore), and the number.
- For international calls from Malaysia dial 00, from Singapore dial 001, and from Brunei 01, followed by the country code, the area code minus the first 0, and the local number.

- Country codes: USA and Canada 1; Australia 61; UK 44; New Zealand 64; France 33.
- Calls between Malaysia and Singapore are considered long-distance, not international calls.
- For interstate calls in Malaysia dial the area code followed by the number. For calls within a state, omit the area code.
- For directory enquiries in Malaysia and Singapore, dial 103; in Brunei, dial 0213.
- For the international operator in Malaysia, dial 108; in Singapore, dial 104.

TRAVEL INFORMATION

Most overseas visitors to Malaysia and Singapore arrive at Kuala Lumpur International Airport (KLIA) and Changi Airport, respectively. Many visitors prefer to arrive overland taking a train or a bus from Thailand, and a few opt for cruise ships. Although most towns in Malaysia are well connected by domestic flights and buses, remote areas in Sarawak and Sabah suffer from poor road conditions. These days, increasing numbers of tourists opt for low-cost carriers, such

as Tigerair in Singapore and AirAsia in Malaysia, to make short hops within Southeast Asia, as well as long-haul flights to Australia, and India. Traveling by rail can be fun, with comfortable sleeper compartments for long journeys, though the network is limited to a couple of lines. Both Singapore and Kuala Lumpur have good public transport services, such as the Light Rail Transit (LRT) and the Mass Rapid Transport System (MRT), that make life easy for visitors to these cities.

Budget airline AirAsia, one of several low-cost options

Arriving by Air

Over 70 international carriers connect Singapore and Malaysia to most continents. These include **Air Canada**, **Cathay Pacific**, **China Airlines**, **Emirates Airlines**, **Japan Airlines**, **Garuda Indonesia**, **British Airways**, **KLM**, **Qantas**, **Thai Airways**, and **United Airlines**.

Low-cost carriers such as **AirAsia**, **Silk Air**, **Tigerair**, **Malindo Air** *(see p332)*, and **Firefly** offer several options for passengers flying in from other countries. There are flights from Singapore to all of Malaysia's regional airports.

Malaysia Airlines (MAS) and **Singapore Airlines**, the national carriers, are well connected to most parts of the world. There is a regular service between Kuala Lumpur and Singapore, operated by both airlines as well as AirAsia and Tigerair. Many international airlines use either **KLIA** or

BALAI KETIBAAN
ARRIVAL HALL

Airport arrival hall sign

Changi Airports as their gateways to Southeast Asia, or as stopover points from Europe to New Zealand and Australia. Both airports are super-modern and well equipped with all the facilities that travelers might need, such as shops, restaurants, and Internet access. KLIA's second terminal, KLIA2, caters primarily to low-cost airlines and is connected to the main terminal by train, which takes 3 minutes. Passengers arriving at Changi Airport, 10 miles (16 km) from central Singapore, have a choice of transport to reach the city, including MRT, limousine services, and airport shuttles.

Air Fares

There is a wide range of tickets available for travel to and around Singapore and Malaysia, but the prices vary seasonally. During the peak months from

July to August, and December to January, prices soar for flights from the USA and Europe.

With over 70 international carriers using the main airports there is stiff competition, and it makes sense to compare rates before booking a flight. For travelers already in Southeast Asia, it is worth considering budget airlines such as Tigerair and AirAsia, which offer fares comparable to those on buses and trains. The ticket price is usually exclusive of international departure tax.

Arriving by Land

Traveling by train is a popular way to enter Malaysia from Thailand, crossing the border at Padang Besar, changing at Butterworth for Penang or continuing to Kuala Lumpur's **KL Sentral** or Singapore's **Woodlands Train Checkpoint**. The **Eastern & Oriental Express (E & O)**, combining luxury with classic sightseeing, covers the route from Bangkok to Singapore, passing through

Luxurious interior of the Eastern & Oriental Express

Kuala Lumpur's KL Sentral. The main route for buses and taxis from Thailand is via Bukit Kayu Hitam at the Malaysian border. A causeway connects Johor Bahru at the southern tip of Malaysia to Singapore. From Pontianak in Kalimantan (Indonesian Borneo), it is possible to enter Sarawak in Malaysian Borneo. The main terminal in Kuala Lumpur is the **Pudu Sentral** station though more and more long-distance buses are using Terminal Bersepadu Selatan (TBS) which is south of the city. Singapore has many different bus stations: check in advance which one you will embark from.

Arriving by Sea

Both countries can be reached by sea. Malaysia has several authorized entry points. Some cruise liners, such as **Star Cruises**,

travel regularly between Singapore, Port Klang, Penang, Pulau Langkawi, and even Phuket in Thailand. A ferry link connects Penang and Melaka on the peninsula with Medan and Dumai in Sumatra (Indonesia). There are regular longboat services between Pulau Langkawi and Satun in South Thailand. Ferries and small boats also connect Singapore to Tanjong Belungkor in the state of Johor in Malaysia.

Organized Tours

The most economical way to visit Malaysia and Singapore is by booking a place on an organized tour. A package deal usually includes flights, hotels, road transport, guides, and admission fee to tourist sights for little more than the cost of a flight. Tour companies such as Borneo Adventure (see p317) offer exciting itineraries.

A cruise liner docked at Langkawi

DIRECTORY

Arriving by Air

AirAsia
Kuala Lumpur.
W airasia.com

Air Canada
Kuala Lumpur.
Tel (03) 2148-8596.
Singapore:
Tel 6256-1198.
W aircanada.ca

British Airways
Kuala Lumpur:
Tel (03) 7712-4747.
Singapore:
Tel 6622-1747.
W britishairways.com

Changi Airport
Singapore. Tel 6542-4422.
W changiairport.com

Cathay Pacific
Kuala Lumpur:
Tel (03) 2035-2777.
Singapore:
Tel 6533-1333.
W cathaypacific.com

China Airlines
Kuala Lumpur:
Tel (03) 2148-9417.
Singapore: Tel 6737-2211.
W china-airlines.com

Emirates Airlines
Kuala Lumpur:
Tel (03) 6207-4999.
Singapore: Tel 6735-3535.
W emirates.com

Firefly
Kuala Lumpur.
Tel (03) 7845-4543.
W fireflyz.com.my

Garuda Indonesia
Kuala Lumpur:
Tel (03) 2162-2811.
Singapore: Tel 6250-2888.
W garuda-indonesia.com

Japan Airlines
Kuala Lumpur:
Tel (03) 2161-1722.
Singapore: Tel 6221-0522.
W jal.com

Jetstar
Singapore. Tel 6822-2288.
W jetstar.com

KLIA
Kuala Lumpur.
Tel (03) 8776-4386.
W klia.com.my

KLM
Kuala Lumpur:
Tel (03) 2711-9811.
Singapore: Tel 6737-7622.
W klm.com

Malaysia Airlines (MAS)
Kuala Lumpur:
Tel (03) 7846-3000.
Singapore:
Tel 6336-6777.
W malaysiaairlines.com

Qantas
Kuala Lumpur:
Tel (03) 6279-5033.
Singapore:
Tel 6415-7373.
W qantas.com.au

Silk Air
Singapore.
Tel 6223-8888.
W silkair.com

Singapore Airlines
Kuala Lumpur:
Tel (03) 2692-3122.
Singapore:
Tel 6223-8888.
W singaporeair.com

Thai Airways
Kuala Lumpur:
Tel (03) 2031-2900.
Singapore:
Tel 1-800 2249-977.
W thaiair.com

Tigerair
Singapore.
Tel 6538-4437.
W tigerairways.com

United Airlines
Kuala Lumpur:
Tel (03) 2161-1433.
Singapore: Tel 6873-3533.
W ual.com

Arriving by Land

E & O Express
W belmond.com

KL Sentral
Kuala Lumpur.
Tel (03) 2279-8888.

Pudu Sentral Bus Station
Kuala Lumpur.
Tel (03) 2274-6063.

Woodlands Train Checkpoint
Singapore.
Tel 6221-3390.

Arriving by Sea

Star Cruises
Malaysia.
Tel (03) 3103-1313.
W starcruises.com

Traveling by Air

Malaysia has a very good network of internal flights, making air travel a comfortable and convenient way of getting around. The national carrier, Malaysia Airlines (MAS), is well connected to almost all popular tourist destinations. Singapore itself is too small to require internal flights. With the advent of budget airlines, such as the hugely successful AirAsia, the much smaller Malindo Air, Firefly and MAS Wings, the cost of flying has reduced considerably. Most big towns in Malaysia now have an airport, and it is easy to get tickets either through local travel agencies or by booking online. Flights are generally punctual, efficient, and inexpensive, which is particularly useful for visitors who want to see as much of the country as possible within a limited period of time.

Passengers waiting to check in at an airport counter

Domestic Airlines

Until recently, Malaysia Airlines *(see p330)* had a virtual mono-poly on all domestic flights throughout Malaysia. The situation has now changed with the arrival of AirAsia *(see p330)* and **MAS Wings** (a subsidiary of Malaysia Airlines), both of which offer low-cost, no-frills flights with limited seating space and payment for in-flight refreshments. AirAsia now flies on long-haul international routes, while MAS Wings operates turbo-propeller plane services in Malaysian Borneo.

Malindo Air flies out of KLIA. Destinations include several cities in Malaysia as well as India, Thailand and Nepal.

Domestic Airports

All Malaysian Airlines domestic flights depart from the state-of-the-art Kuala Lumpur International Airport (KLIA)

(see p330), the largest and most well-connected airport in Malaysia. KLIA2 is the airport's low-cost terminal. The airport connects to KL Sentral via the Express Rail Link. Malindo Air operates some flights from Skypark Sultan Abdul Aziz Shah Airport, Kuala Lumpur's former international airport.

In Peninsular Malaysia, there are airports at Ipoh, Penang, Kuala Lumpur, Alor Setar, Langkawi, Kota Bharu, Kuantan, Kuala Terengganu, and Johor Bahru. Airports in Sarawak include Kuching, Sibu, Mukah, Miri, Bintulu, Belaga, Lawas, Mulu, Ba Kalalan, Long Akah, Long Banga, Long Lellang, Long Seridan, Bario, and Limbang. In Sabah, there are airports at Kota Kinabalu, Labuan, Kudat, Sandakan, Lahad Datu, Tawau, as well as Semporna.

The larger airports in all these states are serviced by both MAS and the fast expanding network of AirAsia.

However, the smaller towns are connected in most cases only by the services of MAS Wings.

Flight Network

While most major Malaysian towns are linked by direct flights, smaller towns also have connecting networks. Johor Bahru provides services to Penang, Ipoh, Kuala Lumpur, Kota Bahru, Kuching, Sibu, Miri, Kota Kinabalu, Sandakan, and Tawau.

In Malaysian Borneo, while the majority of flights originate in the provincial capitals of Kota Kinabalu and Kuching, it is also possible to make short hops without returning to the original point using the rural air services. Several 19-seater and 50-seater planes help maintain communications with the remote provinces. A visitor in Sarawak can therefore go from Kuching to Mulu via Sibu and Miri, or from Kota Kinabalu to Semporna via Sandakan in Sabah. There are also regular direct flights between both Miri and Mulu in Sarawak and Kota Kinabalu in Sabah.

Tickets and Reservations

Tickets for flights on any of the airlines listed in the directory can be purchased from travel agents, although these days it is easier to book online with a credit card. All airlines permit online booking through their websites and e-tickets are the norm. While there is usually

MAS Wings offers budget domestic and regional services

some flexibility about changing dates for reservations with major carriers such as MAS and Singapore Airlines, budget airlines do not allow rescheduling. Changing the date of the flight after making a booking with a budget airline requires payment of a penalty or the purchase of a new ticket.

Fares and Special Discounts

With the introduction of budget airlines in Southeast Asia, travelers have a wide range of travel options. Low-cost carriers connect Malaysia with the Middle East and Australia. Checking in luggage, food, and entertainment cost extra. Also, by the time tax and fuel surcharges are added, flights are no longer as cheap as they first appear. Potential travelers need to weigh the pros and cons of traveling with different carriers. It is also worth checking promotions and offers from MAS and

Singapore Airlines before making any reservations. Passengers arriving by international flights can also get a Visit Malaysia pass issued by MAS, which entitles them to five domestic flights for US$199. AirAsia also does a similar pass that includes flights to its neighboring ASEAN countries. The Singapore Stopover Holiday offered by Singapore Airlines includes free bus rides and entry to several attractions as well as special hotel rates and discounts at shopping outlets.

Travel Agencies

Both countries have travel agents who can assist with travel arrangements, hotel bookings, and guided tours. Travel agency staff should be experts in the region who can advise you as to where to go and where to stay according to your personal requirements. Package holidays are a particularly good idea in Sabah

and Sarawak as these regions can be difficult and time-consuming for independent travelers to get around in. **AD Travel**, **Asian Overland Services**, **Borneo Eco Tours**, **Crest Travel and Tours**, **Discovery Tours** in Sabah, **Discovery Tours and Travel** in Singapore, **East West Executive Travellers**, **Ezz Travel**, **Honeyworld Holidays**, **Planet Travel**, **Malaysia Tourism**, **STA Travel**, **Skyzone Tours and Travel**, **Transtar Travel**, **Pedati Saujana Holidays**, **Star Holiday Mart**, **TDK Travel and Tours**, and **TVI Holidays** offer planned holidays.

Travel agency signboards lining a street in Little India, Georgetown

DIRECTORY

Domestic Airlines

Malindo Air
W malindoair.com

MAS Wings
Tel (03) 7843-3000.
W maswings.com.my

Travel Agencies

AD Travel
112 Jalan Imbi,
Kuala Lumpur.
Tel (03) 2148-4999.
W adtravel.com.my

Asian Overland Services
39–40 Jalan Mamanda 9,
Ampang, Kuala Lumpur.
Tel (03) 4252-9100.
W asianoverland. com. my

Borneo Eco Tours
Lot 1, Pusat Perindustrian,
Kolombong Jaya, Jalan
Kolombong, Kota
Kinabalu, Sabah.
Tel (88) 438-300.

Crest Travel and Tours
111 North Bridge Rd,
05–08 Peninsula Plaza,
Singapore. **Tel** 6337-9189.
W cresttravel.sg

Discovery Tours
Lot G.22, Ground Floor,
Wisma Sabah, Jalan Tun
Fuad Stephens, Kota
Kinabalu, Sabah. **Tel** (88)
257-368. W discovery
tours.com.my

Discovery Tours and Travel
Tel 6733-4333.
W discoverytours.com.
sg

East West Executive Travellers
24 Sin Ming Lane,
03-105 Midview City,
Singapore. **Tel** 6336-6811.
W eastwestplanners.
com

Ezz Travel
62E Ground Floor,
Jalan Genuang, Segamat,
Johor. **Tel** (07) 931-6601.
W ezztravel.com

Honeyworld Holidays
24 Raffles Place,
Singapore.
Tel 6532-2232.
W honeyworld
holidays.com

Malaysia Tourism
17th Floor, Putra World
Trade Center, Jalan Tun
Ismail, Kuala Lumpur.
Tel (03) 2163-0162.
W tourism.gov.my

Pedati Saujana Holidays
2A Bangunan MPSP,
Kedah Darul Aman.
Tel (04) 425-2052.
W pedati-saujana.com

Planet Travel
Block 925 Yishun Central
1, Singapore.
Tel 6286-9009.
W planettravel. com.sg

Skyzone Tours and Travel
Lot 3.05–08 Shaw Parade,
Kuala Lumpur.
Tel (03) 2141-8588.
W skyzone.my

Star Holiday Mart
29/30 Duxton Road,
Singapore. **Tel** 6735-9009.
W starmart.com.sg

STA Travel
400 Orchard Road,
Singapore. **Tel** 6737-7188.
W statravel.com.sg

TDK Travel and Tours
B6 Sri Dagangan 2,
Kuantan, Pahang Darul.
Tel (09) 513-4466.
W tdktravel.blogspot.hk

Transtar Travel
01–15 Golden Mile
Complex, Singapore.
Tel 6299-9009.
W transtar.com.sg

TVI Holidays
1 Park Road, Singapore.
Tel 6533-2533.
W tviholidays.com

Traveling by Train and Boat

While domestic flights are cheap and convenient for visitors with limited time, boat and train travel offers travelers a sense of the geographical variety and richness of Malaysia and Singapore. The railroad connects many major towns in Peninsular Malaysia, while visitors to Sabah can experience rail travel on a short stretch from Kota Kinabalu to Tenom. A range of boats is available to tourists, from dugout canoes to luxury cruise liners. Many, such as the *ekspres* boats of Sarawak, have a distinctive character found nowhere else in Malaysia. Boat and train journeys take longer than flights and are suitable for travelers on an extended holiday.

KTM Komuter train at a Malaysian station

Railroad Network

The Malaysian railroad system, **Keretapi Tanah Melayu Berhad (KTM)**, is a modern, economical, and comfortable mode of transport. The railroad was the only way to get around the country before the construction of the peninsula's road network, and many of the stations in the interior still retain their original colonial architecture.

The network consists of two main lines, with a few minor branches running down to the west coast. From its starting point in Singapore, the West Coast line heads north to Kuala Lumpur, then on to Ipoh and Butterworth, before finally connecting at the border town of Padang Besar with Thai Railways.

The second route is the East Coast line, popularly known as The Jungle Railway *(see p155)*. Branching off the West Coast line at Gemas, about 37 miles (60 km) northeast of Melaka, it heads north through Kuala Lipis to Tumpat on the northeast coast near the Thai border.

In Borneo, the only railroad line is in Sabah, and visitors can ride the short stretch from Kota Kinabalu to Tenom, passing through the long gorge of the Sungai Padas *(see p187)*.

Construction of a high-speed rail link between Kuala Lumpur and Singapore is expected to start in 2016; this should cut the journey time to 90 minutes from the current 8 hours.

Trains

There are two types of trains: express trains that stop only at the main stations, and the slower and cheaper local trains that also stop at smaller stations. Express trains usually consist of first and second class, while local trains are generally third class. All first- and second-class carriages have sleeper berths on overnight trains; they have air conditioning, which is generally very cold, making a jacket or blanket a necessity.

In a class of its own is the **Eastern & Oriental Express (E & O)**. Run by the same people who operate the legendary Venice–Simplon Orient Express, it offers similar five-star service and standards. The train runs a couple of times a month between Singapore and Bangkok, and the journey takes 3 days/2 nights. Traveling in the reverse direction, Bangkok to Singapore, takes 4 days/3 nights. The high prices include a private sleeper, meals, a visit to the Bridge on the River Kwai, and a brief tour of Georgetown in Penang. Travelers have high praise for the bygone glamor and unique experience offered by the company – for many, it's a once-in-a-lifetime trip.

Train Tickets, Fares, and Reservations

Tickets can be purchased at all mainline stations, through the KTM website, or from travel agents. Fares for first-class travel are about double the price of second class, which is approximately double that of third class. Sleeping berths are available for a small charge in addition to the basic fare.

Tourist rail passes offering unlimited train travel are also available. Visitors can pay US$35 for 5 days, US$55 for 10 days, and US$70 for 15 days. The passes are discounted by almost 50 percent for children. The fare from Singapore to Bangkok on the luxurious E & O Express is US$2,280.

Advance booking is advisable for express trains if a sleeping berth is required.

Ticket barrier at a platform in Kuala Lumpur

Passengers boarding ferries on the Batang Rajang

Boat Facilities, Services, and Fares

With regular services to popular destinations, boats and ferries are among the most popular ways to get to riverside towns and offshore islands. Most traditional bumboats have been replaced by faster and sleeker *ekpres* boats that offer basic seating with canopies for protection from the elements. Since they are intended to be used only for short journeys, there are usually no toilets or facilities for buying refreshments.

Although most boats are quite modern, safety precautions can be somewhat lax, with some operators overloading their vessels or not insisting on the use of life jackets. Services are also likely to be temporarily suspended due to inclement weather during the monsoon.

Boat fares vary according to the length of the journey and the condition of the vessel, but an average hour-long journey costs about RM15. Advance booking for tickets is not required, and payment can be made at the jetty or on board.

Boat Routes and Cruises

In Malaysia, many major towns along the coasts and along rivers are connected by ferry, or *ekspres* boats. On the west coast of the peninsula, Butterworth is linked to Pulau Penang by a car ferry, which remains popular despite the existence of a road bridge between the mainland and the island. There is a twice-daily ferry service to Pulau

Langkawi from Penang, and hourly services both from Kuala Kedah and Kuala Perlis. Regular ferries run between Lumut and Pulau Pangkor.

On the east coast, there are several daily ferries from Merang to Pulau Redang and from Kuala Besut to the Perhentian Islands. Visitors to Pulao Tioman can get a ferry from Mersing in Malaysia. There are no boat services connecting Peninsular Malaysia with Malaysian Borneo.

In Sarawak, longboats and *ekpres* boats are the principal methods of travel. They link Kuching with Sibu, Kapit, and Belaga along Batang Rajang, while in the north of the province, they are the main modes of transport along Sungai Baram. While there are no riverboat services in Sabah, a regular ferry runs between Menumbok and Pulau Labuan.

Visitors to Singapore can enjoy a cruise on a traditional bumboat along the Singapore River or around the southern islands. Several companies organize these cruises, including **Riverboat Cruises**, **Singapore River Cruise**, **Singapore River Explorer**, **Singapore Island Cruises**, and **Sindo Ferry**.

Passengers purchasing tickets at a ferry port

Traveling by Road

The roads in Malaysia and Singapore are generally in very good condition and the network is comprehensive, making it easy to get around. There is an extensive and inexpensive bus system, and both state-run and private companies operate services that connect many major towns in Malaysian Borneo and most towns on the peninsula, with good connections to Singapore as well. Long-distance taxis are a good option for group travel, while car hire is reasonably priced and a good alternative for those who prefer flexible itineraries.

Long-distance luxury buses run by Transnasional

Road Network

Peninsular Malaysia's road network is excellent, offering one of the best ways of exploring the country. The main road that runs along the peninsula is the North–South Highway, a six-lane toll road between Johor Bahru in the south and the Thai border. Route 8 goes up the east coast, linking Bentong, near Kuala Lumpur, with Kota Bharu in the north. Route 4 and Route 145 connect the east and west coasts of the peninsula. Various other roads connect towns in the interior.

Due to the rugged terrain, the network in Malaysian Borneo is limited. In Sarawak the only long-distance road runs up the coast between Kuching and Miri, although there are numerous good roads around Kuching itself. Sabah has a comparatively weak network, especially the roads in the interior; however, the road heading north and south along the coast from Kota Kinabalu is good.

Malaysia has two land bridge connections with Singapore – a causeway between Johor Bahru and Singapore and a second link between Tuas in Singapore and Geylang Patah in Malaysia.

Long-Distance Buses

Traveling around Malaysia by bus is fast, comfortable, and cheap. Several private operators, including **Plusliner** and **Transnasional**, run air-conditioned luxury buses between major towns. Buses linking smaller towns make more stops and are not all air-conditioned. In rural areas, regular buses are replaced by minibuses or converted pick-up trucks. Other major bus operators include **Sri Maju**, **Transtar**, **Aeroline**, **Hasry Express**, **Biaramas**, **Tung Ma Express**, and **Dyana Express**.

There are bus services to Singapore from several Malaysian towns, including Kuala Lumpur, Melaka, Ipoh, and Penang. Buses from Malaysia stop at Golden Mile Complex, Kovan Hub, Boon Lay Shopping Centre, The Plaza Beach Road, and Golden Mile Tower. Note

that long-distance bus terminals are often on the outskirts of a town, requiring a local bus or taxi ride to get there, and that long-distance buses tend to set out in the early morning or evening.

Bus Tickets and Fares

It is a good idea to reserve tickets a day ahead, especially during public holidays when many locals are traveling. Most people buy their tickets at the bus company office located at each bus station just before boarding, but to guarantee a place, you can book tickets up to one month ahead on www.easybook.com for bus travel on many different operators across Malaysia and between Malaysia and Singapore. Departure times are displayed on a placard in front of the office. Fares are reasonable and depend on the comfort provided by the bus.

Long-Distance Taxis

Taxi stand sign

Long-distance taxis or share taxis are worth considering, especially when traveling in groups of three or four. Solo travelers will need to wait until the driver has a full complement of four passengers, as these taxis operate on a shared-cost basis. The waiting time is usually not long, and is shorter early in the morning. It is also possible to charter the whole taxi for the price of four single fares. There is usually a long-distance taxi stand right next to the long-distance bus station in each town, with fares for various destinations posted on a board. Taxi fares are about double the bus fare, but the service is much quicker. Night journeys may have an additional fare.

A long-distance taxi

Car and Motorbike Rentals

Renting a car offers travelers the freedom to change their travel plans at will. Rental agencies usually require that drivers be over 23 years of age. Overseas visitors will need a license written in English script.

Car hire rates are higher in Malaysian Borneo than on the peninsula. While insurance is generally included in the price, it is wise to spend extra for Collision Damage Waiver (CDW) insurance, which covers costs resulting from accidents. Even better, buy a rental excess insurance policy ahead of time in your home country. Renting a car in Singapore costs more than in Malaysia, with rental and fuel costing almost double. There are also surcharges for driving hired cars from Malaysia to Singapore and vice versa.

Hiring a motorbike is less formal, and the guesthouse owners or shops who rent them

Motorbikes lined up for hire outside a rental agency

out rarely ask to see a license. If you do not have a license, however, your insurance is invalid. Rental rates are reasonable, and this can be a good way of exploring islands, such as Pulau Penang and Pulau Langkawi, or attractions on the outskirts of cities.

All major rental agencies, including **Budget**, **Hertz**, **Avis**, and **Thrifty** are represented, along with local agencies, such as **Mayflower**, **Orix**, **Hornbill**, **Pronto**, **Extra**, **Kinabalu**, and **Popular**, which sometimes offer

cheaper rates. While renting from a local firm may be tempting, it could be a problem if the vehicle breaks down far from the rental office and the company has no local backup, so enquire about their network before signing a deal. Visitors should note that 4WD vehicles for rent are scarce, so those heading for the hills should employ a reliable tour operator who can provide an appropriate vehicle with a driver.

Rules of the Road

Vehicles drive on the left in both Singapore and Malaysia. The use of seat belts is obligatory, and within cities, the speed limit is 31 mph (50 km/h). Most road signs are self-explanatory, except for the ubiquitous *awas* in Malaysia, meaning "be careful." There are heavy penalties in both countries for those convicted of drinking and driving.

DIRECTORY

Long-Distance Buses

Aeroline
Kuala Lumpur:
Tel (03) 6258-8800.
Singapore:
Tel 6733-7010.
W aeroline.com.my

Biaramas
Lot 2922 & 2923,
Jalan Datuk Tawi Sli,
Kuching,
Malaysia.
Tel (082) 456-999.
W easybus.com

Dyana Express
Northern Bus Terminal,
Kota Kinabalu.
Tel (088) 389-997.

Hasry Express
Cnr Lavender St & Kallang
Bahru Rd, Singapore.
Tel 6294-9306.
W easybus.com

Plusliner
Kuala Lumpur:
Tel (03) 2274-0499.
Singapore:
Tel 6256-5755.
W plusliner.com.my

Sri Maju
Nos. 2, 4, & 6,
Jalan Bendahara, Ipoh,
Malaysia. **Tel** (05) 253-
5367. W srimaju.com

Transnasional
Kuala Lumpur.
Tel (03) 4047-7878.
W transnasional.
com.my

Transtar
Singapore. **Tel** 6299-9009.
W transtar.com.sg

Tung Ma Express
Jalan Padang, Kota
Kinabalu, Malaysia.
Tel (019) 882-7334.

Car and Motorbike Rentals

Avis
B-16, Main Terminal,
KLIA, Malaysia.
Tel (03) 9222-2558.
Terminal 2, Singapore.
Tel 6542-8855.
W avis.com

Budget
Tel 1-800 801-563.
W budget.com

Extra
Beverley Hotel,
Jalan Kemajuan, Kota
Kinabalu, Malaysia.
Tel (088) 218-160.
W e-erac-online.com

Hertz
B10, Terminal Building,
KLIA, Malaysia.
Tel (03) 8776-4507.
W hertz-malaysia.com

15 Scotts Road,
Thong-Teck Building,
Singapore.
Map 1 F2.
Tel 6734-4646. W hertz.
com

Hornbill
Lot 99, Jalan Datuk
Abang Abdul Rahim,
Kuching, Malaysia.
Tel (082) 343-489.
W hbcrsb@streamyx.
com

Kinabalu
Karamunsing Complex,
Kota Kinabalu,
Malaysia.
Tel (088) 232-602.
W kinabalurac.com.my

Mayflower
Mayflower Building,
Kuala Lumpur.
Tel (03) 6252-1888.
W mayflower carrental.
com.my

Orix
Counter C2, Arrival
Level, Main Terminal
Building, KLIA, Malaysia.
Tel (03) 8787-4294.
W orixauto.com.my

Popular
501 Guillemard Road,
Singapore. **Tel** 6742-8888.
W popularcar.com

Pronto
No. 98, Jalan Padungan,
Kuching, Malaysia.
Tel (082) 237-889.
W prontocarrental.com

Thrifty
20 Changi North
Crescent, Singapore.
Tel 6741-6222.
W thrifty.rentals.
com.sg

Getting around KL & Singapore

Both Kuala Lumpur and Singapore are relatively easy to get around, as there is a variety of transport methods at a visitor's disposal. The Light Rail Transit (LRT) and Mass Rapid Transit (MRT) metro systems are swift and efficient. Bus lines cover both cities quite thoroughly, and metered taxis are convenient and easy to find. Though traffic in KL is a growing problem, some trishaws, or three-wheeled bicycle taxis, still ply the streets offering fun but expensive rides for tourists. The most enjoyable way of getting around is walking, if you can cope with the heat, but, while Singapore is pedestrian-friendly, Kuala Lumpur is not easy to walk around.

Fully air-conditioned MRT train traveling on an elevated track

Pedestrians window-shopping in Kuala Lumpur's Chinatown

Walking

All the main areas of interest in Kuala Lumpur, such as the colonial district, Chinatown, and Little India, are close together and can easily be covered on foot. However, as six-lane roads and flyovers divide Kuala Lumpur into sections unconnected by sidewalks, strolling beyond these areas is unviable. Traffic is fast-moving and heavy, so visitors should always be alert.

The situation is better in Singapore. The city center is pedestrian-friendly and conducive to strolling around or window-shopping, especially around Chinatown. The hot and humid climate of both cities requires precautions such as using sunblock, carrying enough drinking water, and limiting walks to a few hours to avoid exhaustion. If you have an iPhone, the handy app GoThere.sg tells you how to get to any destination in Singapore on foot or by taxi, train, or bus.

Metros

In Kuala Lumpur the LRT is a fast and economical way of getting around the city, with trains arriving every 5 to 15 minutes between 6am and 11:20pm. It is possible to pay for a single trip, but it is better to get a myrapid card if you are staying a few days; this stored-value ticket can also be used on Rapid KL buses and the monorail. For tourists, the KL Travel Pass includes the KLIA Ekspres from the airport and all trains and buses in the city. Buy it at the KL Ekspres ticket counter at the airport. Singapore's MRT is often acclaimed as the best metro in the world because of its clean carriages, speedy service, and low prices. The most convenient way to pay is the stored-value ticket, called an EZ-link card worth S$12, which includes a S$5 deposit and is valid on all MRT, LRT, and bus journeys. Any credit on the card can be reclaimed at a card outlet on departure. Tourist day tickets can be bought for 1–3 days of unlimited travel Tickets can be purchased online, at MRT stations and Singapore visitor centers. Smoking, eating, and drinking are prohibited on the MRT.

Buses

Kuala Lumpur is well served by buses, which run at close intervals between 6am and 11pm, although poor signage and problems with route information can occasionally cause visitors some confusion. One of the most useful services for tourists is the Go-KL free shuttle buses that criss-cross the city linking many downtown locations. There are 65 stops in total, on four lines.

In Singapore there are two major bus companies, **SBS Transit** and **SMRT**, who also run train and taxi services. As on the MRT, the easiest way to pay the fare is the EZ-link card, which must be tapped against a machine when boarding and leaving the bus. If paying by cash, on boarding the bus drop the exact fare in the box as no change is given.

Passengers waiting to board a city bus in Kuala Lumpur

Taxis

Taxis can be particularly useful when arriving in an unknown city. In Kuala Lumpur, red and white taxis charge an initial fare of RM3 for the first mile, and 10 cents for every 220 yards (200 m) thereafter. Drivers often decline to use the meter with tourists, and try to agree on a fixed fare that is inevitably higher than the meter rate. It is wise to confirm the usual fare for a planned journey with your hotel before setting out. Most fares in the city should be RM15, but 50 percent extra is charged after midnight. If traveling from KL Sentral or the airport, a coupon system is in place to avoid scams.

Taxis are plentiful on the streets of Singapore. They have a flag fare of S$3 for the first kilometer, and 20 cents for every 400 meters. There are, however, provisions for surcharges. **SBS Transit**, **Comfort Cabs**, **Blue Cab**, **City Cab**, and **Smart** are among the taxi service providers here. The apps MyTeksi and GrabTaxi are local alternatives to Uber.

Organized Tours

Taking an organized tour is the ideal way of seeing a city's major sights in relative comfort, and there are plenty of companies that offer such tours in both Kuala Lumpur and Singapore. In Kuala Lumpur, apart from grand full-day tours or 3-hour city highlight tours, which take in the Petronas

The enormous Petronas Towers, one of the highlights of a city tour

Towers, the Royal Palace, Chinatown, the Lake Gardens, and the National Museum, there are walking tours, architectural tours, and museum tours. **Tour East**, **Kuala Lumpur Travel Tour**, and **Tours by Locals** offer a variety of engaging tour options. **Food Tour Malaysia** devises mouthwatering daytime and evening excursions.

In Singapore tours usually take in Orchard Road, Little India, and Chinatown, though specialist tours are also available, covering themes such as World War II sights, Asian cuisine, and Singapore's throbbing nightlife. For a more personalized tour, with a tailor-made itinerary, it is best to contact the **Registered Tourist Guides Association of Singapore**. **Holiday Tours**, **RMG Tours**, and **SH Tours** also organize packaged excursions of Singapore.

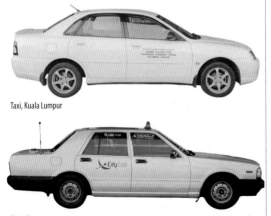

Taxi, Kuala Lumpur

Taxi, Singapore

DIRECTORY

Buses

Rapid KL
No.1 Jalan PJU 1A/46, Petaling Jaya, Selangor, Malaysia.
Tel 1-800 388-228.
Ⓦ rapidkl.com.my

SBS Transit
205 Braddell Road, Singapore.
Tel 1-800 287-2727.
Ⓦ sbstransit.com.sg

SMRT
Singapore.
Tel 1-800 336-8900.
Ⓦ smrt.com.sg

Taxis

Blue Cab
Kuala Lumpur.
Tel (03) 8948-2193.

City Cab
Singapore.
Tel 6552-111.

Comfort Cabs
Kuala Lumpur.
Tel (03) 8024-0507.

SBS Transit
Singapore.
Tel 6555-8888.

Smart
Singapore.
Tel 6485-7777.

Organized Tours

Food Tour Malaysia
Ⓦ foodtourmalaysia.com

Holiday Tours
Singapore. **Tel** 6738-2622.

Kuala Lumpur Travel Tour
Kuala Lumpur.
Tel (01) 7633-0062.
Ⓦ kualalumpurtraveltour.com

Registered Tourist Guides Association of Singapore
Singapore.
Tel 6339-2114.

RMG Tours
Singapore.
Tel 6220-1661.

SH Tours
Singapore.
Tel 6734-9923.

Tour East
Kuala Lumpur.
Tel (04) 227-4522.
Ⓦ toureast.net

Tours by Locals
Ⓦ toursbylocals.com

General Index

Acknowledgments

Dorling Kindersley would like to thank the many people whose help and assistance contributed to the preparation of this book.

Contributors
David Bowden is an Australian expatriate who has worked in Asia for many years. He calls Malaysia home and writes and photographs for some of the leading national and regional newspapers and magazines.

Ron Emmons is a British writer and photographer who has lived in Thailand since the 1990s. He is author of the DK *Top 10 Travel Guide to Bangkok*.

Andrew Forbes has lived in Chiang Mai, Thailand for the past 20 years, where he is editor of CPA Media. He has visited Malaysia regularly over three decades and has contributed to the DK *Eyewitness Travel Guide to Vietnam and Angkor Wat*.

Naiya Sivaraj has been a traveler and writer for as long as she can remember, and has recently started to make a living by combining the two. She is currently pursuing a journalism program at UCLA.

Richard Watkins was born in Wales and is a freelance travel writer. He has written for a number of publications including various newspapers and magazines in the UK, USA, and Australia.

History Consultant
Nicholas White is Reader in Imperial and Commonwealth History at Liverpool John Moores University, UK. He has written a number of books and articles on Malaysian history including (with J.M. Barwise) *A Traveller's History of South East Asia*, published by Windrush/Cassell, 2002.

Phrase Book Writer
E Ulrich Kratz.

Fact Checkers
Erik Fearn, Angelia Teo.

Proofreaders
Shonali Yadav, Stewart J. Wild, Leonie Wilding.

Indexer
Jyoti Dhar.

Design and Editorial
Publisher Douglas Amrine
List Manager Lucinda Smith
Managing Art Editor Jane Ewart,
Managing Editor Kathryn Lane
Project Editor Ros Walford
Senior Art Editor Paul Jackson
Project Art Editor Sonal Bhatt

Jacket Designer Tessa Bindloss
Senior Cartographic Editor Casper Morris
DTP Designers Jenn Hadley, Natasha Lu
Production Controller Inderjit Bhullar

Revisions Team
Louise Abbott, Shruti Bahl, Kiki Deere, Alexandra Farrell, Rhiannon Furbear, Amy Harrison, Helena Iveson, Jacky Jackson, Sumita Khatwani, Maite Lantaron, Jude Ledger, Richard Lim, Hayley Maher, Chris Orr, Catherine Palmi, Rada Radojicic, Lucy Richards, Stuti Tiwari, Helen Townsend, Zoe Ross.

Additional Picture Research
Rachel Barber, Ellen Root.

Additional Cartography
Base mapping for Kuala Lumpur derived from Netmaps.

Additional Photography
Irv Beckman, Simon Bracken, Gerard Brown, Andy Crawford, Peter Chen, Frank Greenaway, Benu Joshi, Barnabas Kindersley, Dave King, Colin Koh, Lawrence Lim, Ian O'Leary, Lloyd Park, Brian Pitkin, Tony Souter.

Special Assistance
Many thanks for the invaluable help of the following individuals: Jo Chua, Baba-Nyonya Heritage Museum; Asma Adnan and Mohamad Redza, Islamic Arts Museum; Rohaya Juli, Money Museum; Noredah Othman, Sabah Tourism Board; Letitia Samuel, Sarawak Tourism Board; Serene Lim Si Si, Singapore Tourism Board; S T Ramish, Tourism Malaysia.

Photography Permissions
Dorling Kindersley would like to thank the following for their assistance and permission to photograph at their establishments:

Islamic Art Museum; Kompleks Budaya Kraf; National Art Gallery; National Museum; Penang Museum and Art Gallery; Royal Museum.

Picture Credits
Key: a=above; b=below/bottom; c=center; f=far; l=left; r=right; t=top.

The Merlion symbol has been used with the kind permission of the Singapore Tourism Board (Reference Number STB/J6/07) 210clb.

The publishers would like to thank the following individuals, companies, and picture libraries for their kind permission to reproduce their photographs:

1-Altitude: 300tl.**123rf.com:** Seow Kai Han 143tl; Jordan Tan 325bl; Morozova Tatiana 188tl; Tktktk 241bl. **23 Love Lane:** Howard Tan 279tr.

Alamy: 1Apix 314br; Age Fotoshock 240tr; AndyLim. com 192cl; Arterra Picture Library 318-319; Banana Pancake 193tl; Robert E. Barber 24bl; Bare Essence Photography 83tr; Beaconstox 310tl; Brandon Cole Marine Photography 314bl; Bruce Coleman Inc. 23bl; Dennis Chang - Singapore 256tl; Comstock Images 24–5c, 201bl; David Noton Photography 78tr, 286cla; Reinhard Dirscherl 25tr, 314cr; David Fleetham 24clb; Simon Grosset 220cl; Chris Hellier 15cl; Gavin Hellier 106bl,150-151; Hemis 27clb; Henry Westheim Photography 118clb; Jack Hobhouse 60tr; David Hosking 22bc; Iconotec 147t; Imagestate Media Partners Limited - Impact pHotos 96br; Images&Stories 159br; Jon Arnold Images 153cr; Jo Kearney 32cl; JTB Media Creation Inc 328cl; Paul Kennedy 215tc; Matthew Lambley 17c; Look Die Bildagentur der Fotografen Gmbh 242; Jenny Matthews 224br; Neil McAllister 66tr, 333cr; Chris McLennan 289cla; Michele Molinari 192tr; David Moore 119cra; Nic Cleave Photography 119crb; North Wind Picture Archives 40bc; Sergio Pitamitz 23cr; Wolfgang Pölzer 314cla; Igor Prahin222t; Robert Harding Picture Library Ltd 27tr, 67tl, 111bc, 184t; Robert Harding World Imagery 17tr, 52-53, 98cl, 109tr, Scenics & Science 67cra; Neil Setchfield 68t, 131bl, 252cl; Nandana de Silva 145t; Slick Shoots 240tr; Nick Simon 34tr; Dave Stamboulis 15tr; Stephen Frink Collection 24tr, 25tl, 25crb; Steve Allen Travel Photography 232clb; Laurie Strachan 288cl; Terry Fincher.Photo Int 179cb; Ozil Thierry 57br; Travelscape Images 15br; Tribaleye Images/ J Marshall 305tr; Carlos Villoch 314bc; Rob Walls 26crb, 42bc; Maximilian Weinzierl 251bl; Terry Whittaker 23tr; David Wootton 27cra; Tengku Mohd Yusof 304cr. **AndyLim Creative**: 137br. **The ASEAN Secretariat**: 50clb. **AsiaExplorers. com**: 101br, 327tc, 327cra, 327c, 327fcra; Timothy Tye 39bl, 327ftr, 327cr. **Timothy Auger**: 223c. **AWL Images**: Jon Arnold 62; Aurora Photos 156; Alan Copson 122, 202-203; Gavin Hellier 97tl.

Baba-Nyonya Heritage Museum: Jo Chua 132clb, 132br, 133ca, 133bl. **Bacchanalia**: 300br; **The Bridgeman Art Library**: Drum, Dong Son style, 2nd-1st century BC (bronze) (see also 232894), Vietnamese School/Musee Guimet, Paris, France, Lauros/Giraudon 39br, Sloane 197br, ff.381v–382r; Plan of the city of Malacca, c.1511 (pen & ink with w/c), Barretti de Resende, Pedro (16th Century)/ British Library, London, UK, © British Library Board. All Rights Reserved 41tr, The port and town of Malacca, Malaysia, illustration from 'Le Costume Ancien et Moderne' by Giulio Ferrario, published c.1820s–30s (coloured engraving), Zancon, Gaetano (1771–1816)/Private Collection, The Stapleton Collection 43crb, Sir Thomas Stamford Raffles (1781-1826), Lonsdale, James (1777-1839)/London Zoological Society, UK 44bl, Borneo: Signing of the Treaty for cession of Labuan, 1846/British Library, London, UK, © British Library Board. All Rights Reserved 46bc. **Brunei Tourism**: 61tr, 158tr, 178cla, 178cl, 178bc, 179tl, 179br.

Calanthe Art Cafe: 285bl. **The Centrepoint**, Singapore: 239c. **Adrian Cheah**: 305cb. **Chez Papa**: 294bl. **China House**: 292tc. **Clifford Pier**: 299tr. **Coral Flyer Zipline**: 185br. **Corbis**: 24cla; Atlantide Phototravel 111cr; Bettmann 50t; Tom Brakefield 157b; EPA/ Ahmad Yusni 34bl,/Pool/Saeed Khan 51bl; Eye Ubiquitous 118cla; Free Agents Limited 205tr; Michael Freeman 37c, 41bl; Farrell Grehan 138; Peter Guttman 27br; Hamish Park 56cr; John Harper 14b; Chris Hellier 28br, 168bl, 169br; Dave G. Houser 306tr; Rob Howard 27cla, 315tl; Hulton-Deutsch Collection 26cra, 48bl, 49bc; Image Source 144bc; So Hing-Keung 34–5c; Earl & Nazima Kowall 26br, 119bc, 304bl; Bob Krist 65br; Frans Lanting 186bl; Charles & Josette Lenars 36cl, 287tl; Yang Liu 305c; Viviane Moos 26cl; Christine Osborne 304clb; Neil Rabinowitz 60cla, 93b; Robert Harding World Imagery/ Louise Murray 176bl; Joel W. Rogers 168cl; Schlegelmilch 56bl; Shamshahrin Shamsudin 79b; Paul Souders 51tr; Stapleton Collection 38; Luca I. Tettoni 40bl; Nik Wheeler 23cl, 27c, 306bl; Lawson Wood 183tr, 200clb; Michael S. Yamashita 61tl; Zefa/Herbert Kehrer 175c,/Photex/Beverly Factor 24br. **CPA Media**: 40tr, 42crb, 44tr, 44cla, 44–5c, 44br, 45tl, 45crb, 45bl, 45br, 46t, 46c, 47tr, 47bl, 47bc, 48tl, 48c, 48br, 49t, 71bl; David Henley 28tr, 117br. **Courtesy of The Thai Silk Company** 98bl.

Dewan Filharmonik Petronas, Kuala Lumpur City Centre, Malaysia: 309br. **DK Images**: FSTOP Pte Ltd, Singapore 209cl, 248br, 249cla, 249cb, 326ca, 334br, 338tr, 339bc. **Dreamstime.com**: Azirull Amin Aripin 308br; Olena Buyskykh 13tl; Chee Siong Chang 97br; Design Mitralhouse 230; Donyanedomam 118tr;Eddietay 2001 239bl; Andrey Goncharov 164tr; Joyfull 81t; Kristofbellens 104-105; Littlewormy 208; Mauhorng 92; Jakub Michankow 141br; Mikewaddell446 17br; Roland Nagy 32tr; Ppy2010ha 298bc; Iryna Rasko 12bl; Ravijohnsmith 70tl; Rodrigolab 12tc; 194-195; Ravindran John Smith 13br.

Eastern and Oriental Hotel: 111cr, 293br.

FLPA: Minden Pictures/Frans Lanting191br; **Forest Research Institute Malaysia**: 82cb.

Gardens by the Bay: 209br. **Getty Images**: Anders Blomqvist 332bl; The Image Bank 2-3; Nora Carol Photography 11tr, 180; Photodisc/Simon Russell 113br; Roslan Rahman 250tr; Stone/Paul Chesley 26bl; Tristan Savatier 16br; Universalimagesgroup 14tr. **GHM Hotels**: 73tc. **Goodwood Park Hotel**: 241c. **The Granger Collection, New York**: 42tc, 43tl, 43bl, 43bc, 45cra, 46br, 163cb, 227tr.

Eric Hunt: 191bl.

ION Orchard: 238br. **Islamic Arts Museum Malaysia**: 74cla, 74clb, 75tl, 75cra, 75cb, 75bc.

Judith Miller: Sloan 305cl.

Lonely Planet Images: Mark Daffey 176cl, 191tl; Richard L'Anson 233bc; Phil Weymouth 233tl.

Kapas Turtle Valley: 281br. **Kuala Lumpur City Gallery:** 67br.

Lyn's Thandoori: 296bc.

Marina Bay Sands Pte Ltd: 217br. **Mary Evans Picture Library:** 47crb. **Masterfile:** Mark Downey 160cl, 312cl; John Foster 169tc; R. Ian Lloyd 35tr, 50br, 55br, 60bl, 140bl, 178tr, 206bc. **Money Museum & Art Mulu Marriott Resort and Spa:** 277t, 282br.

National Archives of Malaysia: 193tr. **National Geographic Image Collection:** Tim Laman 55t, 200cla. naturepl.com: Doug Perrine 23crb. **Centre of Bank Negara Malaysia:** 41bc, 45tc, 45ca. **Negeri Sembilan Tourism Action Council:** Zainal Abidin Abu Samah 127crb, 127bl, 127br. **Nero-Group:** 284bl, 290bc, 291tr. **New Majestic Hotel:** 283tc.

Orient-Express Hotels Trains & Cruises: 330br.

Photographers Direct: 42 Degrees South 41clb; Bare Essence Photography/Chan Tze Leong 60br; Graham Simmons 232tr; Tengku Mohd Yusof Photography 29br. **Photolibrary:** Corbis Corporation 201cra; Digital Vision 132, 274–5; Earth Scenes/ Animals Animals/James J Stachecki 26tr; Staub Frank 139b; Index Stock Imagery/Clineff Kindra 34cla,/Walter Bibikow 36tr; Jon Arnold Images/ Walter Bibikow 33cra; Jtb Photo Communications Inc 33bl, 233cr, 250cl, 303bl, 304tr; David Kirkland 181b; Pacific Stock/Perrine Doug 201tl; Photononstop/Maurice Smith 177br, Robert Harding Picture Library Ltd/ Richard Ashworth 36clb. **Photoshot:** NHPA/Gerald Cubitt 22cb,/John Shaw 23tc;/World Pictures/Eur 82tl.

Rabani: 188b. **Raffles Hotel:** 220bl, 220clb, 221bc, 221cra, 221tl, 276cla. **Resorts World Sentosa:** 250br, 251tl, 251cr. **Reuters:** Zainal Abd Halim 27cb; Jason Lee 34br; Bazuki Muhammad 29crb, 59cr; Stringer Malaysia 29bc. **Ristorante Beccari:** 285tr, 297tr. **Robert Harding Picture Library:** Richard Ashworth 16tl; Reinhard D 200tr, 201crb; Robert Francis 190cl; Gavin Hellier 31c; John Miller 94bl, 95cr; Louise Murray 200bc.

Sabah Tourism Board: 187br, 190bl. **Radin Mohd Noh Saleh:** 32crb, 36bl, 36br, 149cla, 149clb, 149cr, 149crb, 182bl. **Sarawak Forestry:** 169cr. **Sarawak Tourism Board:** 61br, 163tr, 166c, 173c, 173bl, 196tr, 310c, 312br, 314cl, 315br, 316br, 322tl, 323tl. **Sepilok Resort:** 277bc. **Singapore Art Museum:** 219bc. **Singapore Tourism Board:** 205bc, 206cl, 207tr, 207bl. **SuperStock:** age fotostock 54bl, 258br; Steve Vidler 212.

Thai Express: 301tr. **Tioman Cabana:** 295tr. **Tourism Malaysia:** 23bc, 25bl, 25br, 35c, 35bl, 35br, 36–7c, 37tl, 37tc, 37cr, 37bl, 37br, 57tr, 58c, 59bl, 66br, 79tc, 83br, 102c, 149bl, 165cra, 177tl, 304cl, 304cra, 305tl, 305cra, 307cr, 309tr, 310br, 313br, 320cl.

Villa Samadhi: 278bc. **Virtual Malaysia:** 329tc.

Joey CE Wong: 144cla.

YTL Hotels: 276br, 280tc.

Front Endpaper: Left: **AWL Images:** Jon Arnold cr; **Corbis:** Farrell Grehan tr; **Dreamstime.com:** Mauhorng c. Right: **AWL Images:** Aurora Photos c,/ Alan Copson tl, cl; **Getty Images:** Nora Carol Photography tr.

Back Endpaper: **KL Monorail System Sdn Bhd.**

Jacket images: Front: **AWL Images:** Gavin Hellier Main; **DK Images:** Tony Souter bl. Spine: **AWL Images:** Gavin Hellier t.

Phrase Book

Malay belongs to the Austronesian family of languages, whose several hundred distinct variations cover the Indian and Pacific oceans. It is the national language of Malaysia, Brunei, and Singapore, and for many centuries has been the language of learning, diplomacy, and commerce in this region. One of its earliest scripts, a modified Perso-Arabic script called Jawi, was the means by which Islam was disseminated. Jawi is still widely used in Brunei today. Elsewhere, it has been replaced by the Latin script Rumi, which was not spelled uniformly until Malaysia, Indonesia, and Brunei agreed on a standard form of spelling. Prior to the 19th century, international trade and relations would have been unthinkable without the use of Malay, but after 1800, large-scale immigration from China and India resulted in the widespread use of Mandarin Chinese and Tamil in Malaysia. Today, English is widely spoken, mostly in urban centers, but any effort made by visitors to speak Malay is usually appreciated, particularly in more remote parts of the country. Malay, whose official name is Bahasa Melayu, is often incorrectly called Bahasa, which means language.

Malay Pronounciation Guide

There are no strong stresses in the Malay language and most letters are pronounced in the same way as English. As a general rule, beginners are advised to stress the penultimate syllable. However, if this syllable contains a mute e, the stress moves to the final syllable.

a as in f**a**ther
  or as in th**e**
  or as in b**u**t

e like the "a" in m**a**chine when unstressed;
  or as in b**e**ll when stressed

i as in tax**i**
  or as in **A**pril

o as in m**o**rning
  or as in st**o**p

u as in b**oo**t
  or as in g**oo**d

ai as in **i**ce
  .or as two separate sounds, as in Haw**aii**

au as in **ou**t
  or as two separate sounds, as in b**a-u**t

c in between **tu**be and **ch**oose

j in between **d**ue and **J**une

k as English "k" except in a final letter, when it becomes a glottal stop (brief pause)

ng as in si**ng**er

ngg as in lo**ng**er

ny as in in**nu**endo

In an emergency

Help!	**Tolong!**
Stop!	**Berhentilah!**
Call a doctor!	**Panggil doktor!**
Call an ambulance!	**Panggil ambulans!**
Police!	**Polis!**
Fire!	**Api!**
Where is the nearest telephone?	**Di mana telefon yang terdekat?**
Where is the nearest hospital?	**Di mana hospital yang terdekat?**
I am lost!	**Saya sesat!**
Do you need help?	**Awak perlukan pertolongan?**
I've been robbed!	**Saya dirompak!**
Go away!	**Pergi!**
I've had an accident.	**Saya terlibat dalam kemalangan.**

Communication essentials

Yes	**Ya**
No	**Bukan/Tidak**
Hello	**Helo**
Goodbye	**Selamat jalan**
Excuse me/ apologies	**Minta maaf**
Please	**Tolong/silahkan**
Thank you	**Terima kasih**
You are welcome.	**Kembali**
Good morning	**Selamat pagi**
Good afternoon	**Selamat petang**
Good evening	**Selamat malam**
Good night	**Selamat hari**
How are you?	**Apa khabar?**
Madam	**Puan**
Sir	**Encik (Ci')**
Today	**Hari ini**
Tomorrow	**Esok**
Yesterday	**Kelmarin**
Later	**Esok/Nanti**
Now	**Sekarang/Segera**
What?	**Apa?**
When?	**Bila?**
Which one?	**Yang mana?**
Who?	**Siapa?**
Why?	**Mengapa?**

Useful phrases

Do you speak English?	**Apakah berbahasa Inggeris?**
I don't speak Malay.	**Saya belum berbahasa Melayu.**
I don't understand.	**Saya kurang faham.**
I/we want to...	**Saya/kami mahu...**
What is your name?	**Siapakah nama?**
My name is…	**Nama saya…**
Where is…?	**Di mana…?**
Is it close by?	**Sudah dekat?**
Is it far away?	**Masih jauh?**
Could you please speak drive/walk slower?	**Minta perlahan sedikit?**

How do I get to…?	Untuk ke… sebaiknya saya naik apa?
Are children allowed?	Adakah kanak-kanak dibenerkan masuk?
I like...	Saya suka...
I don't like...	Saya tidak suka...

Useful words

address	alamat
Attention!	Awas!
bad	buruk
big	besar
clean	bersih
closed	tutup
cold	sejuk
dirty	kotor
door	pintu
empty	kosong
enough	cukup
entrance	masuk
exit	keluar
full	penuh
good	baik
hot	panas
less	kurang
more	lebih
pull	dorong
push	tolak
open	buka
quick	cepat
slow	perlahan
small	kecil
stairs	tangga

Banks

Is there an ATM?	Ada ATM?
I want to change dollars/ pounds…into Malay ringgit.	Saya mau tukar dollars/ pounds... menjadi ringgit Malaysia.
money	wang/duit
change	wang kecil
change money	tukar wang
exchange rate	kadar pertukaran
traveler's checks	cek kembara

Shopping

Do you have…?	Apakah ada…?
Can I have…?	Minta…?
How many/ much is it?	Berapa harganya?
Do you accept credit cards?	Credit card boleh?
This is too expensive.	Ini terlalu mahal.
buy	beli
cheap	murah
clothes	pakaian
expensive	mahal
market	pasar/tamu

price	harga
sale	jualan (murah)
sell	jual
shoes	kasut
shop	kedai
supermarket	pasar raya

Nature and sightseeing

bay	teluk
beach	pantai
cape/ promontory	tanjung
estuary/town	kuala
hill	bukit
information	penerangan
island	pulau
lake	tasik
mosque	masjid
mountain	gunung
paddy field	sawah
palace	istana/astana
park	taman
river	sungai/batang
square	padang
strait	selat
temple/shrine	kuil
tourist	pejabat
travel agency	agensi pelancongan
village	kampung

Colors

black	hitam
blue	biru
green	hijau
red	merah
white	putih
yellow	kuning

Health

antiseptic	antiseptik
blood pressure	tekanan darah
condom	kondom
contraceptive	kontraseptif/ pencegah hamil
dentist	dokter gigi
diarrhea	diarea/cirit-birit
doctor	dokter
faint	pingsan
fever	panas (badan)
high	tinggi
low	rendah
medicine	ubat
nurse	perawat
pain/ill	sakit
painkillers	ubat penghilang kesakitan
pregnant	hamil
sanitary towels	tuala wanita

Transport

| I would like to reserve a seat. | Saya mahu tempahkan tempat duduk. |

Would you tell me when to get off?	Tolong beritahukan, bila sudah sampai?
How long does it take to get to…?	Berapa lama untuk ke…?
Which bus goes to…?	Bas mana yang ke…?
Where do I pay?	Di mana tempat membayar?
I need a mechanic.	Kami memerlukan mekanik.
I have a flat tire.	Tayarnya kempis.
aeroplane	kapal terbang
boat	perahu
bus	bas
bus stop	stesen bas
car	kereta
car baby seat	tempat duduk bayi
customs	cukai
cycle	naik baisikal
petrol	minyak/petrol
return (trip)	(perjalanan) pergi balik
seat	tiket sehala
single/one way (ticket)	pergi balik
taxi	teksi
timetable	jadual waktu
train	kereta api

Directions

here	di sini
there	di sana
in	(di) dalam
from (where)	dari (mana)
left	kiri
right	kanan
straight on	jalan terus
in front of	di hadapan
behind	di belakang
at the corner	di simpang
near	dekat
far	juah
to	ke
north	utara
south	selatan
east	timur
west	barat
northeast	timur laut
northwest	barat laut
southeast	tenggara
southwest	barat daya

Staying in a hotel

I have a reservation.	Ada tempahan.
Do you have a room?	Ada bilik?
What is the charge per night?	Berapa semalam?

I want a	Saya minta
double/	bilik kelamin/
single room.	bujang.
I am/we are	Saya/kami nak
leaving today.	mendaftar
	kelaur hari ini.
double	kelamin
single	bujang
bed	katil/tempat tidur
key	kunci
lights	lampu
bathroom	bilik mandi
toilet	tandas
soap	sabun
towel	tuala
Open	Buka
Closed	Tutup
Emergency	Pintu
exit	kesemasan

Eating out

A table please.	Minta meja untuk.
May I see the	Minta daftar
menu?	makan?
I would like to	Saya mau
order now.	pesan sekarang.
I am	Saya
vegetarian.	vegetarian.
I don't eat...	Saya tidak makan...
The bill, please.	Minta bil.
breakfast	makan pagi
children's	menu
menu	kanak-kanak
dinner	makan malam
fork	garpu
glass	kaca mata
highchair	kerusi tinggi
knife	pisau
lunch	makan tengah hari
meat	daging
restaurant	restoran
seafood	makanan laut
snack	makanan kecil
spoon	senduk
vegetable	sayur

Menu decoder

asam	sour
ayam	chicken
ayer panas	hot water
ayer sejuk	cold water
ayer teh	tea
buah-buahan	fruit
domba	lamb
garam	salt

gula	sugar
ikan	fish
jus	juice
kelapa	coconut
kopi	coffee
manis	sweet
mee	noodle
merica	pepper
minuman	drink
nasi	steamed rice
pedas	spicy
pedih	bitter
sapi	beef
susu	milk
telur	eggs
udang	prawn/shrimp

Time and day

clock	jam
minute	menit
quarter hour	suku
second	detik
watch	jam tangan
hour	pukul
day	hari
week	minggu
month	bulan
year	tahun
morning	pagi hari
noon	tengah hari
midday	siang hari
afternoon	sore hari
evening/night	malam hari
What is the	Sudah pukul
time please?	berapa?
11.19 in the	pukul sebelas
morning	lewat sembilan
	belas menit pagi
1 o'clock	pukul satu
1.15 in the	pukul satu
early afternoon	lewat suku
(midday)	siang
3.45 in the	pukul empat
afternoon	kurang suku
	sore
6.30 in the	pukul enam
early evening	setengah sore
9.31 in the	pukul sepuluh
evening/	kurang dua
at night	puluh menit
	malam
Monday	hari Isnin
Tuesday	hari Selasa
Wednesday	hari Arba
Thursday	hari Khamis

Friday	hari Jumaat
Saturday	hari Sabtu
Sunday	hari Ahad/
	Minggu

Cardinal numbers

1	satu
2	dua
3	tiga
4	empat
5	lima
6	enam
7	tujuh
8	delapan
9	sembilan
10	sepuluh
11	sebelas
12	dua belas
13	tiga belas
20	dua puluh
21	dua puluh satu
22	dua puluh dua
30	tiga puluh
40	empat puluh
50	lima puluh
60	enam puluh
70	tujuh puluh
80	delapan puluh
90	sembilan puluh
100	seratus
1,000	seribu
2,000	dua ribu
10,000	sepuluh ribu
20,000	dua puluh ribu
100,000	seratus ribu
200,000	dua ratus ribu

Ordinal numbers

1st	pertama
2nd	kedua
3rd	ketiga
4th	keempat
5th	kelima
6th	keenam
7th	ketujuh
8th	kedelapan
9th	kesembilan
10th	kesepuluh
11th	kesebelas
12th	kedua belas
20th	kedua puluh
100th	keseratus
1,000th	keseribu

Kuala Lumpur Integrated Rail Network

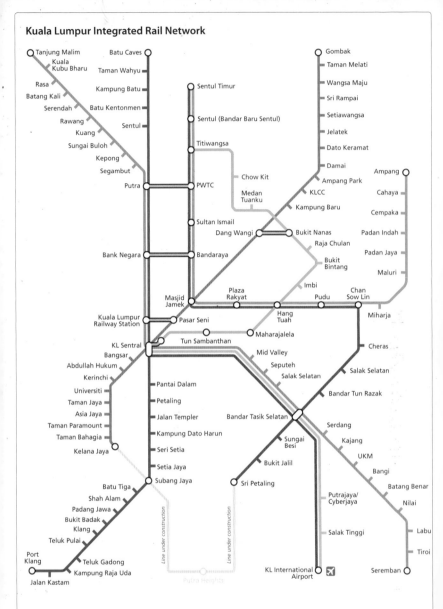

Key

— KTM Komuter Seremban Line
— KTM Komuter Port Klang Line
— Rapid KL's LRT Ampang Line
— Rapid KL's LRT Sri Petaling Line
— Rapid KL's LRT Kelana Jaya Line
— KLIA Ekspres Line
— KLIA Transit Line
— KL Monorail Line
◯ Interchange station
⦿—⦿ Connecting station

Getting Around

Kuala Lumpur is served by an efficient network of Light Rail Transit (LRT) and monorail lines. For visitors, the most useful LRT routes are the Ampang and Sri Petaling lines, linking Plaza Rakyat with Puduraya Bus Station, Masjid Jamek with Merdeka Square, and Bandaraya with Little India. KLCC is on the Kelana Jaya line. The LRT operator, Rapid KL, also runs bus services, and a combined one-day pass for the LRT and bus is available. The separately run KL Monorail is useful for exploring Chinatown and the Golden Triangle. However, very few interchange stations are connected and often new tickets have to be purchased to continue the journey. All trains run from 6am to midnight, but services are less frequent on weekends.